Read this first!

Here's how to find the incredible wedding and special event information in *Here Comes The Guide:*

- ### Event Venues

  Venues are organized by region and city, with illustrated descriptions and details about capacities, fees, and services. To find a specific site, see the index starting on page 415.

- ### Useful Questions to Ask Venues & Event Professionals

  Not sure what to ask a potential event location, photographer, caterer, etc.? Our lists of questions on pages 21–42 will make it easier for you to interview them and help you decide who to hire.

Don't forget to check out
HereComesTheGuide.com!

HereComesTheGuide.com has the most up-to-date information on event venues, services, and bridal fairs—as well as lots of photos and videos. And if you have a certain type of venue or event professional in mind, you'll really appreciate our amazingly useful search engine. We make it easy to find exactly what you're looking for.

What Makes Us Different?

We do most of your homework for you.

1. We've visited 90% of the venues in *Here Comes The Guide*.

We've checked out the majority of our venues in person before including them in *Here Comes The Guide*.

2. We write every venue description with you in mind.

We strive to make each site description informative, accurate, and even entertaining.

3. We provide real pricing for venues, along with nitty-gritty details about each site's capacity, services, and amenities.

This makes it easy to create a list of your top contenders, and by the time you contact or visit a location you're totally informed!

4. We save you a ton of time.

By putting so much comprehensive information all in one place, we save you hours…days…maybe months of searching for event locations. And, you can actually do most of your planning without leaving home!

HereComesTheGuide.com has it ALL:

- **Photos and Videos of Hundreds of Wedding Venues and Services**

  Each location and event professional has their own photo gallery.

- **Fee Info for Every Venue**

  HereComesTheGuide.com provides pricing for facility rental, catering, and other costs.

- **CERTIFIED BY THE GUIDE Event Services**

  We don't just feature any old caterer or DJ. We've carefully checked out each event professional.

- **Local Bridal Shows**

  Find out what events are happening near you, like fab food tastings and fashion shows. Did you have something better to do this weekend?

- **MyGuide**

  Sign up at www.herecomestheguide.com/myguide for the MyGuide email newsletter. Fill out a simple form, and you'll get expert planning advice, deals & discounts, and real wedding inspiration delivered straight to your inbox. (And we never spam!)

- **Guest Accommodations, Honeymoon Locations & Rehearsal Dinner Venues**

  Need to book a block of rooms for your out-of-town guests? Looking for the perfect rehearsal dinner spot or romantic getaway? Find them all on HereComesTheGuide.com.

We're always adding venues to our website, so be sure to check out HereComesTheGuide.com for thousands of wedding locations in California and the rest of the U.S.!

What People Say

"*This is a wonderful website, with all the details that a bride looks for when she's searching for a reception location*. It's well organized and incredibly useful. I wish there were more sites like this one. THANK YOU!!!"
—*Amy, Bride*

"I'm in the process of helping my daughter research sites for her wedding reception and your website has been hugely helpful! The location information is thorough and consistent, making comparing the different locations so easy. *We have found places to check out that we never would have thought of on our own*. Thanks so much for all the work you must have done to put all this information together!"
—*Gail C., Mother of the Bride*

"I cannot stress enough how much help **Here Comes The Guide** was to me. *I was often able to receive more information from your site than from my contacts with the actual locations and vendors!* Especially since I was planning a Southern California wedding from Northern California, you saved me A TON of legwork."
—*Jamie Juster, Bride*

"I have finally found a website that has it all! *I'm planning my wedding from out of state and your event venues search is the best!* I've been looking for a website that has all the information in one place. Thank you!!!"
—*Sarah, Bride*

"I went out and spent the money on your book without hesitation. I'm so glad I did! I've gotten some great ideas and was able to create an outline for my budget. *Not only did I find great reception locations in your book, but I think I found my rehearsal dinner place as well*. It was a gold mine!"
—*Liz Davis, Bride*

"Having recently gotten married, I have a special appreciation for **Here Comes The Guide.** It was extremely helpful during my time of planning. *The quick descriptions painted a beautiful picture of each and every venue, and were very helpful in narrowing down the search by budget, criteria, and location.* I feel this is a very important tool for every busy bride and still recommend it to all my engaged friends."
—*A Southern California Bride*

About Here Comes The Guide

"I just had to let you know how WONDERFUL your website is. *I was amazed to finally find a website with REAL information.* Yours gave me all the nitty-gritty stuff I needed to know to find venues and vendors. With only two sessions at your website, my wedding was planned. Amazing!"

—*Christina R., Bride*

"I have to tell you, I was blown away by your website. It's so beautiful and professionally done. The detail you provide is just enough so that I didn't get bogged down in minutiae. *Your site is such a great resource that I've started telling everybody about it.* I've seen tons of wedding sites, so I know that you've come up with something that's really different."

—*Kimberly P., Bride*

"I went to about ten locations that are in your book and found that the site descriptions were pretty accurate. *I'm amazed at how well you were able to capture the feeling of a place and put it into words.*"

—*Stephanie Stevensen, Bride*

"I completely love your website and look forward to the book. *This is the only resource that is so detailed on California sites, and it makes it so much easier to plan from a long distance.* **Here Comes The Guide** is the best source of information."

—*Jocelyn, Bride*

"*I absolutely love your website. It's warm, feminine, and has what one might call 'simple elegance'.* Great job! I refer friends to your website all the time—for weddings, showers, and birthdays. Keep up the fabulous work."

—*Maria, Bride*

"I love your site! Most other sites that I visited seemed to have a hidden agenda to steer me towards only what benefits them. *This site is non-biased and easy to use. Thank you!*"

—*Elisa Parra, Bride*

"Thanks for providing this invaluable resource! *I'll be using the site for corporate event planning*—I don't know what I did without it!"

—*Mary, Corporate Planner*

We Need Your Help

- **Tell venues that you're using *Here Comes The Guide*.**

  When you contact the places we feature, let them know that you heard about them through *The Guide.*

- **Help us keep our information current.**

  We'd appreciate it if you'd contact us with your comments, corrections, suggestions, and complaints. Your feedback helps us maintain the accuracy of our information.

- **Let us know if you discover a great venue that's not featured in *Here Comes The Guide*.**

  Please call or email us if you find an event site you think we should include in our book and on our website.

Hopscotch Press, Inc.

21 Orinda Way, Ste. C #428, Orinda, CA 94563

510/548-0400   fax 510/439-2674

info@HereComesTheGuide.com

HereComesTheGuide.com

Information Is Always Changing

Everything changes: pricing, services, décor, landscaping, and even ownership.

We've tried to make the information in this book completely accurate, but it's not possible. Locations give us incorrect facts and figures, change ownership or management, revamp their pricing and policies, and sometimes go out of business. Truth is, things in the event industry can turn upside down overnight.

So how can you make sure that you're getting correct information? It's simple:

- When you tour venues, bring your book with you or use your smartphone or tablet to quickly refer to each location's page on **HereComesTheGuide.com** for the most up-to-date info.

- When you contact a location, show or read the information in *Here Comes The Guide* to the facility's representative to verify that it's still current.

- Get everything that's been agreed on in writing, and review it carefully before you sign any contract!

Here Comes The Guide

Sixeenth Edition

Copyright ©2020–2021

Published by Hopscotch Press, Inc.

Orinda, CA
Printed in the U.S.A.

Here Comes The Guide, Southern California®

Sixteenth Edition

Jan Brenner, *Co-Author/Editor-in-Chief*
Jolene Rae Harrington, *Co-Author/Editor*

Meredith Monday Schwartz, *Chief Executive Officer*
Mary Briemle, *Production Associate*
Maggie Munki, *Production Specialist*
Jennifer Ahearn, *Online Media Director*
Angela Mullan, *Regional Sales Lead*
Stephanie Bush, *Regional Sales Manager*
Jessica Robins, *Regional Sales Manager*

Inside Illustrations: *Jon Dalton and Michael Tse*

ISSN (pending)
ISBN 978-0-9988312-2-0

Here Comes The Guide®

Sixteenth Edition

Acknowledgments

Our deepest appreciation goes to our writers, Jolene Rae Harrington (also an invaluable editor), Laurie Turner, and Annie Cooper. Without them none of our books would ever get written.

Our artist, Jon Dalton, penned all the new illustrations for this edition of *Here Comes The Guide*. Using both computer graphics and fine art skills, he transformed photographs of the facilities into the distinctive line drawings that give *The Guide* its unique style.

And as always, we are eternally grateful to our clients and our readers. Your support year in and year out keeps *Here Comes The Guide* a popular resource.

Cover Credits

Photographer: Mary Costa Photography
https://marycostaweddings.com
@marycostaphoto

Floral Designer: Wild Muse Floral Co.
www.wildmusefloral.com
@wildmusefloral

Hairstylist: Sandra J. Robles
@robles.sandraj

Hairpiece: The Fine Art of Design
www.thefineartofdesign.com

Cake Designer: Alana Jones-Mann
http://alanajonesmann.com
@alanajonesmann

Car Rental: Antique Pink Cadillac
@antiquepinkcadillac

Wedding Dress: Etsy
www.etsy.com
@etsy

Groom Attire + Shoes: ASOS
www.asos.com
@asos

Bride: Sam Ushiro
www.awwsam.com
@aww.sam

Groom: Kyle Larsen
@kyleinthewilds

Table of Contents

Really Really Important Information

Questions To Ask

Event Venues

Regional Areas and Cities

Santa Barbara Area

Ventura County

San Fernando Valley

Los Angeles Area

San Bernardino Mountains/Lake Arrowhead

Riverside/Inland Empire

Temecula Wine Country

San Diego Area

Greater Palm Springs

Maps

Index

Preface

When I graduated from college in 1973 (pre-internet), I thought I'd never have to do another endless research project again. Boy, was I wrong. Compared to looking for a place to get married, term papers were a piece of cake. I began my quest optimistically enough, but after a couple of days of frantic and fruitless networking (my wedding date was a mere three months down the road!), the enormity of my task started to sink in. It had taken me 33 years to find the right guy, and it was beginning to look like it might take an equally long time to find the right place.

Going into high gear, I reached out and touched just about everyone I knew, along with quite a few total strangers. Friends and friends of friends didn't have any recommendations that suited our particular needs, and although wedding consultants had information, they were reluctant to part with their lists of sites unless I hired them to plan my wedding. I even called some caterers, florists and cake makers, but they were usually too busy to give me in-depth descriptions of places over the phone. Some chambers of commerce had organized wedding location lists ready to mail out; others had nothing and knew nothing.

After days of phoning, all I had was a patchwork quilt of information. I still hadn't found *the* place, and finally had to face the painful truth: there was no central resource or comprehensive, detailed list. I became anxious. With a full-time job I was hardly free to conduct an exhaustive search, and I realized that I would never be able to find out about the vast majority of interesting or unusual wedding sites, let alone thoroughly evaluate them! My frustration was exacerbated by the fact that it was August and the wedding date in October was drawing closer with each passing day.

As luck would have it, my sister mentioned that her hair stylist had gotten married on a yacht in San Francisco Bay. Hallelujah! That's it! I cried. What a great idea! I'd never even thought about a floating wedding and had no idea you could do such a thing.

We got married on a hot, sunny day behind Angel Island in San Francisco Bay. The captain performed the ceremony on the bow, and afterwards the yacht tooted its horn, the crew let loose multicolored balloons, and a "Just Married" sign was thrown over the stern. As we swept past Alcatraz Island, Sausalito and the Golden Gate and Bay Bridges, our guests relaxed in the sun, enjoying drinks and hors d'oeuvres. What a wonderful day! Even my parents' friends had a great time, and wrote us after the wedding to let us know how much they'd loved their outing on the water.

Serendipity was largely responsible for making my wedding memorable, but you don't have to rely on luck. I created *Here Comes The Guide* so that others wouldn't have to experience what I went through, and I hope it makes your search for the perfect location easy and painless.

Lynn Broadwell
Founder

Really, Really Important Information

Introduction

Little did we know when we wrote *Here Comes The Guide, Northern California* in 1989 that we would receive such an overwhelming response from our readers. The first edition sold out in less than a year, and as public demand grew we launched our Southern California edition. Thanks to our enthusiastic readership of engaged couples, savvy party hostesses, and event planners, *The Guide* continues to be a bestseller!

So what makes this book so popular?

We've done most of your homework for you.

We present comprehensive, solid information: a full description and illustration of each location, plus details about fees, capacities, and services. Our wide selection of facilities includes delightful places that you might not have found on your own.

This book cuts your search time by 90%.

Instead of having to call or email dozens of facilities and ask the same questions over and over again, you can look up many of the answers in *The Guide*. Once you've narrowed down your list of potential sites, you can contact them to schedule an in-person visit. Not only does *The Guide* save you time, it often saves you money by letting you comparison shop!

We screen our venues.

We personally evaluate most of the venues in *Here Comes The Guide,* sending a professional writer to 90% of them to make sure they meet our criteria. (Yes, we actually turn down locations that don't satisfy our requirements.)

We're experienced.

We've been writing and publishing *Here Comes The Guide* since 1989. We're proud that our publication has become the essential resource for weddings—and just about any kind of event—in California.

If you can't find the perfect venue in *Here Comes The Guide,* check out our website at HereComesTheGuide.com.

You'll have access to all the information in the *Here Comes The Guide* book online and a lot more:

- **More Southern California venues,** along with photos and videos. You'll be able to tour hundreds of sites in your pajamas!

- **Even more venues in other regions of the U.S.,** like Northern California, New England, Chicago, and Hawaii, just to name a few.

- **Plenty of event services,** with lots of photos of floral designs, cakes, makeup, and hair—you name it!

- **Bridal Fair Calendar** with details about upcoming extravaganzas and wedding showcases.

- **Venues for Rehearsal Dinners, Etc.** Need a place to hold your rehearsal dinner, bridal shower, day-after brunch, or other intimate gathering? We've got lots of suggestions (with photos and details, of course!)

- **Guest accommodations/room block options** plus photos and details.

- **Honeymoon destinations,** including romantic photos and practical info.

Navigation is a snap, and our searchable database lets you find event venues by city, type, capacity, view, etc., and event professionals by company name, region, or service category.

And check back often—we regularly update our website with event locations and services that aren't featured in the book!

Understanding Our Information

Explanation of Main Headings

Each venue description in *Here Comes The Guide* follows the same format. To help you understand the information presented, we've provided an explanation of the main headings in the same order as they appear.

Description

Once you've selected a geographical area and you're clear about your needs, then thoroughly review all the sites listed in your area of preference. The descriptions are written to give you a sense of what places are like, from ambiance to physical layout. However, before reading the descriptions, you may want to check the *Capacity* and *Fees & Deposits* sections to determine which places seem to be a good fit from a size and budget perspective. If a facility is still a viable option after you've read the entire two-page editorial, flag it for easy reference when planning to contact and visit sites later on.

Ceremony Capacity

Standing and seated capacities are sometimes included for ceremonies since these numbers may be totally different than the corresponding numbers for receptions.

Reception Capacity

By now you should have a rough idea of how many people will be attending. If not, it's time to zero in on the number, since many facilities want a deposit based on an estimated head count. Look at the capacity figures for each event location. Seated or sit-down capacity refers to guests seated at tables. Standing capacity refers to a function where the majority of guests are not formally seated, such as a champagne/hors d'oeuvres reception (though there may be cocktail tables and/or lounge furniture). Keep track of those facilities that are compatible with your guest count. If you're planning well in advance and don't have your guest list whittled down yet, then you'll just have to estimate and refine the count as the date draws near. There is a world of difference in cost and planning effort between an intimate party of 60 and a large wedding with over 200 guests, so pin down your numbers as soon as you can.

Meeting Capacity

In general, the seated capacity for meetings is listed as a range or a maximum. Sometimes, specific spaces are named along with their individual capacities. Occasionally, seating configurations are also provided: *theater-style* (auditorium row seating with chairs arranged closely together), *classroom-style* (an organized table-and-chair arrangement, usually in rows) and *conference-style* (seating around tables).

Prices

We've tried to make the information regarding costs as accurate as possible. However, keep in mind that we can't list the fees for all of the services a venue offers. Also, while packages tend to be more inclusive, they may not cover the full cost of your event—especially when you add in extras like appetizers or rentals. It's important to find out as soon as possible exactly what is—and isn't—included with any service or package you're considering in order to accurately assess how your venue choice will impact your budget.

It's a good idea to confirm pricing with the facility you're calling. If you're planning far in advance, anticipate price increases by the time you contract with a venue. Once you're definite about your location, you should lock in your fees in a contract, protecting yourself from possible rate increases later. Make sure you ask about every service provided and are clear about all of the extras that can really add up. Facilities may charge you for tables, chairs, linens, plateware and silverware, glassware and additional hours. Don't be surprised to see tax and service charges in fixed amounts applied to the total bill if the facility provides restaurant or catering services.

Sometimes a deposit is nonrefundable—a fact you'll definitely want to know if the deposit is a large percentage of the total bill. And even if it's refundable, you still need to read the cancellation policy thoroughly. Make sure you understand the policies that

> **Look at the information regarding pricing and remember that it changes regularly and usually in one direction—up!**

will ensure you get your cleaning and security deposit returned in full and, again, get everything in writing.

Food costs vary considerably. Carefully plan your menu with the caterer, event consultant, or chef. Depending on the style of service and the type of food being served, the total food bill can vary dramatically—even if you're getting quotes from the same caterer. If, for example, you're having a multi-course seated meal, expect it to be the most expensive part of your event.

Alcohol is expensive, too, and you may be restricted in what you can serve and who can serve it. Some venues don't allow you to bring your own alcoholic beverages, and even if they do permit it you may be limited to beer, wine, or champagne. Many places discourage you from bringing your own (BYO) by charging an exorbitant corkage fee to remove the cork and pour. Other places have limited permits that don't allow them to serve alcohol or restrict them from serving certain kinds; some will let you or the caterer serve alcohol, others require someone with a license. Make sure you know what's allowed. Decide what your budget is for alcohol and determine what types you're able to provide. And keep in mind that the catering fees you are quoted rarely include the cost of alcohol. If you provide the alcohol, make sure you keep your purchase receipts so you can return any unopened bottles.

So how much will your event cost? Hopefully not more than you can afford! There are a lot of variables involved in coming up with an estimated total for your event. Just make sure you've included them all in your calculations and read all the fine print before you sign any contract.

Availability

Some facilities are available 7am to 2am; others offer very limited "windows". If you'd like to save some money, consider a weekday or weeknight reception, or think about having your event in the off-season (often November, or January through March, but varies depending on the region). Even the most sought-after places have openings midweek and during non-peak months—and at reduced costs. Facilities want your business and are more likely to negotiate terms and prices if they have nothing else scheduled. Again, read all the fine print carefully and mark those facilities that have time slots that meet your needs. If the date you have in mind is already booked, it doesn't hurt to ask if someone actually confirmed that date by paying a deposit or signing a contract. If they haven't, you may be in luck.

Services/Amenities and Restrictions

Most facilities provide something in the way of services and many have limitations that may affect your function. For instance, they may not allow you to have amplified music outdoors or bring your own caterer.

We've attempted to give you a brief description of what each venue has to offer and what is restricted. Because of space limitations, we've shortened words and developed a key to help you follow our abbreviated notations. Once you're familiar with our shorthand, you'll be able to read through all the data outlined at the bottom of each entry and flag each facility that meets your requirements.

Services/Amenities Key

CATERING

- **in-house:** the facility provides catering (for a fee)
- **in-house, no BYO:** the facility provides catering; you cannot bring in your own
- **preferred list:** you must select your caterer from the facility's approved list
- **in-house or BYO:** the facility will provide catering or you can select an outside caterer of your own
- **BYO, licensed:** arrange for your own licensed caterer

KITCHEN FACILITIES

- **ample** or **fully equipped:** large and well-equipped with major appliances
- **moderate:** medium-sized and utilitarian
- **minimal:** small with limited equipment; may not have all the basic appliances
- **setup** or **prep only:** room for setup and food prep, but not enough space or utilities to cook food
- **n/a:** not applicable because facility provides catering or doesn't allow food

TABLES & CHAIRS

- **some provided** or **provided:** facility provides some or all of the tables and chairs
- **BYO:** make arrangements to bring your own

LINENS, SILVER, ETC.

- same as above

RESTROOMS

- **wheelchair accessible** or
- **not wheelchair accessible**

DANCE FLOOR

- **yes:** an area for dancing (hardwood floor, cement terrace, patio) is available
- **CBA, extra charge:** a dance floor can be brought in for a fee

DRESSING AREA

- **yes:** there is an area for changing
- **no:** there's no area for changing
- **limited:** smaller space, not fully equipped as changing room
- **CBA:** can be arranged

PARKING

- **CBA:** can be arranged

  other descriptions are self explanatory

ACCOMMODATIONS

If overnight accommodations are available on site, the number of guest rooms is listed.

- **CBA:** the facility will arrange accommodations for you

OUTDOOR NIGHT LIGHTING

- **yes:** there is adequate light to conduct your event outdoors after dark
- **access only** or **limited:** lighting is sufficient for access only

OUTDOOR COOKING FACILITIES

- **BBQ:** the facility has a barbecue on the premises
- **BBQ, CBA:** a barbecue can be arranged through the facility
- **BYO BBQ:** make arrangements for your own barbecue
- **n/a:** not applicable

CLEANUP

- **provided:** facility takes care of cleanup
- **caterer:** your caterer is responsible
- **caterer or renter:** both you and/or your caterer are responsible for cleanup

AUDIOVISUAL/MEETING EQUIPMENT

- **full range:** facility has a full range of audiovisual equipment
- **no:** no equipment is available
- **BYO:** bring your own equipment
- **CBA:** equipment can be arranged
- **CBA, extra fee:** equipment can be arranged for an extra fee

VIEW

We've described what type of view is available for each facility.

- **no:** the facility has no views to speak of

OTHER

Description of any service or amenity that is not included in above list.

Restrictions Key

ALCOHOL

- **in-house, no BYO:** the facility provides alcoholic beverages (for a fee) and does not permit you to bring your own
- **BYO:** you can bring your own alcohol
- **corkage, $/bottle:** if you bring your own alcohol, the facility charges a fee per bottle to remove the cork and pour
- **licensed server:** the server of alcohol must be licensed

SMOKING

- **allowed:** smoking is permitted throughout the facility
- **outside only:** smoking is not permitted inside the facility
- **not allowed:** smoking is not permitted anywhere on the premises
- **designated areas:** specific areas for smoking have been designated

MUSIC

Almost every facility allows acoustic music unless stated otherwise. Essentially, restrictions refer to amplified music.

- **amplified OK:** amplified music is acceptable without restriction
- **outside only:** no amplified music allowed inside
- **inside only:** no amplified music permitted outside
- **amplified OK with limits or restrictions:** amplified music is allowed, but there are limits on volume, hours of play, type of instruments, etc.

WHEELCHAIR ACCESS

Accessibility is based on whether the event areas (not necessarily the restrooms) of a facility are wheelchair accessible or not.

- **yes:** the facility is accessible
- **limited:** the facility is accessible but with difficulty (there may be a step at the entrance, for example, but all of the rooms are accessible)
- **no:** the facility is not accessible

INSURANCE

Many facilities require that you purchase and show proof of some insurance coverage. The type and amount of insurance varies with the facility, and some facilities offer insurance for a minimal charge.

- **liability required, certificate required,** or **proof of insurance required:** additional insurance is required
- **not required:** no additional insurance is required
- **may be required:** sometimes additional insurance is required

Valuable Tips

Selecting an Event Venue

Before you jump into the venue descriptions in *Here Comes The Guide,* identify what kind of celebration you want and establish selection criteria early. Here are some basics:

Your Venue's Geographical Location

For many couples, it's important that the location they select is easy for the majority of their guests to get to. However, whether you're hosting your event close to home or planning a destination wedding in another city, state, or country, you need to think about the logistics of getting everyone to your event site.

Special Considerations in Southern California

Guests may be traveling a considerable distance by car to your party destination. While they'll most likely be using their vehicle's navigation system to get there, be sure to provide additional instructions, tips, etc. if you think they'll be helpful.

If you're having a Friday evening event, take commuters into account, especially if your event site is in an area that gets bumper-to-bumper traffic. One solution is to schedule your get-together after 7pm when freeways are less congested.

Even if you have few constraints when picking a location, it's still worth considering the total driving time to and from your destination. When it's more than two hours, an overnight stay may be necessary, and you may be limited to a Saturday night event, since your nearest and dearest won't be able to spend hours on the road during the week. If you're going to need lodging for some of your guests during your celebration, be sure to check out the "Guest Accommodations/Room Blocks" section on HereComesTheGuide.com for suggestions and info. If you have guests arriving by plane, it's certainly helpful if there's an airport nearby, and if your co-workers, friends or family enjoy drinking try to house them close to the event site or have contact numbers handy for transportation via taxis, Uber, or another ride service.

There's no reason why you can't contemplate a special event in the San Diego mountains or in a wine cave in Santa Ynez. Just remember that if you're planning a wedding that's not local, a venue's on-site coordinator or a wedding planner can really help: Many are experienced in handling destination events and can be a great asset.

Budget

Many couples aren't very experienced with event budgeting and don't know how to estimate what locations, products, and services will ultimately cost. If you're not sure what you can realistically afford, we recommend talking to a professional event planner or wedding coordinator early in the planning stages. You don't have to make a big financial or time commitment to use a professional; many will assist you on an hourly basis for a nuts-and-bolts session to determine priorities and to assign costs to items on your wish list.

Part of being realistic involves some simple arithmetic. Catering costs, for example, are usually calculated on a per-person basis. The couple who has $10,000 and wants to invite 250 guests should know that $40 per guest actually won't go very far. Tax and gratuity combined usually consume 23–33% of the food & beverage budget. If you subtract that 30% from $40, you have $28 left. If you also serve alcohol at $12/person, you're down to $16/person for food. That's usually not enough for appetizers and a seated meal, let alone location rental fees, entertainment, flowers, printed invitations, photography, etc.

Before you make any major decisions or commit any of your funds for specific items, take a serious look at your total budget, make sure it can cover all your anticipated expenses, and leave a little cushion for last-minute items. If your budget doesn't cover everything, it's time for some hard decisions. If you have a very large guest list and a small pocketbook, you may need to shorten the list or cut back on some of the amenities you want to include. No matter who foots the bill, be advised that doing the homework here really counts. Pin down your costs at the beginning of the planning stage and get all estimates in writing.

> **The important point is that if you know what kind of event you want and are clear about your budget, your search will be faster and easier.**

Style

Do you know what kind of event you want? Will it be formal or informal? A traditional wedding or an innovative party? Will it be held at night or during the day? Indoors or outdoors? Is having a garden ceremony or gourmet food a deal breaker? By identifying the geographical area and the most important elements of your dream wedding before you start looking for a venue, you can really narrow down your search.

Guest Count

How many people are anticipated? Many facilities request a rough estimate 60–90 days in advance of your function—and they'll want a deposit based on the figure you give them. A confirmed guest count or guarantee is usually required 72 hours prior to the event. It's important to come up with a solid estimate of your guest list early on in order to plan your budget and select the right ceremony or reception spot.

It's also important to ensure that the guest count you give the facility *before* your event doesn't change *during* your event. Believe it or not, it's possible to have more people at your reception than you expected. How? Some folks who did not bother to RSVP may decide to show up anyway. In one case we know of, the parents of the bride got an additional bill for $1,200 on the event day because there were 30 "surprise" guests beyond the guest count guarantee who were wined and dined. To prevent this from happening to you—especially if you're having a large reception where it's hard to keep track of all the guests—it's a good idea to contact everyone who did *not* RSVP. Let them know as politely as possible that you will need to have their response by a given date to finalize food & beverage totals.

Seasonal Differences

Southern California, for all its (pardon the expression) faults, has got some great advantages weather-wise. Outdoor special events, ceremonies, and receptions can take place throughout most of the year, and from September to November you can anticipate sunny skies and warm temperatures. However, when the mercury rises in inland areas, watch out. A canopy or tables with umbrellas are essential for screening the sun. In fact, you should ask each facility manager about the sun's direction and intensity with respect to the time of day and month your event will take place. Guests will be uncomfortable facing into the sun during a ceremony, and white walls and enclosed areas bounce light around and can hold in heat. If your event is scheduled for midday in July, for example, include a note on your location map to bring sunglasses, hat, and sunscreen. If you also mention words like "poolside," "yacht deck" or "lawn seating" on the map, it will help guests know how to dress. In summer, you might want to consider an evening rather than a midday celebration. Not only is the air cooler, but you may also get an extra bonus—a glorious sunset.

If you're arranging an outdoor party November through April, or in the foothills or mountain areas, expect cooler weather and prepare a contingency plan. Despite our region's favorable Mediterranean climate, it has rained in May, June, and July, so consider access to an inside space or a tent (and factor in any additional cost that might require).

Special Requirements

Sometimes places have strict rules and regulations. If most of your guests smoke, then pick a location that doesn't restrict smoking. If alcohol is going to be consumed, make sure it's allowed and find out if bar service needs to be licensed. If dancing and a big band are critical, then limit yourself to those locations that can accommodate them and the accompanying decibels. Do you have children, seniors or disabled guests, vegetarians or folks who want kosher food on your list? If so, you need to plan for them, too. It's essential that you identify the special factors that are important for your event before you sign a contract.

Locking in Your Event Date

Let's say it's the first day of your hunt for the perfect spot, and the second place you see is an enchanting garden that happens to be available on the date you want. You really like it but, since you've only seen two locations, you're not 100% sure that this is *the* place. No problem. You decide to keep your options open by making a tentative reservation. The site coordinator dutifully pencils your name into her schedule book and says congratulations. You say thanks, we have a few more places (like 25) to check out, but this one looks terrific. Then off you go, secure in the knowledge that if none of the other sites you visit pans out, you still have this lovely garden waiting for you.

The nightmare begins a couple of weeks, or perhaps months, down the road when you've finished comparison-shopping and call back the first place you liked to finalize the details. So sorry, the coordinator says. We gave away your date because a) oops, one of the other gals who works here erased your name by mistake (after all, it was only *penciled* in), b) we didn't hear back from you soon enough, or c) you never confirmed your reservation with a deposit.

For the tiniest instant you picture yourself inflicting bodily harm on the coordinator or at least slapping the facility with a lawsuit, but alas, there's really not much you can do. Whether a genuine mistake was made or the facility purposely gave your date to another, perhaps more lucrative, party (this happens sometimes with hotels who'd rather book a big convention on your date than a little wedding), you're out of luck. To avoid the pain (and ensuing panic) of getting bumped, here's what we suggest: Instead of just being penciled in, ask if you can write a refundable $100–250 check to hold the date for a limited time. If the person in charge is willing to do this but wants the full deposit up front (usually nonrefundable), then you'll need to decide whether you can afford to lose the entire amount if you find a more appealing location later on. Once the coordinator or sales person takes your money, you're automatically harder to bump. Make sure you get a receipt that has the event date, year, time, and space(s) reserved written on it, as well as the date your tentative reservation runs out. Then, just to be on the safe side, check in with the facility weekly while you're considering other sites to prevent any possible "mistakes" from being made. When you finally do commit to a place, get a signed contract or at least a confirmation letter. If you don't receive written confirmation within a week, hound the coordinator until you get it, even if you have to drive to the sales office and stand there until they hand it over to you. And even after you've plunked down your money and have a letter and/or contract securing your date, call the coordinator every other month to reconfirm your reservation. It pays to stay on top of this, no matter how locked in you think you are. If you don't hear back from your contact in a reasonable time frame despite repeated attempts, you should contact the facility or catering sales department directly to confirm that your coordinator still works

> **If you try to pick a venue before you've made basic decisions, selection will be a struggle and it will take longer to find a spot that will make you happy.**

there. If she/he doesn't, find out who is responsible for managing your event, and verify that your contract (and the must-have details) are still in place.

Parking

Parking is seldom a critical factor if you get married outside an urban area, but make sure you know how it's going to be handled if you're planning a party in a parking-challenged place like downtown Los Angeles, Pasadena, or Santa Monica.

A map is a handy supplement to any invitation, and there's usually enough room on it to indicate how and where vehicles should be parked. Depending on the location, you may want to add a note suggesting carpooling or mention that a shuttle service or valet parking is provided. If there's a fee for parking, identify the anticipated cost per car and where the entry points are to the nearest parking lots. The last thing you want are surprised and disgruntled guests who can't find a place to stash their car, or who are shocked at the $20–40 parking tab.

Professional Help

If you're a busy person with limited time to plan and execute a party, pick a facility that offers complete coordination services, from catering and flowers to decorations and music. Or better yet, hire a professional event or wedding coordinator. Either way, you'll make your life much easier by having someone else handle the details. And often the relationships these professionals have with vendors can end up saving you money, too.

Food and Alcohol Quality

Food and alcohol account for the greatest portion of an event's budget; consequently, food & beverage selections are a big deal. Given the amount of money you will spend on this category alone, you should be concerned about the type, quantity, and quality of what you eat and drink. If in-house catering is provided, we suggest you sample different menu options prior to paying a facility deposit. If you'd like to see how a facility handles food setup and presentation, ask the caterer to arrange a visit to someone else's party about a half hour before it starts. It's wise to taste wines and beers in advance, and be very specific about hard alcohol selections.

Hidden Costs

This may come as a surprise, but not all services and event equipment are covered in the rental fee, and some facilities hide the true cost of renting their space by having a low rental fee. It's possible to get nickeled and dimed for all the extras: tables, chairs, linens, dance floor, cake cutting, valet service and so forth. You can also end up paying more than you expected for security and cleanup. All these additional charges can really add up, so save yourself a big headache by understanding exactly what's included in the rental fee and what's not before you sign any contract.

Bonus Info

If you're not sure what to ask potential venues and event professionals, check out our "Questions to Ask" section starting on page 21. We've put together lists of questions that come in very handy when you're interviewing potential event locations, photographers, caterers, etc.

Tips for Previewing a Venue

Make Appointments.

If you liked what you read about a venue in *The Guide,* then we recommend you make an appointment to see that location rather than just driving by. Sometimes an unremarkable-looking building will surprise you with a secluded garden or hidden courtyard. And sometimes the opposite is true—you'll love the stunning façade, but the interior isn't your style.

Incidentally, we've withheld the addresses of privately owned properties. Should you happen to know where any of these facilities is located, we urge you to respect the owner's or manager's privacy and make an appointment instead of stopping by.

When you do call for an appointment, it's not a bad idea to ask for specific directions, including cross streets. GPS is great when it works, but sometimes it doesn't so it's useful to have directions as a backup (you can also look up the location on *HereComesTheGuide.com* and print out a detailed street map). Try to cluster your visits so that you can easily drive from one place to another without backtracking. Schedule at least an hour per facility and leave ample driving time. You want to be efficient, but don't over-schedule yourself. It's best to view places when you're fresh and your judgment isn't clouded by fatigue.

Bring along *The Guide* or use your phone or tablet to access our website.

We've listed the street address for each site, and our illustrations in the book often make it easier to identify the venues you're planning to see. And if you bring the book or use your smartphone or tablet to look up venues on HereComesTheGuide.com, you can double-check our information with the site representative.

Bring a notebook—paper or digital!

You can make notes in your copy of *Here Comes The Guide,* but have a small notebook or digital device handy, too. Keep track of the date, time and name of the person providing the information, and then read back the info to the site representative to confirm that what you heard is correct. Remember to have your notes with you when you review your contract, and go over in detail what you were told versus what's in the contract before you sign anything.

Take pictures.

Video is particularly useful for narrating your likes, dislikes and any other observations while you're shooting a venue. However, if you're just taking still photos, make sure you have a system for matching shots to their respective locations. You'd be surprised how easy it is to confuse photos. Make sure your phone or other gear is charged and bring whatever else you need to make it all work properly.

File everything.

Many facilities will hand you pamphlets, menus, rate charts and other materials. Develop a system for sorting and storing the information that keeps your notes, photos and handouts together, clearly labeled and easily accessible.

Bring a checkbook or credit card.

Some of the more attractive venues book a year to 18 months in advance. If you actually fall in love with a location and your date is available, plunk down a deposit to hold the date.

Working With a Venue

Confirm All the Details

When you make the initial phone call or email, confirm that the information presented in *Here Comes The Guide* is still valid. Show or read the information in our book to the site's representative, and have him or her inform you of any changes. If there have been significant increases in fees or new restrictions that you can't live with, cross the place off your list and move on. If the facility is still a contender, request a tour.

Once you've determined that the physical elements of the place suit you, it's time to discuss details. Ask about services and amenities or fees that may not be listed in the book and make a note of them. Outline your plans to the representative and make sure that the facility can accommodate your particular needs. If you don't want to handle all the details yourself, find out what the facility is willing and able to do, and if there will be an additional cost for their assistance. Venues often provide planning services for little or no extra charge. If other in-house services are offered, such as flowers or wedding cakes, inquire about the quality of each service provider and whether or not substitutions can be made. If you want to use your own vendors, find out if the facility will charge you an extra fee. For more help with working with a location, see our "Questions to Ask a Wedding Venue" on page 26.

The Importance of Rapport

Another factor to consider is your rapport with the person(s) you're working with. Are you comfortable with them? Do they listen well and respond to your questions directly? Do they inspire trust and confidence? Are they warm and enthusiastic or cold and aloof? If you have doubts, you need to resolve them before embarking on a working relationship with these folks—no matter how wonderful the facility itself is. Discuss your feelings with them, and if you're still not completely satisfied, get references and call them. If at the end of this process you still have lingering concerns, you may want to eliminate the facility from your list even though it seems perfect in every other way.

On the other hand, don't let your rapport with a banquet coordinator or site rep sway you to book a venue you aren't in love with—there's a lot of turnover in the hospitality industry, and you may call Brittany one day only to—surprise!—be referred to Brian. So if Brittany was your main reason for choosing this place, you could be in for a big disappointment if you and Brian don't hit it off and suddenly the venue's shortcomings really stand out.

Signing a Contract

It's easy to get emotionally attached to a venue, but remember that it's not a done deal until you sign a contract. Now's the time to be businesslike and put your emotions aside. If you can't do that, get a non-emotional partner, friend, or relative to help you review the small print and negotiate changes before you sign. Remember all those notes you took when you first visited the venue? Compare them with what's actually written in the contract. No matter what someone told you about the availability of a dance floor, the price of pastel linens, or the ceremony arch, you can't hold the facility to it until the contract is signed. Places revise their prices and policies all the time, so assume that things may have changed since you originally saw the site or talked to a site representative.

If you're not happy with the contract, prepare to negotiate. Before your appointment with whoever has the power to alter the contract, make an itemized list, in order of importance, of the changes you want. Decide what you're willing to give up, and what you can't live without. If in the end the most important things on your list cannot be addressed to your satisfaction, this is probably not the right place for you. It's better to find another location than to stay with a facility that isn't willing to work with you.

Insurance Considerations

Nowadays, if someone gets injured at an event or something is damaged at or near the event site, it's likely that someone will be sued.

In order to protect themselves and spread the risk among all parties involved, facilities often require additional insurance and/or proof of insurance from service professionals and their clients.

Event venues and service professionals (such as caterers) are very aware of their potential liability and all have coverage of one kind or another. Many of the properties we represent will also require you, the renter, to get extra insurance.

What's funny (or not so funny) is that as more and more event sites require extra liability and/or a certificate of insurance, fewer insurance companies are willing to issue either one—even if you're covered under a homeowner's policy. At this point, insurance carriers don't want to attach extra clauses to your policy to increase coverage for a single event, and most, if not all, companies are unwilling to add the event site's name to your existing policy as an additional insured.

Don't despair. Even though it's hard to come by, you can get extra insurance for a specified period of time, and it's relatively inexpensive.

Obtaining Extra Insurance

- **The first thing to do is read your rental contract carefully.** Make sure you understand exactly *what's* required and *when* it's required. Most facilities want $1,000,000–2,000,000 in extra liability coverage. If you don't pay attention to the insurance clauses early in the game, you'll have to play catch-up at the last moment, frantically trying to locate a carrier who will issue you additional insurance. And, if you don't supply the certificate to the facility *on time,* you may run the risk of forfeiting your event site altogether.

- **The second thing is to ask your event site's representative if the site has an insurance policy through which you can purchase the required extra coverage.** If the answer is yes, then consider purchasing it—that's the easiest route (but not necessarily the best!). The facility's extra insurance coverage may not be the least expensive and it may not provide you with the best coverage. What you need to ask is: "If one of my guests or one of the professionals working at my event causes some damage to the premises or its contents, will this extra insurance cover it?" If the answer if yes, get it in writing.

- **The third thing, if the answer is no, is to find your own coverage.** We suggest you avoid random searches online and call one of these two insurance providers:

  1) WedSafe at 877/723-3933. This company insures weddings and private events. You can reach them at their toll free number or online at wedsafe.com. They offer coverage for wedding cancellation and/or liability.

  2) WedSure®, a division of R.V. Nuccio & Associates, Inc. at 1-800-ENGAGED or www.WedSure.com. They specialize in insuring special events. Their website FAQs outline what's offered, and you can also contact them to clarify details and get a personalized quote.

  Coverage starts at $95 for a wedding; the total cost will depend on what you want. Rob Nuccio's coverage is underwritten by Fireman's Fund.

Here are some of the items a typical policy might cover:

- Cancellation or postponement due to: weather, damage to the facility, sickness, failure to show of the caterer or officiant, financial reasons—even limited change-of-heart circumstances!

- Photography or videography: failure of the professional to appear, loss of original negatives, etc.

- Lost, stolen, or damaged gifts

- Lost, stolen, or damaged equipment rentals

- Lost, stolen, or damaged bridal gown or other special attire

- Lost, stolen, or damaged jewelry

- Personal liability and additional coverage

- Medical payments for injuries incurred during the event

If you use this service, call or email to let us know whether you're happy with them. We'd love to get your feedback.

It Can't Happen To Me

Don't be lulled into the notion that an event disaster can't happen to you. It could rain when you least expect it. Or your well-intentioned aunt might melt your wedding dress while ironing out a few wrinkles. Wouldn't it be nice to know that your dress, wedding photos, equipment rentals, and gifts are covered? Naturally, a New Year's Eve party or a high school prom night is riskier than a wedding, but we could tell you stories of upscale parties where something did happen and a lawsuit resulted.

So even if extra insurance is not required, you may still want to consider additional coverage, especially if alcohol is being served. *You are the best predictor of your guests' behavior.* If you plan on having a wild, wonderful event, a little additional insurance could be a good thing.

Recycling

Do Your Part!

If you're wondering why we're including a brief item about recycling in a book like *Here Comes The Guide,* it's because parties and special events often generate recyclable materials as well as leftover food and flowers.

You and your caterer can feel good by donating the excess, and recycling plastic bottles, glass, paper, etc. An added benefit is that food donations are tax deductible for either you or the caterer. And if you recycle, the cost for extra garbage bins can be eliminated or reduced. Call your local recycling center to arrange a pickup.

Food donations can be distributed to teenage drop-in centers, youth shelters, alcoholic treatment centers, rescue missions, and AIDS hospices, as well as senior, homeless, and refugee centers. Flowers will brighten the day of patients or residents at your favorite local hospital, hospice or senior center.

IMPORTANT: There are regulations that apply to the kinds of foods that can be donated and how they need to be packaged. If you plan to donate your leftovers, it's best to talk to your caterer about it or call the places where you'd like to donate *prior* to your event to find out what their requirements for preparation and drop-off are. Look online to find Southern California food banks and homeless shelters that take food donations.

For more valuable tips about going green, read our article "It's A Nice Day for a Green Wedding." You'll find it in the Wedding Ideas section on HereComesTheGuide.com!

Working With Event Professionals

Hiring a Caterer: Get References and Look for Professionalism

If you're selecting your own caterer, get references from friends and acquaintances or, better yet, contact any of the caterers featured on HereComesTheGuide.com. We've thoroughly screened these companies and can assure you that they're in the top 5% of the industry in terms of quality and service. We keep all of their references on file, so you can contact us and ask questions about them.

Every caterer is different. Some offer only preset menus while others will help you create your own. Menus and prices vary enormously, so try to have a good idea of what you want and what you can spend before interviewing prospective caterers. After you've talked to several caterers and have decided which ones to seriously consider, request references from each one and call them. Ask not only about the quality of the food, but about the ease of working with a given caterer. You'll want to know if the caterer is professional—fully prepared and equipped, punctual and organized. You may also want to know if the caterer is licensed, prepares food in a kitchen approved by the Department of Health, or carries workmen's compensation and liability insurance. And don't forget to inquire about the cleanup—did the staff remove all the equipment and garbage in a matter that was acceptable? Although this level of inquiry may seem unnecessary, responses to these questions will give you a more complete picture of how a caterer runs his or her business, and will help you determine which one is best suited for your event.

Facility Requirements for Caterers

Facilities often have specific requirements regarding caterers—they may have to be licensed and bonded, out by 11pm, or fastidiously clean. Before you hire a caterer, make sure that he or she is compatible with your site. In fact, even if the facility does not require it, it's a good idea to have your caterer visit the place in advance to become familiar with any special circumstances or problems that might come up. You'll notice throughout *Here Comes The Guide* the words "in-house" or "select from list" after the word *Catering*. Sites that have an exclusive caterer or only permit you to select from a preferred list do so because each wants to eliminate most of the risks involved in having a caterer on the premises who is not accustomed to working in that environment. Exclusive or preferred caterers have achieved their exalted status because they either provide consistently good services or they won the catering contract when it went out to bid. Whether you're working with one of your facility's choices or your own, make sure that your contract includes everything you have agreed on before you sign it.

Working with an Event Planner or Wedding Coordinator

Opting to hire a professional planner may be a wise choice. A good consultant will ask you all the right questions, determine exactly what you need, and take care of as much or as little of your affair as you want. If you'd like to feel like a guest at your own event, have the consultant manage everything, including orchestrating the day of the event. If you only want some advice and structure, hire a planner on a meeting-by-meeting basis.

Most of the principles used in selecting a caterer apply to hiring an event coordinator. Try to get suggestions from friends or facilities, follow up on references the coordinators give you, compare service fees and make sure you and the coordinator are compatible. The range of professionalism and experience varies greatly, so it really is to your advantage to investigate each coordinator's track record. You can save a lot of time by starting with the coordinators featured on HereComesTheGuide.com.

Again, once you've found someone who can accommodate you, get everything in writing so that there won't be any misunderstandings down the road. Although engaging a professional to "manage" your event can be a godsend, it can also be problematic if you turn the entire decision-making process over to them. Don't forget that it's your party, and no one else should decide what's right for you.

For lists of questions to ask potential wedding venues and vendors, see the next section. You can also find them on HereComesTheGuide.com.

Questions To Ask
Venues and Event Professionals

(including Here Comes The Guide's Wedding Checklist)

Here Comes The Guide's Wedding Checklist

10–12 Months To Go...

☐ Visit HereComesTheGuide.com and start planning your wedding!

☐ Work out your budget and establish your top priorities—where to save/where to splurge.

☐ Get your creative juices flowing. Start browsing our Wedding Ideas, Real Weddings, and Pinterest, as well as bridal blogs and magazines to identify your wedding style and color palette.

☐ Compile your preliminary guest list (you'll need that guest count!).

☐ Choose your wedding party—who do you want by your side at the altar?

☐ Sign up for MyGuide. We'll send you useful—and sassy!—wedding planning emails.

☐ Find a venue for your ceremony and reception, and reserve your date. Know what questions to ask when evaluating a wedding venue (see page 26).

☐ Do you need wedding insurance? It's something to think about. Check with your venue about Liability Insurance and consider other options, like cancellation insurance.

☐ Now that you have a date, tell everyone to save it! For destination weddings or weddings around a holiday, consider sending out Save-the-Date cards or emails. Or create your own wedding website, and let your invitees know about it.

☐ Say yes to your wedding dress (or tux!) and begin assembling the perfect accessories. Need inspiration? Attend a trunk show or bridal fair.

☐ Already feeling overwhelmed? Consider hiring a Wedding Coordinator.

☐ Assemble an all-star vendor team. We'd start with:
- Caterer
- Photographer/Videographer
- Officiant

When you hire a vendor, get all the details in writing!

☐ Another way to minimize stress: Start dreaming up your honeymoon...and check out our "Plan A Honeymoon" section on HereComesTheGuide.com.

6–9 Months To Go...

☐ Continue researching, interviewing and booking vendors. And don't forget, when you hire one, make sure to put everything in writing!
- Decide on arrangements with your Floral Designer.
- Do a tasting and choose your wedding cake with your Cake Designer.
- Hire the DJ/Entertainment for your ceremony, cocktail hour and reception.
- Discuss the style and wording of your wedding invitations with a Stationer.

☐ Create your gift registry (and don't forget to update your wedding website!).

☐ Arrange hotel room blocks for out-of-town guests and book your own suite for the wedding night. See HereComesTheGuide.com for room block options.

☐ Shop for bridesmaid/flower girl dresses and give your attendants clear instructions on how to place their orders.

☐ Arrange and book any necessary transportation.

☐ Go over bridal shower/bachelorette details and the guest list with the person(s) hosting your party.

3–5 Months To Go...

☐ Book the rehearsal and rehearsal dinner locations (see HereComesTheGuide.com for rehearsal dinner options). If you're including entertainment or specialty details like a groom's cake, now's the time to lock in these elements.

☐ Put together your rehearsal dinner guest list.

☐ Make childcare arrangements for your guests'

kids.

☐ Reserve all necessary party rentals and linens.

☐ Order wedding favors for your guests.

☐ Shop for and reserve men's formalwear.

☐ Concentrate on finalizing the:
- Guest list. Get everyone's mailing address.
- Invitation wording. Confirm your invitation text with the Stationer, and consider additional stationery (programs, menu cards, place cards, thank-you cards, etc.). Schedule a pickup date for your invites.
- Ceremony readings and vows.
- Menu, beverage and catering details.
- Timeline of the reception formalities.

☐ Do a Makeup & Hair trial and book your stylists. While you're at it, come up with your own beauty and fitness regimen to be camera-ready for the big day.

☐ Shop for and purchase your wedding rings.

☐ Finalize honeymoon plans and obtain all necessary documents (are you sure your passports are up to date?).

6–8 Weeks To Go...

☐ You're getting close...mail out those invitations! Have a game plan for recording the RSVPs and meal choices.

☐ Touch base with your vendors to confirm date, deposits and details.

☐ Start researching marriage license requirements and name-change paperwork.

☐ Begin your dress fittings. Be sure to buy the appropriate undergarments beforehand.

☐ So you think you *can't* dance? Consider taking a dance lesson with your fiancé—a good way to break in your bridal shoes!

☐ Give the wedding party a nudge—make sure they've ordered all necessary attire.

☐ Write thank-you cards for shower gifts and any early wedding gifts received.

3–5 Weeks To Go...

☐ Send out rehearsal dinner invitations. If your get-together will be informal, feel free to send an Evite.

☐ Finalize and confirm:
- Wedding vows and readings with your Officiant.
- Shot list with your Photographer/Videographer.
- Song list for ceremony, cocktail hour and reception with your DJ and/or Band/Musicians.
- Timeline for the reception and who's giving the toasts.
- Wedding night and honeymoon accommodations.

☐ Obtain marriage license and complete name-change documents, if applicable.

☐ Pick up your wedding rings and proofread any engraving!

☐ If you're the traditional type, do you have something old, new, borrowed and blue?

☐ Purchase your guest book, toasting flutes, cake servers, unity candle, and all that good stuff.

☐ Buy gifts (optional) for the wedding party and parents of the wedding couple.

☐ Have your final dress fitting. Bring your shoes and accessories for the full impact.

☐ Sigh. Hunt down whoever hasn't RSVP'd yet.

1–2 Weeks To Go...

☐ Give your caterer/venue the final guest count.

☐ Arrange seating and create the seating chart and/or place cards.

☐ Pick up your gown. Swoon.

☐ Confirm arrival times and finalize the wedding timeline with vendors and the wedding party—make sure your MOH has a copy, too.

☐ Put together your own Bridal Emergency Kit.

☐ Speaking of emergencies: Check the weather report, and if things look iffy contact your venue to make sure a contingency plan is in place.

☐ Start packing for your honeymoon. (See "weather report" above.)

☐ In desperate need of a facial or massage? Now's the time to squeeze one in.

The Day Before...

☐ Make sure all wedding-day items are packed/ laid out and ready to go! (Don't forget the rings and marriage license!)

☐ Figure out tips and final payments for vendors. Put them in clearly marked envelopes and give them to the Best Man or another person you trust to hand out at the reception.

☐ Assign someone to pack up your gifts/ belongings after the reception (don't forget the top tier of your cake!).

☐ Thank your BFF for agreeing to return your groom's tux and other rental items the day after the wedding.

☐ Enjoy a mani-pedi.

☐ Attend the rehearsal and dinner. Now's the time to give out wedding party gifts.

☐ Try to go to bed early…you need your beauty sleep tonight.

Wedding-day advice...

☐ Allow plenty of time to get ready.

☐ Do the rounds at your wedding—greet everyone and thank them for coming.

☐ Take a deep breath. Stop to appreciate your new spouse and the day that you spent so much time planning!

After the Honeymoon/Back to Reality...

☐ Write and send thank-you cards. (Don't procrastinate!)

☐ Complete your registry and exchange any unwanted or duplicate gifts.

☐ Have your wedding dress cleaned and preserved by a reputable company.

☐ Keep in touch with your Photographer/ Videographer to work on albums, DVDs, etc.

☐ Enjoy wedded bliss…

Questions to Ask a Wedding Venue

Here Comes The Guide is a fantastic resource to help you find the location to host your wedding, rehearsal dinner or company party. Even with all the info we provide, though, you'll need to address your specific needs with each venue you visit to come up with a winner. Which is why we've come up with this comprehensive list of questions to ask your venue!

The following list of questions and tips will help you navigate through your location search (for a printable version, go to HereComesTheGuide.com). Use them as a guide while you're talking with a site contact or reviewing a site information packet. Feel free to add questions that relate to your particular event (e.g. "Can my dog be the ring bearer in my ceremony?") Make sure to get everything in writing in your final contract!

Don't forget to have a notebook, digital device or your planning binder handy so that you can record answers to all these questions.

1. What dates are available in the month I'm considering?

2. How many people can this location accommodate?

3. What is the rental fee and what is included in that price? Is there a discount for booking an off-season date or Sunday through Friday?

4. How much is the deposit, when is it due, and is it refundable? What's the payment plan for the entire bill?

5. Can I hold my ceremony here, too? Is there an additional charge? Is the ceremony site close to the reception site? Are there changing areas for the bride and groom? How much time is allocated for the rehearsal?

6. Is the site handicap accessible? (To be asked if you have guests with mobility issues.)

7. What's the cancellation policy? *NOTE: Some places will refund most of your deposit if you cancel far enough in advance, since there's still a chance they can rent the space. After a certain date, though, you may not be able to get a refund—at least not a full one.*

8. What's your weather contingency plan for outdoor spaces?

9. How long will I have use of the event space(s) I reserve? Is there an overtime fee if I stay longer? Is there a minimum or maximum rental time?

10. Can I move things around and decorate to suit my purposes, or do I have to leave everything as is? Are there decoration guidelines/restrictions? Can I use real candles? *TIP: Keep the existing décor in mind when planning your own decorations so that they won't clash. If your event is in December, ask what the venue's holiday décor will be.*

11. What time can my vendors start setting up on the day of the wedding? Is it possible to start the setup the day before? How early can deliveries be made? How much time will I have for décor setup? Does the venue provide assistance getting gifts or décor back to a designated car, hotel room, etc. after the event has concluded?

12. Do you provide a coat check service (especially important for winter weddings)? If not, is there an area that can be used and staffed for that purpose?

13. Is there an outdoor space where my guests can mingle, and can it be heated and/or protected from the elements if necessary? Is there a separate indoor "socializing" space?

14. Do you have an in-house caterer or a list of "preferred" caterers, or do I need to provide my own? Even if there is an in-house caterer, do I have the option of using an outside caterer instead?

15. If I hire my own caterer, are kitchen facilities available for them? *NOTE: Caterers charge extra if they have to haul in refrigerators and stoves.*

16. Are tables, linens, chairs, plates, silverware and glassware provided, or will I have to rent them myself or get them through my caterer?

17. What is the food & beverage cost on a per-person basis? What is the tax and service charge?

18. Can we do a food tasting prior to finalizing our menu selection? If so, is there an additional charge?

19. Can I bring in a cake from an outside cake maker or must I use a cake made on the premises? Is there a cake-cutting fee? If I use a cake made on site is the fee waived? Do you provide special cake-cutting utensils?

20. Can I bring my own wine, beer or champagne, and is there a corkage fee if I do? Can I bring in other alcohol?

21. Are you licensed to provide alcohol service? If so, is alcohol priced per person? By consumption? Are there additional charges for bar staff? Is there a bar minimum that must be met before the conclusion of the event? What is the average bar tab for the number of people attending my

event? *NOTE: Some facilities (private estates and wineries in particular) aren't licensed to serve hard alcohol. You may need to get permission from the location to bring in an outside beverage catering company.*

22. Are there restrictions on what kind of music I can play, or a time by which the music must end? Can the venue accommodate a DJ or live band? *TIP: Check where the outlets are located in your event space, because that will help you figure out where the band can set up and where other vendors can hook up their equipment. You don't want the head table to block the only outlet in the room.*

23. Is there parking on site? If so, is it complimentary? Do you offer valet parking, and what is the charge? If there is no parking on site, where will my guests park? Are cabs easily accessible from the venue?? If a shuttle service is needed, can you assist with setting it up? *TIP: You should have the venue keep track of the number of cars parked for your event and add the total valet gratuity to your final bill so that your guests won't have to tip.*

24. How many restrooms are there? *TIP: You should have at least 4 restrooms per 100 people.*

25. Do you offer on-site coordination? If so, what services are included and is there an additional charge for them? Will the coordinator supervise day-of? How much assistance can I get with the setup/décor?

26. What security services do you offer? Do I need to hire my own security guards, or does the site hire them or have them on staff? *TIP: In general, you should have 2 security guards for the first 100 guests and 1 more for every additional 100 guests.*

27. Does the venue have liability insurance? *NOTE: If someone gets injured during the party, you don't want to be held responsible—if the site doesn't have insurance, you'll need to get your own. For info on insurance go to page xx.*

28. Can I hire my own vendors (caterer, coordinator, DJ, etc.), or must I select from a preferred vendor list? If I can bring my own, do you have a list of recommended vendors? *TIP: Check out the prescreened vendors featured on HereComesTheGuide.com. They're all top event professionals who have passed our extensive reference check and been Certified By The Guide.*

29. What overnight accommodations do you provide? Do you offer a discount for booking multiple rooms? Do you provide a complimentary room or upgrade for the newlyweds? What are the near-est hotels to the venue? *TIP: Some venues have partnerships with local hotels that offer a discount if you book a block of rooms.*

30. Do you have signage or other aids to direct guests to my event?

31. Do you have a recycling policy?

More Tips:

- If you really love the site, ask the venue representative to put together a proposal with all the pricing and policies—including the tax and service charge—so you have an idea of the basic cost.

- Use your cell phone (or a digital camera) to take photos or videos of the locations you visit, so that you have a record of what you liked or didn't like about them. And if you're planning to visit more than a few venues, it's a good idea to snap a photo of each one's sign when you arrive—that way you won't get confused about which place is which when you review your photos later.

- Pay attention to the venue as a whole: Check out everything, including the restrooms, the foyer, the dressing rooms, the outdoor lighting and even the kitchen. You want to be sure your vision can be realized at this location. If possible, make arrangements with the site representative to visit the venue when it's set up for a wedding.

- GET EVERYTHING IN WRITING. Your date is not officially reserved until you sign a contract and, in many cases, give a deposit—even if a site contact says you don't need to worry about it. Once you've found THE PLACE, make sure you ask what is required to get your booking locked in and then follow through on satisfying those requirements. And don't assume that just because the site coordinator said you can have 4 votive candles per table you'll get them. Before you sign a contract, read the fine print and make sure it includes everything you and the site contact agreed on. As new things are added or changed in your contract, have the updated version printed out and signed by you and the site representative. Also, document all your conversations in emails and keep your correspondence.

Questions to Ask a Wedding Photographer

You've put so much time and effort into planning your wedding you'll want every special moment captured in photos. But how do you know which photographer is right for you? Whether you're considering any of our *Certified By The Guide* wedding photographers or another professional, you need to do your homework.

Here are the questions you should ask those photographers who've made your short list, to ensure that the one you ultimately choose is a good fit for you and your wedding.

The Basics

1. Do you have my date available? *NOTE: Obviously, if the answer is NO and you're not willing or able to change your date, don't bother asking the rest of these questions.*

2. How far in advance do I need to book with you?

3. How long have you been in business?

4. How many weddings have you shot? Have you done many that were similar to mine in size and style?

5. How would you describe your photography style (e.g. traditional, photojournalistic, creative)? *NOTE: It's helpful to know the differences between wedding photography styles so that you can discuss your preferences with your photographer. For descriptions of the various styles, see the next page.*

6. How would you describe your working style? *NOTE: The answer should help you determine whether this is a photographer who blends into the background and shoots what unfolds naturally, or creates a more visible presence by taking charge and choreographing shots.*

7. What do you think distinguishes your work from that of other photographers?

8. Do you have a portfolio I can review? Are all of the images yours, and is the work recent?

9. What type of equipment do you use?

10. Are you shooting in digital or film format or both? *NOTE: The general consensus seems to be that either format yields excellent photos in the hands of an experienced professional, and that most people can't tell the difference between film and digital images anyway. However, film takes longer to process than digital.*

11. Do you shoot in color and black & white? Infrared? *NOTE: Photographers who shoot in a digital format can make black & white or sepia versions of color photos.*

12. Can I give you a list of specific shots we would like?

13. Can you put together a slideshow of the engagement session (along with other photos the couple provides) and show it during the cocktail hour? What about an "instant" slideshow of the ceremony?

14. What information do you need from me before the wedding day?

15. Have you ever worked with my florist? DJ? Co-ordinator, etc.? *NOTE: Great working relationships between vendors can make things go more smoothly. It's especially helpful if your videographer and photographer work well together.*

16. May I have a list of references? *NOTE: The photographer should not hesitate to provide this.*

The Shoot

17. Are you the photographer who will shoot my wedding? If so, will you have any assistants with you on that day? If not, who will be taking the pictures and can I meet them before my wedding? *NOTE: You should ask the questions on this list of whoever is going to be the primary photographer at your event, and that photographer's name should be on your contract.*

18. Do you have backup equipment? What about a backup plan if you (or my scheduled photographer) are unable to shoot my wedding for some reason?

19. If my wedding site is out of your area, do you charge a travel fee and what does that cover?

20. Are you photographing other events on the same day as mine?

21. How will you (and your assistants) be dressed? *NOTE: The photographer and his/her staff should look professional and fit in with the style of your event.*

22. Is it okay if other people take photos while you're taking photos?

23. Have you ever worked at my wedding site before? If not, do you plan to check it out in advance? *NOTE: Photographers who familiarize themselves with a location ahead of time will be prepared for any lighting issues or restrictions, and will know how best to incorporate the site's architectural elements into the photos.*

24. What time will you arrive at the site and for how long will you shoot?

25. If my event lasts longer than expected, will you stay? Is there an additional charge?

Packages, Proofs and Prints

26. What packages do you offer?

27. Can I customize a package based on my needs?

28. Do you include engagement photos in your packages?

29. What type of album designs do you offer? Do you provide any assistance in creating an album?

30. Do you provide retouching, color adjustment or other corrective services?

31. How long after the wedding will I get the proofs? Will they be viewable online?

32. What is the ordering process?

33. How long after I order my photos/album will I get them?

34. Will you give me the negatives or the digital images, and is there a fee for that?

Contracts and Policies

35. When will I receive a written contract? *TIP: Don't book a photographer—or any vendor—who won't provide a written contract.*

36. How much of a deposit do you require and when is it due? Do you offer a payment plan?

37. What is your refund/cancellation policy?

38. Do you have liability insurance?

Questions to Ask Yourself:

1. Do I feel a connection with this photographer as well as his/her photos? Are our personalities a good match?

2. Am I comfortable with this person's work and communication style?

3. Has this photographer listened well and addressed all my concerns?

Check references. *Ask the photographer for at least 5 references, preferably of couples whose weddings were similar to yours in size and/or style. Getting feedback from several people who have actually hired the photographer in question can really help you decide if that person is right for you. Be sure to check out the photographers on HereComesTheGuide.com. They're some of the best in the business and have all been Certified By The Guide.*

Photography Style Glossary

Though there are no standard "dictionary definitions" of photographic styles, it's still a good idea to have an understanding of the following approaches before you interview photographers:

Traditional, Classic: The main idea behind this timeless style is to produce posed photographs for display in a portrait album. The photographer works from a "shot list," ensuring he or she covers all the elements the bride and groom have requested. To make sure every detail of the shots is perfect, the photographer and his/her assistants not only adjust their equipment, but also the background, the subject's body alignment, and even the attire.

Photojournalism: Originally favored by the news media, this informal, reality-based approach is the current rage in wedding photography. Rather than posing your pictures, the photographer follows you and your guests throughout the wedding day, capturing events as they unfold to tell the story of your wedding. He or she has to be able to fade into the background and become "invisible" in order to snap these candid or unposed photos, and must also possess a keen eye and a willingness to do what it takes to get the shot.

Illustrative Photography: This style, which is often used for engagement photos, is a pleasing blend of traditional and photojournalistic, with an emphasis on composition, lighting and background. The photographer places subjects together in an interesting environment and encourages them to relax and interact. Illustrative captures some of the spontaneity of candids, while offering the technical control of posed shots.

Portraiture: Traditional photographers generally excel at the precision required in portraiture—formal, posed pictures that emphasize one or more people. Couples interested in a more edgy result may prefer Fine Art Portraiture, with its dramatic lighting, unique angles and European flavor.

High Fashion: Commercial photographers excel at creating striking, simple photographs that dramatize the subject—and, of course, her clothes! Though not a style generally included in wedding photography, you may want to choose a photographer with high fashion experience if looking artsy and glamorous while showing off your dress is important to you.

Natural Light: Rather than using a camera flash, photographers use the natural light found in a setting, usually daylight. The look is warm and, well, natural—yet the photographer must be skilled to deal with shadows and other lighting challenges.

Questions to Ask a Wedding Planner

In the first flush of joy after your engagement, you probably began browsing wedding websites, social media sites like Pinterest, and magazines. If you soon felt buried by a blizzard of checklists and a daunting array of decisions, you and your fiancé might want to think about hiring a professional wedding planner.

Depending on your budget and needs, you can contract:

- a full-service planner to arrange every detail

- someone to assist you only in choosing your wedding location and vendors

- a day-of coordinator (which really means 30 days before your wedding)

NOTE: Many locations have in-house coordinators, but make sure you're clear on exactly what level of service they provide. Venue coordinators usually just handle day-of issues and offer a list of their preferred vendors, so having your own planner may still be a great help.

Even though hiring a planner is an added cost, they often end up saving you money in the long run. And no doubt about it—the right wedding planner can definitely save you time and stress (priceless!).

Before interviewing potential wedding planners, you and your fiancé should have an idea of:

- How much money you have in your budget

- How many people you would like to invite

- Your preferred wedding date

- Your vision for your wedding *(NOTE: If you aren't sure yet don't worry—getting help with this is one of the reasons why you're hiring a wedding planner!)*

After each interview is complete, ask yourselves:

- Did we feel heard?

- Does the planner understand our vision?

- Did we get a strong sense he/she will work with our budget?

- Was there a good connection and did our personalities mesh well?

Listen to your gut. If an interview doesn't feel right, then maybe that person just isn't a good fit for you. Your wedding planner is the vendor you'll be spending the most time with, so it's important to pick someone who's compatible with you and your fiancé.

Now, here are THE QUESTIONS!

Getting to Know a Planner

1. Do you have our wedding date open? If so, do you anticipate any issues with the date such as weather, travel for our guests, difficulty booking a venue, etc.?

2. What made you want to be a wedding planner?

3. Describe the most challenging wedding you planned and how you handled the problems that came up.

4. How would you rate your problem-solving skills?

5. How would you rate your communication skills?

6. Are you a certified wedding planner? If so, where did you get certified? What is your educational background?

7. Are you a member of any wedding association(s)? If so, does your association require you to satisfy yearly education requirements?

8. How long have you been in business? Do you have a business license?

9. How many full-scale weddings have you planned? When was your last one?

10. How many wedding clients do you take on in a year? How many do you expect to have during the month of our wedding?

11. Is wedding planning your full-time job? If it's part-time, what is your other job?

Working With the Venue

12. Have you ever worked at the venue we've chosen?

13. If our event is outdoors, what contingency plan would you have for bad weather? (Describe an event where you had weather issues and how you resolved them.)

Hiring Other Vendors

14. Are we required to book only the vendors you recommend or do we have the freedom to hire someone even if you haven't worked with them before?

15. Do you take a commission or discount from any of the vendors you would refer us to?

16. Will you be present at all of the vendor meetings and will you assist us in reviewing all of the vendor contracts and making sure everything is in order?

17. Will you invoice us for all the vendor fees or will we need to pay each one of them ourselves?

18. For the vendors who will be on site the day of our wedding, can I provide you with checks for final payment that you will distribute to them?

19. If issues arise with the vendors before, during or after our wedding, will you handle them or are we responsible for this?

Scope of Work

20. What kind planning do you offer? Logistical only (i.e. organizational—handling things like the timeline and floor plan) or Design and Logistical (i.e. bringing a client's vision to life as well as taking care of all the organizational aspects of the wedding)?

21. If you just do logistical planning, can you refer us to a vendor who can assist us with event design? *(NOTE: Floral designers often do full event design, as do vendors who specialize in design.)*

22. Will you handle every aspect of the planning or can we do some things on our own? In other words, what parts of the planning will we be responsible for?

23. Will you be the person on site the day of our wedding or will it be another planner? How many assistants will you have?

24. In case of an emergency that prevents you from being at our wedding, who will be the backup planner? What are their qualifications?

25. What time will you arrive and depart on the day of our wedding?

26. Will you stay on site after our wedding to make sure everything has been broken down and all vendors have left the location?

27. Will you provide us with a timeline of the wedding and a floor plan of the wedding venue?

28. Do you offer different package options or is everything customized based on what we're looking for?

29. How many meetings and phone calls are included in our package?

30. Is the wedding day rehearsal included in your services?

31. Do any of your packages include planning the rehearsal dinner and/or post-wedding brunch? If not, would you provide that service and what would be the extra cost to include it in our contract?

32. Do any of your packages include honeymoon planning? If not, would you provide that service and what would be the extra cost to include it in our contract?

33. Do any of your packages include assistance with finding my wedding dress and wedding party attire? If not, would you provide that service and what would be the extra cost to include it in our contract?

Getting Down to Business

34. Once we book with you, how quickly can we expect to receive the contract?

35. After we give you our budget, will you provide us with a breakdown of how the money is going to be allocated?

36. As changes are made to our plans, will you update us with a revised estimate and updated contract?

37. How do you charge for your services? Hourly, percentage of the wedding cost, or flat rate?

38. Can you provide a detailed list of all the items included in your fee?

39. What is your payment policy? Do you accept credit cards?

40. How much of a deposit is required to book your services? When is the final payment due?

41. Are there any fees that won't be included in your proposal that we should be aware of?

42. What is your refund or cancellation policy?

43. Can you provide a list of references? *NOTE: Any experienced coordinator should be able to give you plenty of references. For a list of Coordinators/ Wedding Planners you can trust, see the ones we've featured on HereComesTheGuide.com. They've all passed our difficult certification process with flying colors! Brides and grooms told us how much they loved working with them, so we wanted to recommend them to you.*

44. Can you provide us with a portfolio and/or video of weddings you have done?

Questions to Ask a Caterer

Besides your venue, the food and drink for your wedding bash will probably consume the largest portion of your wedding budget. Catering costs are usually presented as "per-person" charges, sometimes abbreviated in wedding brochures as "pp" after the amount. But be aware—the per-person charge often doesn't include everything: Tax and the gratuity (sometimes called the "service charge") might be extra, and there may also be separate per-person charges for the meal, drinks, hors d'oeuvres, and even setup. So your actual per-person charge might end up being considerably more than you expect. Bring your calculator along when meeting with potential caterers to help you arrive at the real bottom line.

There's more to consider. Nowadays, many caterers offer a range of services in addition to catering. Some are actual "event producers," providing props, special effects, décor—in other words, complete event design. They might also be able to assist in finding a location, coordinating your affair, or lining up vendors. One thing a caterer can't do, however, is cook up a 5-course Beef Wellington dinner for $20 per person. When planning your menu, be realistic about what you can serve given your budget and the size of your guest list.

A lot of factors come into play when selecting a caterer, so don't be afraid to ask as many questions as you need to. You can refer to the following list, whether your potential caterer works at your event facility or you're hiring them independently.

The Basics

1. Do you have my date open?

2. How many weddings do you do per year, and how long have you been in business?

3. Have you done events at my location? *TIP: If you haven't chosen your location yet, ask the caterer if they can help you select one.*

4. Are you licensed by the state of California? Are you licensed to serve alcohol?

5. Will I need any permits for my event? If so, will you handle obtaining them?

6. Will you provide a banquet manager to coordinate the meal service or an on-site coordinator who will run the entire event?

7. Can you assist with other aspects of the wedding like selecting other vendors, event design (e.g. specialty lighting, elaborate décor, theme events, etc.)?

Food & Presentation

8. Given my budget, guest count and event style, what food choices would you recommend? Do you specialize in certain cuisines?

9. Do we have to work off a preset menu or can you create a custom menu for our event? If I have a special dish I'd like served, would you accommodate that?

10. Do you offer event packages or is everything à la carte? What exactly do your packages include?

11. Do you use all fresh produce, meat, fish, etc.? Can you source organic or sustainably farmed ingredients?

12. Can you accommodate dietary restrictions, such as kosher, vegan, etc.?

13. What décor do you provide for appetizer stations or buffet tables?

14. Do you offer package upgrades such as chocolate fountains, ice sculptures, espresso machines or specialty displays?

15. Can you do theme menus (e.g. barbecue, luau, etc.)? Would you also provide the décor?

16. What's the difference in cost between passed appetizers and appetizer stations? What's the price difference between a buffet and a sit-down meal? If we have a buffet, are there any stations that cost extra, like a carving station? *NOTE: Don't automatically assume that a buffet is going to be the less expensive option. Ask your caterer which type of service is more affordable for you, given the menu you're planning.*

17. How much do you charge for children's meals?

18. How much do you charge for vendor meals?

19. Do you do wedding cakes? If so, is this included in the per-person meal price or is it extra?

20. Can you show me photos of cakes you've done in the past?

21. If I decide not to serve cake, can you provide a dessert display instead?

22. If we use an outside cake designer, do you charge a cake-cutting fee?

23. Do you do food tastings and is there an extra charge for this?

24. Do you handle rental equipment such as tables, chairs, etc.?

25. What types of linens, glassware, plates and flatware do you provide? *NOTE: Some low-budget caterers have basic packages that use disposable dinnerware instead of the real thing, so make sure you know exactly what you'll be getting.*

26. Can you provide presentation upgrades such as chair covers, lounge furniture, Chiavari chairs, etc.? What would be the additional fees?

27. What is your policy on cleanup? *TIP: Be very clear about what "cleanup" means and who's responsible for handling it—and be sure to get it in writing. We've heard many tales about caterers that left dirty dishes, trash and uneaten food behind. In most cases, when you rent a location it will be YOUR responsibility to leave the place in acceptable condition. You want to spend your wedding night with your honey, not picking up empty bottles from the lawn!*

28. If there is leftover food from my event, can we have it wrapped up for guests to take home or have it delivered to a local shelter?

Drink

29. Do you provide alcoholic beverages and bartenders? Can you accommodate specialty cocktails?

30. What brands of alcohol will be served?

31. Can we provide the alcohol and you provide the bar labor?

32. Do you charge a corkage fee if we provide our own wine or champagne?

33. How do you charge for alcoholic and non-alcoholic beverages? Per consumption or per person? Which is more cost-effective?

34. Is the champagne toast after the ceremony included in your meal packages or is it extra?

35. Will your staff serve the wine with dinner?

36. How long will alcohol be served?

37. Is coffee and tea service included with the per-person meal charge? What brands of each do you offer and do they include decaf and herbal tea options?

Business Matters

38. What is the ratio of servers to guests?

39. How will the servers be dressed?

40. How is your pricing broken down (e.g. food, bar, cake-cutting, tax, gratuity)? *NOTE: Usually tax and a service charge are tacked on to your final cost. The service charge, which can range 18–23%, is used to tip the staff. And in many states, the service charge itself is taxable.*

41. How much time do you require for setting up and breaking down my event, and are there extra fees for this?

42. If my event runs longer than contracted, what are your overtime fees?

43. What is the last date by which I can give you a final guaranteed guest count?

44. What is your payment policy? Do you accept credit cards?

45. How much of a deposit is required to hold my date? When is the final payment due?

46. Are there any fees that won't be included in the proposal that we should be aware of?

47. Once we book with you, how quickly can we expect a contract? And if we make changes to menu choices or other items, will you update us with a revised estimate and contract?

48. What is your refund or cancellation policy?

49. Can you provide a list of recent references? *TIP: See the caterers we feature on HereComesTheGuide. com. These pre-screened companies provide great food and service, and they all passed our rigorous certification process with flying colors.*

Questions to Ask a Floral Designer

Floral designers do much more than just supply the bouquet! They help create the look and mood for your wedding ceremony, as well as centerpieces and other table decorations for the reception. They add the floral flourishes for the wedding party (don't forget that corsage for Grandma!), and some may even work with your cake designer to provide embellishments.

Before sitting down with a floral designer, you should already have reserved your ceremony and reception venue. That way you'll be able to discuss how much additional floral décor will be needed to either achieve a specific look at your site or complement an existing garden and/or room aesthetic.

Another must: Don't design the wedding bouquet until you've ordered your wedding dress. Since that task will hopefully be completed at least 6 months before your wedding date (hint, hint!), you should have plenty of time to work out the details of both your accessories and floral décor.

So where to start? Do a little research prior to interviewing floral artists by visiting the websites or shops of vendors you're considering. You want to know that whomever you hire can create bouquets and arrangements that suit your style. (And do explore our "Brides Want to Know: Bouquet Brainstorm" article on HereComes-TheGuide.com for more GUIDElines and inspiration.)

Once you've compiled your short list of contenders, use these questions to zero in on your final choice:

The Basics

1. Do you have my date open?

2. Have you done events at my ceremony and reception location(s) before? If not, are you familiar with the sites?

3. How long have you been in business?

4. How many weddings have you done?

5. Where did you receive your training?

6. How many other weddings or events will you schedule on the same day?

7. Will you be doing my arrangements yourself or would it be another floral designer?

8. What design styles (e.g. ikebana, traditional, modern, trendy, European, Oriental) do you work in?

9. Can you work with my budget?

10. What recommendations can you give me to maximize my budget?

11. Do you offer specific packages or is everything customized?

12. Can you provide me with 3–4 recent wedding clients that I can contact for references?

The Flowers

13. What flowers are in season for the month I am getting married?

14. Based on my color scheme and budget, what flowers do you recommend?

15. Is there a difference in price if I use one type of flower vs. a mixed arrangement or bouquet?

16. If I request it, can you provide any organic, pesticide-free or sustainably grown varieties? *TIP: Organic roses cost more, but last so much longer!*

17. What are the different kinds of wraps (called "collars" in florist-speak) you can do for my bouquet?

18. What about coordinating boutonnières, bridesmaid flowers, and centerpieces? Can you suggest anything special to coordinate with the theme/venue/season of my event?

19. What other décor can you provide (aisle runner, candelabras, trees, arches, votives, mirrors, etc.)? How will these items affect the overall cost?

20. If I give you a picture of a bouquet and/or arrangement that I like, can you recreate it?

21. Do you have photos or live examples of florals designed in the style I want?

22. Can you do sketches or mockups of the arrangements you've described before I sign the contract? If so, is there an additional fee for this?

23. Will you work with my cake designer if I decide to add flowers to my wedding cake? If so, is there an additional setup fee for this?

24. How far in advance of the wedding will you create the bouquets and arrangements, and how are they stored?

25. Can you assist me in the preservation of my bouquet after the wedding? If not, can you recommend someone?

The Costs

26. Do you charge a delivery fee?

27. Do you have an extra charge for the setup and breakdown of the floral décor?

28. Is there an extra fee if I need you to stay throughout the ceremony to move arrangements to the reception site?

29. Are there any additional fees that have not already been taken into account?

The Contract

30. How far in advance do I need to secure your services? What is the deposit required to secure my date?

31. Will you provide me with an itemized list of all the elements we've discussed, along with prices?

32. When can I expect to receive my contract from you?

33. What is your refund policy if for some reason I need to cancel my order?

Useful Tips:

- Prior to meeting with potential floral designers: have your color scheme finalized; create a list of the kinds of flowers you like; and have some examples (pictures from magazines, the web, etc.) of the kind of bouquets and arrangements that appeal to you.

- After you've met with each floral designer ask yourself, "Did the florist answer all my questions to my satisfaction?" "Do I feel like the florist really listened and understood my vision?" "Am I comfortable with this person?"

- Once you've booked your floral designer you'll want to provide them with a picture of your dress and swatches or photos of the bridesmaids dresses and the linens you'll be using.

Don't forget to browse our Floral Designers on HereComesTheGuide.com! They all got rave reviews during our rigorous certification process, and received the Certified By The Guide seal of approval.

Questions to Ask a Cake Designer

Next to your dress, the cake is probably a wedding's most important icon. And whether you want a traditional multi-tiered confection, a miniature Statue of Liberty (hey, that's where he proposed!) or a cupcake tower, your wedding cake should reflect your personality. Use the following questions as a guide when evaluating a potential cake designer. If you're not familiar with cake terms, please see the cake glossary on the next page.

Business Matters

1. Do you have my wedding date open?

2. How many wedding cakes do you schedule on the same day? *NOTE: You want to feel comfortable that your designer is sufficiently staffed to handle the number of cakes they've scheduled to deliver and set up on your date.*

3. How do you price your cakes? By the slice? Does the cost vary depending on the design and flavors I choose?

4. What is your minimum per-person cake cost?

5. What recommendations can you give me to maximize my budget?

6. Do you have a "menu" of cakes and prices that I can take with me?

7. What are the fees for delivery and setup of the cake? Do you decorate the cake table, too?

8. What do you do if the cake gets damaged in transit to or at my reception site?

9. Do you provide or rent cake toppers, a cake-cutting knife, cake stands, etc.? What are the fees?

10. How far in advance should I order my cake?

11. How much is the deposit and when is it due?

12. When is the final payment due?

13. Are there any additional fees that I should be aware of?

14. What is your refund policy if for some reason I need to cancel my order? What if I'm not happy with the cake?

15. When can I expect to receive my contract from you?

Background Check

16. How long have you been in business? Are you licensed and insured?

17. How many weddings have you done?

18. Where did you receive your training?

19. Can you provide me with 3–4 recent wedding clients that I can contact for references? *TIP: Check out the cake vendors featured on* HereComesTheGuide.com. *They're some of the best cake designers in Southern California and they've all been Certified By The Guide.*

The Cake

20. Do you have a portfolio of your work I can view, and did you make all the cakes in it?

21. What are your specialties?

22. Can you design a custom cake to match my theme, dress or color scheme, or do I select from set designs?

23. If I provide you with a picture of what I'd like, can you recreate it? Does it cost extra for a custom design?

24. I have an old family cake recipe. Can you adapt it for my wedding cake design?

25. If I don't have a clear vision of what I would like, can you offer some design ideas based on my theme and budget?

26. What flavors and fillings do you offer?

27. What are the different ingredients you typically use? Do you offer all organic or vegan options? *TIP: Quality ingredients cost more, but the investment is worth it—the cake will taste better.*

28. Do you have cake tastings? Is there a charge?

29. Do you do both fondant and buttercream icing?

30. Are there any other icing options I should consider? Which do you recommend for my cake design?

31. Can you create sugar paste, gum paste or chocolate flowers? If I decide to have fresh flowers on my cake will you work with my florist or will you obtain and arrange the flowers yourself?

32. Will you preserve the top tier of my cake for my first wedding anniversary or do you provide a special cake for the occasion?

33. Can you make a groom's cake? Is this priced the same as my wedding cake?

34. How much in advance of the wedding is the cake actually made? Do you freeze your cakes? *NOTE: Wedding cakes usually take at least a couple of days to make.*

Useful Tips:

- Arrange a consultation with your potential cake designer in person, and do a tasting before you sign a contract. *NOTE: Not all cake tastings are complimentary.*

- Make sure your cake designer specializes in wedding cakes. A wedding cake is generally much more elaborate than a birthday cake from your local bakery. Your cake professional should have special training in constructing this type of cake.

- In general, you should order your cake 6–8 months prior to your wedding.

- You might be able to save money by choosing one overall flavor for your cake, or by having a small cake for display and the cake cutting accompanied by a sheet cake to serve to your guests. Some cake designers may even offer a "dummy" or fake cake layer (usually made from styrofoam) to add an extra tier (or more) to your cake without too much extra expense. Talk to your cake designer to see how you can get the most bang for your wedding cake buck.

Wedding Cake Glossary

Icings

Buttercream: It's rich and creamy, is easily colored or flavored, and is used for fancy decorations like shells, swags, basketweaves, icing flowers, etc. Since it's made almost entirely of butter (hence the name), buttercream has a tendency to melt in extreme heat, so it's not recommended for outdoor weddings.

Fondant: Martha Stewart's favorite. This icing looks smooth and stiff and is made with gelatin and corn syrup to give it its helmet-like appearance (it's really very cool looking). It looks best when decorated with marzipan fruits, gum paste flowers, or a simple ribbon, like Martha likes to do. Although not as tasty as buttercream or ganache, fondant does not need refrigeration so it's the perfect icing to serve at your beach wedding.

Royal Icing: A mix of confectioner's sugar and milk or egg whites, royal icing is what the faces of gingerbread men are decorated with. It's white, shiny and hard, and does not need to be refrigerated. It's used for decorations like dots and latticework.

Ganache: This chocolate and heavy cream combination is very dark, and has the consistency of store-bought chocolate icing. It can be poured over cakes for a glass-like chocolate finish or used as filling (it stands up wonderfully between cake layers). Due to the ingredients, however, it's unstable—don't use it in hot or humid weather or the icing will slide right off the cake.

Whipped Cream: Delicious, but by far the most volatile, fresh whipped cream is usually not recommended for wedding cakes because they have to be out of the fridge for so long. If you really want to use it (it looks extremely white and fresh, which goes beautifully with real flowers) just keep it in the fridge until the very last second.

Decorations

Marzipan: An Italian paste made of almonds, sugar and egg whites that is molded into flowers and fruits to decorate the cake. They're usually brightly colored and very sugary. Marzipan can also be used as icing.

Gum Paste: This paste, made from gelatin, cornstarch, and sugar, produces the world's most realistic, edible fruit and flower decorations. Famous cake designers like Sylvia Weinstock are huge fans of gum paste. One nice benefit: these decorations last for centuries in storage.

Piping: Piping is ideal for icing decorations like dotted Swiss, basketweave, latticework, and shells. It comes out of a pastry bag fitted with different tips to create these different looks, which can range from simple polka dots to a layered weave that you'd swear is a wicker basket.

Pulled Sugar: If you boil sugar, water, and corn syrup it becomes malleable and the most beautiful designs can be created. Roses and bows that have been made from pulled sugar look like silk or satin—they're so smooth and shiny.

Dragees: These hard little sugar balls are painted with edible gold or silver paint, and they look truly stunning on a big ol' wedding cake.

Questions to Ask a DJ or Live Entertainment

Too often choosing the entertainment is left to the end of your overwhelming "Wedding To-Do List"—but it shouldn't be. Not only does music set the appropriate mood, but a skilled Master or Mistress of Ceremonies will gracefully guide your guests from one spotlight moment to another. And practically speaking, the best performers are often booked well in advance—so shake your groove thing, or you may be stuck doing the chicken dance with Uncle Edgar.

To get you started, we've put together this list of questions that will help you evaluate a DJ, band, or other entertainer. Note that rather than interviewing a specific performer or DJ yourself, you might be dealing with an entertainment agency rep.

The Basics

1. Do you have my date open?

2. Have you done events at my ceremony and/or reception location before? If not, are you familiar with them?

3. How long have you been in business? *NOTE: If you are interviewing a live band, you'll want to ask how long the musicians have played together. However, if you work with a reputable agency, instead of booking a specific band you'll most likely be getting seasoned professionals brought together for your event. Even though all the band members may not have played together before, they're professional musicians who are able to work together and sound fantastic anyway. The key is to make sure you book the specific singer and/or bandleader that you liked in the demo. The players will take their cues from them.*

4. How many weddings have you done? How many do you do in an average weekend?

5. What sets you apart from your competition?

6. Are there any other services that you provide, such as lighting design?

7. How far in advance do I need to secure your services?

8. Can you provide me with 3–4 recent wedding clients that I can contact for references?

Pricing and Other Business Details

9. What is your pricing? Does this include setup and breakdown between ceremony and reception locations?

10. How much is the deposit and when is it due? When is the final payment due?

11. If the event lasts longer than scheduled, what are the overtime charges?

12. What is the continuous music charge? *NOTE: For bands, bookings traditionally run for 4 hours divided into 4 sets, each lasting 45 minutes with a 15-minute break. If you want "continuous music," i.e. with band members trading breaks, there is usually an additional charge.*

13. When can I expect to receive my contract from you?

14. Are there any additional fees that could accrue that I am not taking into account, like travel expenses or charges for special musical requests? (One performer was asked to prepare an entire set of songs from *Phantom of the Opera!* Yes, he charged extra.)

15. What is your refund policy if for some reason I need to cancel or alter my date?

16. Do you carry liability insurance? *NOTE: This usually only applies to production companies that also supply lighting, effects, etc.*

17. If I hire musicians for the ceremony and want them to play at the wedding rehearsal, what is the extra charge?

The Music

18. Do you have a DVD of your music or a video link to a prior wedding where you performed?

19. Can you assist me in choosing the music for my processional, recessional, father-daughter dance, etc.?

20. How extensive is your music library or song list? What genres can you cover? Can I give you a specific list of songs I want or don't want played?

21. Are we guaranteed to have the performer(s) of our choice at our event? *SEE NUMBER 3 ABOVE. As mentioned, many bands hired by an agency are made up of members who may not play together regularly. Even set bands often have substitute players. If there are specific performers (singer, harpist, guitarist, etc.) that you want, make sure that your contract includes them. Of course, illness or other circumstances may still preclude their being able to perform at your event.*

22. If the DJ or one of the band members scheduled for my event is unable to perform for some reason, do you have a backup replacement ready to go?

23. Can you provide wireless mics for the ceremony?

24. Does any of your equipment require special electrical outlets that I need to inform my wedding site about?

25. Do you bring backup equipment?

26. What kind of space or stage do you require for the DJ or band? If my site doesn't provide what you need, will you make arrangements for the stage or am I responsible for renting it? *NOTE: A band will require a specific amount of square feet per band member.*

27. How much time will you need for setup, sound check and breakdown on the day of the event?

28. What music will be provided during the breaks? *NOTE: If you have a preference, make it known. If you want them to play your own digital music, be sure to inquire about system compatibility with your CD, iPod, etc.*

29. How many people will you staff for my event?

Useful Tips:

- Discuss with your site manager any restrictions that might affect your event, like noise limits, a music curfew and availability/load of electrical circuits. Also check with your facility and caterer about where and what to feed the performers.

- All professional entertainers have access to formalwear (if they don't, that's your first clue they're not professionals!) However, it is YOUR responsibility to be specific about how you expect your performers to be dressed. Any extraordinary requests (period costumes, all-white tuxes, etc.) are normally paid for by the client.

- Make notes of your general music preferences before you meet with your DJ, bandleader, etc. For example: "Classical for the ceremony, Rat Pack-era for the cocktail hour and a set of Motown during the reception." Not only will this help you determine which entertainment professionals are a good match for you, it will guide them in preparing your set list. *TIP: The DJs and Entertainers on HereComesTheGuide.com are first-rate. They all got great reviews during our certification process, and we're happy to recommend them.*

Questions to Ask When Ordering Your Wedding Invitations

Letterpress, thermography, engraved, matte, jacquard, glassine… ordering invites will mean learning a few new vocabulary words (see page 42). You'll also need to learn about all the components that you might want to include in your invitation, as well as what other printed materials could be part of your wedding scenario. With so many details to consider, you'll depend on a creative wedding invitation professional to clue you in on the jargon, and guide you in choosing invites that reflect your wedding style. After all, nothing sets the tone for an event like an impeccably designed wedding invitation.

This list of questions has been compiled to help ensure that no detail is left unaddressed (no pun intended), whether you're working with a stationery boutique, an online vendor, or a graphic designer.

Getting To Know Your Invitation Professional

1. How long have you been in business?

2. What is your design background? *NOTE: This may or may not involve formal training. Remember, "good taste" isn't necessarily something that can be taught!*

3. What types of printing processes do you offer and which do you specialize in? Which do you recommend for my budget and style?

4. Is your printing done in-house or do you outsource it? *NOTE: Printing is usually less expensive if it's outsourced. However, a possible benefit of in-house printing is a quicker turnaround time, which could come in especially handy if any reprinting (say, due to an error) is required.*

5. Do you offer custom invitations as well as templated styles? Is there a fee if I want to order a sample of either an existing invitation style or a custom design? If so, how much?

6. If I choose a custom wedding invitation, what are my options for color, paper type, ink and fonts? What is the word limit for the text?

7. Can I also order my table numbers, place cards, escort cards, ceremony programs, menus, etc. from you?

8. Do you offer a package or a discounted price if I order all of the invitation components at the same time? (For a complete list of what might be included, see the next page.)

9. If I want to include a picture or graphic on my save-the-date card or invitation, can you accommodate that? If so, does the image need to be saved in a specific format? Do you have photo retouching available, and if so, what is the price range? Can your photo specialist also convert color images to black & white or sepia? Is there an additional cost?

10. Are there any new styles, trends and color combinations I might consider? Which are the most popular? What kinds of handmade or artisanal paper do you offer? *NOTE: The answers to these questions will give you a sense of how creative and up-to-the-minute your invitation professional is.*

11. Can my invitations be printed on recycled paper and/or with soy-based ink?

12. Based on the paper I select and the number of pieces involved, what would it cost to mail my wedding invitation? *NOTE: If you use a non-standard sized envelope, postage may be more expensive.*

Getting Down To Business

13. Once I place my order, how long will it take to have the completed invitations delivered? Do you have rush-order available and what are the extra fees? If you are ordering from an online company, ask: What are the shipping methods available to me, and their respective costs?

14. If the invitation involves multiple pieces, can you assemble them? If so, is there an additional fee? How will the assembly affect my delivery date?

15. Do you offer an invitation addressing service? If so, what is the charge for this? What lettering style options are available? Will the lettering push back my delivery date?

16. When is payment due?

17. I will have an opportunity to sign off on my invitation proof before you send my order to print, right?

18. Once I've signed off on the proof, I expect the printed invitations to match the approved sample. If they don't (i.e. an error was made after I signed off on the proof), will my invitations be corrected and reprinted at no additional cost? How much additional time will it take to redo my order if there is a problem with it?

19. What is your refund policy if for some reason I need to cancel my order?

20. When can I expect to receive my contract from you?

21. Can you provide me with the contact information of 3–4 recent wedding clients who I can call or email for references?

Possible Printed Invitation Components

(Don't panic… most of the extra elements are OPTIONAL!!)

- Save-the-Date Cards

- Wedding Announcement

- Wedding Invitation Components:
  - Outer Envelope
  - Optional Inner Envelope
  - Optional Belly Band
  - Invitation
  - Reception Card, if held at a different location than the ceremony
  - Directions/Map
  - Response Card & SASE (self-addressed stamped envelope)

- Thank-You Cards

- Shower Thank-You Cards

- Other Invites:
  - Engagement Party
  - Shower
  - Bachelor/Bachelorette Party
  - Rehearsal Dinner
  - After Party

- Wedding Program

- Pew Cards

- Place Cards

- Table Cards

- Menus

- Napkins, Matchbooks or Labels for favors

Useful Tips:

- Ordering your invitations over the phone increases the possibility of mistakes, so order in person if possible. If you order your invitations from an online company, make sure your contract states that they will correct mistakes they make for free.

- Insist on getting a proof. Have at least two other people review all your proofs before you sign off on them—it's amazing what a fresh pair of eyes will see!

- If ordering online, remember that color resolution can vary drastically between computers. The best way to guarantee the exact color you want is to ask that a sample be snail-mailed to you.

- Order 20–30 extra save-the-dates and/or invitations with envelopes in case you have to add to the guest list or you make a mistake when assembling or addressing the envelopes.

- Save-the-date cards should be sent out 6–9 months prior to your wedding.

- Invitations should be sent out 6–8 weeks prior to your wedding.

- Consider working with one stationer or graphic designer for all of your printed materials. He or she will guide you in making sure all of the components convey a consistent design concept. Not that they have to be identical, but as Joyce Scardina Becker observes in *Countdown to Your Perfect Wedding,* "It's like making a fashion statement: All of the accessories in your wardrobe should coordinate and fit together nicely."

- To Evite or not to Evite? For the main event, even we progressives at *Here Comes The Guide* come down on the side of tradition and say go with real paper and snail mail—even if your budget determines that you have to DIY. However, if your overall wedding style is relaxed and casual, then we think Evites are fine for the supporting events, such as your Bachelorette Party. We like Evite's built-in RSVP system and creative style options.

- Save your sanity. Put a little number on the back of your RSVP cards that corresponds to your own numbered guest list. With this number system, if a guest fails to write their name(s) on their RSVP card, and all you know is 2 people are coming and they both want the chicken, you'll still be able to figure out whose RSVP it is without having to hunt anyone down.

- For more about wedding invitations, see "Inviting Elements: Invitation Basics" on HereComesTheGuide.com.

Invitations Glossary

A glossary of common printing terms.

Printing Terms

Letterpress: Letterpress printing dates back to the 14th century, and involves inking the raised surface of metal type or custom-engraved plates and then applying the inked surface against paper with a press. When used with the right paper (thick, softer paper results in a deeper impression), typefaces and colors, letterpress creates an elegant product with a stamped, tactile quality. This process offers lots of options, but can cost more than other methods. Also, photographs and metallic inks generally don't work well with letterpress.

Embossing: Using a metal die, letters and images are pressed into the paper from behind, creating a raised "relief" surface, imparting added dimension to the invitation design. Usually used for large initials or borders. Ink or foil may be applied to the front of the paper so that the raised letters and images are colored.

Blind embossing: No ink or foil is applied, so the embossed (raised) image is the same color as the paper.

Thermography: This popular printing method uses heat to fuse ink and resinous powder, producing raised lettering. Though it looks almost exactly like engraved printing, thermography is much less expensive. This process will not reproduce detail as sharply as engraving will. The powder is added after the ink is applied, generally with an offset press, so the use of paper or metal offset plates affects quality here, too.

Engraving: Engraving is generally the most formal and expensive printing option. The image is etched into a metal plate, and the ink held in the etched grooves is applied to the paper with a press. The resulting raised image is comprised entirely of ink sitting on the surface of the paper. The ink applied is opaque, making it possible to print a lighter colored ink on a darker colored paper. Engraving is not the best printing choice if you have a photo or illustration that requires a screen.

Offset printing: Most printing these days is offset, which means the original image is transferred from a plate to a drum before it is applied to the paper. This process produces print that sits flat on the surface. There are many levels of quality with this method: If your printer uses paper printing plates, the job will cost less but the result may be fuzzy, inconsistent lettering. Metal plates yield much sharper, crisper type.

Digital printing: In this method the computer is linked to the printing press and the image is applied to paper or another material directly from a digital file rather than using film and/or plates. Digital is best for short-run, quick jobs. This can also be a good option if you want to use full color.

Foil stamping: Foil is applied to the front side of the paper, stamped on with a metal die. Foils can be metallic or colored, shiny or dull. They are usually very opaque, and this is a great way to print white on a dark colored paper.

Calligraphy: This is the perfected art of writing by hand. Often associated with fancy, curlicue script, calligraphy can be done in several genres and styles.

Paper Terms

Matte: A paper coating that's flat and non-reflective (no gloss).

Jacquard: Screen-printed paper that creates an illusion of layering; for example, paper that looks like it's overlaid with a swatch of lace.

Parchment paper: This paper is somewhat translucent and often a bit mottled to mimic the appearance of ancient, historical documents made out of animal skin. It's excellent for calligraphy.

Linen finish: Paper with a surface that actually mimics linen fabric. If you look closely, you see lines of texture going both horizontally and vertically on the surface.

Rice paper: Not actually made of rice, this paper is extremely thin and elegant.

Glassine: A very thin, waxy paper. Thinner than vellum (see below), its surface is slick and shiny, whereas vellum is more translucent. Glassine is best suited for envelope use, while vellum is sturdy enough to be printed on directly for invitation use.

Vellum: A heavier, finely textured, translucent paper made from wood fiber. Similar to parchment, it was originally made from the skin of a calf, lamb or baby goat and used for writing and painting during the pre-printing age.

HereComesTheGuide.com

Find your California wedding venue →

Want to look somewhere else? Click here.

Photo: Palm Event Center in the Vineyard | Avec L'Amour Photography | Engaged Photo: Imagery by Marianne

Take a deep breath...

Throw on your sweats, grab some coffee (or wine, depending on what time it is), and get comfy.

Let's plan your wedding together!

xo,
The Guide Gals ♥

You've gotta visit our website!
Here's what you'll find:

- A fast and easy way to search for the perfect venues and vendors.

- Information about new venues that aren't in the book!

- Lots of locations for rehearsal dinners, honeymoons, and accommodations (room blocks!) for your event.

- More great wedding and special event services!

- Deals and discounts!

- Tons of photos and videos. Real Wedding galleries, too!

- Information about bridal fairs.

Event Venues

Southern California

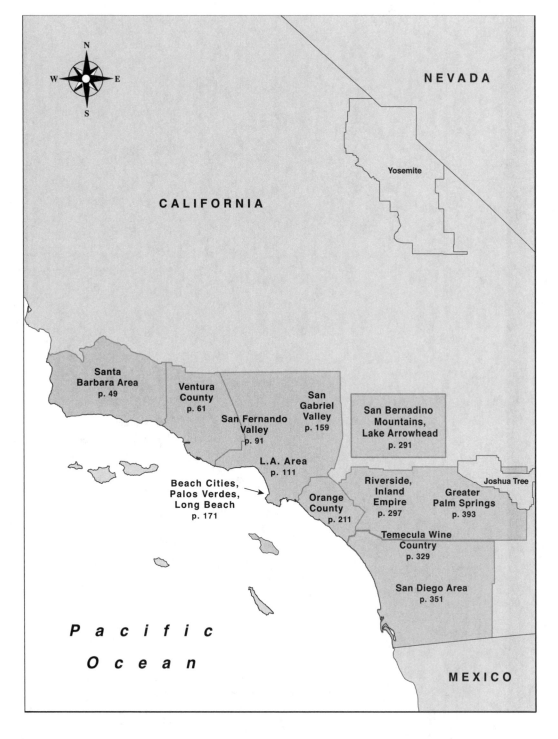

N
W E
S

NEVADA

CALIFORNIA

Yosemite

Santa
Barbara Area
p. 49

Ventura
County
p. 61

San Fernando
Valley
p. 91

San
Gabriel
Valley
p. 159

San Bernadino
Mountains,
Lake Arrowhead
p. 291

L.A. Area
p. 111

Beach Cities,
Palos Verdes,
Long Beach
p. 171

Orange
County
p. 211

Riverside,
Inland
Empire
p. 297

Greater
Palm Springs
p. 393

Joshua Tree

Temecula Wine
Country
p. 329

San Diego Area
p. 351

Pacific

Ocean

MEXICO

Santa Barbara Area

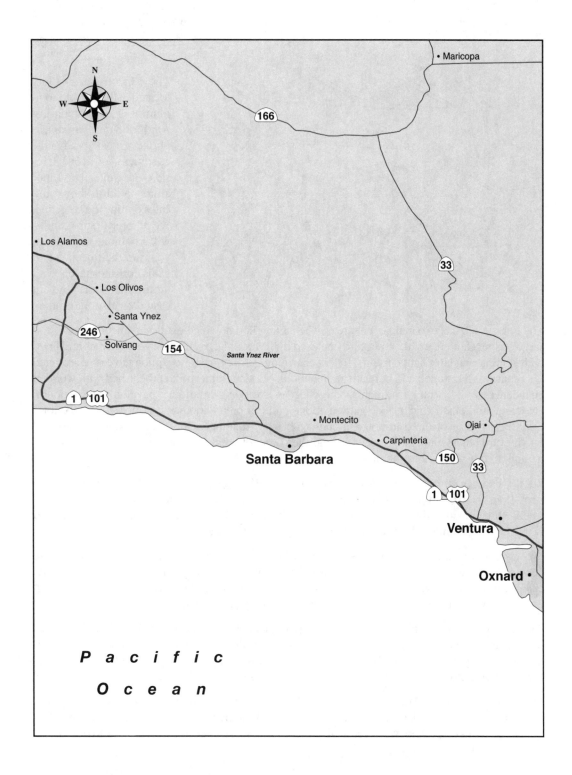

Rincon Beach Club

3805 Santa Claus Lane, Carpinteria

805/566-9933

eventsbyrincon.com
sales@eventsbyrincon.com

Waterfront Event Facility

● Rehearsal Dinners	● Corporate Events
● Ceremonies	● Meetings
● Wedding Receptions	● Film Shoots
● Private Parties	Accommodations

The Rincon Beach Club, located in the seaside community of Carpinteria just south of Santa Barbara, is bound to make you smile as soon as you arrive: It resides on "Santa Claus Lane" amid colorful shops and cafés dotting the shoreline. We're pretty sure smiles will continue throughout your time at Rincon, a gracious, private haven with mountain vistas and an easy, coastal sophistication.

The Beach Club has two main event areas: The Dining Room, which exudes a quiet elegance; and the Wedding Garden, a leafy courtyard enclosed by 10-foot-high walls of flowering vines and lined with shimmering fairy light curtains. In this charming outdoor oasis, reception tables are arranged on a spacious flagstone patio beneath an ingenious wooden framework embellished with wooden chandeliers and Tuscan string lights. The effect is like being in an airy pavilion that's modern, yet warm, and oh-so-chic. A rose garden at one end is a pretty spot for ceremonies (and couples have their choice of three in-house arches with ivory draping). Guests are comfortably seated on vineyard chairs with ivory cushions, and the sound of breaking waves in the background is a natural accompaniment to the momentous occasion.

But if it's an oceanfront ceremony that you crave, the RBC has you covered! It's just a five-minute stroll from the club to the beach, where Rincon's experienced style squad will personalize your setting: Imagine a wedding aisle lined with seashells and driftwood, or a bamboo arch draped with tropical garlands—they can even lay grass sod right on the sand!

Everyone returns to the club for cocktail hour, where a mahogany bar on the garden's West Patio becomes a social hub for some guests, while others mingle or lounge on couches next to a "succulent garden" fountain. An open-air garden reception beneath a starry sky is utterly enchanting, especially with the sweet scent of jasmine and refreshing sea breezes.

For dancing or a more formal reception, the adjacent Dining Room is perfect. French doors on two sides let in the garden view, and the room's clean, uncluttered style provides a refined backdrop for personalized décor. The club has a collection of furniture, props, classy uplighting, and other accoutrements to create whatever atmosphere you envision.

At Rincon Beach Club, you get much more than a picturesque venue: Expert planning, event production, and palate-pleasing cuisine are also part of the package. This full-service approach is not only a time—and money—saver, it also results in a more cohesive expression of your vision.

Rincon's experienced professionals know how to craft a celebration that reflects your style and taste. This is especially evident when it comes to your menu, which they'll customize from aperitif to dessert. From global-inspired delicacies to the latest food trends, absolutely nothing intimidates these culinary artists!

Minutes from Santa Barbara, yet "miles from conventional", Rincon Beach Club and Catering's impressive presentation and devotion to details really sets them apart. As one satisfied bride put it: "I was so relaxed—I just showed up and had fun!"

CEREMONY CAPACITY: The site holds 250 seated guests outdoors.

EVENT/RECEPTION CAPACITY: The club can accommodate 130 seated or 350 standing guests indoors, and 250 seated or 350 standing outdoors.

MEETING CAPACITY: The club can accommodate up to 350 guests.

PRICES: WHAT'S THIS GOING TO COST?

Rental Fee: $6,200/event
- The rental fee varies depending on the day of the week and time of year.
- Special pricing for weekday and daytime events may apply.
- Note that the in-house Wedding Coordinator is required.

Meals (when priced separately): $41–75/person

AVAILABILITY: Year-round, daily, anytime.

SERVICES/AMENITIES:

Catering: in-house
Kitchen Facilities: n/a
Tables & Chairs: provided
Linens, Silver, etc.: provided
Restrooms: wheelchair accessible
Dance Floor: portable provided
Bride's & Groom's Dressing Areas: yes
AV/Meeting Equipment: some provided, CBA
Other: in-house wedding cake, groom's lounge, event coordination, day-of and full-service wedding planning

Parking: on street
Accommodations: no guest rooms
Outdoor Night Lighting: provided
Outdoor Cooking Facilities: BBQ on site; food action stations available
Cleanup: provided
View: coastline, fountain, garden, landscaped grounds, mountains, ocean

RESTRICTIONS:

Alcohol: full in-house bar
Smoking: allowed on patio only
Music: amplified OK

Wheelchair Access: yes
Insurance: liability required

This is important! Tell locations you're reading HERE COMES THE GUIDE and ask if our information is still current.

51

The 1880 Union

362 Bell Street, Los Alamos

805/344-2744

1880Union.com
guestrelations@1880union.com

Historic Hotel & Event Facility

- Rehearsal Dinners
- Ceremonies
- Wedding Receptions
- Private Parties
- Corporate Events
- Meetings
- Film Shoots
- Accommodations

From humble beginnings as a Wells Fargo stagecoach station, and later a turn-of-the-century hotel and saloon, the modern-day 1880 Union has been reborn as a luxurious and incredibly unique celebration retreat that artfully retains the venue's historic charm. The weathered wooden façade is right out of a Hollywood Western, and the Saloon, with its whimsical Old West memorabilia, foodie fare, and signature microbrew, is now a lively Santa Barbara Wine Country hotspot. But all that's for the public…

For you and your in-crowd, the rest of the 1880 Union becomes your exclusive, private playground to live out your wedding weekend fantasy. While it's tempting to simply cowboy (or cowgirl!) up, the minute you step into the extravagant lobby your imagination goes upscale. Taking in the opulent crystal chandeliers, heirloom grandfather clock, and satin loveseats clustered around the hearth, you quickly realize that this is the kind of place where Gold Rush dandies and their grande dames once hung their lace-trimmed hats. A grand piano and an old-fashioned reception desk with an antique cash register stand ready to make your own "welcome to my party" statement to greet your arriving guests.

Ceremonies are held in the estate's enchanting backyard, accessed through a discreet iron gate that opens to a vine-covered arbor and serene rose garden. Just beyond, a white wrought-iron gazebo atop a raised dais crowns a lush sweep of lawn. Sheltered by magnolia trees on one side and an ivy-cloaked brick wall on the other, it's an exceptionally romantic spot to exchange vows. Afterwards, while you explore the property's intriguing photo ops, your guests enjoy the social hour in a neighboring brick courtyard, aglow with bistro lights and the flames from the huge outdoor fireplace flickering softly in the twilight.

Continue the festivities al fresco, or invite guests inside to the lavish Dining Room, where nostalgia elegantly merges with high style and French windows capture pretty garden views. Chandeliers in beaded cages, a jazzy Art Deco bar, and an eclectic mix of wood and marble tables with plush velvet chairs banishes any thought of an ordinary reception. And expect out-of-the-ordinary cuisine as well: Your personal gourmet chef will craft a menu inspired by local ingredients and your own culinary sensibilities.

After-party, anyone? Just head upstairs to the Mezzanine, where a trio of giant leather couches welcomes you to a quirky entertainment lounge, featuring an antique chess set, a Victrola, a poker room, and even a retro pinball arcade. When it's finally time to retire, nine imaginatively decorated rooms lodge your nearest and dearest, but reserve the seductive Presidential Suite for yourselves.

Surrounded by exquisite period furnishings, dramatic chandeliers, and a cozy fireplace, you'll feel utterly indulged—especially after a soak in the magnificent claw-foot copper tub. And spoiler alert: A sliding bookcase reveals a secret Bride's Room, chicly outfitted with multiple mirrors and a gorgeous stained-glass door that leads to a balcony overlooking the courtyard—so perfect for an end-of-evening bouquet toss!

Naturally, this fun and fascinating landmark has attracted its share of celebrities. 1880 Union knows how to roll out the red carpet, so rest assured that their experienced, dedicated event team will treat you and your group like privileged VIPs.

CEREMONY CAPACITY: The site seats 30 indoors and 300 outdoors.

EVENT/RECEPTION CAPACITY: The facility can accommodate 50 seated or 150 standing guests indoors, and 300 seated or standing outdoors.

MEETING CAPACITY: The venue seats up to 50 guests.

PRICES: WHAT'S THIS GOING TO COST?

Rental Fee: $6,000–11,000/event
- The rental fee varies depending on the day of the week and time of year.
- Saturday or weekend wedding packages require a buyout of 1880 Union's 9 historic guest rooms for an additional fee. You may opt to have your guests cover the cost of their own rooms.

Meals (when priced separately): $55/person and up
- Customized menus include taxes, gratuities, staffing, event insurance, and day-of wedding coordination.
- Food & beverage minimums apply.

AVAILABILITY: Year-round. There's an 11pm event curfew, but your overnight guests can continue the party later than that.

SERVICES/AMENITIES:

Catering: in-house
Kitchen Facilities: n/a
Tables & Chairs: provided
Linens, Silver, etc.: provided
Restrooms: wheelchair accessible
Dance Area: yes
Bride's & Groom's Dressing Areas: yes
AV/Meeting Equipment: some provided, CBA
Other: event coordination, grand piano, picnic area

Parking: on street
Accommodations: 9 guest rooms
Outdoor Night Lighting: decorative, landscape, and string lighting
Outdoor Cooking Facilities: BBQ CBA
Cleanup: provided
View: fountain, garden, landscaped grounds, fields, hills

RESTRICTIONS:

Alcohol: in-house or BYO with corkage fee
Smoking: designated areas only
Music: amplified OK with restrictions

Wheelchair Access: limited
Insurance: included

Montecito Club

Private Club

920 Summit Road, Santa Barbara

805/624-5153

www.montecitoclub1918.com/special-events
slehmberg@montecitoclub1918.com

● Rehearsal Dinners	● Corporate Events
● Ceremonies	● Meetings
● Wedding Receptions	● Film Shoots
● Private Parties	Accommodations

Named "one of the best places to visit" by *Travel & Leisure,* Montecito boasts breathtaking scenery, fabulous weather, and an effortless style. All of this also makes it one of the country's top choices for a destination wedding—especially now that the gorgeous renovation of the historic Montecito Club is complete.

Situated between the Santa Ynez Mountains and Pacific Ocean, this century-old property affords panoramic ocean, city, and mountain views. The recent three-year remodel has retained the club's Spanish architecture, while incorporating beautiful Andalusian design elements and Moroccan influences. The grounds have been enhanced, too, with an abundance of lush greenery and meticulous landscaping. Although Montecito Club is a private facility, outside weddings and events are welcome.

A short drive along the club's treelined golf course takes you to the Clubhouse and Event Lawn. The expansive lawn, which has spectacular, unobstructed views of the Santa Barbara harbor, downtown, and Santa Ynez Mountains, is a favorite spot for exchanging vows. But it's also popular for an al fresco cocktail reception or dinner—in fact, you can host all three phases of your wedding here if you like!

The Clubhouse has plenty of its own charms to offer. Guests are welcomed through a private entrance into an ornate and colorful vestibule that opens into the Ballroom. Appointed with hand-carved African mahogany doors, a gold-leafed ceiling, antiques, and imported sconces, it's ideal for larger parties. The adjoining Great Room, aptly named for its sumptuous décor and view overlooking the golf course and Pacific Ocean, provides a dramatic backdrop for a ceremony or cocktail reception. The space's 10-foot sandstone fireplace, Swarovski crystal chandeliers, exotic furnishings, and hand-painted ceiling all contribute to the sense of epic grandeur.

An excellent choice for an intimate reception or rehearsal dinner is the Rotunda, a marvelous, circular space featuring a series of arched windows that showcase a 180-degree panorama of the golf course, Pacific Ocean, and Channel Islands. It's often used in combination with the Ballroom, designed with a soaring trestle-beamed ceiling, vintage wrought-iron chandeliers, fireplace, and marble bar. An interior balcony does triple duty as a wonderful photo op, a nook for your DJ, or a place to toss the bouquet. The adjacent Lounge is perfect for dancing the night away.

Montecito Club's renowned chef, Jamie West, will create a reception menu that's as impressive as the club's event spaces and views. With his extensive experience at some of the top dining establishments in the country, he's able to offer a wide variety of cuisines. All dishes can be paired with vintages from a curated wine list thanks to the assistance of the club's sommelier.

Additional benefits include a private bridal suite (complete with champagne and small bites), access to the grounds for photo ops, artisan chocolates to take home, and the undivided attention of the staff—they only host one event per day! If what you're looking for is an A-list venue and VIP treatment, you'll find that and much more at the the Montecito Club.

CEREMONY CAPACITY: The venue seats up to 150 guests indoors and 250 outdoors.

EVENT/RECEPTION CAPACITY: The site can accommodate 250 guests indoors or outdoors.

MEETING CAPACITY: Meeting spaces can seat up to 250.

Rental Fee: $4,000–9,500/event
  • The rental fee varies depending on the guest count and type of event.

Ceremony Fee: $4,000/event
  • Ceremonies without a reception on site are $6,000.

Meals (when priced separately): $70–120/person

Service Charge or Gratuity: 22%

AVAILABILITY: Year-round. Events must end by 11pm indoors and 10pm outdoors.

SERVICES/AMENITIES:

Catering: in-house
Kitchen Facilities: n/a
Tables & Chairs: provided
Linens, Silver, etc.: provided
Restrooms: wheelchair accessible
Dance Floor: yes
Bride's Dressing Area: yes
AV/Meeting Equipment: BYO

Parking: on-site lot, valet or shuttle service required
Accommodations: no guest rooms
Outdoor Night Lighting: access only; market lighting package available
Outdoor Cooking Facilities: none
Cleanup: provided
View: fairways, hills, ocean

RESTRICTIONS:

Alcohol: in-house
Smoking: not allowed
Music: amplified OK with some restrictions

Wheelchair Access: yes
Insurance: not required

Santa Barbara Zoological Gardens

500 Ninos Drive, Santa Barbara
805/566-9933
eventsbyrincon.com/zoocateringbyrincon
angie@eventsbyrincon.com

Waterfront Zoological Gardens

- Rehearsal Dinners
- Ceremonies
- Wedding Receptions
- Private Parties
- Corporate Events
- Meetings
- Film Shoots
- Accommodations

Sure, plenty of zoos have the requisite elephant or lion…but the Santa Barbara Zoo has something more: 30 acres of lush gardens laced with majestic ocean views. This isn't your typical wedding venue, and this isn't a typical zoo, either. For one thing, the meticulously maintained park rests between the beach and a bird sanctuary. For another, it's got a surprisingly pleasant aroma, a mixture of roses, jasmine and the sea. This zoo also has experienced event pros who are particularly attentive and enthusiastic about helping make your day special.

Arriving wedding guests are escorted along a landscaped path to Palm Garden, a stunning ceremony site tucked away in a sunken, grassy courtyard. Surrounded by palm trees, agapanthus and leafy green thickets, it has the exotic air of a tame jungle hideaway. Couples tie the knot in front of a cluster of palms, sometimes adding a *chuppah* or bamboo arch, with a hint of ocean in the distance.

Next, while you and your wedding party pose for photos in the park's scenic gardens, your guests take refreshments on nearby Lower Hilltop, a broad grassy "porch" set with cocktail tables and a bar. To make this time even more memorable, you might arrange some novel entertainment: Invite some flamingoes to join the party; hire the zoo train to take everyone on a tour (cocktails welcome); or have guests take turns feeding Michael and Audrey, Masai giraffes who unfurl long purple tongues as they gently accept their food. Now that's something most wedding guests don't get to experience!

When it's time to serve dinner to your friends and family, a short flight of stone steps leads to Upper Hilltop, a circular expanse of lawn gorgeously arrayed for the reception. Since the field is so spacious, the event staff creates "outdoor rooms" to lend a feeling of intimacy, using a variety of optional amenities—a dance floor, tenting, chandeliers, market lights, heat lamps, specialty linens, lounge furniture, and props. They stage the festivities either overlooking Lower Hilltop, which offers glimpses of the Pacific through the palm fronds in one direction and the Santa Ynez Mountains in the other; or on the interior section, which enjoys two different Pacific vistas plus a pergola and splashing fountain. The event team will personalize your wedding, whether you prefer traditionally elegant styling or something imaginative. (One couple recently had an Alice in Wonderland-themed gala!) Pretty much anything you can dream up, the zoo staff will help you pull off.

The same is true of the cuisine. *Zoo Catering Services by Rincon (ZCS)* boasts "Wild Flavors with Civilized Service", and they're equally adept at delivering a relaxed barbecue or a sophisticated candlelit affair, global fusion, or the freshest California cuisine. You're in good hands with these culinary superstars!

The Santa Barbara Zoological Gardens is a private, nonprofit organization, which is perfect for green weddings—your special event fees help support the zoo's conservation and education efforts. With its picturesque setting and impeccable service, this unique location is a "natural" for out-of-the-ordinary celebrations.

CEREMONY CAPACITY: The facility holds up to 250 seated guests outdoors.

EVENT/RECEPTION CAPACITY: The site can accommodate 600 seated or 1,000 standing outdoors.

MEETING CAPACITY: The Discovery Pavilion can seat 200.

PRICES: WHAT'S THIS GOING TO COST?

   Rental Fee: $5,200/event

   Meals (when priced separately): $32/person and up

   Service Charge or Gratuity: 18%

AVAILABILITY: Year-round.

SERVICES/AMENITIES:

Catering: in-house
Kitchen Facilities: n/a
Tables & Chairs: CBA
Linens, Silver, etc.: CBA
Restrooms: wheelchair accessible
Dance Floor: CBA
Bride's Dressing Area: yes
AV/Meeting Equipment: CBA
Other: picnic area, event coordination, animal options, zoo train options

Parking: provided, large lot
Accommodations: no guest rooms
Outdoor Night Lighting: CBA
Outdoor Cooking Facilities: BBQ on site; food action stations available
Cleanup: provided
View: fountain, garden, courtyard, landscaped grounds; panorama of hills, mountains, ocean and coastline

RESTRICTIONS:

Alcohol: in-house
Smoking: designated areas only
Music: amplified OK

Wheelchair Access: yes
Insurance: liability required

Unitarian Society of Santa Barbara

Historic Church & Event Facility

1535 Santa Barbara Street, Santa Barbara
805/965-4583 X223
www.ussb.org/love
facilities@ussb.org

- Rehearsal Dinners
- Ceremonies
- Wedding Receptions
- Private Parties
- Corporate Events
- Meetings
- Film Shoots
- Accommodations

Directly across from the blossom-filled Alice Keck Park Memorial Garden is the Unitarian Society of Santa Barbara, a historic, nondenominational church with a long tradition as a wonderful wedding location. Their beautiful Sanctuary evokes a peaceful sense of divine mystery, and the congregation's inclusive philosophy makes this venue a congenial gathering place, perfectly suited for life's celebrations. Unitarian Universalists support one another on their various spiritual paths, and are nonjudgmental, compassionate and socially conscious. As you and your soul mate begin your own lifelong journey together, consider letting the tranquil surroundings of the Unitarian Society provide you with a memorable send-off.

The Unitarian Society campus includes the Sanctuary, a Reception hall, a Terrace and two Gardened Courtyards. Designed and built in 1930 in the city's signature Spanish-Revival style, the Sanctuary's rustic glamour is enhanced by antique architectural elements: Vintage lantern-style light fixtures are suspended from the vaulted ceiling's open beams. The original wooden pews are flanked by lofty, rectangular stained-glass panels in subdued shades of pale blue and honey, each inscribed with the name of a famous Unitarian freethinker like essayist Ralph Waldo Emerson. At the front of the Sanctuary, the chancel is softly illuminated by a breathtaking stained-glass rose window in radiant jewel tones; a smaller rose window looks out over balcony seating at the rear. The Sanctuary conveys a momentous yet joyful ambiance, and its quality acoustics make music sound even more dramatic. Hire one of their recommended musicians, and walk down the aisle to the impressive sound of the Sanctuary's genuine 1,500-pipe organ or Steinway concert piano. Couples of any faith or sexual orientation are invited to pledge their love in this glorious space, a welcome solution for interfaith marriages and same-sex unions.

Following the ceremony, guests often enjoy an open-air social hour in the pretty Jefferson Courtyard. A brick patio flanked by twin lawns crowned with olive saplings is a delightful spot to toast the newlyweds; then, while refreshments are served, bridal parties can sneak across the street for photos in the park. A second-story terrace lets guests survey the festivities below. Tucked in one corner of the courtyard, a semiprivate enclave with a labyrinth and small amphitheater invites cozy conversations.

Outdoor receptions are usually held in the Parish Courtyard at the front of the facility. Lovely and serene, this bricked garden plaza offers a spacious yet intimate environment for up to 200 guests. Well-placed foliage provides filtered shade, and at the right time of year a grand magnolia tree shows off delicately fragrant flowers. A triple-arched breezeway is a perfect place for the bar and, once the sun sets, ambient lighting lends a romantic luster to the idyllic setting.

Through the breezeway lies the newly refurbished Parish Hall, an attractive banquet room with a high ceiling. Earth-toned walls bring out the room's Mission-style flavor and complement a large stained-glass window (similar to the Sanctuary panels). The hardwood floor is great for dancing, and a proscenium stage puts the entertainment on display. Recent upgrades include an audiovisual system, and behind the scenes your caterer cooks up a feast in a professional kitchen.

Flexible, welcoming, and aesthetically pleasing, the Unitarian Society continues its legacy as host to unforgettable events.

CEREMONY CAPACITY: The Sanctuary holds 285 seated guests; the courtyard 200 seated.

EVENT/RECEPTION CAPACITY: Indoors, the site holds up to 110 seated; outdoors 200 seated.

MEETING CAPACITY: Spaces are available that seat up to 150 guests.

PRICES: WHAT'S THIS GOING TO COST?
   Rental Fee: $1,250–3,850/event
      • The rental fee varies depending on the time of day, space reserved, and event duration.

AVAILABILITY: Year-round, daily. Monday–Saturday 9am–10pm; Sunday 3pm–10pm.

SERVICES/AMENITIES:

Catering: select from list or BYO
Kitchen Facilities: new commercial kitchen
Tables & Chairs: CBA
Linens, Silver, etc.: BYO
Restrooms: wheelchair accessible
Dance Floor: provided indoors
Bride's Dressing Area: yes
AV/Meeting Equipment: some provided

Parking: on street and valet CBA
Accommodations: no guest rooms
Outdoor Night Lighting: CBA
Outdoor Cooking Facilities: BBQ CBA
Cleanup: CBA
View: gardens, park, mountains
Other: grand piano; vocalists and organist CBA

RESTRICTIONS:

Alcohol: BYO, licensed server only
Smoking: not allowed
Music: amplified OK with restrictions

Wheelchair Access: yes
Insurance: one-day liability policy required

Overwhelmed? Use the search criteria on www.HereComesTheGuide.com to narrow down your choices.

59

Ventura County

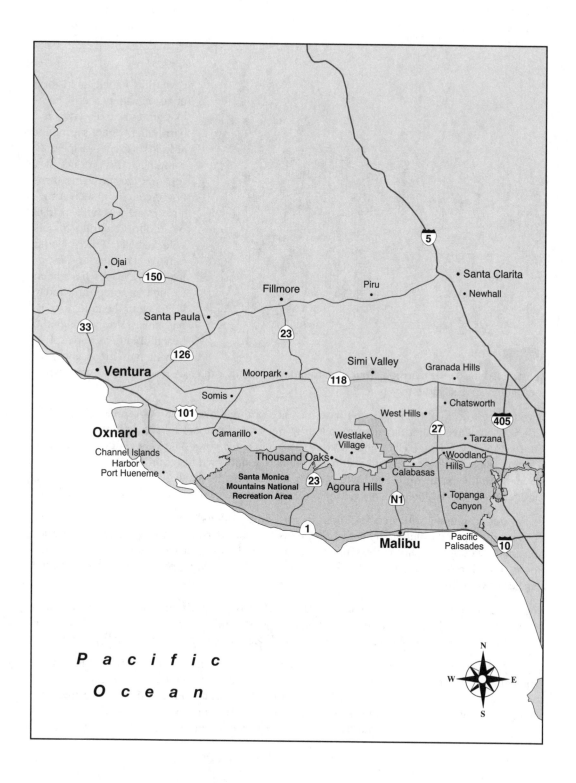

Camarillo Ranch

201 Camarillo Ranch Road, Camarillo

805/383-5697

www.cityofcamarillo.org
camarilloranch@cityofcamarillo.org

● Rehearsal Dinners	● Corporate Events
● Ceremonies	● Meetings
● Wedding Receptions	● Film Shoots
● Private Parties	Accommodations

Camarillo Ranch, a historic mansion with peaceful, park-like grounds and a jazzy red barn, offers a rare setting for all kinds of events—especially weddings. The product of a romantic gesture, this turn-of-the-century Queen Anne-style estate was built in 1892 by Adolfo Camarillo for his wife Isabella. The splendid heritage structure and its remaining 4.5 acres have been lovingly restored, and today visitors tour the ranch's original stables, stroll through the beautiful gardens, and explore a living museum expertly reconstructed inside the mansion. Your own friends and family can enjoy the same diversions when they attend special gatherings here.

If you come to wed at the ranch, you have a choice of three lovely outdoor ceremony sites. The East Garden, a manicured lawn surrounded by trees and luxuriant foliage, is highlighted by a bronze-roofed gazebo—a charming backdrop for exchanging vows. The West Garden, located on the opposite side of the mansion, features a fountain and its own lush border of trees. For larger ceremonies, the expansive Estate Lawn is the perfect setting. It's shaded by mature trees—one in particular, a fabulous Moreton Bay fig, displays an intricate root system, symbolic of a knot well tied!

Follow your ceremony with a cocktail hour in one of the gardens while you snap a few photos as newlyweds. A grand staircase in the mansion's foyer is a wonderful place to stage group portraits, and an alcove opposite showcases stained glass and scrollwork. You'll also appreciate the Bride's Room, a luxurious and modern salon where you and your wedding party can put the finishing touches to your finery.

Want to continue the festivities outdoors? The Estate Lawn is also an ideal spot for hosting a reception. Here, 600 or more guests can dine beneath magnificent trees, and this verdant space adapts to whatever mood you envision, from a posh garden soirée to a festive family occasion.

If you prefer to bring the party inside, then you can get your glam on in the ranch's Red Barn. Originally constructed in 1905, a recent renovation has preserved the look of the classic American structure, complete with a brick-red façade trimmed in white and a whimsical weathervane on top. The barn's rustic-chic ambiance is coupled with 21st-century amenities, so your guests won't have to rough it. The neutral décor and soaring wooden rafters beg for your own elegant embellishments—antique chandeliers or icicle lights, for example. Spacious enough to hold 250 for a reception and still allow for dancing on the sealed concrete floor, the barn also boasts two sets of double doors and windows that can be opened to the country breeze.

The ranch's exclusive caterer is both skilled and seasoned, and will deliver your preferred culinary experience with grace and style. Whether you're dreaming of a nostalgic Victorian-inspired fête or a trendsetting bash with modern décor, this unique property provides a flexible, scenic venue for your landmark celebration.

CEREMONY CAPACITY: The Estate Lawn accommodates 1,000 seated guests; the East Garden and West Garden seat up to 300 each. Indoors, the Red Barn can hold 250.

EVENT/RECEPTION & MEETING CAPACITY: The Estate Lawn holds 1,000 seated or standing guests. Indoors, the Red Barn accommodates 250 seated or 600 standing guests.

PRICES: WHAT'S THIS GOING TO COST?

Rental Fee: $4,950/event and up
- The rental fee varies depending on the day of the week, space reserved, and guest count.
- Venue rental includes use of the Red Barn and garden lawns, a Bridal Suite, and escorted access to the Ranch House for wedding photography.
- For Saturday weddings, add $5/person.
- A 10% discount for active-duty military is available.

Meals (when priced separately): $75/person and up
- Custom catering packages include: tables, upgraded chairs, linens, etc.; all tableware, glasses, servingware, etc.; lighting; dance floor; bartenders; staffing; and setup and cleanup. Other details can be arranged.

Service Charge or Gratuity: 15%

AVAILABILITY: Year-round, daily, 9am–11pm event curfew. Renters have until midnight for room cleanup and breakdown.

SERVICES/AMENITIES:

Catering: Provided
Kitchen Facilities: prep only
Tables & Chairs: CBA
Linens, Silver, etc.: provided
Restrooms: wheelchair accessible
Dance Floor: barn or CBA
Dressing Area: yes
AV/Meeting Equipment: CBA through exclusive vendor, extra fee

Parking: 30-car lot on site; more CBA
Accommodations: no guest rooms
Outdoor Night Lighting: CBA
Outdoor Cooking Facilities: BBQ CBA
Cleanup: provided
View: mountains, garden, fountain, landscaped grounds
Other: picnic area

RESTRICTIONS:

Alcohol: licensed server
Smoking: not allowed
Music: amplified OK

Wheelchair Access: barn and first floor of Ranch House
Insurance: liability required

Rancho de Las Palmas

3566 Sunset Valley Road, Moorpark
805/529-6699
www.ranchodelaspalmas.com
ranchodelaspalmas@gmail.com

Private Estate

- Rehearsal Dinners
- Ceremonies
- Wedding Receptions
- Private Parties
- Corporate Events
- Meetings
- Film Shoots
- Accommodations

As soon as you step into Rancho de las Palmas, the word "oasis" comes to mind. With its spring-fed lagoon, stunning fountains, and thousands of palm trees, it comes as close as we've ever seen to the literal definition of a tropical oasis. Developed over the past two decades by the Cassar family, this one-of-a-kind, 420-acre private estate combines a garden setting with a vintage, country club flair.

The focal point of Rancho is the huge lagoon, which features sparkling fountains and a marvelous island that's connected to the shore by a twinkle-lit bridge. Encircled by weeping willows and stalwart palm trees, the area surrounding the lagoon is great for open-air entertaining.

There are many ceremony locations at Rancho de las Palmas. You can exchange vows on the grass beneath a lovely vintage arch, in front of the two-tiered waterfall, atop the curved brick stairway facing the lagoon, or at the estate's newest spot where the bride walks down a 100-foot-long aisle and through a series of ornate archways decorated with flowers to say "I do".

From here, it's only a few steps to the estate's grand Pavilion for dinner and reception. This unique, circular space comes alive when the sun goes down!—organza draped from the top of the center pole is embedded with glowing twinkle lights, creating a charming and romantic ambiance.

One of your greatest pleasures at Rancho de las Palmas will be taking a stroll around the grounds. As you do, you'll enjoy the beautiful gathering areas—and might even find a nice private spot to seal your night with a sweet kiss. You may also notice how the palm and pepper trees, flowers, fountains, and verdant gardens all come together naturally in this lush wonderland. With photo opportunities everywhere, it's no surprise that photographers and videographers love this place!! And, if children are included in your celebration, they'll be enchanted (and occupied) by a Swiss Family Robinson-style treehouse, complete with slide and swings. Even childcare can be provided on request.

Among the many benefits of having your celebration at Rancho is that they only host one event per day. This means you and your bridal party will have plenty of time to get ready in the air-conditioned bridal room, toast the occasion with a few drinks on the patio, and truly relax before the festivities begin. Oh, and we should mention that they haven't overlooked the guys: Groom's Island is a cool hangout for the groom and his entourage.

In addition to weddings, Rancho de las Palmas hosts numerous movie shoots, luaus, casino nights, bar mitzvahs, birthdays, small graduations, fundraisers, and memorial services. So if renting a ballroom or banquet hall simply isn't your style, pay a visit to Rancho de Las Palmas—it's as refreshing as an oasis in the desert!

CEREMONY CAPACITY: Ceremony areas hold 232 seated guests. Special outdoor events of up to 1,000 guests may be held on a limited number of dates.

EVENT/RECEPTION & MEETING CAPACITY: The covered Pavilion can accommodate up to 232 seated guests. For corporate events, the site holds up to 232 guests.

PRICES: WHAT'S THIS GOING TO COST?

Rental Fee: *$2,500–4,000/event*
- The site rental fee varies depending on the day of the week.

Package Prices: *$69/person and up*
- Wedding packages include use of the property, a buffet or dinner, hors d'oeuvres, unlimited social bar & champagne toast, chairs, tables, and tableware.

Service Charge or Gratuity: *17%*

AVAILABILITY: Year-round, daily including holidays, 9am–11pm.

SERVICES/AMENITIES:

Catering: in-house, no BYO
Kitchen Facilities: n/a
Tables & Chairs: provided
Linens, Silver, etc.: provided
Restrooms: wheelchair accessible
Dance Floor: rental available
Bride's Dressing Area: yes
AV/Meeting Equipment: BYO

Parking: large, paved, lighted lot
Accommodations: no guest rooms
Outdoor Night Lighting: yes
Outdoor Cooking Facilities: through caterer
Cleanup: caterer
View: tropical botanical gardens, freshwater lake, turtle rescue sanctuary, palm trees, fountains

RESTRICTIONS:

Alcohol: in-house, or BYO
Smoking: designated areas
Music: amplified OK outdoors

Wheelchair Access: mostly yes
Insurance: extra insurance CBA
Other: no rice or confetti

Newhall Mansion

829 Park Street, Piru
805/398-5042
www.newhallmansion.com
guestrelations@newhallmansion.com

Historic Mansion & Garden

- Rehearsal Dinners
- Ceremonies
- Wedding Receptions
- Private Parties
- Corporate Events
- Meetings
- Film Shoots
- Accommodations

Despite its decades-long popularity as a location for film and TV shoots, you've probably never heard of Piru before. Yet the quiet agricultural community on the Eastern fringe of scenic Heritage Valley is a mere 10 minutes from Valencia's Magic Mountain. The town is emerging from its relative obscurity, however, thanks to the spectacular renovation of its crown jewel, Newhall Mansion. This enchanting Queen Anne-style hilltop residence, set on nine landscaped acres, was originally built in 1890 by Piru's founder, publishing magnate David C. Cook, as a gift for his wife. The ensuing years saw a series of owners, a fire and two earthquakes, until at last the mansion was rescued in 2013. The current proprietors have completely transformed the Ventura County landmark, adding modern amenities, lush gardens and exquisite décor that accentuates its vintage glamour.

Passing through the mansion's imposing wrought-iron gates, you're greeted by a citrus grove flanking a long, rose-lined promenade. Next comes the Park, a lovely hedged lawn in front of the mansion with a splashing fountain and panoramic mountain view. The estate's fairy-tale façade, featuring wraparound verandas, intricate scrollwork and a stone tower, makes a grand backdrop for exchanging vows.

A stroll to the backyard reveals a tiled Courtyard that's a delightful locale for dining and dancing under the stars. Extras include a fire pit, a swimming pool with white cabanas, and an old-fashioned pagoda to showcase the wedding cake, sweetheart table or bar. Specialty lighting throughout the grounds adds to the evening's magic. The terraced gardens and rolling lawns that overlook the Courtyard hold more wedding options. An illuminated stairway makes a dramatic wedding aisle, and the couple exchanges vows in front of a twinkle-lit arch. Groves of olive, pomegranate, apricot and fig trees form a leafy background, a legacy of David Cook's "Second Garden of Eden". In the tranquil twilight, the romantic milieu does seem a lot like paradise.

The best way to indulge in all the mansion's luxuries is to spend the weekend, which also lets you expand your event into the breathtaking 12,000-square-foot interior. Each room is lavished with period details, antiques and artistic restorations. The Ballroom's magnificent stained-glass transom frames a glorious view, and is a favorite spot for bridal portraits. The Dining Room, with its stunning coffered ceiling, and the stately fire-lit Library offer classic Victorian elegance. And the new Bridal Hospitality Suite on the top floor provides 3,000 square feet of seclusion and queenly comforts.

The mansion's most imaginative entertainment option is the Tavern, an underground man-cave whose circular stone entryway recalls a Gothic castle. A series of brick-walled salons radiate an aura of mystery, and a giant flat-screen TV, custom redwood bar and cool stylings make the Tavern a novel setting for a cocktail reception, bachelor party or rehearsal dinner. A hidden bedroom will have you feeling like characters in a romance novel. Seven sumptuous bedrooms in the main house boast a collective assortment of deluxe treats: a fireplace, an extravagant stone shower with carved mermaids, a wooden Jacuzzi and a huge stained-glass oriel window.

Newhall Mansion welcomes you to celebrate in complete privacy amid nostalgic opulence, all while surrounded by nature. Not only has this historic charmer put Piru on the map—it's also a treasure of a wedding venue.

CEREMONY & EVENT/RECEPTION CAPACITY: The facility can accommodate 50 seated or standing guests indoors and 300 seated or standing outdoors.

MEETING CAPACITY: Meetings do not take place at this facility.

PRICES: WHAT'S THIS GOING TO COST?

Rental Fee: $7,000-11,000/event
- The rental fee varies depending on the day of the week and time of year.
- Saturday or weekend wedding packages require a buyout of Newhall Mansion's 8 historic guest rooms for an additional fee. You may opt to have your guests cover the cost of their own rooms.

Meals (when priced separately): $65/person and up
- Customized menus include taxes, gratuities, staffing, event insurance, and day-of wedding coordination.
- Food & beverage minimums apply.

Additional Info: Indoor usage is only available when overnight accommodations are booked.

AVAILABILITY: Year-round. There's an 11pm event curfew, but your overnight guests can continue the party later than that.

SERVICES/AMENITIES:

Catering: in house, or BYO with approval
Kitchen Facilities: limited
Tables & Chairs: provided
Linens, Silver, etc.: in house
Restrooms: wheelchair accessible
Dance Area: provided
Bride's Dressing Area: yes
AV/Meeting Equipment: some available
Other: picnic area

Parking: large complimentary lot
Accommodations: 8 guest rooms, including a new 3,000 sq. ft. bridal suite
Outdoor Night Lighting: provided
Outdoor Cooking Facilities: BBQ on site
Cleanup: caterer or renter
View: canyon, forest, fountain, garden, landscaped grounds, pool, vineyards

RESTRICTIONS:

Alcohol: in-house, or BYO with approval
Smoking: designated areas only
Music: amplified OK with restrictions

Wheelchair Access: yes
Insurance: included

Quail Ranch

Private Ranch

Address withheld to ensure privacy. Simi Valley

805/328-4928

quailranchevents.com
joanne@quailranchevents.com

- Rehearsal Dinners
- Ceremonies
- Wedding Receptions
- Private Parties
- Corporate Events
- Meetings
- Film Shoots

Accommodations

Perched high on a hill, Quail Ranch is a hidden private estate and 70-acre avocado ranch in Eastern Ventura County, just outside of Los Angeles.

Built in 1933, the historic Ranch House is an authentic Spanish-style home featuring the original red-tile roof, huge picture windows that frame the grounds, and a hacienda-style layout complete with splashing tiled fountains. The artfully designed grounds and interior create a serene world of rustic elegance that showcases the ranch's charms.

Ceremonies are held in the estate's lemon orchard, where a sprawling 5,000-square-foot terrace hosts romantic "I do"s. For her entrance, the bride descends a grand staircase flanked by olive trees and bougainvillea to the brick terrace below. The couple exchanges vows beneath a majestic oak tree, while the sweet scent of lemon blossoms fills the air.

Afterwards, guests gather for cocktails on the front lawn, which is surrounded by star pines and ancient oaks. As evening descends, the party moves to the other side of the home for a reception on another expansive tree-lined lawn. A dark wood bar beneath an arbor laced with wisteria and bistro lights contributes to the mood of relaxed elegance.

Chic bridal party hideaways include a bride-friendly retreat with luxe furnishings and a lofty stone fireplace; and The Ranch Lodge, a true "groom's room", outfitted with leather sofas, bar and pool table.

Farm-to-table cuisine is also part of the Quail Ranch experience. A variety of delicious dishes featuring locally grown produce are beautifully presented by their exclusive "Certified By The Guide" caterer, *Command Performance*. Menus are customized with each client's tastes and budget in mind.

Infused with gracious living and warm hospitality, Quail Ranch is an inspiring choice for your landmark celebration.

CEREMONY & EVENT/RECEPTION CAPACITY: The facility holds up to 300 seated or standing guests outdoors.

MEETING CAPACITY: Meeting spaces can seat up to 200.

PRICES: WHAT'S THIS GOING TO COST?

Rental Fee: $6,900/event and up
- The rental fee varies depending on the day of the week, time of year, and guest count.

Package Prices: $104.95/person and up
- Custom catering packages include: tables, upgraded chairs, linens; all tableware, glasses, servingware; lighting; dance floor; bartenders and wooden bar; staffing, setup, and cleanup. Other details can be arranged.

AVAILABILITY: Year round, daily. Hours are flexible.

SERVICES/AMENITIES:

Catering: provided by preferred caterer
Kitchen Facilities: n/a
Tables & Chairs: provided
Linens, Silver, etc.: provided
Restrooms: not wheelchair accessible
Dance Floor: yes
Bride's & Groom's Dressing Areas: yes
AV/Meeting Equipment: BYO
Other: groom's room with pool table and private patio; fire pit, fireplaces

Parking: valet required
Accommodations: no guest rooms
Outdoor Night Lighting: CBA
Outdoor Cooking Facilities: no
Cleanup: caterer or renter
View: fountain, garden, landscaped grounds, fields; panorama of orchards, cityscape, hills, and mountains

RESTRICTIONS:

Alcohol: BYO
Smoking: designated areas only
Music: amplified OK outdoors with restrictions

Wheelchair Access: limited
Insurance: liability required

Want to know WHAT TO ASK a potential location or vendor? Check out our Questions to Ask starting on page 21.

The Vineyards

2525 Stow Street, Simi Valley
805/583-2525
www.thevineyardsimi.com
soroor@thevineyardsimi.com

Garden Event Facility

● Rehearsal Dinners ● Corporate Events
● Ceremonies ● Meetings
● Wedding Receptions ● Film Shoots
● Private Parties Accommodations

Hidden among the Simi Valley foothills on 8 acres, The Vineyards is a lavish special event oasis that includes almost every romantic element you can imagine: sunsets and starlight, grapevines and gardens, waterfalls and whimsical fountains, as well as glamorous interiors that make you feel like movie stars. Yet perhaps the venue's most standout attribute is their service-oriented banquet managers, who thoughtfully orchestrate each phase of your celebration, right from your guests' arrival at the main center's waterfall entryway.

The friendly staff (and the personalized signage) directs them to either a rustic or contemporary ceremony site, depending on your preference. A stroll to the former follows a serpentine garden path shaded by twinkle-lit, vine-covered arbors down a hillside to a forested dell. As fragrant blooms perfume the air, you exchange vows in front of a profusion of lush greenery and willowy trees. The namesake vineyards are spread out below the garden, and newlyweds are often photographed holding hands among the grapevines.

For a different yet equally invigorating experience, wed on the Waterfall Terrace atop a stunning stone stage framed by a redwood pergola, to the hypnotic accompaniment of rushing water. Behind you, water spills over two landscaped stone tiers that flank the stage steps where your bridal party holds court. Your loved ones enjoy this refreshing tableau, seated beneath café lights and portable white-wood pergolas fashioned with adjustable canopies and sheer drapes—an innovation that's both practical and pretty.

Several enchanting patios encircle the main building, each lending its own charms to al fresco gatherings (think fire tables, custom-built fountains, a fetching footbridge and more!) Or bring the social hour inside to the ultra-swanky Mountain View Room, whose décor epitomizes unique chic. Outfitted in the venue's signature creamy white (always in style, darling), the bi-level room dazzles with crystal chandeliers, luminarias and sparkly accents. On the upper level, silver banquettes dressed with retro fur pillows are the perfect spot to admire breathtaking wraparound windows that double as transparent water walls, a clever design that elevates the space's hip factor.

Elegant galas are sure to impress in the neighboring Grandview Room, which boasts a similar aesthetic—taken up a notch. Chiffon ceiling canopies entwined with rope lights showcase dining tables and gold Chiavari chairs. A built-in stage stands ready for your entertainment, and theatrical lighting delivers a range of color enhancements that add dramatic flair to your reception.

The venue's most novel space is the rotunda-shaped Star View Room, centered around a circular copper bar ringed with trendy acrylic stools. Overhead, an elaborate chandelier hangs from a soaring coved ceiling that displays a scintillating faux starscape. With its nightclub attitude and intimate white leather-clad enclaves, the Star View's mood is at once sultry and cool, just the thing for cocktails, an after-party or an out-of-the-ordinary rehearsal dinner.

If it's all a bit dizzying, don't worry. The Vineyards' seasoned event pros will skillfully integrate your vision with their value-filled packages. Versatile, original and accommodating, this is definitely one of those places you have to experience to fully appreciate, so be sure it's on your "must see" list. You won't be disappointed.

CEREMONY & MEETING CAPACITY: The facility holds 250 seated guests indoors and 300 seated outdoors.

EVENT/RECEPTION CAPACITY: The facility can accommodate up to 300 seated indoors and 300 seated or standing outdoors.

PRICES: WHAT'S THIS GOING TO COST?

Package Prices: $139/person
- Pricing is $139/person for the first 100 guests and $115 for each additional.
- Packages include meals, alcohol, facility, coordinator; photographer, DJ, florist, & cake may be included.
- Note that there is a 100-guest minimum.

Service Charge or Gratuity: 20%

AVAILABILITY: Year-round, daily, 9am–midnight.

SERVICES/AMENITIES:

Catering: in-house
Kitchen Facilities: n/a
Tables & Chairs: provided
Linens, Silver, etc.: provided
Restrooms: wheelchair accessible
Dance Floor: yes
Dressing Area: yes
AV/Meeting Equipment: CBA
Other: in-house event coordination, wedding cake, florals, photographer, and DJ

Parking: large complimentary lot; valet available, extra fee
Accommodations: no guest rooms
Outdoor Night Lighting: yes
Outdoor Cooking Facilities: BBQ CBA
Cleanup: caterer or renter
View: panorama of hills and mountains; canyon, forest, fountain, garden, landscaped grounds, waterfall, vineyards

RESTRICTIONS:

Alcohol: in-house
Smoking: outdoors only
Music: amplified OK

Wheelchair Access: yes
Insurance: liability required

Wood Ranch Golf Club

Golf Club

301 Wood Ranch Parkway, Simi Valley

805/527-9663 X207

www.countryclubreceptions.com
eventdirector@woodranchgc.com

● Rehearsal Dinners	● Corporate Events
● Ceremonies	● Meetings
● Wedding Receptions	● Film Shoots
● Private Parties	Accommodations

Framed by the rugged Santa Susanna Mountains, the upscale Simi Valley community of Wood Ranch, located a stone's throw from the Reagan Library, is prized for its quiet lifestyle, wide boulevards, and manicured lawns. At its center lie the verdant greens of the exclusive Wood Ranch Golf Club and its striking contemporary clubhouse, reminiscent of the work of Frank Lloyd Wright.

Masterfully marrying nature and architecture, the building's exterior incorporates elements of Wright's enduring designs, such as cast cement bricks, wood beams, and strong clean lines softened by feathery ferns and colorful blooms. Step under the porte-cochère and you'll feel like you're visiting a sleek, private lodge. That feeling is enhanced when a greeter welcomes your guests and directs them down the walkway to the left, which takes them to a scenic knoll for your ceremony. Shaded from the afternoon sun by a tall stand of trees and brightened by an ever-changing landscape of flowering plants, the site's large lawn and gazebo overlook a glistening lake below.

Once vows have been exchanged, it's time to move inside to the beautifully appointed clubhouse. The foyer's cool slate floor and the enormous barrel-shaped skylight overhead set the tone for the Arts and Crafts touches throughout each room. The Main Lobby, where cocktails are served, makes generous use of luxury materials for an understated elegance: The slate and marble fireplace, for example, is adorned with a large metallic artwork and contributes a modern focal point to the room. Mahogany accents not only add richness to the space, but also mirror the warm wood of the grand piano. A massive chandelier hangs from the high ceiling and reflects the best of Craftsman style in burnished copper, which is picked up again in the room's distinctive copper-and-glass-enclosed wine cellar to your right. The entire room is flooded with light filtering in from the Grand Ballroom, just beyond the tall silk drapes that separate the two spaces (but allow your guests a peek at what's in store for them during the reception).

The Ballroom's most arresting feature is its wall of floor-to-ceiling windows. Over 20 feet tall, they provide a panorama of the golf course below, fringed by the mountains beyond it. For smaller groups, there's the Lakeview Room to the left, which has an outdoor terrace overlooking the gazebo, lawns, and lakes of the signature 18th hole.

Wood Ranch Golf Club's seamless combination of timeless design, modern sensibilities, and first-class service creates a beautiful setting for a most memorable wedding celebration.

CEREMONY CAPACITY: The Gazebo Lawn holds up to 350 seated guests; the Ballroom up to 220 seated.

EVENT/RECEPTION & MEETING CAPACITY: The Club accommodates up to 220 seated or 400 standing guests indoors or outdoors.

PRICES: WHAT'S THIS GOING TO COST?

Package Prices: $72/person and up
- Pricing varies based on food, beverage, and rental inclusions. Food & beverage minimums will apply. Menus and packages can be customized to fit your needs and budget. Pricing does not include additional site fees, mandatory service charge, gratuity, and current sales tax.

AVAILABILITY: Year-round, daily, anytime. Closed on Christmas Day.

SERVICES/AMENITIES:

Catering: in-house
Kitchen Facilities: n/a
Tables & Chairs: provided
Linens, Silver, etc.: provided
Restrooms: wheelchair accessible
Dance Floor: provided
Bride's Dressing Area: provided
AV/Meeting Equipment: some provided

Parking: large lot, valet required for parties over 100 guests
Accommodations: no guest rooms
Outdoor Night Lighting: access only
Outdoor Cooking Facilities: BBQ
Cleanup: provided
View: fairways, hills, lakes, landscaped grounds
Other: grand piano, secluded gazebo, reception lawn

RESTRICTIONS:

Alcohol: in-house
Smoking: outside only
Music: amplified OK

Wheelchair Access: yes
Insurance: not required

Hartley Botanica

4465 Balcom Canyon Road, Somis
805/532-1997
www.hartleybotanica.com
barbara@hartleybotanica.com

Botanical Gardens

● Rehearsal Dinners	● Corporate Events
● Ceremonies	● Meetings
● Wedding Receptions	● Film Shoots
● Private Parties	Accommodations

Just beyond the hills of Camarillo in the peaceful Las Posas Valley you'll find the small hamlet of Somis, home to generations of family farmers. Somis has so far managed to escape the pressure of development, and boasts one post office, one store, and the oldest wooden gas station in California. It's the kind of place that makes you want to slow down for a while, stop and smile at a stranger, and breathe in the fresh country air that seems to make all that grows here flourish.

At Hartley Botanica, not only do the plants and flowers thrive, they also end up in beautiful shapes and clever arrangements. That's because this Somis nursery doubles as a landscaping company, and throughout the property you'll discover artistic examples of garden design. Nowhere is this more impressive than in the wedding area, a spectacular garden oasis that owes its creation to a proud father's love.

It all started when owner Barbara Goodrich took over the place in 1995. Her interest in landscaping came from her parents, creative types whose 30 years of experience include such notable clients as Janet Jackson and Michael Landon. When Barbara got engaged, Mom offered to make her a fabulous wedding gown. Not to be outdone, Dad took advantage of the nursery's natural beauty to create a dream ceremony and reception site for his daughter's wedding. Now Barbara wants to share her fantasy garden with you for your own wedding or special event.

Party guests are free to explore the nursery's novelties, like its rock waterfall with grotto, peacocks, and sculptured rose garden. Yet the celebration grounds themselves are shielded from the public by custom-designed metal gates. The bride has her own changing room to prepare for the walk down the aisle—and you've never seen an aisle quite like this one!

A dramatic, sweeping promenade winds around an expanse of verdant lawn. Along the way you pass under no fewer than 18 vine-covered archways set in bases of flowering stone urns. The rose-colored walkway is embellished with real leaves pressed into the concrete, and caged songbirds add to the magical effect. To the left, a pond featuring an aquatic garden and a cascading waterfall accompany you until you reach the final stretch of the aisle. Then a delicate canopy of tree branches laden with honeysuckle leads to your groom, standing at the center of an enormous daisy permanently etched right into the aisle. (A smaller daisy just beyond can hold an accompanist.) Your guests enjoy the spectacle from the lawn, with the rolling hills as a picturesque backdrop.

A row of shrubs marks the rear of the Ceremony Garden, and on the other side lies the reception area, an even larger swath of lawn dotted with trees, decorative statuary, and pots overflowing with colorful flowers. A stand of Chinese pistache trees shelters a long bar fashioned of smooth stones; its countertop, embedded with leaves, is the ideal spot to serve drinks and a buffet. Each botanical treatment features built-in seating areas, and some offer intriguing surprises: In the center of the lawn, for example, a lush forest environment of eucalyptus trees serves as a natural aviary for cockatiels and doves.

After a short time at the Gardens, your cares seem to float away on a gentle rose-scented breeze. Everything here is fresh, green, and blossoming—an enchanting environment for a celebration of new beginnings.

CEREMONY CAPACITY: The Wedding Area holds 375 guests.

EVENT/RECEPTION CAPACITY: The Reception Area holds 375 guests.

MEETING CAPACITY: Several spaces accommodate up to 375 guests.

PRICES: WHAT'S THIS GOING TO COST?

Rental Fee: $3,250/event and up

Package Prices: $78/person and up
 • Wedding catering packages include use of the property, valet parking, catering options (from champagne brunch to candlelight dinner), 4 to 4½ hours of beverage service, catering staff and bartender, non-alcoholic beverages, choice of linens, tableware, coffee bar, spacious bride's room & man cave for the groom, and day-of event coordination.

Service Charge or Gratuity: 18%

AVAILABILITY: Year-round, Saturday or Sunday, 8am–2:30pm or 3:30pm–midnight.

SERVICES/AMENITIES:

Catering: in-house
Kitchen Facilities: n/a
Tables & Chairs: provided
Linens, Silver, etc.: provided
Restrooms: wheelchair accessible
Dance Floor: provided
Bride's Dressing Area: yes
AV/Meeting Equipment: BYO

Parking: valet parking
Accommodations: no guest rooms
Outdoor Night Lighting: yes
Outdoor Cooking Facilities: no
Cleanup: caterer or renter
View: gardens, waterfalls, foothills, pond
Other: DJ, florist, cake

RESTRICTIONS:

Alcohol: BYO, no corkage fees
Smoking: designated areas
Music: amplified OK outdoors

Wheelchair Access: yes
Insurance: liability required
Other: no rice, birdseed, or confetti

The Saticoy Club

Golf Club

4450 Clubhouse Drive, Somis
805/485-4956 x19
www.thesaticoyclub.com
agalaviz@thesaticoyclub.com

● Rehearsal Dinners	● Corporate Events
● Ceremonies	● Meetings
● Wedding Receptions	● Film Shoots
● Private Parties	Accommodations

The road that leads to The Saticoy Club gently winds its way up the hillside, and as you approach your destination you're likely to pass acres of colorful foliage in full bloom. Upon arrival, you may notice the faint aroma of strawberries, carried on a light sea breeze. A tranquil landscape of farmland spreads out below, with the Pacific coastline in the distance. As you take in the beauty of your surroundings, it's easy to understand why the club's founders chose this scenic spot.

The first club in Ventura County, Saticoy opened in 1921 and over the ensuing decades has become a social center for distinguished residents and visiting celebrities. A recent renovation ensures the club's aesthetic is anchored in the modern era, and given its illustrious pedigree, visitors are pleasantly surprised by Saticoy's welcoming, unpretentious atmosphere—just one of the things that make it a standout venue for affordable weddings and events.

Arriving guests are escorted to one of two pretty ceremony sites: Intimate vows are celebrated in front of a cascading waterfall, atop a garden lawn just below the Dining Room Terrace. A short walk away is a lush lawn poised on a bluff ringed by lofty hedges, where guests enjoy a spectacular panorama of miles of bountiful fields beneath a gorgeous sunset. On a clear day, the ocean view stretches all the way to the Channel Islands! A rose-petal aisle and floral arrangements to mark the altar are included with all ceremony packages.

As the newlyweds explore the photogenic grounds, friends and family mingle on the Terrace, where lounge furniture, fire-pit tables, and golf course vistas create a congenial social hour. Two adjustable monitors are often used to display slideshows of the bride and groom.

When it's time to dine, everyone steps inside the recently updated Dining Room, which boasts a high, open-beamed ceiling. A tulle-and-light canopy can be added for extra glamour, but a wall of windows that captures the setting sun and starry skies offers plenty of visual appeal. A fireplace warms one end of the room, while at the opposite end the head table gets prime placement in front of a huge picture window. Sophisticated table settings can be complemented by optional pewter Chiavari chairs that give off a subtle glow beneath graceful chandeliers. A sizable dance floor encourages everyone to show off their best moves.

The cornerstone of the club's excellent reputation is its service-oriented philosophy. Food & Beverage Manager Alex Galaviz has worked here for over 20 years, and treats everyone as if they were guests in his own home. Known for his careful consideration of each couple's particular wishes, Alex oversees your event from your first meeting through the big day. During your complimentary tasting, courtesy of the club's award-winning chef, he'll guide you towards menu selections and wine pairings that suit your palate and budget. Linens in a range of colors are included with your booking, and Alex even provides a tablescape preview: "We want to make sure our couples get exactly what they've envisioned," he says.

Such high-caliber service at a premier venue usually comes with a high price, but at The Saticoy Club you'll be delighted by the reasonable cost. And the personal attention and staff smiles are always on the house!

CEREMONY CAPACITY: The facility seats 100 guests indoors and 265 outdoors.

EVENT/RECEPTION CAPACITY: The facility can accommodate 280 seated or 325 standing indoors and 75 seated or 150 standing outdoors. Dancing can be held outdoors for up to 300 guests (a dance floor is included with the rental).

MEETING CAPACITY: Meeting spaces hold up to 150 guests.

PRICES: WHAT'S THIS GOING TO COST?

Rental Fee: $2,000/event

Ceremony Fee: $1,500/event
- The ceremony fee includes white bistro garden chairs, an archway or columns with floral arrangements, and a rose petal aisle.

Meals (when priced separately): $42/person and up

Service Charge or Gratuity: 20%

AVAILABILITY: Year-round, daily, until 11pm.

SERVICES/AMENITIES:

Catering: in-house
Kitchen Facilities: n/a
Tables & Chairs: provided
Linens, Silver, etc.: provided
Restrooms: wheelchair accessible
Dance Floor: portable provided
Dressing Area: yes
AV/Meeting Equipment: some provided

Parking: large lot, on street
Accommodations: no guest rooms
Outdoor Night Lighting: yes
Outdoor Cooking Facilities: BBQ CBA
Cleanup: provided
View: hillsides, fairways; waterfalls; panorama of Pacific coastline and cityscape

RESTRICTIONS:

Alcohol: in-house
Smoking: outdoors only
Music: amplified OK with restrictions

Wheelchair Access: yes
Insurance: required for outside vendors
Other: no rice, birdseed, or confetti

The wedding vendors on our website are the best in the business. How do we know? Read page 425.

Palm Garden Hotel

Hotel

495 North Ventu Park Road, Thousand Oaks
805/716-4335

www.palmgardenhotel.com
sales@palmgardenhotel.com

- Rehearsal Dinners
- Ceremonies
- Wedding Receptions
- Private Parties
- Corporate Events
- Meetings
- Film Shoots
- Accommodations

First-time visitors to Palm Garden Hotel are always pleasantly surprised to discover this suburban Conejo Valley oasis tucked amidst a bustling neighborhood just minutes from the 101. The rest of the world instantly melts away once you step inside and are greeted by your experienced on-site coordinator: From the get-go, she'll be your personal guide as you explore this freshly renovated property and together craft your vision of your all-inclusive wedding weekend.

The heart of the hotel is a sun-washed garden courtyard that encircles a sparkling swimming pool and spa, with plush loungers and cabanas beckoning from the pool deck. While it's tempting to kick off your shoes and stay awhile, continue along a flower-lined path to the property's two premier suites. These cool hangouts can host your bachelor and bachelorette party, and also serve as your wedding-day basecamp. The guys favor the chic Hollywood Suite, which boasts a vintage pool table surrounded by cocktail seating and a custom bar, plus two TVs, a kitchenette, and a private master bedroom. The lovely Garden Suite, with its comfortable living room, kitchenette and roomy makeup area, is a tranquil haven for your bridal party preparations. As newlyweds, you can spend your wedding night in the adjoining gardenview master bedroom, which includes a romantic soaking tub—the hotel will even surprise you with champagne and chocolate-covered strawberries!

Hold your dreamy ceremony on the nearby Garden Lawn, sheltered by hedges, palm trees, and trellises entwined with bougainvillea and fragrant jasmine. A wedding aisle lined with rose petals leads to a quaint white wood gazebo fringed in pink and red roses: You might be inspired to enhance this already picturesque site with your own creative touches, such as personalized signage or lanterns, but it's got plenty of built-in allure.

After the vows, while you and your new spouse pose for photos around the scenic property, your guests will stroll to the Poolside Patio for the cocktail hour. It's accented with lush greenery, and provides cushioned seating clustered around copper-lined fire pits for some lively conversation. The adjoining Terrace, a cheerful, light-filled room, has a wall of French doors that can be left open so your guests can easily wander in and out. The Terrace is also a pretty place for your bridal shower or rehearsal dinner and may even be combined with the Patio for an intimate outdoor reception.

If you're planning a large gala, you'll love the spacious Ballroom, outfitted with wooden plantation shutters, chrome fixtures, and a dance floor (included!)—all of which brings a breezy sophistication to your special occasion.

The hotel's on-site culinary team is at your service as well. Their chefs can whip up delicious dishes in a range of customized menus and serving styles, from a festive buffet to a formal, 4-course plated dinner. They're also on hand for welcome refreshments and day-after brunches.

Indeed, Palm Garden Hotel makes it easy to gather your loved ones (and their pets!) under one roof for an extended celebration. And with all the freebies—like a full hot breakfast for overnight guests and on-site parking—it's not only a great value for you, but for your friends and family as well. With its convenient location just minutes from Malibu and its effortless charm, the new Palm Garden Hotel seems destined to become a classic.

CEREMONY, EVENT/RECEPTION, & MEETING CAPACITY: The facility holds 200 seated guests indoors or outdoors.

PRICES: WHAT'S THIS GOING TO COST?

Rental Fee: $500/event and up
  • The rental fee varies depending on the space reserved.

Meals (when priced separately): $35–75/person

Service Charge or Gratuity: 21%

AVAILABILITY: Year-round, daily, anytime.

SERVICES/AMENITIES:

Catering: in-house
Kitchen Facilities: n/a
Tables & Chairs: provided
Linens, Silver, etc.: provided
Restrooms: wheelchair accessible
Dance Floor: portable provided
Bride's Dressing Area: yes
AV/Meeting Equipment: provided

Parking: large lot
Accommodations: 150 guest rooms
Outdoor Night Lighting: provided
Outdoor Cooking Facilities: none
Cleanup: provided
View: garden, landscaped grounds, mountains, pool area

RESTRICTIONS:

Alcohol: full in-house bar
Smoking: outdoors only
Music: amplified OK

Wheelchair Access: yes
Insurance: not required

Sherwood Country Club

Country Club

320 West Stafford Road, Thousand Oaks

805/496-3036

www.sherwoodcatering.com
cateringinfo@sherwoodcc.com

- Rehearsal Dinners
- Ceremonies
- Wedding Receptions
- Private Parties
- Corporate Events
- Meetings
- Film Shoots
- Accommodations

Your name has to be "on the list" to gain entrance to the gated, ultra-exclusive Lake Sherwood neighborhood. We felt privileged to be admitted, but the geese that waddled across our path seemed to take their VIP status for granted. This lush, luxe enclave tucked against the Santa Monica Mountains is indeed nature-friendly, even while impressive celebrity-owned mansions line its serene lanes.

Sherwood owes its name to the 1922 film, *Robin Hood*, when the picturesque, oak-covered grounds where the club would later be built, doubled as Sherwood Forest. With such a cinematic pedigree, it's not surprising that Sherwood Country Club itself, opened in 1989, is often featured in movies, too, including (appropriately) the hit comedy, *Bridesmaids*. In real life, the club is also a sought-after wedding location.

A grand circular drive leads to the Clubhouse, a stunning example of classic Georgian architecture. The immaculate bricked façade and stately white-columned portico create a pronounced sense of occasion, a feeling that increases inside the elegant lobby: Tastefully curated antiques and paintings lining the walls are perfectly complemented by a herringbone-patterned wood floor and a coved ceiling awash in *trompe l'oeil* clouds.

The ambiance is even more heavenly outside on the Canopy Terrace, a favorite ceremony spot with a romance all its own: A semi-circular, cream-colored colonnade forms a rotunda, topped with a pergola and overhead canopy that provides year-round shade. Star jasmine perfumes the perimeter, and chandeliers, garlands, or draping can easily be added. Guests gaze out on a panorama of green fairways, rolling hillsides and blue horizon, all of which makes an enchanting backdrop for wedding vows.

While the bridal party strolls to the members-only rose garden for photos in front of a cascading waterfall, friends and family enjoy the cocktail hour on the sun-splashed brick Garden Patio adjacent to the terrace. For guests who prefer to mingle inside, French doors open into the Conservatory, a refined hideaway outfitted with a baby grand piano, fireplace and plush furnishings.

Outdoor receptions are staged on the Croquet Lawn, an expanse of crisply trimmed grass below the patio, edged with manicured hedgerows and twinkle-lit trees. The space adapts well to tents, lounge furniture, string lights and whatever other décor you fancy, but whether it's decorated or left au naturel, guests are treated to a rosy-pink sunset above the hills and after-dinner dancing under glittering stars.

Yet once you get a look at Sherwood's pretty-as-a-picture ballroom, you might decide to host the party indoors instead. Not your typical square banquet space, this ballroom has a curved wall of windows that frame the club's lovely views. Dazzling beaded crystal chandeliers, suspended from the coffered ceiling, cast an ethereal glow over your reception. At the room's far end, a separate lounge area is just the place to add a cappuccino bar. Consider heightening the magic with the club's customizable lighting packages or other event enhancements. From wedding-cake spotlights to signature cocktails, the accomplished event managers will help you sort through all the options—including Sherwood's enticing menus.

Every inch of Sherwood Country Club is meticulously maintained, and weddings here receive the same careful attention to detail. Even your most selective guests will be impressed, and all you and your new spouse have to do is enjoy being the center of attention.

CEREMONY CAPACITY: The site seats 200 guests indoors and 300 outdoors.

EVENT/RECEPTION CAPACITY: The facility can accommodate 250 seated or 500 standing indoors and 300 seated or 1,000 standing outdoors.

MEETING CAPACITY: Meeting spaces hold 300 seated guests.

PRICES: WHAT'S THIS GOING TO COST?

Package Prices: $100/person and up
- Wedding packages may include bar packages, hors d'oeuvre reception, served meal, complimentary self-parking, tables, chairs, linens and silver, and time for your rehearsal.

Service Charge or Gratuity: 20%

AVAILABILITY: Year-round, daily. Call for details.

SERVICES/AMENITIES:

Catering: in-house, or BYO
Kitchen Facilities: fully equipped
Tables & Chairs: provided
Linens, Silver, etc.: provided
Restrooms: wheelchair accessible
Dance Floor: portable provided
Bride's Dressing Area: yes
AV/Meeting Equipment: provided, CBA

Parking: large lot
Accommodations: no guest rooms
Outdoor Night Lighting: CBA
Outdoor Cooking Facilities: BBQ CBA
Cleanup: provided
View: forest, fountain, garden, pond, landscaped grounds, waterfall; panorama of fairways and Santa Monica mountains
Other: grand piano

RESTRICTIONS:

Alcohol: in-house
Smoking: designated areas only
Music: amplified OK with restrictions

Wheelchair Access: yes
Insurance: liability required

Sunset Hills Country Club

Country Club

4155 Erbes Road North, Thousand Oaks
805/495-6484 X241

www.countryclubreceptions.com
events@sunsethillsclub.com

● Rehearsal Dinners	● Corporate Events
● Ceremonies	● Meetings
● Wedding Receptions	● Film Shoots
● Private Parties	Accommodations

Nestled in the rolling hills of Thousand Oaks, Sunset Hills Country Club is just outside Los Angeles but feels like it's worlds away. The club is spread over 85 lush acres, whose gently rolling hills are dotted with majestic oaks, mature elms, and a wealth of other trees. In addition to a clubhouse and golf shop, the property features an 18-hole golf course and an Olympic-sized swimming pool.

Situated on three separate levels with interconnecting stairways, the two clubhouse buildings and Pro Shop are arranged in a horseshoe around the sparkling pool. With their arched façades and red-tile roofs, these one-story stuccos reflect a contemporary melding of California and Spanish architecture.

Sunset Hills welcomes events of all kinds—weddings, birthday parties, and golf tournaments to name a few. If marriage is on your mind, two sites are available for ceremonies. For a big wedding, the best place to tie the knot is in a flat green valley surrounded by stately oaks that affords ample room for theater-style seating. More intimate ceremonies take place at the crest of a little hill beneath overarching alder branches.

After saying "I do" outdoors, bring your festivities inside the Sunset Hills Ballroom, located on the clubhouse's upper level. This spacious, L-shaped venue comes with a parquet dance floor and features an arching, adobe-style brick fireplace. Wrought-iron chandeliers and sconces illuminate earth-tone walls adorned with Tuscan-style artwork, imparting a tasteful elegance. If your event calls for more space, a movable wall rolls easily aside, allowing the ballroom and the lounge to combine into a single large room overlooking the patio and pool.

Sunset Hills offers a variety of wedding packages, all of which can be customized. Their executive chef is happy to personalize your menu, and the on-site event manager will work with you and/or your wedding planner to choreograph your affair from start to finish.

The team at Sunset Hills Country Club is experienced at hosting all types of celebrations. Their expertise and marvelous esprit de corps will ensure that yours will be a resounding success.

CEREMONY CAPACITY: The lawn area holds 200 seated guests.

EVENT/RECEPTION CAPACITY: The Ballroom accommodates 200 seated with dance floor.

MEETING CAPACITY: The Ballroom holds 200 guests seated theater-style.

PRICES: WHAT'S THIS GOING TO COST?

Package Prices: $68/person and up
- Pricing varies based on food, beverage, and rental inclusions. Food & beverage minimums will apply. Menus and packages can be customized to fit your needs and budget. Pricing does not include additional site fees, mandatory service charge, gratuity, and current sales tax.

AVAILABILITY: Year-round, daily, 6pm–midnight. Earlier events can be arranged.

SERVICES/AMENITIES:

Catering: in-house
Kitchen Facilities: n/a
Tables & Chairs: provided
Linens, Silver, etc.: provided
Restrooms: wheelchair accessible
Dance Floor: yes
Bride's Dressing Area: yes
AV/Meeting Equipment: CBA

Parking: ample, large lots
Accommodations: no guest rooms
Outdoor Night Lighting: yes
Outdoor Cooking Facilities: none
Cleanup: provided
View: pool

RESTRICTIONS:

Alcohol: in-house
Smoking: outside only
Music: amplified OK indoors, outdoors with restrictions

Wheelchair Access: yes
Insurance: not required

Crowne Plaza Ventura Beach Hotel

Hotel

450 East Harbor Boulevard, Ventura
805/652-5108
www.cpventura.com
JWagner@cpventura.com

- Rehearsal Dinners
- Ceremonies
- Wedding Receptions
- Private Parties
- Corporate Events
- Meetings
- Film Shoots
- Accommodations

Living is easy in Ventura, California, a laid-back coastal town midway between the hectic Los Angeles scene and pricey Santa Barbara resorts. Ventura's beaches are picturesque even when the morning fog swirls above the breakers; on its many sunny days, beachcombers can spy the Channel Islands—a necklace of atolls—etched on the horizon.

As the only beachfront hotel in Ventura, this Crowne Plaza provides everything you need for a beach wedding ceremony right on the powdery sand. Their event team will arrange white folding chairs beside the aisle, and set a ceremonial arch in front of the surf so that you can exchange vows just steps from the shore—a microphone and speaker are included, too. Afterwards, your photographer captures shots of the two of you walking off into a glorious sunset, while friends and family begin the party on the Lanai Patio, a private terrace that faces the sea. As twilight descends, everyone moves indoors for your reception.

The versatile San Miguel Ballroom is conveniently located right on the first floor, and can accommodate a party of 200 or be sectioned off for more intimate gatherings. Alternatively, take the elevator 12 stories up to the most spectacular ballroom in the county. The circular Top of the Harbor Ballroom looks out on a captivating panorama through floor-to-ceiling glass: the Ventura hills in one direction and the sinuous shoreline in the other. At twilight, wisps of mist play along the crashing waves; as night descends, the city lights and the illuminated Ventura pier vie with a star-filled indigo sky in a contest of sparkle. The ballroom's contemporary styling, like the rest of the hotel, is both relaxed and confident and suits the soothing surroundings.

The venue's catering packages include many amenities that enhance your celebration at a very good value, such as custom floral centerpieces, table linens, chair covers, wine with dinner, custom wedding cake, and an oceanview bridal suite. If you want to pamper your guests even more, consider adding hand-rolled cigars, an espresso cart, or a decadent chocolate fountain—or save these treats for your rehearsal dinner or post-wedding brunch. The California-inspired cuisine showcases fresh, local ingredients complemented by an outstanding wine list. We were delighted with the meal we sampled, and bet your guests will be, too. (And yes, the chef is happy to customize your menu!) Other dining temptations include the new NOM Tequila Grill, which offers casually upscale authentic Mexican cuisine for any of your guests staying for the weekend.

Speaking of staying here: Guests will appreciate their oceanview accommodations, which feature the Crowne's "Seven Layers of Comfort" bed. As the newlyweds, you get to sleep in and then enjoy room service delivery of your complimentary breakfast. Eventually, though, you'll want to venture forth and explore the area's attractions. The hotel is walking distance to downtown, and you can also take an easy stroll along the promenade and watch the surfers ply the waves. Other diversions include kayaking around the Channel Islands (adventurous) or renting an on-site bicycle (fun), visiting the hotel's art gallery (cultured), or simply lounging by the oceanfront swimming pool (sublime!).

Every step of the way, the Crowne Plaza Ventura Beach will contribute to a scenic and stress-free wedding weekend.

CEREMONY CAPACITY: The hotel holds 400 seated guests, indoors or out.

EVENT/RECEPTION CAPACITY: The hotel accommodates 350 seated in the Ballroom, or 100 seated or standing on the Lanai.

MEETING CAPACITY: Meeting spaces seat 400 guests indoors.

PRICES: WHAT'S THIS GOING TO COST?

Rental Fee: $2,500/event and up
  • The rental fee varies depending on the day of the week, time of day, and space reserved.

Meals (when priced separately): $45–120/person

Service Charge or Gratuity: 22%

AVAILABILITY: Year-round, daily, hours vary depending on the event.

SERVICES/AMENITIES:

Catering: in-house
Kitchen Facilities: fully equipped
Tables & Chairs: provided
Linens, Silver, etc.: provided
Restrooms: wheelchair accessible
Dance Floor: provided
Bride's Dressing Area: yes
AV/Meeting Equipment: some provided

Parking: large lot, covered garage
Accommodations: 235 guest rooms
Outdoor Night Lighting: yes
Outdoor Cooking Facilities: BBQ
Cleanup: provided
View: cityscape and panorama of the ocean, coastline, and mountains; pool area
Other: beach ceremonies

RESTRICTIONS:

Alcohol: in-house
Smoking: outdoors only
Music: amplified OK

Wheelchair Access: yes
Insurance: required for vendors only

Serra Cross Park

Brakey Road, Ventura
www.serracrosspark.org
Please contact the venue through their website.

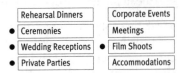

Rehearsal Dinners	Corporate Events
● Ceremonies	Meetings
● Wedding Receptions	● Film Shoots
● Private Parties	Accommodations

What California bride doesn't fantasize about getting married in a beautiful, natural setting with a sweeping ocean view? Yet for some couples, it seems that the right to gaze out to sea during their most important celebration is reserved for those with a lavish budget. Don't despair! You'll feel like you've landed on Easy Street when you learn about our latest discovery: Serra Cross Park, a hilltop aerie with a breathtaking coastal panorama, a modest pricetag, and a rich history.

It all started back in 1782. Shortly after Father Junipero Serra founded the San Buenaventura Mission, a large wooden cross was placed on a neighboring hillside as a guidepost for travelers. Over the years, the original cross and a series of replacements were lost to the elements, but locals never gave up. The current cross has stood atop its circular stone pedestal since 1941, and today the Serra Cross Conservancy and community volunteers are committed to maintaining and improving the park for everyone's enjoyment. Serra Cross Park also has a romantic legacy—throughout the years, countless couples have been married here, making this a particularly cherished piece of local heritage.

From a side street behind Ventura's handsome City Hall, the short but sinuous drive to the park begins. Once you and your guests reach the top, expect wide eyes and open mouths as the awe-inspiring view unfolds. In one direction, a curve of beach embraces the crashing surf; in another, the Channel Islands are etched against a billowing stretch of blue; behind you are the multilayered contours of chaparral-cloaked hills. Taking it all in from your exalted perch, you're filled with a sense of humility and wonder—even reverence. For many, these powerful feelings are symbolized by the simple wooden cross, poised atop its stone platform.

It's on this small stage that you'll exchange your vows, with a filigree of olive trees and the watery vista in the background. Champagne toasts follow, and if you want to continue the party, you'll be treated to a magnificent sunset. As evening falls, the moon, the stars, and the city lights set the horizon aglow. Reserve the park in the month of August, and you'll get the best seat in the house for a stunning fireworks display, courtesy of the Ventura County Fair! It's hard to imagine a more exhilarating finale than this exuberant, multicolored spectacle.

With its dramatic vantage, friendly pricing, and enduring tradition, Serra Cross Park just might be the answer to your wedding prayers.

CEREMONY & EVENT/RECEPTION CAPACITY: The site holds 300 seated or 450 standing outdoors.

MEETING CAPACITY: Meetings do not take place at this location.

PRICES: WHAT'S THIS GOING TO COST?

Rental Fee: $600/event and up
- The rental fee varies depending on the event duration.
- The pricing is for a 2-hour event. Additional hours can be added at $300/hour.

AVAILABILITY: Year-round, daily, 10am–8pm in set blocks of time.

SERVICES/AMENITIES:

Catering: BYO, recommendations available
Kitchen Facilities: n/a
Tables & Chairs: through caterer
Linens, Silver, etc.: through caterer
Restrooms: none on site, portable restroom rentals CBA
Dance Floor: CBA
Bride's & Groom's Dressing Area: no
AV/Meeting Equipment: n/a

Parking: large lot
Accommodations: no guest rooms
Outdoor Night Lighting: access only, additional through caterer
Outdoor Cooking Facilities: BBQ CBA
Cleanup: through caterer
View: garden, landscaped grounds; panorama of coastline, hills, canyon, and mountains
Other: site coordination

RESTRICTIONS:

Alcohol: through caterers
Smoking: not allowed
Music: amplified OK outdoors with restrictions
Other: security required for large events

Wheelchair Access: limited
Insurance: $1 million liability policy required for catered events

Westlake Yacht Club

Yacht Club

32129 Linden Canyon, Westlake Village
818/889-4820

www.westlakeyc.org
privaterental@westlakeyc.org

● Rehearsal Dinners	● Corporate Events	
● Ceremonies	● Meetings	
● Wedding Receptions	● Film Shoots	
● Private Parties	Accommodations	

Just a half hour north of Los Angeles sits Westlake Village, an idyllic, upscale neighborhood cradled by the Santa Monica Mountains and acres of greenspace. The centerpiece of this serene enclave is its scenic 125-acre lake, the site of the newly remodeled Westlake Yacht Club. Founded in 1969 as a private sporting hub, these days the casually elegant venue plays host to unforgettable waterfront celebrations for members and nonmembers alike.

The jaunty, Cape Cod-inspired clubhouse is perched on a landscaped knoll overlooking the lake promenade. Arriving guests might be greeted by a scampering white-tailed rabbit or a few geese, but you can provide a more conventional welcome by placing signage beneath the club's bright blue awning.

The recently enlarged interior features oak walls, a soaring beamed ceiling, and a neutral color scheme that easily adapts to your own stylings. Both formal and laid-back get-togethers work equally well here. There's a Bridal Suite available that's outfitted with mirrors, a vanity, and a couch and chairs. Most impressive, however, are the tall windows along the three sides that bathe the space in natural light and contribute to its expansive ambiance. French doors opposite the entry frame a view of the lake and open onto the roomy club deck.

Most wedding couples can't resist holding a ceremony out here: The picturesque lakefront panorama is edged with forested hills and almost perennial blue skies. A parade of sailboats and watercraft, along with a variety of shorebirds, provides a tranquil yet invigorating vista. The setting is made all the more dreamy by the sight of graceful swans gliding along the water. Time your vows for dusk, and a magnificent sunset will complete the picture-postcard backdrop.

After the first kiss, the bridal party poses for fun photos on the boardwalk. Meanwhile guests meander toward the other side of the deck for a twilight cocktail hour. Friends and family can also mingle around a large bar that commands one side of the clubhouse, a convivial spot for refreshments and conversation.

Receptions spread out inside the spacious clubhouse, with ample room for 150 guests and a dance floor. But if you can't resist dining al fresco, then have your social hour around the bar while the staff prepares the deck for dinner under the stars.

Speaking of dinner, your loved ones are in for a treat: The venue's preferred caterer is the neighboring Boccaccio's Restaurant, a local culinary favorite that's been delivering crowd-pleasing cuisine and exemplary service for over 50 years. You can also choose from a curated list of the venue's other tried-and-true catering pros, or even bring in your own. In other words, you've got options!

And while you're envisioning the possibilities, think beyond the wedding…the club's deck is also a great place for a romantic rehearsal dinner or anniversary party. In fact, we can imagine many couples getting married here, and then returning for their 10th, 25th or even 50th-year celebration to relive the wonderful memories!

CEREMONY CAPACITY: The facility seats 150 guests indoors and 250 outdoors.

EVENT/RECEPTION & MEETING CAPACITY: The facility accommodates up to 150 guests either indoors or outdoors, and up to 250 when the indoor and outdoor spaces are combined.

PRICES: WHAT'S THIS GOING TO COST?

Rental Fee: $1,500–4,000/event
- The rental fee varies depending on the day of the week and guest count.

Package Prices:
- A wide range of hosted and non-hosted alcohol packages is available, including corkage. Tax and gratuity are not included.

AVAILABILITY: Year-round, daily, 7am–10pm outdoors and until midnight indoors. Availability on Friday nights is limited.

SERVICES/AMENITIES:

Catering: preferred caterer, or BYO
Kitchen Facilities: fully equipped
Tables & Chairs: provided
Restrooms: wheelchair accessible
Dance Floor: yes
Bride's Dressing Area: yes
AV/Meeting Equipment: some provided

Parking: large complimentary lot
Accommodations: no guest rooms
Outdoor Night Lighting: yes
Outdoor Cooking Facilities: BBQ on site
Cleanup: provided with fee
View: panorama of lake and hills

RESTRICTIONS:

Alcohol: in-house
Smoking: outdoors only
Music: amplified OK with restrictions

Wheelchair Access: yes
Insurance: liability required

San Fernando Valley

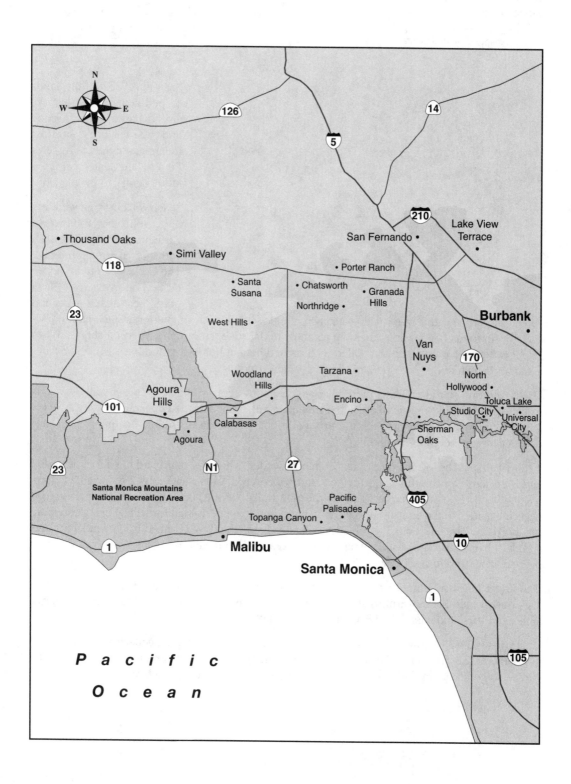

Calamigos Equestrian

480 Riverside Drive, Burbank
818/972-5940
www.calamigosequestrian.com
info@calamigosequestrian.com

Equestrian Center

- Rehearsal Dinners
- Ceremonies
- Wedding Receptions
- Private Parties
- Corporate Events
- Meetings
- Film Shoots
- Accommodations

Set on 74 beautifully land-scaped acres in the historic Griffith Park area near Disney and Warner Bros. studios, Calamigos at the Los Angeles Equestrian Center brings a little country to the big city.

When you host your wedding here, you have a choice of garden ceremony sites, each with its own reception venue. The Cottage, a quaint house nestled on five acres of lush grass, features a treelined ceremony garden with a water-wall—a truly romantic setting. With an interior designed for today's bride, it serves as her spacious dressing room or bridal suite. From here, it's just a short stroll to The Polo Room for the reception. Filled with natural light, it boasts a grand bar, chandeliers, and a wall of French doors that open to a large cocktail patio.

The Grand Prix Garden offers a more intimate ceremony spot, with its own water-wall as well as tropical palms, wild bougainvillea, and a mountain view. The attached cocktail breezeway leads guests into the vintage-inspired Grand Prix Ballroom, where three striking, floating-prism chandeliers capture everyone's attention.

A third option is the lovely Equestrian Ceremony Garden. This cozy courtyard has a rock waterfall and is enclosed by colorful bougainvillea- and ivy-covered walls, shaded by a retractable canvas "ceiling", and aglow with market lights overhead. A wall of floor-to-ceiling sliding glass panels connects the garden to the Equestrian Ballroom, providing a wonderful California Living-style indoor/outdoor flow. The ballroom, a sophisticated space highlighted by bronzed iron chandeliers and a built-in bar, also comes with a wraparound breezeway with cabanas where guests can mingle over cocktails and hors d'oeuvres.

Planning a rehearsal dinner or intimate wine tasting event? The Little Barn is the perfect place! This fresh venue has a warm, rustic-chic ambiance thanks to custom wood tables, wine-barrel tables and bars, and chandeliers hanging from the rafters.

Calamigos is a well-known, family-owned and operated company with a collective of operations in Southern California. They're dedicated to creating an amazing experience for you and your guests, so go ahead and relax while they expertly handle your entire celebration!

CEREMONY CAPACITY: The Cottage holds up to 350 seated guests, Hunt Field Lawn seats up to 1,000, and the Equestrian Terrace up to 250 seated guests.

EVENT/RECEPTION CAPACITY: The facility has a variety of areas that accommodate up to 550 seated or 1,200 standing indoors, and 250 to 5,000 seated outdoors.

MEETING CAPACITY: The Equestrian Ballroom (divisible into 4 sections) holds 120–800 guests. The Grand Prix Room (divisible into 3 sections) holds 800 guests. The Cottage can accommodate up to 500 guests, seated theater-style.

PRICES: WHAT'S THIS GOING TO COST?

Package Prices: $109-119/person
- Package prices vary depending on the package chosen.
- Wedding packages include: 1-hour wedding rehearsal; room rental fees; stationary hors d'oeuvres; plated meals; 3-hour hosted champagne, wine, and beer package; cake-cutting, and Chiavari chairs.

Service Charge or Gratuity: 21%

Additional Info: For other kinds of special events, please contact the venue for custom pricing.

AVAILABILITY: Year-round, daily, 7am–1am.

SERVICES/AMENITIES:

Catering: in-house, no BYO
Kitchen Facilities: n/a
Tables & Chairs: Chiavari chairs provided
Linens, Silver, etc.: provided
Restrooms: wheelchair accessible
Dance Floor: provided
Dressing Areas: yes
AV/Meeting Equipment: not provided
Other: coordination, horse-drawn carriage

Parking: complimentary, self-parking in ample lot
Accommodations: no guest rooms
Outdoor Night Lighting: yes
Outdoor Cooking Facilities: CBA
Cleanup: provided
View: mountains, landscaped grounds, waterfalls, trees

RESTRICTIONS:

Alcohol: in-house
Smoking: not allowed
Music: amplified OK indoors, outdoors with restrictions

Wheelchair Access: yes
Insurance: liability required for vendors

Pickwick Gardens

Garden

1001 West Riverside Drive, Burbank

818/845-5300 X171

www.pickwickgardensconferencecenter.com
info@pickwickgardens.com

- Rehearsal Dinners
- Ceremonies
- Wedding Receptions
- Private Parties
- Corporate Events
- Meetings
- Film Shoots

Accommodations

For anyone who only knows Pickwick Gardens from their sign on Riverside Drive, walking through the wrought-iron gate in the back will be a revelation, because this has to be one of the most idyllic outdoor wedding spots in the San Fernando Valley.

This area was once the bustling aquatic section of a public recreation complex, but today it's an expansive, two-and-half acre, woodland oasis that's at the very heart of any event at Pickwick Gardens. Paved walkways lit by old-fashioned street lamps meander through the lawns. The varied landscape of this bucolic retreat combines towering pines, graceful jacarandas, spiky palms, and majestic oak trees. Old stone fountains serve as multitiered planters, and colorful flowerbeds punctuated with rose bushes and seasonal blooms line the walkways. At the center of the garden is a huge tented pavilion with overhead fans. A raised stage at one end is anchored by a curving, river rock wall that would make a beautiful altar backdrop for your ceremony…or you can exchange vows on a lawn, shaded by trees. Afterwards, serve cocktails under the pavilion as the late afternoon and evening breezes come off the Santa Monica Mountains in nearby Griffith Park.

Bordering the gardens are several special event rooms, each with a private bridal room where you and your attendants can get ready. Most have full-on, outdoor views and awning-covered patios. The very popular Rose Garden Room features a unique rotunda and circular parquet dance floor set against tall windows, while the charming, newly renovated Magnolia Terrace Room is bright with a white, woodbeamed ceiling, white wainscoting, and golden candelabra chandeliers. Just outside the windows you can see the room's own private mini-garden.

At 8,500 square feet, the Royal Ballroom can comfortably accommodate 550 guests for a sit-down dinner and dancing. Decorated in rich tones of garnet and gold paisley, its regal ambiance is further established by windows draped with swags and valances, and huge chandeliers dripping with crystals.

Whether you desire a formal dinner, a buffet with ethnic specialties, or more casual fare for a bridal shower or rehearsal dinner, an executive chef is on site to help you customize your menu.

CEREMONY CAPACITY: The site seats 800 guests indoors and 500 outdoors.

EVENT/RECEPTION CAPACITY: The site accommodates 550 seated or 800 standing guests indoors and 700 seated or 1,000 standing outdoors.

MEETING CAPACITY: Meeting spaces hold 800 seated guests.

PRICES: WHAT'S THIS GOING TO COST?

Rental Fee: $1,500–8,500/event
   • The rental fee varies depending on the guest count.

Meals (when priced separately): $36–90/person

Service Charge or Gratuity: 21%

AVAILABILITY: Year-round, daily, 7am–midnight.

SERVICES/AMENITIES:

Catering: in-house
Kitchen Facilities: n/a
Tables & Chairs: provided
Linens, Silver, etc.: provided
Restrooms: wheelchair accessible
Dance Floor: provided in special event rooms
Bride's Dressing Area: yes
AV/Meeting Equipment: some provided

Parking: large lot
Accommodations: no guest rooms
Outdoor Night Lighting: no
Outdoor Cooking Facilities: no
Cleanup: provided
View: garden, mountains, landscaped grounds
Other: grounds are available until 10pm

RESTRICTIONS:

Alcohol: in-house
Smoking: in designated areas only
Music: amplified OK with restrictions

Wheelchair Access: yes
Insurance: liability required
Other: no sparklers, confetti, glitter, birdseed, or rice

Want to find more venues and services? Check out our informative website, www.HereComesTheGuide.com.

95

Saddle Peak Lodge

419 Cold Canyon Road, Calabasas
818/222-3888 x14

www.saddlepeaklodge.com
Events@saddlepeaklodge.com

Restaurant

● Rehearsal Dinners	● Corporate Events
● Ceremonies	● Meetings
● Wedding Receptions	● Film Shoots
● Private Parties	Accommodations

Saddle Peak Lodge is one of the more intriguing event sites we've ever seen. Steeped in California history, this turn-of-the-century hunting lodge began over 100 years ago as a small one-room cabin where cowboys, miners, fishermen and oil riggers imbibed the local "Hillbilly Punch" and swapped tall stories. Later the lodge carved a new identity, first as a way-stop and general store and then as a summer resort. In the '30s and '40s, Saddle Peak became the in-vogue hangout for movie stars such as Errol Flynn, Clark Gable and Charlie Chaplin. Today it prospers as a restaurant specializing in exotic game, and is renowned as an extraordinary place to host any special occasion.

As you enter the lodge, the antler door pulls and three-hoofed lamp in the foyer signal that you're in for a unique dining experience. The provocative aroma of roasting elk, venison, buffalo and mesquite lingers in the air—so tantalizing it gives you pangs of hunger in anticipation.

With its rough-hewn, tall-timbered interior, Saddle Peak is warm and elegantly rustic in its décor. An antique pistol collection gleams in a display case, while old western saddles and riding tack are slung casually over large beams. Populating the wood walls is an amusing mix of mounted trophy heads—deer, moose, pronghorn, eland—as well as authentic saloon paintings from the 1800s.

Saddle Peak's log-cabin ambiance lends itself beautifully to weddings: With hurricane lamps glowing on white tablecloths and a fire crackling in the Main Dining Room's massive rock hearth, the lodge is a wildly romantic setting.

Most weddings are celebrated on the lodge's picturesque and secluded Far Patio, just a short walk from the Main Dining Room. Couples exchange vows on a circular, two-tiered slate rock area that overlooks a spectacular view of Santa Monica Mountains' rolling hills and canyons. Note that as an added perk when you buy out the lodge, the third-floor Loft is transformed into a bridal suite where the bride can get ready for her walk down the aisle. French doors open to a stone walkway that leads past a cascading waterfall to the ceremony site.

Post ceremony, guests sip wine under the shade of pine and eucalyptus trees, or relax fireside in the dining room in handsome, handmade willow chairs. Small parties may want to savor hors d'oeuvres in the upstairs Den or Library—cozy pine-paneled rooms lined with windows and eclectically decorated with collectibles, antique books, and relics of the Old West. Dinner and dancing take place in the Main Dining Room, or al fresco on the Main Patio under a canopy of trees with the natural sounds of the nearby waterfall in the background.

The restaurant's extensive menu includes seafood, poultry, lamb and beef in addition to game, and they're perfectly happy to prepare vegetarian entrées as well. Not only is the food award winning (earning "best-of" honors from the *Los Angeles Times* and *Conde Nast Traveler,* as well as the highest ratings from ZAGAT, DiRoNA and Four Diamond AAA), but the lodge also boasts an award-winning domestic wine collection. Plus the staff are incredibly friendly and accommodating, making you feel like you're part of the Saddle Peak family.

From their distinctive cuisine and impeccable service to the incredible vistas, Saddle Peak Lodge earns rave reviews.

CEREMONY & EVENT/RECEPTION CAPACITY: The facility holds 150 seated or 175 standing guests indoors and 150 seated or 200 standing outdoors.

MEETING CAPACITY: Meeting spaces seat 90 guests indoors.

PRICES: WHAT'S THIS GOING TO COST?

Rental Fee: $350–2,500/event
- The rental fee varies depending on the day of the week, time of day, and space reserved.
- A food & beverage minimum applies. Please inquire about pricing for a full restaurant buyout.

Food & Beverage Minimum:
- The food & beverage minimum varies depending on the space(s) reserved, day of the week, and time of day.

Meals (when priced separately): $75–145/person
- Reception pricing starts at $75/person for lunch and $95/person for dinner.

Service Charge or Gratuity: 21%

AVAILABILITY: Year-round. Daytime and evening events are available.

SERVICES/AMENITIES:

Catering: in-house
Kitchen Facilities: n/a
Tables & Chairs: provided
Linens, Silver, etc.: provided
Restrooms: wheelchair accessible
Dance Floor: CBA
Bride's Dressing Area: yes
AV/Meeting Equipment: CBA

Parking: large lot, valet only
Accommodations: no guest rooms
Outdoor Night Lighting: provided
Outdoor Cooking Facilities: no
Cleanup: provided
View: canyon, fountain, garden, landscaped grounds; panorama of mountains, forest, and hills

RESTRICTIONS:

Alcohol: full in-house bar
Smoking: designated areas only
Music: amplified OK with restrictions

Wheelchair Access: yes
Insurance: not required

Knollwood Country Club

Country Club

12024 Balboa Boulevard, Granada Hills
818/360-2101 X1

www.countryclubreceptions.com
privateeventdirector@knollwoodgc.com

● Rehearsal Dinners	● Corporate Events
● Ceremonies	● Meetings
● Wedding Receptions	● Film Shoots
● Private Parties	Accommodations

When Granada Hills was founded in 1927, town members chose the name "Granada" after its sister city Granada, Spain. Although separated by thousands of miles, the two communities have similarities: Both are in the foothills of mountain ranges, and both have temperate climates—a quality making them prime candidates for outdoor weddings.

One of this city's best-known wedding locations is Knollwood Golf Course, an affordable public golf course and clubhouse with a friendly attitude. Ceremonies are held outside on a trim lawn backed by pine trees and the rolling fairways. You can say your vows under the open sky beneath a wooden arch that can be ornamented with flowers, tulle or even pine boughs. And, speaking of pines, there are so many around here you can almost imagine you're getting married in a quiet mountain meadow.

After the ceremony, guests walk over to the clubhouse, an unpretentious fieldstone-faced building with three event spaces. Here, they sip cocktails in the private bar area while you and your new spouse have your pictures taken under the trees. The reception follows in the spacious Granada Room. With its unadorned white walls, this room easily adapts to your event theme and color scheme. Light streams in through floor-to-ceiling windows during the day, while faux-candle fixtures hanging from the high ceiling provide illumination at night. The Granada Room also has its own large built-in dance floor with a crystal chandelier and draping overhead.

If your event is more intimate or you need additional space, there are two other smaller banquet rooms: the Gallery and the Fairway. Both are neutral-toned with floor-to-ceiling windows; the larger Gallery Room also has a fieldstone wall and its own bar.

Next to the relaxed golf-club setting, it's the ease of planning an event here that draws couples to Knollwood. The venue provides a wide selection of wedding packages, and the event staff is happy to customize one to meet your specific needs.

Knollwood offers another perk that's especially popular with the men in your group: You can integrate a little golf into your event! Grooms frequently schedule a morning tee time to loosen up with family and friends on the wedding day.

Granada Hills is known as the "Valley's Most Neighborly Town," and you might say that Knollwood is its most neighborly wedding site. You don't have to be a member—or even a golfer—to get married here, and they take such good care of you, you may end up feeling that you've definitely hit a wedding hole in one.

CEREMONY CAPACITY: The lawn holds 250 seated guests; the indoor areas hold 300 seated.

EVENT/RECEPTION & MEETING CAPACITY: The clubhouse accommodates 300 seated or 400 standing guests.

PRICES: WHAT'S THIS GOING TO COST?

Package Prices: $60/person and up
- Pricing varies based on food, beverage, and rental inclusions. Food & beverage minimums will apply. Menus and packages can be customized to fit your needs and budget. Pricing does not include additional site fees, mandatory service charge, gratuity, and current sales tax.

AVAILABILITY: Year-round, daily.

SERVICES/AMENITIES:

Catering: in-house
Kitchen Facilities: n/a
Tables & Chairs: provided
Linens, Silver, etc.: provided
Restrooms: wheelchair accessible
Dance Floor: provided
Bride's Dressing Area: yes
AV/Meeting Equipment: some provided, more CBA

Parking: large complimentary lot
Accommodations: no guest rooms
Outdoor Night Lighting: CBA
Outdoor Cooking Facilities: no
Cleanup: provided
View: fairways, mountains, garden
Other: event coordination

RESTRICTIONS:

Alcohol: in-house
Smoking: outside only
Music: amplified OK, subject to management approval

Wheelchair Access: yes
Insurance: not required

Middle Ranch

Country Club

11700 Little Tujunga Canyon Road, Lake View Terrace
818/897-4029
www.middleranch.com
information@middleranch.com

Rehearsal Dinners	●	Corporate Events
● Ceremonies	●	Meetings
● Wedding Receptions	●	Film Shoots
● Private Parties		Accommodations

Surrounded by the San Gabriel Mountains and bordered by the Angeles National Forest on three sides, Middle Ranch's civilized lawns and attractive buildings are a pleasant surprise in the midst of this rugged landscape.

The 650-acre property, known primarily as an exclusive equestrian country club, is also a spectacular place for a wedding. Ceremonies are held on the expansive front lawn with a backdrop of trees and mountains. The venue's main building, the award-winning Lodge, harmonizes nicely with its surroundings and has been recognized for its architectural style. Beneath its Spanish tile roof you'll find a large "living room" that's ideal for socializing over cocktails and hors d'oeuvres. The ambiance here is very relaxed, with a lofty, open-beamed ceiling, an abundance of warm natural wood, terracotta-tile floors and a handsome, two-sided fieldstone fireplace. Leather couches and chairs, along with antique Oriental carpets, complete the décor.

French doors open out to a lovely and spacious garden patio. Partly shaded by fragrant eucalyptus trees, it's an intimate spot for an al fresco reception. A few steps uphill, there's a pool with a large deck backed by an untamed hillside. You and your guests can sit by the water enjoying cocktails, or dine at tables set up on the patio.

The contrast between the wild, natural setting and the effortless elegance of the venue itself makes Middle Ranch a very special—and distinctly Californian—place to celebrate.

CEREMONY CAPACITY: The outdoor area can accommodate 350+ seated guests.

EVENT/RECEPTION CAPACITY: The Lodge accommodates 250 seated or standing; the outdoor areas hold 350+ seated or standing guests.

MEETING CAPACITY: The Lodge holds 150 seated, the conference room up to 30 seated.

PRICES: WHAT'S THIS GOING TO COST?

Rental Fee: *$5,000/event and up*
- The rental fee varies depending on the day of the week and guest count.
- The rental fee includes: tables, chairs, linens and choice of linen color, place settings, dance floor, outdoor heaters, facility personnel, and 6.5 hours of facility rental time.
- The ceremony package includes chairs, wedding arch, bridal suite, and rehearsal time for no additional charge.

Meals (when priced separately): *$55/person and up*
- Alcohol, tax, and service charge are additional. Please contact the venue for a customized catering quote.

AVAILABILITY: Year-round, daily, until midnight.

SERVICES/AMENITIES:

Catering: in-house
Kitchen Facilities: fully equipped
Tables & Chairs: provided
Linens, Silver, etc.: linens, silver, and china provided
Restrooms: wheelchair accessible
Dance Floor: 12' x 21', included
Bride's & Groom's Dressing Area: yes
AV/Meeting Equipment: BYO

Parking: large lot
Accommodations: no guest rooms
Outdoor Night Lighting: yes
Outdoor Cooking Facilities: n/a
Cleanup: provided
View: sprawling lawns, landscaped patio and pool area; Angeles Forest

RESTRICTIONS:

Alcohol: in-house, no BYO
Smoking: designated area only
Music: amplified OK

Wheelchair Access: yes
Insurance: not required for social functions; required for business functions

Porter Valley Country Club

Country Club

19216 Singing Hills Drive, Porter Ranch
818/360-1071 X2122

www.portervalley.com
contactus@portervalley.com

● Rehearsal Dinners	● Corporate Events
● Ceremonies	● Meetings
● Wedding Receptions	Film Shoots
● Private Parties	Accommodations

Nestled in the foothills of the Santa Susana Mountains, Porter Valley Country Club is a lushly land-scaped private club surrounded by green rolling hills. An abundance of trees, flowers, lawns, and water features makes you feel like you're in paradise.

Weddings take place at your choice of two locations: The first is the rose garden at the west end of the clubhouse. Here, most couples exchange vows under an arbor adorned with flowers, timing the ceremony to coincide with a gorgeous sunset. Seating on the lawn and Clubhouse Terrace affords guests an excellent view of the fairways as well as the nearby lake with its sparkling fountain. The second ceremony site is on the first tee overlooking the lake. This option gives the bride a more dramatic entrance, as all eyes are on her as she walks from the clubhouse down a path and up a long aisle to the elevated tee.

After the ceremony, the bride and groom are welcome to pose for photographs on the greens or alongside the club's impressive arched portico with the lake in the background.

At the same time, guests can gather for the reception in the newly remodeled Pinehurst Room, a setting that's both classic and elegant. Painted in pale cream and soft dove grey hues, it's illuminated by contemporary dome chandeliers suspended from the coffered ceiling. Floor-to-ceiling windows frame views of the verdant fairways, and glass doors open directly onto the adjoining terrace. A beautiful grey planked wood floor is perfect for dancing the night away, while lovely wall sconces provide a romantic atmosphere. More intimate events are held in the Homestead Room, which features two walls of windows overlooking the golf course and pool.

Porter Valley Country Club's warm and welcoming staff is known for their expertise, and they're especially adept at hosting large events. They've orchestrated hundreds of weddings, corporate functions, private parties and, of course, golf tournaments, so you can rest assured you'll be in skilled hands.

CEREMONY CAPACITY: The outdoor terrace holds up to 200 seated guests, and the 1st tee comfortably accommodates 350 seated.

EVENT/RECEPTION CAPACITY: Banquet rooms can host intimate events of 20 guests to large parties of up to 350.

MEETING CAPACITY: There are 3 areas that accommodate 20–300 seated guests.

PRICES: WHAT'S THIS GOING TO COST?

Package Prices: $30/person and up
  • Luncheon packages start at $30/person, dinner packages at $64/person. Wedding packages can include: hors d'oeuvres, wine and beverages, bar service, champagne toast, cake, 2-course meal, and coffee or tea.

Meals (when priced separately): $27/person and up
  • À la carte luncheons start at $27/person and dinners start at $29/person.

Service Charge or Gratuity: 20%

Additional Info: Room rental fees for business functions or meetings vary depending on the time frame. Food & beverage services are provided.

AVAILABILITY: Year-round, daily. Luncheons 11am–4pm, 11:30am–4:30pm or noon–5pm; dinners 6:30pm–11:30pm or 7pm–midnight. Additional hours are available for a nominal fee. Business functions or meetings can take place anytime; private golf tournaments can be held on Mondays.

SERVICES/AMENITIES:

Catering: in-house, no BYO
Kitchen Facilities: n/a
Tables & Chairs: Chiavari chairs provided for reception
Linens, Silver, etc.: provided
Restrooms: wheelchair accessible
Dance Floor: provided
Bride's Dressing Area: CBA
AV/Meeting Equipment: LCD screen, VCR, TVs, flip charts, microphone, podium

Parking: complimentary large lot, valet CBA, security provided
Accommodations: no guest rooms, hotels nearby
Outdoor Night Lighting: yes
Outdoor Cooking Facilities: BBQ
Cleanup: provided
View: fairways, lake with wildlife, Santa Susana Mountains
Other: photo booth, coordination, flowers, vendor referrals

RESTRICTIONS:

Alcohol: in-house
Smoking: outside only
Music: amplified OK with volume limits

Wheelchair Access: yes, elevator
Insurance: not required
Other: no rice, confetti, glitter, or birdseed; votive candles OK, decorations must be approved

---

This is important! Tell locations you're reading HERE COMES THE GUIDE and ask if our information is still current.

Braemar Country Club

4001 Reseda Boulevard, Tarzana
818/345-6520
www.braemarclub.com
braemarevents@clubcorp.com

Country Club

- Rehearsal Dinners | Corporate Events
- Ceremonies | ● Meetings
- Wedding Receptions | ● Film Shoots
- Private Parties | Accommodations

Nestled in the canyons and arroyos along the northern slopes of the Santa Monica Mountains, Braemar Country Club offers an oasis of peace away from the hustle and bustle of the city. The beautifully designed clubhouse is an elegant, modern setting for all types of events. One walks on cool, creamy marble through an open floor plan flooded with natural light. There are graceful columns along every hallway, lots of French doors, and a tiled deck that wraps around the entire structure. The pleasing architectural elements are perfectly complemented by the natural colors of the carpeting and comfortable furniture.

Outdoor ceremonies are held on the brick Terrace, where you have a breathtaking panoramic view of the golf course and San Fernando Valley. During evening celebrations, city lights glitter in the distance, and for more sparkle you may want to add candles and twinkle lights. Customized cocktail bars and buffet stations can be set up here, making it the perfect place for guests to mingle on a balmy night. The Terrace is also popular for al fresco rehearsal dinners.

Larger receptions can be hosted poolside, or in the clubhouse. You may choose the Ballroom, or a versatile suite of three rooms, each of which overlooks a spectacular view of the emerald hills of the golf course in the foreground, and the mountains in the background. Laid out in an L-shape with floor-to-ceiling windows, the rooms can be opened up to allow for a very large party or partitioned into five separate spaces that collectively serve as ceremony site, cocktail area, and banquet hall with dance floor.

Flexibility is the name of the game here, and no matter how you orchestrate your celebration, nature—and stunning views—are always within reach.

CEREMONY CAPACITY: The Club seats 75–250 guests indoors or outdoors.

EVENT/RECEPTION CAPACITY: The Main Dining Room holds 200 seated or 300 standing. The entire Clubhouse holds 300 seated or 500 standing.

MEETING CAPACITY: 3 areas accommodate 25–250 seated guests.

PRICES: WHAT'S THIS GOING TO COST?

Packages:

- Inclusive wedding packages range $65–125/person and include a 6-hour block, the ceremony and reception, room rental, linens, dance floor, and cake-cutting fee. Package upgrades are available that may include a DJ, photography, videography, décor & design. Pricing varies depending on the day of the week, time of year, and guest count. Overtime is $375/hour. Tax and service charge are additional.

Service Charge or Gratuity: 22%

Additional Info: The ceremony includes a rehearsal, white folding chairs, microphone, and speakers. All-day meeting packages that include breakfast, lunch, & afternoon snack start at $60/person. Tax and service charge are additional. For other types of special events like mitzvahs, anniversaries, birthdays, and golf tournaments, please contact the venue for pricing.

AVAILABILITY: Year-round, daily, in 5-hour blocks.

SERVICES/AMENITIES:

Catering: in-house; outside caterers may be permitted

Kitchen Facilities: n/a

Tables & Chairs: provided

Linens, Silver, etc.: provided

Restrooms: wheelchair accessible

Dance Floor: provided

Dressing Areas: yes

AV/Meeting Equipment: full range

Parking: complimentary self-parking, valet CBA extra fee

Accommodations: no guest rooms

Outdoor Night Lighting: yes (brick Terrace and poolside)

Outdoor Cooking Facilities: BBQs CBA

Cleanup: provided

View: golf course, valley, and distant mountains

Other: full event planning and coordination, additional fee

RESTRICTIONS:

Alcohol: in-house, no BYO

Smoking: outdoors only

Music: amplified OK

Wheelchair Access: yes

Insurance: required

Other: no rice or birdseed outdoors

Sheraton Universal

333 Universal Hollywood Drive, Universal City
818/509-2726 Catering Department
www.sheratonuniversal.com
sciccarelli@sheratonuniversal.com

- ● Rehearsal Dinners
- ● Ceremonies
- ● Wedding Receptions
- ● Private Parties
- ● Corporate Events
- ● Meetings
- ● Film Shoots
- ● Accommodations

A gleaming tower that rises up from the back lot of famed Universal Studios Hollywood, the Sheraton Universal has provided a swank place to stay for an impressive roster of actors and actresses. Celebrity patrons have earned it the nickname "The Hotel of the Stars," and a similar moniker could be applied to its most spectacular wedding spot—the Starview Room on the 21st floor. In this case, however, "The Wedding Site of the Stars" derives its sparkle not from Hollywood's brightest, but from the heavenly bodies glittering in the night sky.

A botanical haven, the Starview Room is a glassed-in aerie with wraparound views of the Hollywood Hills and the San Fernando Valley as far as the eye can see. At night, twinkling lights in the ceiling compete with the great L.A. Basin light show.

If a sky-high perch isn't what you had in mind, the first floor offers a series of handsome banquet facilities, starting with the Grand Ballroom. It features rich woodwork, beveled mirrors, sparkling chandeliers, and carpeting in subdued shades of taupe and ocean blue. The Ballroom's foyer—aptly named the Great Hall—is a terrific prefunction space, with six crystal chandeliers and floor to-ceiling windows framed in flowing, sheer white fabric. They overlook a garden ringed with magnolia trees. You can tie the knot in the Grand Ballroom, although some couples prefer to have their ceremony outside in the garden.

There are several other spacious banquet rooms, all with a similarly refined décor. And for a small wedding, you might want to reserve the Terrace Room, which opens onto a terracotta patio next to the pool.

The Sheraton Universal offers a full range of gourmet menus that can be customized for each client—and it's one of the few event sites in L.A. that can provide glatt kosher catering. As we discovered, there's a great deal of choice and flexibility here, and this is one place where the sky is, quite literally, the limit.

CEREMONY CAPACITY: The Starview Room seats 300 guests indoors and the Ballroom Garden seats 500 outdoors.

EVENT/RECEPTION CAPACITY: Indoor spaces accomodate 150–850 seated or 250–1,200 standing. Outdoors, the site holds up to 500 seated or 600 standing.

MEETING CAPACITY: 3 areas accommodate 150–1,200 seated guests.

PRICES: WHAT'S THIS GOING TO COST?

Ceremony Fee: $1,000/event

Meals (when priced separately): $48/person and up
  • Reception luncheons start at $48/person, dinners at $54/person. Each event is customized.

Service Charge or Gratuity: 22%

AVAILABILITY: Year-round, daily. Meetings take place 8am–5pm; weddings are held noon–4pm or 6:30pm–12:30am.

SERVICES/AMENITIES:

Catering: in-house, no BYO
Kitchen Facilities: n/a
Tables & Chairs: provided
Linens, Silver, etc.: provided
Restrooms: wheelchair accessible
Dance Floor: provided
Bride's & Groom's Dressing Areas: yes
AV/Meeting Equipment: full range, in-house audiovisual company

Parking: self-parking or valet, extra charge
Accommodations: 451 guest rooms
Outdoor Night Lighting: yes
Outdoor Cooking Facilities: no
Cleanup: provided
View: city view from Starview Room; San Fernando Valley skyline, Hollywood Hills skyline
Kosher: glatt kosher kitchen
Other: event coordination

RESTRICTIONS:

Alcohol: in-house, no BYO
Smoking: outdoors only
Music: amplified OK indoors

Wheelchair Access: yes
Insurance: required

Woodland Hills Country Club

Country Club

21150 Dumetz Road, Woodland Hills

818/347-1511

www.woodlandhillscc.org
rebecca@woodlandhillscc.org

- Rehearsal Dinners
- Ceremonies
- Wedding Receptions
- Private Parties
- Corporate Events
- Meetings
- Film Shoots
- Accommodations

A long curved road lined with towering eucalyptus trees takes you to Woodland Hills Country Club, a secluded hilltop wedding venue that offers some of the best panoramic views in the valley.

The clubhouse entrance is impressive, with its prominent porte-cochère covered in climbing vines. Beautiful landscaping is a priority here, and throughout the grounds you'll find a profusion of greenery and colorful flowers.

Ceremonies take place at a serene site next to the clubhouse. This manicured lawn is actually the first tee box and is bordered by tall hedges and seasonal blooms. You'll have your choice of three in-house ceremony arches to frame your vows, but what really makes this a star setting is the view: To the right, your guests are treated to a verdant vista of the rolling green fairways, while the ceremony backdrop is a layered panorama of cypress trees and the oak-covered foothills of the Santa Monica Mountains. Spectacular sunsets are an added perk! If you like, hold an al fresco cocktail reception on the neighboring terrace, or move inside to one of several attractive spaces.

Host the cocktail hour in The Main Lobby, which can be staged with chairs and couches for a lounge effect. Afterwards, the Terrace Ballroom welcomes your guests for the main reception. This spacious banquet area has a built-in dance floor and raised stage for your band, DJ, or cake table display. Decorated in muted, neutral tones, the room boasts a marble-topped bar where friends and family can mingle for conversation, as well as a small back patio overlooking the putting green and distant hills.

If you're planning a more intimate affair, the Sunset Room on the opposite side of the clubhouse is a little gem. A warmly inviting spot with a wall of natural stone and floor-to-ceiling windows, it's ideal for a rehearsal dinner. It can also be used as a cocktail and/or dance area for the larger, adjacent Oak Room, replete with oak-beamed ceiling and breathtaking views.

Myriad photo ops take advantage of the lovely surroundings: You can arrange to pose beside picturesque sites on the fairways, like a stone bridge, waterfall, or pond floated with lily pads.

There are many options available in planning your celebration here, and the staff takes pride in helping each couple determine their ideal wedding—and stay within their budget. After all, this is a location built on dreams!

CEREMONY CAPACITY: The site holds 180 seated guests indoors and 250 seated outdoors.

EVENT/RECEPTION CAPACITY: The facility accommodates 250 seated or 325 standing guests indoors.

MEETING CAPACITY: Meeting spaces hold up to 325 seated guests.

PRICES: WHAT'S THIS GOING TO COST?

Package Prices: $45–114/person
  • Wedding packages vary and may include the room rental, meals, liquor, and linens.

AVAILABILITY: Year-round, daily.

SERVICES/AMENITIES:

Catering: in-house
Kitchen Facilities: n/a
Tables & Chairs: provided
Linens, Silver, etc.: provided
Restrooms: wheelchair accessible
Dance Floor: provided
Bride's Dressing Area: yes
AV/Meeting Equipment: some provided, more CBA

Parking: large lot
Accommodations: no guest rooms
Outdoor Night Lighting: CBA
Outdoor Cooking Facilities: BBQ CBA
Cleanup: provided
View: garden patio; panorama of mountains, valley, cityscape, hills, and fairways; fountain, landscaped grounds
Other: coordination, in-house florals

RESTRICTIONS:

Alcohol: in-house
Smoking: outdoors only
Music: amplified OK

Wheelchair Access: yes
Insurance: not required

Los Angeles Area

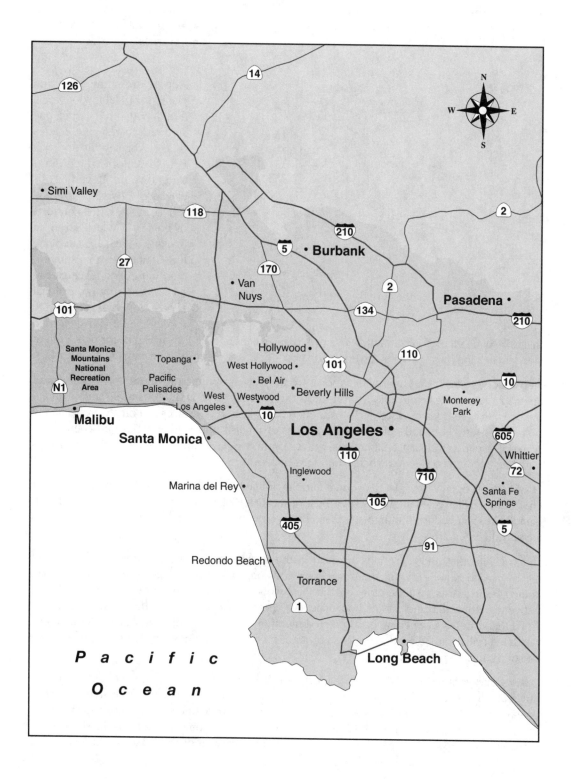

Lawry's The Prime Rib

Restaurant

100 N. La Cienega Boulevard, Beverly Hills
310/360-6281
www.lawrysonline.com/lawrys-primerib/beverly-hills
nnavarro@lawrysonline.com

● Rehearsal Dinners	● Corporate Events
● Ceremonies	● Meetings
● Wedding Receptions	● Film Shoots
● Private Parties	Accommodations

Not far from the glitz and glamour of Hollywood you'll find the other red carpet: one steeped in seven decades of Los Angeles history, rich British/American culinary tradition and Beverly Hills elegance. Lawry's The Prime Rib combines the comforts of home—if you lived in an expansive English estate along the Thames—with a sumptuous dining experience executed flawlessly by professional servers who treat you like royalty. And if you're worried that this venue's famed Restaurant Row location or opulent English Edwardian décor puts it out of your league, don't be—Lawry's The Prime Rib provides classic sophistication with Old World prices.

Step inside the foyer and the contemporary world fades away into a timeless, softly lit realm of amenable luxury. Tasteful period furniture in the cocktail room and adjacent bar area complements wainscoted, jewel-toned walls. Antique chandeliers and sconces illuminate eye-catching polished silver pieces and gold-framed paintings of English nobles, dignitaries and countryside scenes. Despite its formal accoutrements, the atmosphere is warm and relaxed—perfect for guests mingling over hors d'oeuvres while awaiting your arrival.

Double doors open to reveal a step-down into the brilliant, emerald-colored Oak Room, a popular choice for smaller celebrations. Here, a bust of the Duke of Wellington and a bas-relief of William Shakespeare adorn the fireplace mantel, while the mixed-shade parquet flooring highlights a colorful coat of arms.

Larger ceremonies and receptions are held in the spacious main dining room, where a pair of majestic wooden lions evocative of regal courtyards presides over your grand entrance. An uplit, domed ceiling casts a subtle glow on the dark wooden columns and beveled glass, lending a festive nighttime ambiance at any hour. The sweetheart table is housed in the "garden," a central space that features a sweeping hand-painted mural overhead. The adjacent Vintage Room, a private wine cellar, can be used as a bride's room or for rehearsal dinners and post-reception family traditions, including tea ceremonies.

Lawry's The Prime Rib's reputation for great food has stood the test of time. One of the oldest single-family-owned restaurants in Los Angeles, it has served its signature British-style dinner of slow-roasted Midwestern prime beef, mashed potatoes and Yorkshire pudding alongside flavorful gravy, horseradish, and its original seasoning salt since 1938. The almost-theatrical tableside service includes spinning salad prepared on a bed of ice and a carving of the roast from a 500-pound silver cart inspired by London's famous Simpsons-in-the-Strand restaurant. The meal finishes with a selection of traditional British and American desserts, including an ice cream sundae made with C.C. Brown's hot fudge sauce, a secret recipe bought by the Lawry family from Hollywood's most legendary but now-defunct ice cream parlor.

From their family to yours, Lawry's The Prime Rib serves up the most authentic Anglo-British (and award-winning) culinary experience this side of the pond, lending its cherished traditions to your celebration.

CEREMONY CAPACITY: The restaurant can accommodate 250 seated guests indoors.

EVENT/RECEPTION & MEETING CAPACITY: The restaurant holds 450 seated or standing guests indoors.

PRICES: WHAT'S THIS GOING TO COST?

Ceremony Fee: $500/event

Meals (when priced separately): $44–90/person

Service Charge or Gratuity: 3% service charge or admin fee and 18% gratutity

AVAILABILITY: Year-round, daily, 4pm–11pm, except Christmas. Luncheon hours are Monday–Saturday 7am–3pm, and Sunday 7am–2:30pm.

SERVICES/AMENITIES:

Catering: in-house
Kitchen Facilities: n/a
Tables & Chairs: provided
Linens, Silver, etc.: provided
Restrooms: wheelchair accessible
Dance Floor: CBA, extra charge
Bride's Dressing Area: yes
AV/Meeting Equipment: provided

Parking: large lot, valet required
Accommodations: no guest rooms
Outdoor Night Lighting: CBA
Outdoor Cooking Facilities: no
Cleanup: provided
View: no
Other: clergy on staff, event coordination

RESTRICTIONS:

Alcohol: in-house
Smoking: not allowed
Music: amplified OK indoors

Wheelchair Access: yes
Insurance: not required

Overwhelmed? Use the search criteria on www.HereComesTheGuide.com to narrow down your choices.

113

Montage Beverly Hills

Hotel & Resort

225 North Canon Drive, Beverly Hills

310/860-7890

www.montagehotels.com/beverlyhills/gatherings/weddings
mbhcatering@montage.com

- Rehearsal Dinners
- Ceremonies
- Wedding Receptions
- Private Parties
- Corporate Events
- Meetings
- Film Shoots
- Accommodations

Find the magic in every location…then create unforgettable experiences. That's the hallmark of the exclusive Montage Hotels and Resorts collection, and nowhere is it more evident than at Montage Beverly Hills.

Ideally situated in the heart of Southern California's Golden Triangle, this luxurious urban retreat is surrounded by city splendor and stunning views. Add to this the area's glamorous history and vibrant arts, entertainment, and culinary scene, and it's an ideal choice for a destination wedding, whether you and your guests live locally or are flying in from around the world.

Start with some premium pampering at their world-class Spa Montage, where treatments can be customized for the entire wedding party. Follow with a soak in their mineral pool, some yoga or Pilates, or simply relaxing in a cabana by the rooftop pool. There's also a fitness center with personal trainers, plus a full-service salon and barbershop to make you feel your best for the big day.

Fabulous al fresco ceremonies take place on the Montage Terrace, which features Mediterranean-inspired inlaid tile and architectural details that reflect the grand estates of the 1920s. This elevated expanse also overlooks the lush vistas of the Beverly Canon Gardens and plaza fountains. After saying "I do", host your cocktail hour and reception under the stars, or head inside to one of their opulent ballrooms. (But not before posing for that must-have album photo on their curved grand staircase!)

The wonderfully elegant, Spanish Colonial-style Marquesa Ballroom is fit for the gala of your dreams. Its regal proportions include a soaring ceiling hung with elaborate candelabra chandeliers, and a series of opera balconies that overlook the main floor as well as a large foyer where guests can mingle over cocktails. For a more intimate and flexible option, reserve the Contessa Ballroom. It also comes with a separate foyer, boasts elaborate wall coverings, and can be divided into three individual spaces, allowing you to create a stylish lounge, dining room, and dance area.

The light, bright, glass-enclosed conservatory is a total charmer, offering rooftop dining with panoramas of the city and the lights of the Hollywood Hills behind you. Accommodating up to 70, it's perfect for a smaller reception, rehearsal dinner, or bridal shower. There are several other private dining spaces for pre- and post-event gatherings, but one in particular is quite special: Kitchen Table. Here, you and your "inner circle" can savor a curated, foodie-heaven adventure.

Wherever you celebrate, you'll appreciate the attention to detail and personalized service that takes Montage Beverly Hills to a higher level. This includes the cuisine, which showcases locally sourced, fresh ingredients and is artfully prepared, presented, and accompanied by inspired wine pairings. With all-inclusive packages and customized events, the staff is there for you from initial planning to arranging sumptuous accommodations, excursions, and local transportation for your guests. Your experience at this exceptional hotel will be so much more than just VIP treatment... you'll come away with your own beautiful "montage"—a collection of moments, images, emotions, and memories that linger for a lifetime.

CEREMONY & EVENT/RECEPTION CAPACITY: The hotel can accommodate 300 seated or standing guests indoors or outdoors.

MEETING CAPACITY: Meeting spaces seat up 350.

PRICES: WHAT'S THIS GOING TO COST?

Rental Fee: $2,500/event and up
  • The rental fee varies depending on the space reserved.

Food & Beverage Minimum: $25,000/event and up

Meals (when priced separately): $125/person and up

Service Charge or Gratuity: 23%

AVAILABILITY: Year-round, daily.

SERVICES/AMENITIES:

Catering: in-house
Kitchen Facilities: n/a
Tables & Chairs: some provided
Linens, Silver, etc.: some provided
Restrooms: wheelchair accessible
Dance Floor: portable provided
Dressing Areas: CBA
AV/Meeting Equipment: CBA, extra fee

Parking: large on-site lot; garage and nearby lot, valet available
Accommodations: 201 guest rooms
Outdoor Night Lighting: CBA
Outdoor Cooking Facilities: no
Cleanup: provided
View: Hollywood Hills, Beverly Canon Gardens
Other: grand piano, in-house wedding cake, in-house florals, picnic area, event coordination (extra charge)

RESTRICTIONS:

Alcohol: in-house
Smoking: not allowed
Music: amplified OK indoors

Wheelchair Access: yes
Insurance: not required

City Club Los Angeles

555 Flower Street, 51st Floor, Los Angeles
213/620-9662
www.cityclubla.com
ernest.nicodemus@clubcorp.com

● Rehearsal Dinners	● Corporate Events
● Ceremonies	● Meetings
● Wedding Receptions	Film Shoots
● Private Parties	Accommodations

One look is worth a thousand words, so if you're planning a wedding or special event in Los Angeles you definitely want to check out this stylish, 51st-floor venue that delivers jaw-dropping views of the city and coastline.

After 25 years on Bunker Hill and a multimillion-dollar reinvention, the City Club Los Angeles has relocated to the Gold LEED Certified City National Plaza Tower situated in the heart of L.A.'s thriving central business district. Your guests will love exploring this area, which is home to the fabulous Staples Center and the L.A. Live entertainment complex with its glamorous theaters, restaurants, and hotels.

Step into the City Club itself and you enter a world of privacy and exclusivity—one where all of the spaces reflect a unique interpretation of Los Angeles' diverse districts. Elevators whisk guests up to the dramatic lobby, whose chic furnishings, art, and 3-D jewel-toned wall convey the spirit of the Jewelry District.

The spectacular Angeles Ballroom is truly a room with a view: 280 degrees of top-of-the-world vistas through its floor-to-ceiling windows. Chandeliers that look like delicate clusters of stars drop from the beautiful white, coffered ceiling. The room's brilliant mélange of posh and trendsetting touches, no doubt inspired by the nearby Fashion District, includes luxurious champagne and icy-blue colorations, as well as striking wall and carpet designs whose intersecting lines and angles suggest the freeway system that crisscrosses L.A.

If you use the entire ballroom, its vast dimensions make it ideal for ultra-grand functions with multiple bars, stages, dining areas and dance floors, but it also breaks into three more intimate chambers, each overlooking the tower's picturesque surround. The Santa Monica Room, Harbor Room, and Hollywood Ballroom can be used individually or in combination to create varying environments for your function. You might start by exchanging vows in the Harbor Room with its Pacific or sunset views, and then progress to the Hollywood Ballroom and Santa Monica Room for cocktails and/or dining enhanced by the gorgeous nighttime cityscape glittering all around you.

If you're planning a weekend extravaganza, there are additional entertainment areas you can add to the mix. The club's vibrant Anytime Lounge, outfitted with "spotlight" chandeliers, a bar top that resembles a grand piano, and a lush red wall framing a giant TV screen, brings to mind the Theater District. In the Private Dining Room, which looks out on the Hollywood sign, walls "blooming" with faux orchids evoke the Flower District. Even the hallway leading to the lounge showcases art from the private collections of L.A. residents—a nod to the city's Art Walk.

And don't forget, City Club Los Angeles has 25 years of experience in superior service and fine dining. You can sample your proposed menu's mouthwatering selections at a private tasting.

What more can you ask for? Oh, yes, a great time before, during, and after your party! Whether you and your guests are locals or out-of-towners, we guarantee you'll find plenty of terrific places to stay and loads of fun things to do in this club's one-of-a-kind setting.

CEREMONY CAPACITY: The Angeles Room holds 360 seated guests. The Hollywood Room accommodates up to 250 for a ceremony.

EVENT/RECEPTION CAPACITY: The Santa Monica, Hollywood, and Harbor Rooms combined hold up to 360 guests seated with a dance floor or 600 for a cocktail reception. They can also be broken out to accommodate a smaller more intimate wedding.

MEETING CAPACITY: 11 rooms can accommodate 5–600, including a screening room that seats 15.

PRICES: WHAT'S THIS GOING TO COST?

Package Prices: $150–195/person
- All-inclusive packages include: standard rentals, 2-hour hosted house brand bar and sparkling wine toast, tray-passed hors d'oeuvres for cocktail hour, plated or buffet dinner and gourmet wedding cake, choice of white or black dance floor, tax and service charge, and more!
- Package customization is available.

Food & Beverage Minimum:
- There is a food & beverage minimum for all events; tax and service charge are not included.

AVAILABILITY: Year-round, 7am–2am.

SERVICES/AMENITIES:
Catering: in-house, no BYO
Kitchen Facilities: n/a
Tables & Chairs: provided
Linens, Silver, etc.: provided
Restrooms: wheelchair accessible
Dance Floor: available
Bride's & Groom's Dressing Areas: yes
AV/Meeting Equipment: full range

Parking: in-house garage, valet on weekdays, self-park on weekends
Accommodations: no guest rooms, hotels nearby
Outdoor Night Lighting: n/a
Outdoor Cooking Facilities: n/a
Cleanup: provided
View: panorama of Los Angeles
Other: full event coordination, private screening room

RESTRICTIONS:
Alcohol: in-house
Smoking: not allowed
Music: amplified OK

Wheelchair Access: yes
Insurance: required for vendors only

The Ebell of Los Angeles

4400 Wilshire Boulevard, Los Angeles
323/931-1277
www.ebellofla.com
inquiry@ebelloflosangeles.com

Historic Landmark

Rehearsal Dinners	● Corporate Events
● Ceremonies	● Meetings
● Wedding Receptions	● Film Shoots
● Private Parties	Accommodations

Love at first sight. That's what so many couples feel when they walk through the imposing front doors of this historic, architectural masterpiece, located right in the heart of Los Angeles.

Built in 1927 as the final home of the Wilshire Ebell Women's club, the building is a stunning example of the Italian-Renaissance style. All of the elegantly designed rooms, which feature a wealth of elaborate period details, will truly take your breath away. You're welcome to rent the entire venue, but most weddings are held in either the North or South half of the property.

If you choose the North "wing", you'll most likely host your ceremony and reception in The Lounge, a magnificent space with a high, gilded ceiling; dramatic floor-to-ceiling windows; wrought-iron chandeliers; and a mezzanine and grand staircase. It also comes with a grand piano and outdoor patio! The adjoining Art Salon is ideal for your cocktail hour, as well as a treat for the eyes with its tall archways and fabulous art exhibits.

Opt to have your wedding in the South "wing" and you'll enjoy an indoor-outdoor celebration. Ceremonies and cocktail parties take place in the Garden, an expansive courtyard enclosed by picturesque arcades and lined with flowering shrubs and trees. There's a sunny, elevated terrace on one side, and a lower-level lawn with a graceful fountain and statue at its center. When it's time for dinner and dancing, everyone gathers in the adjacent Dining Room. This light-filled space is notable for its carved columns, stage, and bank of tall French doors that open to the courtyard.

The Ebell's warm, attentive Special Events team will work with your coordinator and provide hands-on assistance from beginning to end. And, as you'd expect, the cuisine here is as exceptional as the venue: It showcases local, sustainable, and seasonal ingredients, and the executive chef is happy to customize your menu. Talented mixologists are also available to create handcrafted cocktails.

Whether you're planning a traditional wedding or a more unconventional affair, it's sure to be unique at the Ebell of Los Angeles. As one bride described her magical experience, "From the beautiful venue to the impeccable 5-star service and absolutely delicious food, the Ebell team went above and beyond our dreams to deliver the most perfect, memorable day—one that we will always cherish."

CEREMONY CAPACITY: The Garden seats approximately 250 guests, while The Lounge can seat 250–300.

EVENT/RECEPTION & MEETING CAPACITY: Indoor spaces hold 100–250 seated with dance floor or 200–400 for a standing cocktail reception. The Garden accommodates up to 200 seated or 400 standing.

PRICES: WHAT'S THIS GOING TO COST?

Package Prices: *$200–250/person*

• Packages include menus, bar and beverages, personnel, setup fee, room rental fee, tasting, security, lighting, linens, place settings, in-house tables, banquet chairs, and parking.

Food & Beverage Minimum: *$15,000/event and up*

Service Charge or Gratuity: *21%*

AVAILABILITY: Year-round, anytime until midnight.

SERVICES/AMENITIES:

Catering: in-house only

Kitchen Facilities: fully equipped

Tables & Chairs: provided

Linens, Silver, etc.: provided

Restrooms: wheelchair accessible

Dance Floor: hardwood floors

Dressing Area: yes

AV/Meeting Equipment: some provided

Parking: ample

Accommodations: no guest rooms

Outdoor Night Lighting: limited

Outdoor Cooking Facilities: no

Cleanup: provided

View: no

RESTRICTIONS:

Alcohol: all in-house

Smoking: allowed in Garden

Music: amplified OK; time restrictions in Garden Courtyard

Wheelchair Access: yes

Insurance: certificate required

Other: no rice, birdseed, glitter, or confetti

Hilton Los Angeles Airport

Hotel

5711 West Century Boulevard, Los Angeles
310/410-6128
www.losangelesairport.hilton.com
gloria.urbina@hilton.com

● Rehearsal Dinners	● Corporate Events
● Ceremonies	● Meetings
● Wedding Receptions	● Film Shoots
● Private Parties	● Accommodations

Standing at the gateway to California's largest and arguably most diverse city, the Hilton Los Angeles Airport combines a soothing sophistication with artistic flourishes. Located just a quarter mile outside of LAX and within an easy drive to downtown, the beaches or Beverly Hills, it's the perfect destination for gathering your far-flung friends and relatives for an upscale wedding celebration.

This world-class hotel, while managed by the Hilton organization, is privately owned and much of the décor has been hand-picked by the owners. That attention to detail is evident as soon as you enter the lobby, which balances its three-story-high proportions with lots of human-scaled conversation areas. Gleaming marble floors and granite consoles are softened with richly patterned rugs and velvet armchairs, all layered in a neutral palette of cream, gold and honey. At the far end of the lobby an impressive center staircase, all glass and gold railings, makes a stellar backdrop for wedding photos.

Just beyond the staircase are two of the hotel's premier banquet rooms, which are often used together for a seamless affair. If you have your ceremony on site, the palatial-sized International Ballroom is an excellent choice—it has ample room for a traditional or ethnic ceremony, even when divided in two. Done in warm shades of wine and gray with silver accents, it's a modern and quite elegant space. The high, coffered ceiling enhances the dramatic impact of the enormous, rectangular, icicle-crystal chandeliers.

After you've said "I do," invite everyone across the foyer to the similarly themed (same colors) but smaller Pacific Ballroom, a somewhat more intimate setting for mingling over cocktails. Then it's back to the International Ballroom for a sumptuous dinner and dancing, taking advantage of the venue's full 11,000 square feet of splendor. (Although the hotel has an extensive catering menu, you're free to bring in ethnic or specialty foods from an outside caterer.)

For something quite different, head up to the La Jolla Room and Foyer on the mezzanine level. Along the way, take a moment to enjoy the aerial views of the lobby below, then check out the display of dazzling accoutrements that you pass en route to the event spaces: a framed golden brocade, Asian tapestries and gorgeous geodes of amethyst and crystal—all arranged using the principles of Feng Shui. Cocktails and hors d'oeuvres are served in the warmly inviting La Jolla Foyer, followed by dinner in the La Jolla Room, which is adorned with unusual chandeliers that look like flower petals descending from the ceiling, and mirrored French doors along the back wall.

There are several other options for weddings of 50 or fewer, and the staff will happily work with you to design an event that suits your style and budget. Your out-of-town guests can relax at the hotel (there's a pool, sports bar, fitness center and restaurants) or they can visit many of the local attractions. And when their stay at the Hilton is over, it's just a quick trip back to the airport.

CEREMONY CAPACITY: The site seats 450 guests, indoors or outdoors.

EVENT/RECEPTION CAPACITY: The facility can accommodate 800 seated or standing guests indoors, and up to 600 standing outdoors.

MEETING CAPACITY: Meeting spaces hold up to 1,000 seated guests.

PRICES: WHAT'S THIS GOING TO COST?

Rental Fee: $800–5,000/event
  • The rental fee varies depending on the space reserved.

Meals (when priced separately): $40–100/person

AVAILABILITY: Year-round, daily.

SERVICES/AMENITIES:

Catering: in-house, or BYO
Kitchen Facilities: limited
Tables & Chairs: provided
Linens, Silver, etc.: provided
Restrooms: wheelchair accessible
Dance Floor: portable provided
Bride's Dressing Area: CBA
AV/Meeting Equipment: available

Parking: large lot, self park or valet available
Accommodations: 1,234 guest rooms
Outdoor Night Lighting: yes
Outdoor Cooking Facilities: no
Cleanup: provided
View: no

RESTRICTIONS:

Alcohol: in-house, or BYO with glass rental
Smoking: outdoors only
Music: amplified OK indoors

Wheelchair Access: yes
Insurance: liability required

Want to know WHAT TO ASK a potential location or vendor? Check out our Questions to Ask starting on page 21.

Los Angeles Zoo

Zoological Gardens

5333 Zoo Drive, Los Angeles
323/644-4781
www.lazoo.org
events@lazoo.org

● Rehearsal Dinners		● Corporate Events	
Ceremonies		● Meetings	
● Wedding Receptions		Film Shoots	
● Private Parties		Accommodations	

Remember how much fun you had the first time you went to the zoo? Whether it was years ago or last month, the memories always linger. So it makes perfect sense that you'd want to share that feeling of joy with friends and family on one of the biggest days of your life—especially if you're welcomed as an "after hours VIP".

The Los Angeles Zoo—with over 130 acres, 1,400 animals, and 800 species of plants—is a top SoCal landmark attracting droves of locals and tourists alike. Naturally, the photogenic residents get plenty of press, but the zoo's dedicated staff believes your wedding deserves a lot of attention too. And with three unique venues in a fabulous setting, they'll turn your special evening at the zoo into a wildly successful affair.

Now, can we talk about the elephant in the room? Or, more precisely, that majestic, Asian pachyderm grazing just beyond the covered deck of the CAMBODIA PAVILION, where you and your guests are sipping cocktails. It's an unforgettable sight, especially against a backdrop of lush greenery and the Hollywood Hills. You can also have an intimate al fresco dinner here, or opt for the two-story STILT HOUSE.

The place itself evokes a rustic lodge on an exotic adventure, while the ceramic lily pads out front hint that you're in for a few aquatic treats. A wall of glass on the first floor features a fish tank filled with South American piranhas and a view of the rock-strewn stream outside. Up on the second floor, the space boasts a high, beamed ceiling and open-air sides—the better for watching the antics of river otters playing in the water. You can easily host both cocktails and dinner here for up to 50...or move to TREETOPS TERRACE, the zoo's largest reception venue.

Big, bright and airy, this pavilion feels like a geodesic dome with its soaring, asymmetrical ceiling, skylights, and windows. It's great for all the party animals on your list because the staff can bring in a stage, dance floor, and bar, as well as help with lighting, décor, setup, and choosing a menu from their in-house caterer, *Taste of the Wild*.

Book any of the three venues or feel free to combine them, because they're just steps away from each other (golf carts and trams are available as well). Plus, you'll want to seriously consider their not-to-be-missed add-ons, like animal encounters where zoo handlers bring exotic birds, reptiles, and other animals for you to experience up close and personal.

CEREMONY CAPACITY: This is a reception-only venue.

EVENT/RECEPTION CAPACITY: The facility can accommodate 500 seated or standing guests in an open-air setting.

PRICES: WHAT'S THIS GOING TO COST?

Package Prices: $50–100/person
  • Prices vary depending on the guest count and package chosen.

Meals (when priced separately): $55/person and up
  • Meal pricing varies depending on the meal style and food stations chosen.

AVAILABILITY: February–October, daily.

SERVICES/AMENITIES:

Catering: in-house
Kitchen Facilities: fully equipped
Tables & Chairs: provided
Linens, Silver, etc.: yes, extra fee may apply
Restrooms: wheelchair accessible
Dance Floor: CBA
Dressing Area: no
AV/Meeting Equipment: some provided, extra fee may apply

Parking: large lot
Accommodations: no guest rooms
Outdoor Night Lighting: yes
Outdoor Cooking Facilities: no
Cleanup: provided
View: forest/wooded areas, landscaped grounds
Other: picnic area

RESTRICTIONS:

Alcohol: in-house
Smoking: not allowed
Music: amplified OK outdoors

Wheelchair Access: yes
Insurance: liability required

Luxe Sunset Boulevard Hotel

Hotel

11461 Sunset Boulevard, Los Angeles

310/691-7510

www.luxehotels.com
judith@luxehotels.com

- Rehearsal Dinners
- Ceremonies
- Wedding Receptions
- Private Parties
- Corporate Events
- Meetings
- Film Shoots
- Accommodations

It can be difficult to find tranquility in Los Angeles, but the Luxe Sunset Boulevard Hotel will make you feel like you've left the city behind.

Located on seven hilltop acres, this urban oasis is truly secluded, and yet it's just minutes from the Getty Center and a short drive to other favorite L.A. sites like Santa Monica Beach, UCLA, and the Skirball Cultural Center.

If you have a romantic ceremony in mind, get married under the stars on the Luxe Sunset Terrace. As you walk down the central aisle of this intimate courtyard, lacy elm trees provide a natural canopy and frame views of the "fountain wall" backdrop. Afterwards, serve cocktails in the adjoining Sunset Foyer, an urban garden lined with olive trees and twinkle lights. This unique space features built-in stone lounges for mingling and conversation, accompanied by the soothing background sounds of a lovely water fountain.

Host your reception in the understated Luxe Sunset Ballroom. Sophisticated, yet inviting, it's designed like a home away from home with a neutral color palette of taupe, cream, and bronze that complements any décor. Dramatic lighting, provided by modern chandeliers, recessed lights, and wall sconces, along with state-of-the-art audiovisual equipment, lets you create just the right mood for your event.

Your out-of-town guests will find the hotel an extremely comfortable and enjoyable place to stay. Guest rooms and suites are quite spacious, and most have windows or doors that open to the outside. They're decorated in warm, natural shades with custom-made furniture, and include amenities like free WiFi and high-speed internet, designer bedding, and a Keurig Single Cup Brewer with complimentary coffee and tea. In-room dining is available 24 hours a day, and Luxe also offers daily turndown service and plush cotton robes.

The Luxe Sunset Boulevard Hotel is a stylish L.A. getaway for a memorable celebration. They only host one major event at a time, so your wedding will be their top priority and you'll get the full attention of the Catering Department. Of course, this boutique property is also perfect for a weekend "vacation". After you unpack your bags, the serene setting and accommodating staff will quickly help you relax and unwind. Take a stroll through the gardens...have a great meal in the redesigned Sirrocco restaurant...work out in the newly designed gym and then cool off in the mountainview pool. Once you're here, you really can get away from it all!

CEREMONY & EVENT/RECEPTION CAPACITY: The Luxe Sunset Ballroom holds 300 seated guests and the Luxe Terrace seats 250.

MEETING CAPACITY: Six rooms accommodate 10–300 seated guests.

PRICES: WHAT'S THIS GOING TO COST?

Packages: $130–225/person
- Three wedding packages range $130–195/person for lunch and $145–225/person for dinner and include: hosted premium bar, wine served with 3-course meal, use of the Garden Terrace for ceremony rehearsal and ceremony, parquet dance floor and stage, ballroom lighting, bridal dressing room, wedding-night accommodations with breakfast for two, and preferred room rates for wedding guests.

Service Charge or Gratuity: 13%

AVAILABILITY: Year-round, daily, 6am–midnight.

SERVICES/AMENITIES:

Catering: in-house, no BYO
Kitchen Facilities: n/a
Tables & Chairs: provided
Linens, Silver, etc.: provided
Restrooms: wheelchair accessible
Dance Floor: CBA, $600 fee
Dressing Areas: yes
AV/Meeting Equipment: full range, extra fee
Other: off-site catering also provided

Parking: valet only, $14/car
Accommodations: 162 guest rooms
Outdoor Night Lighting: yes
Outdoor Cooking Facilities: n/a
Cleanup: provided
View: garden, hills, landscaped grounds, pool area
Kosher: kosher catering provided (kosher kitchen on site)

RESTRICTIONS:

Alcohol: in-house, or wine corkage $27/bottle
Smoking: outside only
Music: amplified OK indoors, until 10pm outdoors

Wheelchair Access: yes
Insurance: liability required
Other: no rice or birdseed

The MacArthur

607 South Park View Street, Los Angeles

213/381-6300

themacarthur.com
tawni@themacarthur.com

● Rehearsal Dinners	● Corporate Events
● Ceremonies	● Meetings
● Wedding Receptions	● Film Shoots
● Private Parties	Accommodations

One of the most iconic architectural treasures in Los Angeles, The MacArthur consistently dazzles. Originally conceived in 1925 as a lavish Elks Lodge, it later became the Park Plaza Hotel and now, after meticulous retrofitting and restoration, this historical-cultural monument is an absolutely stunning special event and filming venue (with boutique hotel accommodations to come in the near future!)

Its Neo-Gothic design and Art Deco flourishes display a glamour and exuberance unique to the MacArthur, while providing a wealth of fabulous photo backdrops like the enormous angels perched around the building's exterior or the brass-and-glass arched entry, topped by a set of brass elk antlers (the last ones remaining from the venue's stint as an Elks Lodge). Inside, the Lobby will take your breath away. Its cathedral ceiling, elaborate murals, and Renaissance chandelier evoke the grandeur of a centuries-old Italian villa.

The Garden, a private courtyard surrounded by potted trees and blooms, is an ideal place to exchange your vows. Follow with cocktails al fresco here, then segue through a set of glass doors into the adjacent Plaza Ballroom for the reception. Awash with natural light, this stately space features an Art Deco bar, Corinthian columns crowned in copper leaf, and glittering chandeliers. Best of all, after dinner and dancing you can head back to the Garden for a nightcap under the stars.

For a totally different perspective, host your ceremony and cocktail reception on the Rooftop Deck, where you can revel in the panoramic views of downtown Los Angeles. Planning a smaller gathering? Reserve The Lounge, with its large bar, warm woods, high ceiling, and columned entry—it's just right for an intimate dinner celebration.

If you're thinking full-tilt gala, the MacArthur has two stellar choices. The Grand Ballroom, located off the Lobby mezzanine, is a true showstopper. Patterned after a palace in Florence, it's rich with columns, arches, floor-to-ceiling windows, and wrought-iron chandeliers dripping with crystals and suspended from an intricate wood-beamed ceiling. Looking for something even more extravagant? Then prepare to be wowed by Elks Hall. The venue's largest space pays homage to early Art Deco motifs, like elaborate sunburst sconces, a soaring, hand-decorated ceiling, and a spectacular chandelier that resembles a giant version of a Tiffany diamond pendant. With room for 350 seated or 700 standing, you don't have to leave anyone off your guest list.

All these settings are, of course, quite beautiful, but they're even more fabulous when paired with exceptional cuisine. Fortunately, The MacArthur has partnered with *The Copper Key*—a highly-acclaimed culinary team with worldwide experience from a Michelin-starred restaurant in Amsterdam to cooking in Rome, Barcelona, London, San Francisco, and Los Angeles—to create and customize the best of contemporary global fare to suit your needs and your event.

CEREMONY CAPACITY: The venue seats 350 indoors and 300 outdoors.

EVENT/RECEPTION CAPACITY: The facility can accommodate 350 seated or 750 standing guests indoors and 270 seated or 600 standing guests outdoors.

MEETING CAPACITY: Please contact the venue for meeting capacities.

PRICES: WHAT'S THIS GOING TO COST?

- Pricing was being updated at press time and was not available. Please contact the venue for details.

AVAILABILITY: Year-round.

SERVICES/AMENITIES:

Catering: in-house
Kitchen Facilities: fully equipped, kosher kitchen CBA
Tables & Chairs: provided, or BYO
Linens, Silver, etc.: provided, or BYO
Restrooms: wheelchair accessible
Dance Floor: provided for most spaces
Dressing Areas: yes
AV/Meeting Equipment: CBA, extra fee

Parking: valet parking or nearby public lots
Accommodations: no guest rooms
Outdoor Night Lighting: yes
Outdoor Cooking Facilities: no
Cleanup: provided, extra fee
View: cityscape, garden patio/courtyard, park
Kosher: provided

RESTRICTIONS:

Alcohol: in-house
Smoking: outdoors only
Music: amplified OK with restrictions

Wheelchair Access: yes
Insurance: liability required for all events

MountainGate Country Club

Country Club

12445 Mountaingate Drive, Los Angeles
310/476-6215 x104
www.countryclubreceptions.com
privateeventdirector@mtngatecc.com

● Rehearsal Dinners	● Corporate Events
● Ceremonies	● Meetings
● Wedding Receptions	● Film Shoots
● Private Parties	Accommodations

Situated at the gateway to the Santa Monica Mountains, at the top of a scenic road that heightens expectations as you ascend, MountainGate does not disappoint. The country club—the jewel of a private residential development—is a breath of fresh air for couples seeking panoramic views and a location that's convenient to both Beverly Hills and the Valley.

Fronted by a cobblestone entryway and a white porte-cochère, the clubhouse is embraced by a grove of tall conifers and native trees. The building evokes Frank Lloyd Wright's aesthetic, with its geometric configuration and interior use of natural wood and glass. In contrast to the angular architectural lines, the entry walkway is surrounded by cascading waterfalls, ferns, bougainvillea, azaleas, birds of paradise, and other tropical plants. It's a calming and inviting environment, and guests take time to appreciate it before stepping into the building's foyer. Needless to say, this gorgeous setting is a favorite for individual or group photos.

The best spot for outdoor ceremonies is a picturesque, perfectly manicured tee box at the edge of an expansive golf course that constitutes MountainGate's backyard. The ceremony site, which overlooks a serene panorama of rolling hills, is shaded by a cluster of birch trees.

Indoor receptions are held in the club's newly renovated event space, which is beautifully designed in neutral tones with a vaulted ceiling and grand chandeliers. Wraparound floor-to-ceiling windows and a light-filled atrium frame wonderful views of the Garden Terrace's walls of greenery, the verdant golf course, and the Santa Monica Mountains.

MountainGate is known for its outdoor garden areas. The North Lawn, set with cocktails tables and hors d'oeuvres prepared by the on-site chef, is ideal for mingling. Afterwards, guests head to the romantic Garden Terrace to continue the festivities. Lined with trees, flowers, and a wall of greenery, it's a lovely canvas on which to create whatever style reception you envision. At night, bistro string lights and a sky full of glittering stars provide a glowing finishing touch.

In addition to the smart architecture and attractive landscaping, what really makes a MountainGate wedding so memorable is the hospitable attitude that prevails among staffers: Everyone goes out of his or her way to make your event feel special. And, thanks to the club's policy of hosting only one wedding at a time, you'll receive the personal attention that every couple deserves.

CEREMONY CAPACITY: The site can accommodate up to 250 seated guests indoors or 350 outdoors.

EVENT/RECEPTION CAPACITY: The indoor event space holds 250 seated guests with a dance floor, 300 without, or 350 standing guests. The Garden Terrace (which can be tented) accommodates 400 seated with a dance floor, and 420 without.

MEETING CAPACITY: The Main Dining Room can accommodate 150 guests classroom-style or 250 theater-style.

PRICES: WHAT'S THIS GOING TO COST?

Package Prices: $95/person and up
 • Pricing varies based on food, beverage, and rental inclusions. Food & beverage minimums will apply. Menus and packages can be customized to fit your needs and budget. Pricing does not include additional site fees, mandatory service charge, gratuity, and current sales tax.

AVAILABILITY: Year-round, Tuesday–Sunday.

SERVICES/AMENITIES:

Catering: in-house or BYO
Kitchen Facilities: fully equipped
Tables & Chairs: provided
Linens, Silver, etc.: provided
Restrooms: wheelchair accessible
Dance Floor: provided
Bride's & Groom's Dressing Areas: yes
AV/Meeting Equipment: microphone, screen, other CBA

Parking: on site; valet included with some packages
Accommodations: no guest rooms
Outdoor Night Lighting: yes
Outdoor Cooking Facilities: n/a
Cleanup: provided
View: hills and golf fairways
Other: wedding cake

RESTRICTIONS:

Alcohol: in-house
Smoking: outside only
Music: amplified OK until 11pm outdoors or 2am indoors

Wheelchair Access: yes
Insurance: not required
Other: no rice, glitter, confetti, or birdseed

The wedding vendors on our website are the best in the business. How do we know? Read page 425.

Natural History Museum of L.A. County

Museum

900 Exposition Boulevard, Los Angeles
213/763-3221
www.nhmlac.org/host-event
specialevents@nhm.org

● Rehearsal Dinners	● Corporate Events
● Ceremonies	● Meetings
● Wedding Receptions	Film Shoots
● Private Parties	Accommodations

The Natural History Museum is one of Los Angeles' most beloved institutions and for good reason. The halls of this spectacular 1913 jewel boast an impressive and eclectic blend of styles—Spanish Renaissance trimmings, Romanesque arched windows, a Beaux Arts-inspired layout, and intricate Art Nouveaux fixtures. When you combine all of this stunning architecture with the museum's revered collections and breathtaking exhibits… well, this place really must be seen to be believed.

At the heart of the museum is the dramatic Haaga Family Rotunda, which is part of the original building. It rises to a dizzying height (the dome alone is 58 feet tall!), and is accented by Corinthian pillars, walls of Italian marble, and a mosaic tile floor. With the stained-glass dome's luminous skylight overhead and the renowned bronze statue of the "Three Muses" in the center providing a graceful focal point, this is truly an unforgettable spot for a ceremony or reception.

In the striking Grand Foyer, guests are welcomed by two distinguished museum ambassadors: the towering skeletons of a Triceratops and Tyrannosaurus Rex, locked in fierce battle. Let these dueling dinos preside over the festivities as you dine beneath soaring 40-foot marble columns and dance on the elegant travertine floor.

Celebrations can also be held in the African and North American Mammal Halls, where the walls are lined with the museum's cherished dioramas. Just imagine sipping champagne next to a family of giraffes or nibbling casually on a canapé as a grey wolf lurks beside you in the tall prairie grass.

The Otis Booth Pavilion is one of the museum's modern additions, and it's a showstopper. Three stories high and completely enclosed in glass, it overlooks the Nature Gardens and waterfall, and features the colossal skeleton of a 63-foot fin whale suspended from the ceiling.

Outdoor spaces abound here, too, and each one is uniquely lovely. Consider the Pond and Pollinator Garden, with its deck overlooking the water and bountiful plants chosen to attract hummingbirds, honeybees, and butterflies. Or opt for the Glazer Family Edible Garden, where an ever-changing array of seasonal vegetables, fruits, and herbs surround a secluded courtyard.

Through an arrangement with Exposition Park Management, ceremonies may also be held in the sunken Rose Garden, which is within view of the LA's iconic Memorial Coliseum. Afterwards, your guests simply stroll through the museum's east gate to your reception inside.

Having so many amazing choices may make it hard to pick a favorite venue, but no matter where you decide to host the main event you get an extra bonus: the option to add access to the galleries of your choice, so that you and your guests can appreciate the extraordinary collections that makes this world-class museum so special.

CEREMONY CAPACITY: The Rotunda seats 150 guests; the Grand Foyer seats 200; and the African and North American Mammal Halls each seat 250.

EVENT/RECEPTION CAPACITY: The Rotunda holds 140 seated or 250 standing guests; the Grand Foyer 160 seated or 400 standing; the African Mammal Hall 225 seated and 350 standing; and the North American Mammal Hall 250 seated and 400 standing. The most popular wedding package includes the use of the Grand Foyer and both Mammal Halls for a ceremony and reception of up to 250 guests. These spaces can also host corporate and nonprofit events for up to 610 seated and 800–1,150 standing, or up to 2,000 standing with a full buyout. The Nature Gardens seat up to 500, and the Otis Booth Pavilion ground floor accommodates 150 seated or 200 standing. Please contact the museum for additional capacity information and package suggestions for non-wedding related events.

MEETING CAPACITY: Meetings do not take place at this venue.

PRICES: WHAT'S THIS GOING TO COST?

Rental Fee: $7,500/event and up
- The rental fee varies depending on the space reserved and guest count.
- The fee covers an 8-hour time block including: setup and cleanup (4pm load-in to midnight), a 1-year VIP membership to the Natural History Museum Family of Museums, operations, security, housekeeping, event management staffing, and all taxes and service charges. A portion of the fee is tax deductible.

AVAILABILITY: Year-round, daily, 6pm–11pm. Extended hours are available.

SERVICES/AMENITIES:

Catering: Select from list or BYO, extra fee
Kitchen Facilities: none
Tables & Chairs: some provided
Linens, Silver, etc.: through caterer
Restrooms: wheelchair accessible
Dance Floor: some areas available for dancing
Bride's & Groom's Dressing Area: no
AV/Meeting Equipment: no
Other: museum tours; "Dinosaur Encounters" CBA, extra fee

Parking: complimentary for event guests in adjacent lots
Accommodations: no guestrooms
Outdoor Night Lighting: access only
Outdoor Cooking Facilities: through caterer
Cleanup: caterer or renter
View: nature gardens, pond, nearby rose garden

RESTRICTIONS:

Alcohol: licensed server and permit required
Smoking: not allowed
Music: amplified OK

Wheelchair Access: yes
Insurance: required for renters and vendors

Taglyan Cultural Complex

Cultural Center

1201 Vine Street, Los Angeles

323/978-0005

www.taglyancomplex.com
info@taglyancomplex.com

Rehearsal Dinners	● Corporate Events
● Ceremonies	● Meetings
● Wedding Receptions	● Film Shoots
● Private Parties	Accommodations

Opened to great fanfare in 2008, the Taglyan Arts and Cultural Complex offers a dazzling combination of Old World opulence and cutting-edge audiovisual technology. Located mere blocks from the world-famous intersection of Hollywood and Vine, this venue may be new to the event scene, but with its stately limestone façade it looks like it's been part of the neighborhood for years.

As soon as you enter the massive iron gates on a quiet side street, you feel like you've been transported to a European villa. Italian cypress, magnolia and olive trees, along with vintage-look streetlamps, dot the property. Immediately on your right is the formal brick courtyard, anchored by the kind of huge two-tiered fountain you might find in an Italian piazza, complete with figural fish and turtles spouting water. A formal garden containing white roses encircles the fountain, creating a very romantic spot for wedding ceremonies. As an added enhancement, the historic French Normandy-style building across the street acts as a charming backdrop. Taglyan's upper patio, which could serve as an alternate ceremony site or for cocktails, overlooks the courtyard and has its own cherub fountain with two small gardens and marble pillars.

Inside the building itself, it's obvious that no expense has been spared in workmanship or materials. The dramatic Grand Foyer is a feast for the eyes, highlighted by an Italian marble floor inlaid with various patterns—the first one symbolizing eternity, which seems rather fitting for couples who've just exchanged vows. This palatial-sized space has natural light streaming in through tall windows draped in rich green velvet, as well as filtering in through stained-glass inserts in the high, coffered ceiling. Along one wall you can set up couches in front of faux fireplaces, creating a cozy area for small-group mingling. Another option for intimate conversation is the outdoor flagstone patio, which makes a perfect bar and lounge setting.

But the *pièce de résistance* is the Main Ballroom—truly a "grand" ballroom. Set off by green marble pillars and elaborate, cascading crystal chandeliers, its 7,050-square-foot, circular stained-glass ceiling is flat-out, jaw-droppingly beautiful. And as if its artistry alone wasn't mesmerizing enough, it can even be programmed to shift colors with an elaborate lighting system. In fact, the entire facility incorporates state-of-the-art audiovisual equipment, including scrims and projectors with screens that descend around the room so you can screen personal movies, then take it up a notch by bathing the stage and dance floor in sound and light.

Taglyan Complex has devoted just as much attention to every detail behind the scenes as well, from its two top-of-the-line kitchens to the ample underground parking and luxurious bridal room (and large groom's room). Their exclusive in-house caterer, *Divine Food & Catering,* will customize your menu whether you desire a multicultural meal, Continental fare, or something in between. When you're here, all you have to do is relax, revel in your surroundings and get ready for a very memorable event.

CEREMONY CAPACITY: The foyer and garden each seat up to 250 guests.

EVENT/RECEPTION CAPACITY: The site accommodates 500 seated or 800 standing guests in the ballroom. Standing cocktail receptions of up to 400 may be held in the foyer or the garden.

MEETING CAPACITY: Meeting rooms seat 100–500 guests.

PRICES: WHAT'S THIS GOING TO COST?

Package Prices: $135/person and up
- Package prices vary depending on the day of the week, time of day, time of year, and guest count.
- Packages include: the venue rental (use of the ballroom, foyer, and garden until 2am), special event lighting and sound equipment, custom projection, furniture, linens, dance floor, staging, cake cutting/serving, and in-house catering.

Service Charge or Gratuity: 18%

Additional Info: There's a 150-guest minimum for a Friday or Sunday event, and a 250-guest minimum for a Saturday event.

AVAILABILITY: Year-round, daily.

SERVICES/AMENITIES:

Catering: in-house or BYO
Kitchen Facilities: fully equipped
Tables & Chairs: provided
Linens, Silver, etc.: provided
Restrooms: wheelchair accessible
Dance Floor: portable provided
Bride's Dressing Area: yes
AV/Meeting Equipment: provided

Parking: large lot, valet required
Accommodations: no guest rooms
Outdoor Night Lighting: yes
Outdoor Cooking Facilities: BBQ CBA
Cleanup: provided
View: garden courtyard, landscaped grounds

RESTRICTIONS:

Alcohol: in-house
Smoking: in designated areas only
Music: amplified OK with restrictions

Wheelchair Access: yes
Insurance: not required

Calamigos Ranch Malibu

Ranch and Conference Center

327 South Latigo Canyon, Malibu
818/889-6280
www.calamigos.com
weddings@calamigos.com

- Rehearsal Dinners
- Ceremonies
- Wedding Receptions
- Private Parties
- Corporate Events
- Meetings
- Film Shoots
- Accommodations

Although Calamigos bills itself as a country ranch set amongst 130 acres of rolling hills, verdant meadows, lakes, ancient oaks, and its own vineyard, most of its event facilities are far from rustic.

There are four different ceremony options, each with its own reception site. The Redwood Room—the most historic venue on the property—opens to a peaceful and private area to exchange vows.

Shaded by trees, guests are seated on either side of a stone aisle, facing a redwood arbor adorned with flowers where the couple says "I do". Afterwards, everyone moves into the Redwood Room itself, a delightful, sun-filled space thanks to light streaming in through "walls" of French doors. One of the room's remarkable features is its romantic "waterfall", a curtain of water that descends like a light rain just outside the glass doors.

The Oak Room is popular for intimate ceremonies. Rows of chairs are arranged in front of a wood arbor with a rock waterfall directly behind it, framed by a backdrop of eucalyptus, pine, and oak trees. Couples who get married here usually have their reception in the nearby dining room. Like the Redwood Room, it has French doors that maximize light and views of the outdoors. Crisp white table linens contrast nicely with the warm pine ceiling beams and doorframes, while ferns and ficus trees provide indoor greenery. Buffets are often served on the adjoining deck, which is partially shaded by oak branches.

A third option is the Pavilion at North Point, a secluded little meadow ringed by trees and natural landscaping. Couples tie the knot on an earthen terrace beneath a majestic spreading oak, or next to a clear pond at the base of a river rock waterfall. Dining and dancing takes place under an elegant white tent draped with sheer fabric and enhanced by twinkle lights.

Lastly, the Birchwood Room is a charming venue for more intimate gatherings. Ceremonies unfold on a grassy field bordered by roses, plum trees, and a large cascading waterfall. The reception can be held on the private, multilevel deck just steps away. Surrounded by nature—including a couple of streams—this spot is beautiful and calm. Sunset and evening events are lovely here, especially when the thousands of twinkle lights lacing the trees add their sparkle.

And if you've come to the ranch for one of their legendary western-style celebrations (yes, they host Barn Mitzvahs!), check out The Barn. It's the real thing: The floor is covered with sawdust, and bales of hay are scattered about.

The newest addition to the ranch is the Calamigos Guest Ranch and Beach Club. This inviting getaway lets you extend your stay with 70 luxurious guest rooms that bring you closer to nature: Each one has its own terrace—some offer a mountain view and others are designed as enclosed interior spaces that are open to the sky and stars.

Calamigos Ranch has some truly unique event facilities, and the staff are topnotch professionals when it comes to helping you plan your wedding. They'll work with you to create a celebration that reflects your personal vision, and coordinate everything down to the last detail.

CEREMONY CAPACITY: Indoors, the ranch holds up to 500 seated guests; outdoors up to 800 seated.

EVENT/RECEPTION CAPACITY: Indoor areas accommodate 50–500 seated or 150–600 standing guests. The smallest site has a 50-guest minimum.

MEETING CAPACITY: The site accommodates 35–600 guests for conferences.

PRICES: WHAT'S THIS GOING TO COST?

Package Prices: $156–160/person
  • Packages can be customized.

Additional Info: For day conferences, all-inclusive packages range $75–105/person.

AVAILABILITY: Year-round, daily, including holidays. Conferences and other corporate events are by arrangement.

SERVICES/AMENITIES:

Catering: in-house, or BYO (buyout may be required)
Kitchen Facilities: fully equipped
Tables & Chairs: provided
Linens, Silver, etc.: provided
Restrooms: wheelchair accessible
Dance Floor: provided
Bride's Dressing Area: yes; groom's CBA
AV/Meeting Equipment: CBA, extra fee

Parking: large lot, free valet
Accommodations: 70 guest rooms
Outdoor Night Lighting: yes
Outdoor Cooking Facilities: BBQs
Cleanup: provided
View: Santa Monica Mountains
Other: ceremony coordination & rehearsal

RESTRICTIONS:

Alcohol: in-house, BWC corkage $10/bottle
Smoking: outdoors only
Music: amplified OK until 11pm

Wheelchair Access: yes
Insurance: liability required
Other: no rice, confetti, or sparklers

Duke's Malibu

21150 Pacific Coast Highway, Malibu

310/317-6204

www.dukesmalibu.com
events@dukesmalibu.com

Oceanfront Restaurant

- Rehearsal Dinners
- Ceremonies
- Wedding Receptions
- Private Parties
- Corporate Events
- Meetings
- Film Shoots

Accommodations

Duke's picturesque waterfront location, fun-loving yet professional staff, and fresh coastal cuisine will tempt you to celebrate on Malibu's famous shores. This legendary restaurant and its private event spaces enhance all types of occasions—wedding ceremonies, receptions, rehearsal dinners, day-after brunches, and more—with gracious hospitality and breathtaking views. It's the perfect atmosphere for old friends and new families to come together and create timeless memories.

Guests are greeted with a welcoming aloha spirit, and ushered through a private entrance into the versatile Ocean Room, which is well suited for a casual celebration or can easily be transformed into a beautiful setting for a stylish affair. This lovely space has two walls of beachfront windows that are just steps away from the splashing surf, and doors that open onto a balcony right over the sand where guests may enjoy a quiet moment away from the festivities—perhaps to take in one of Malibu's extraordinary sunsets!

For more intimate celebrations, like bridal and baby showers, Duke's Malibu can accommodate your group in its "Board" Room (as in surfboard). This private, oceanview room is located in the restaurant and seats 33. As with the Ocean Room, mahogany Chiavari chairs, a choice of linens in various colors, and votive candles are provided for your event.

Just as satisfying as the view are Duke's coastal-inspired special event menus. They feature fresh fish and premium steaks, offered in plated, buffet, and family-style options.

When your heart's set on treating friends and family to an oceanfront experience, Duke's Malibu is the ideal spot for a truly unique and memorable gathering.

CEREMONY CAPACITY: The Ocean Room holds 150 seated guests.

EVENT/RECEPTION CAPACITY: The Ocean Room accommodates 250 seated or 400 standing guests.

MEETING CAPACITY: The Ocean Room holds 250 seated, the Board Room 33 seated.

PRICES: WHAT'S THIS GOING TO COST?

Rental Fee: *$100–1,500/event*
- The rental fee varies depending on the day of the week, the time of year, and space reserved.
- The Ocean Room ranges $500–1,500 and the Boardroom ranges $100–250. There is also a food & beverage minimum that varies depending on the day of the week and time of year.
- There is a ceremony fee of $1,000.

Meals (when priced separately): *$35–79/person*

Service Charge or Gratuity: *20%*

AVAILABILITY: Year-round, daily, until midnight. Closed Christmas Day.

SERVICES/AMENITIES:

Catering: in-house, no BYO
Kitchen Facilities: n/a
Tables & Chairs: provided
Linens, Silver, etc.: provided
Restrooms: wheelchair accessible
Dance Floor: yes
Dressing Area: CBA, extra charge
AV/Meeting Equipment: CBA or BYO

Parking: valet
Accommodations: no guest rooms
Outdoor Night Lighting: access lighting only
Outdoor Cooking Facilities: n/a
Cleanup: provided
View: 180-degree panorama of the Pacific Ocean, beach, and sunsets

RESTRICTIONS:

Alcohol: in-house; wine and champagne corkage $20/750 ml bottle, $35/1.5 l bottle
Smoking: designated area outdoors
Music: amplified OK indoors

Wheelchair Access: yes
Insurance: not required

Want to find more venues and services? Check out our informative website, www.HereComesTheGuide.com.

137

Malibu West Beach Club

Private Beach Club

30756 West Pacific Coast Highway, Malibu
310/457-0195
www.malibuwestbeachclub.com
events@malibuwestbc.com

- Rehearsal Dinners
- Ceremonies
- Wedding Receptions
- Private Parties
- Corporate Events
- Meetings
- Film Shoots

Accommodations

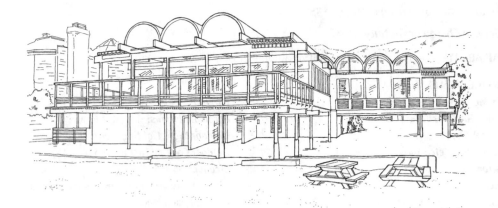

Standing at the edge of the ocean between Zuma State Beach and Broad Beach, the Malibu West Beach Club presides over one of the most desirable slices of real estate in Southern California. Glorious white sand stretches 100 yards from the clubhouse to the breaking surf, and from the second-floor deck there's a 180-degree panorama of the vast Pacific and miles of Malibu coastline. When it's clear, you can even see all the way to Catalina Island and the Channel Islands! As an added treat, whales migrate close to shore in the winter months, and almost daily you'll spot dolphins leaping out of the water as they swim by.

The unassuming two-story structure is partially screened from the street behind some evergreen trees, so you'd never know it was there if you didn't go looking for it. The large event space, which occupies the top floor and opens onto the spacious deck, is a bright and airy room with a high vaulted and arched ceiling. It features a driftwood-colored floor, walls and ceiling enhanced by white Georgette chiffon draping and twinkle lights, and three crystal chandeliers. Of course, the sunsets, visible through the club's glass façade, complement any décor.

Ceremonies are held on the 50-foot oceanfront deck, with that glorious ocean panorama as a backdrop. Afterwards, the newlyweds may go down to the beach for photos, while their guests remain on the deck to mingle during the cocktail hour and savor the view.

Dinner and dancing take place inside, where everyone can enjoy the fabulous ocean vista through the wall of floor-to-ceiling glass that separates the banquet room from the deck. And throughout the evening, diners are free to step outside to sip wine or champagne, linger over the setting sun or watch the stars come out in the night sky.

In addition to the banquet room, Malibu West also offers a versatile oceanfront bride's room. The club has outfitted it with thoughtful amenities to help the ladies primp and prepare—mirrors, vanities, dress racks and a blow dry bar. After the ceremony, it's also a quiet retreat where the bride and groom can have a moment alone together before the festivities begin, and during the reception this space can be set up as a kiddies' play area.

As if all this weren't enough, Malibu West also boasts a knowledgeable, friendly staff that will assist you in selecting vendors that match your vision and your budget. Given its beachfront location, genial ambiance and affordable prices, the Malibu West Beach Club is understandably in demand.

CEREMONY CAPACITY: The oceanview deck holds 150 seated guests.

EVENT/RECEPTION & MEETING CAPACITY: The site holds up to 150 seated or 200 standing guests. 150 or fewer is suggested for weddings, if you want everyone in the same room at the same time.

PRICES: WHAT'S THIS GOING TO COST?

Rental Fee: $6,250–7,850/event
- The rental fee varies depending on the guest count.
- Pricing is for weekend and holiday events. Midweek rates start at $3,650. An on-site representative is required for the duration of the event and is included in the rental fee.

AVAILABILITY: Year-round, daily, 8am–1am, in 12-hour blocks.

SERVICES/AMENITIES:

Catering: select from extensive list
Kitchen Facilities: most appliances
Tables & Chairs: provided, 170 chairs and tables for up to 200 guests
Linens, Silver, etc.: caterer or BYO
Restrooms: two are wheelchair accessible
Dance Floor: included
Bride's Dressing Area: yes
AV/Meeting Equipment: BYO

Parking: limited on-street, 7 spaces at the club; valet or shuttle required for larger parties
Accommodations: no guest rooms
Outdoor Night Lighting: access lighting only
Outdoor Cooking Facilities: BYO
Cleanup: through caterer
View: panoramic ocean views and sunsets, Catalina & Channel Islands, Malibu coastline
Kosher: kosher kitchen CBA

RESTRICTIONS:

Alcohol: BYO; server bonded and licensed
Smoking: outdoors only
Music: amplified OK indoors until 10pm, volume reduced until midnight

Wheelchair Access: ramp
Insurance: liability required
Other: no rice, staples, nails, birdseed, or confetti

The Sunset Restaurant

6800 Westward Beach Road, Malibu
310/589-2027
www.thesunsetrestaurant.com
eventsdirector@thesunsetrestaurant.com

Waterfront Restaurant

● Rehearsal Dinners	● Corporate Events
● Ceremonies	● Meetings
● Wedding Receptions	● Film Shoots
● Private Parties	Accommodations

You can have it all—a romantic setting, delectable cuisine, and gracious service—at the Sunset Restaurant, tucked against the Malibu bluffs just steps from Zuma Beach. Housed in an updated version of a classic beach bungalow, the two-story restaurant breathes with space and light, thanks to the expanse of windows along the ocean-facing front wall. One of the many benefits of staging your wedding at the Sunset is the ease of having everything in one package. This venue is particularly event-friendly, with distinct areas that coordinate with each phase of a wedding celebration.

First, say your marriage vows right on the beach. For a fee that includes the city permit, the Sunset arranges a platform walkway, runner and a wood stage area with the blue Pacific as a vibrant backdrop. Other elements further enhance this idyllic place: Sailboats drift across the horizon, dolphins play in the surf, the sound of the waves is in soothing harmony with the music of your accompanist. As you walk down the aisle, a light breeze lifts your veil, which floats around you like sea foam. Your guests are entranced, and the fun is only beginning. (This writer knows from personal experience: She had her wedding here, and the guests are still raving!)

After the ceremony, your photographer captures dramatic photos of the bridal party during one of Malibu's enchanting sunsets. Meanwhile, your friends and family gather on the outdoor patio that adjoins the Event Room. Here they enjoy the cocktail hour and scrumptious hors d'oeuvres, while mingling around cocktail tables or relaxing on couches. You can add your own festive touches with colored paper lanterns, string lights or vibrant throw pillows.

When it's time for the reception, everyone moves into the Event Room. Its understated, yet classy, décor adapts easily to your own vision...but this room has a couple of tasteful features that add to your celebration: The white fabric lining the ceiling lends a wavy softness to the space, and a row of view-filled windows curves shoreward, like a long ripple in the nearby surf. At some point during your festivities, you might drift outside with your sweetheart to stroll on the sugary sand and soak up a bit of moonlight.

The Sunset Restaurant, which is open for weekend brunch as well as lunch and dinner every day, has a large number of regular (and often celebrity!) clientele and attracts more loyal fans every day. After paying a visit to this divine seaside locale, you're bound to become a regular, too.

CEREMONY CAPACITY: The beach site holds up to 150 seated guests.

EVENT/RECEPTION & MEETING CAPACITY: Indoors, the restaurant accommodates 120 seated with a dance floor or 150 without, or 200 standing guests. Outdoors the parking lot may be tented for 200 seated or 300 standing. The entire restaurant can be rented for larger parties.

PRICES: WHAT'S THIS GOING TO COST?

Rental Fee: $2,500–10,000/event
   • The rental fee varies depending on the space reserved, guest count, and event duration.

Meals (when priced separately): $40/person and up

Service Charge or Gratuity: 20% administrative fee

AVAILABILITY: Year-round.

SERVICES/AMENITIES:

Catering: in-house; outside kosher and ethnic caterers allowed with approval, call for details

Kitchen Facilities: fully equipped

Tables & Chairs: provided

Linens, Silver, etc.: provided

Restrooms: wheelchair accessible

Dance Floor: yes

Bride's Dressing Area: CBA

AV/Meeting Equipment: BYO

Parking: valet

Accommodations: no guest rooms

Outdoor Night Lighting: string lights on patio

Outdoor Cooking Facilities: CBA

Cleanup: provided

View: Malibu coastline, ocean

Other: beach ceremony

RESTRICTIONS:

Alcohol: in-house for hard liquor only; corkage fee for wine and champagne

Smoking: outside only

Music: amplified OK

Wheelchair Access: yes

Insurance: not required

California Yacht Club

Yacht Club

4469 Admiralty Way, Marina del Rey
310/448-4771 Catering Department

www.calyachtclub.com
cycater@calyachtclub.net

● Rehearsal Dinners	● Corporate Events
● Ceremonies	● Meetings
● Wedding Receptions	● Film Shoots
● Private Parties	Accommodations

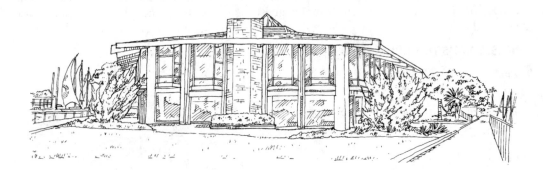

Cleverly designed in an octagonal shape with glass walls that showcase a panoramic view of the harbor, California Yacht Club is a great place for a waterside wedding.

Lovers of the sea will naturally want to get married as close to the ocean as possible, and the Club has a stellar site: a triangular expanse of lawn that advances from the building and tapers to a rounded point in front of the water's edge. Couples exchange vows here, while their guests enjoy the sea air, glittering Pacific and the colorful parade of boats that pass by just beyond the point. After the ceremony, everyone strolls over to the adjacent patio for cocktails and hors d'oeuvres.

The Club itself is a handsome, two-story building that devotes its entire first floor to celebrations. Receptions take place in the spacious Fireside Room, named for its beautiful brick fireplace, which is set into a wall of windows. Before the dining begins, all eyes are on the bride, who makes a dramatic entrance as she gracefully descends a sweeping atrium staircase. The room's décor is completely up to your imagination—anything from a Polynesian buffet with tiki torches, hula dancers and a fire show (held outdoors), to a formal Black & White Ball. No matter where you sit you're virtually on the water, and the 180-degree view allows every guest to watch the sun set over the ocean.

The accommodating staff will customize every detail, so you'll get the event that you want along with a lovely location. This is a place where water surrounds you, flocks of sea birds fly overhead, and ships slip quietly in and out of the harbor. Set sail together at California Yacht Club.

CEREMONY CAPACITY: The Club's outdoor lawn holds 250 seated; the indoor Fireside Room seats 160.

EVENT/RECEPTION CAPACITY: The Fireside Room can accommodate 160 seated with a dance floor or 250 for a cocktail reception.

MEETING CAPACITY: The Gallery Room holds up to 36 seated; the Fireside Room up to 180 seated.

PRICES: WHAT'S THIS GOING TO COST?

Meals (when priced separately): *$27/person and up*
- Luncheons range $27–45/person, dinners or buffets $45–85/person.

Service Charge or Gratuity: *22%*

AVAILABILITY: Year-round, daily, 8am–1am. The Club is closed on Mondays and Tuesdays and is available for a buyout on those days.

SERVICES/AMENITIES:

Catering: in-house
Kitchen Facilities: yes
Tables & Chairs: provided
Linens, Silver, etc.: provided
Restrooms: wheelchair accessible
Dance Floor: portable provided, extra fee
Bride's & Groom's Dressing Area: yes
AV/Meeting Equipment: CBA, extra fee

Parking: valet parking or guest lot available
Accommodations: no guest rooms
Outdoor Night Lighting: access only
Outdoor Cooking Facilities: BBQs CBA
Cleanup: provided
View: marina, Pacific Ocean

RESTRICTIONS:

Alcohol: in-house, or corkage $20/bottle
Smoking: outdoors only
Music: amplified OK indoors until 1am, outdoors until 11pm

Wheelchair Access: yes
Insurance: required of all vendors
Other: no rice or birdseed

Hornblower Cruises & Events

Yachts

13755 Fiji Way, Marina del Rey

310/301-6000

www.hornblower.com/marina-del-rey/weddings
mdr@hornblower.com

● Rehearsal Dinners	● Corporate Events
● Ceremonies	● Meetings
● Wedding Receptions	● Film Shoots
● Private Parties	● Accommodations

If boats could talk, what tales the Hornblower Cruises & Events fleet could tell! Collectively, the five Marina del Rey-based yachts have entertained movie stars, politicians, playboys, and proletariat alike.

Set foot on a Hornblower Cruises & Events yacht and you encounter a classy operation: Each vessel is meticulously maintained—it's as sleek and well-groomed as a thoroughbred. Mahogany and teak boiseries gleam; brass railings sparkle. Quality is the byword here, and it defines all aspects of a Hornblower Cruises & Events event, from the gracious uniformed staff to the meals, which are exquisite in taste as well as presentation.

Weddings on board are exhilarating—exchange vows dockside or while the yacht's underway, plying the harbor's gentle waters. And if you want to take full advantage of the maritime motif, enlist the ship's captain to perform your ceremony.

Entertainer boasts two large, fully enclosed decks, each with a full bar and dance floor. With a full galley, high-quality sound system, and open-air lounge deck, she can accommodate 400 guests for seated dining or 550 for cocktails and a buffet. The aft deck provides a "back porch", additional deck space for guests who want to take in the sea air or dance under the stars!

Hornblower's nostalgic *Zumbrota* is a Roaring Twenties masterpiece rich in history: Mae West and Douglas Fairbanks both took their turns at ownership. The *Zumbrota* is a truly majestic vessel, showcasing walls paneled in Burmese teak, a bar with whimsical brass elephant-head fixtures, and the wheelhouse's original compass.

The impressive *Just Dreamin'* is a 110-foot mega-yacht that's custom-designed for high-style special events. Her three comfortable cabins, open aft deck, built-in dance floor and, of course, air conditioning and heating will make your guests feel totally pampered. A long list of assets has made her one of Southern California's most sought-after yachts.

Hornblower Cruises & Events has other luxurious yachts in its fleet, so if none of these seems to fit your needs, let them match you up with just the right vessel for your celebration. Through the years, the seasoned Hornblower Cruises & Events staff has hosted more than 50,000 events!

And besides, what better way to begin life's journey together than with a buoyant send-off on a beautiful boat? It doesn't get much better than this.

CEREMONY & EVENT/RECEPTION CAPACITY: The yachts can accommodate 10–550 guests.

MEETING CAPACITY: The yachts hold up to 408 seated guests.

PRICES: WHAT'S THIS GOING TO COST?

Package Prices: *$78/person and up*
- Wedding packages include: boat rental, food, cake, non-alcoholic beverages, and a ceremony by the captain.
- Intimate weddings start at $550 for up to 20 guests. There is an additional cost for dinner cruise tickets, which range $75–99/person. Packages include: dockside ceremony, performed by the ship's captain; bouquet for bride & boutonnière for groom; a champagne toast with two commemorative flutes; 4-course seated meal; wedding cake; and more!

Additional Info: Hourly boat rental rates and à la carte services can also be arranged.

AVAILABILITY: Year-round, daily.

SERVICES/AMENITIES:

Catering: in-house, no BYO
Kitchen Facilities: n/a
Tables & Chairs: provided
Linens, Silver, etc.: provided
Restrooms: wheelchair access varies
Dance Floor: provided
Dressing Areas: available on some yachts
AV/Meeting Equipment: provided

Parking: fee lots near dock
Accommodations: available on some yachts
Outdoor Night Lighting: yes
Outdoor Cooking Facilities: no
Cleanup: provided
View: ocean, bay
Other: event coordination

RESTRICTIONS:

Alcohol: in-house, no BYO
Smoking: not allowed
Music: amplified OK

Wheelchair Access: limited
Insurance: not required

This is important! Tell locations you're reading HERE COMES THE GUIDE and ask if our information is still current.

145

Hotel MdR-DoubleTree by Hilton

Hotel

13480 Maxella Avenue, Marina del Rey
310/577-6064

hotelmdr.com
gloria.estrada@hotelmdr.com

● Rehearsal Dinners	● Corporate Events
● Ceremonies	● Meetings
● Wedding Receptions	Film Shoots
● Private Parties	● Accommodations

An ambiance of modern, relaxed sophistication strikes just the right note at this trendy hotel with a boutique vibe. Located at the nexus of Silicon Beach (home to L.A.'s top tech firms), and some of SoCal's most appealing seaside communities (Marina del Rey, Santa Monica, and Venice Beach), Hotel MdR is the perfect spot to get away, stay connected, and host an event that everyone will remember.

The long, palm-lined driveway leads to a sleek porte-cochère entry where you step into an airy, open-concept lobby that flows from one sexy-chic conversation area to the next. Sinuous couches and comfy contemporary chairs invite people to mix and mingle, while off to the side the "Energy Room", outfitted with a ping pong table, can get the party started.

The lobby's glass walls provide gorgeous views of the grounds and open up to several stunning event spaces that can be used individually or combined. The romantic Haven Patio features twinkle lights and lots of greenery, ideal for a wedding ceremony. Follow with cocktails and a very Cali-cool reception staged at their poolside cabanas and adjacent Cove Patio. Or, sip drinks on the Barbianca Patio, next to their fabulous Barbianca Local Kitchen Restaurant and stylish Lounge. Its emphasis on healthy, locally sourced ingredients and Italian/Mediterranean cuisine served with an innovative Napa Valley panache has won it high praise. Barbianca would make an excellent place to begin your celebration with a welcome party, rehearsal dinner, or intimate reception. There's even a private dining room for your select group of 24.

Couldn't possibly leave anyone off your guest list? Then the upscale Panache Ballroom, which can easily accommodate 200 for dinner and dancing, is for you. Their staff is happy to help you personalize the space with dramatic lighting and decorative touches to suit the occasion, whether it's a wedding, corporate gala, graduation bash, or new startup launch.

They offer three wedding packages that include extensive menu options and food station displays, as well as a pre-event menu tasting, an on-site coordinator, and a complimentary wedding-night bridal suite. Your guests will love the tech-savvy accommodations—complete with balconies—not to mention digging into their scrumptious breakfasts. They'll also be grateful for the fitness center, pool, and easy stroll to the marina to take in the colorful boats.

Speaking of strolling, check out nearby Abbot Kinney Boulevard for unique boutiques and the Marina Marketplace for fun shops and eateries. Need more enticement? Hotel MdR is totally pet friendly, so bring your best buddy along for the walk!

CEREMONY CAPACITY: The site can accommodate 250 seated guests indoors and 100 outdoors.

EVENT/RECEPTION CAPACITY: The facility holds 200 seated or 300 standing guests indoors and 80 seated or 200 standing outdoors.

MEETING CAPACITY: The venue can seat up to 200 guests.

PRICES: WHAT'S THIS GOING TO COST?

Rental Fee: $500–2,500/event
- The rental fee varies depending on the space reserved, event duration, package chosen, and type of event.

Meals (when priced separately): $48/person and up

Package Prices: $60/person and up
- Packages include the venue rental, food, and alcohol.
- Pricing is based on the package chosen.

Service Charge or Gratuity: 15%

AVAILABILITY: Year-round, 6am-midnight.

SERVICES/AMENITIES:

Catering: in-house, BYO allowed for religious reasons
Kitchen Facilities: n/a
Tables & Chairs: provided, extra fee may apply
Linens, Silver, etc.: some provided
Restrooms: wheelchair accessible
Dance Floor: provided
Bride's & Groom's Dressing Areas: CBA
AV/Meeting Equipment: some provided, extra fee may apply

Parking: large lot
Accommodations: 283 guest rooms
Outdoor Night Lighting: yes, market lighting
Outdoor Cooking Facilities: no
Cleanup: provided
View: water feature, pool area
Other: event coordination

RESTRICTIONS:

Alcohol: in-house
Smoking: designated area only
Music: amplified OK, with restrictions

Wheelchair Access: yes
Insurance: not required

Marina City Club

4333 Admiralty Way, Marina del Rey
310/578-4906 x2

www.marinacityclubevents.com
viviana@marinacityclub.net

Private Waterfront Club

● Rehearsal Dinners		● Corporate Events	
● Ceremonies		● Meetings	
● Wedding Receptions		● Film Shoots	
● Private Parties		Accommodations	

Rising up near the water's edge, the distinctive curved towers of the Marina City Club keep watch over the marina like a band of giant sentries. Residents of this exclusive condominium complex enjoy unbeatable marina views, and access to several event spaces that take full advantage of them. And, as luck would have it, non-residents are invited to share in their good fortune.

Celebrations take place on the Third Floor, and on weekends you have exclusive use of the entire space. There are two main rooms that flow into each other and, of course, face the marina. Couples typically have their ceremony in the Dockside Room and their reception in the Galaxy Room, but you're free to choreograph your event in whatever way works best for you.

If you get married in the Dockside Room, you'll exchange vows under a flower-festooned gazebo or chuppah in front of a unique slanted wall of glass, reminiscent of those wonderful New York City or Paris penthouse windows. During the day, natural light flows in through the windows; at night the "city" of boats bobbing in the marina provide their own mini-light show. If you like, hire a pianist to play during the ceremony and cocktail hour on the baby grand piano provided. In the center of the room, a circular black marble bar is not only convenient for serving cocktails, it also makes a chic buffet table. An abundance of palms and other trees add softness and color, while gleaming brass accents add a touch of glamour. You can use the room's existing square tables and comfortable black lacquer chairs, or have Club staff replace them with round tables and gold Chiavari banquet chairs.

The Galaxy Room, which also has floor-to-ceiling windows overlooking the marina, is designed with a platform for a band or sweetheart table, a spacious parquet dance floor, and a raised area that's perfect for mingling while sampling hors d'oeuvres, or enjoying a buffet or seated dinner. The space is well suited for hosting meetings, too.

A few more things that couples planning their wedding should know: The facility's health club, beauty salon, dressing rooms, and other services are at your disposal. If your vehicle of choice is a boat, the Club Dock Master will provide a Club slip so that you can sail in and out of the marina at your convenience.

All of the Marina City Club's event spaces can be reserved for private parties, as well as for corporate retreats, seminars, and training. The Club has hosted hundreds of wedding receptions, and they have extensive experience in organizing theme parties such as a Casino Night, Mardi Gras, Texas Barbecue, and Comedy Night. Shuttle service can be arranged to and from the L.A. Airport (a 15-minute drive), and attractions like Venice Beach, Oceanfront Walk, and the 3rd Street Promenade are just minutes away. No wonder the residents love living at the Marina City Club—they have everything they could possibly want right here.

CEREMONY CAPACITY: The Galaxy Room or cocktail area can accommodate 150–200 seated guests.

EVENT/RECEPTION CAPACITY: The Third Floor holds 300 seated guests and 400 standing.

MEETING CAPACITY: The Galaxy Room seats 100 guests classroom-style, the Quasar Room accommodates up to 40 guests theater-style, and the Nova Room seats 12 guests conference-style.

PRICES: WHAT'S THIS GOING TO COST?

Rental Fee: $1,750–4,000/event
  • The rental fee varies depending on the space reserved.

Meals (when priced separately): $39–62/person

Service Charge or Gratuity: 23%

Additional Info: Banquet packages and customized menus are available. A cake-cutting fee of $2.50/person is additional.

AVAILABILITY: For special events, year-round; 7am–11:30pm.

SERVICES/AMENITIES:

Catering: in-house or BYO
Kitchen Facilities: n/a
Tables & Chairs: basic round or long banquet tables and 200 gold Chiavari chairs provided
Linens, Silver, etc.: provided
Restrooms: wheelchair accessible
Dance Floor: provided
Bride's Dressing Area: yes
AV/Meeting Equipment: full range available for rent

Parking: 30 or more guests require a valet
Accommodations: no guest rooms
Outdoor Night Lighting: access only
Outdoor Cooking Facilities: no
Cleanup: provided
View: marina
Other: on-site spa facilities and health club; guests can arrive and depart by boat

RESTRICTIONS:

Alcohol: in-house, or WC corkage $15/bottle (requires management's prior approval)
Smoking: outdoors only
Music: amplified OK indoors until 11pm

Wheelchair Access: yes
Insurance: required
Other: no rice, birdseed, confetti, or sparklers

Marina del Rey Hotel

Hotel

13534 Bali Way, Marina del Rey
424/289-8214
www.marinadelreyhotel.com
weddings@marinadelreyhotel.com

- Rehearsal Dinners
- Ceremonies
- Wedding Receptions
- Private Parties
- Corporate Events
- Meetings
- Film Shoots
- Accommodations

They say "location, location, location" is the be-all of real estate, but when it comes to wedding venues, "views, views, views" tops even that. Fortunately, Marina del Rey Hotel has both!

Fresh off a $25 million renovation, this iconic boutique hotel is not only way cooler than ever, it also boasts a prime harborfront location that showcases a romantic tableau of luxurious yachts, sleek sailboats, and gulls soaring on gentle sea breezes.

Topping the list of new perks is the waterfront Ceremony Lawn. This expansive, curving swath of grass enjoys wide-angle vistas of the entire marina, with a stand of towering palms that serves as a shady altar for exchanging vows. And if you time it right, you'll be treated to a colorful sunset backdrop during cocktails.

Another great spot for a ceremony and/or social hour is the Waterfront Patio, which has equally beautiful nautical sightlines from a different perspective. An adjacent banquet space with walls of windows is perfect for an intimate reception or even a private rehearsal dinner. For larger celebrations, take your choice of the Marina, Edgewater, or Regatta Rooms—or combine all three into one grand ballroom setting. Floor-to-ceiling windows and double glass doors provide lots of natural light during daytime parties, and tulip-shaped chandeliers softly illuminate sophisticated soirées. Plus, since all of the rooms open to adjoining shaded terraces that overlook the harbor, guests can wander out any time they like and raise their wine glasses to that fabulous So Cal scenery.

The photo ops are terrific outside, but there are some great ones inside, too. The hotel lobby has a waterside motif, with textured walls that evoke gentle waves. A stunning mobile of sea birds by the main entry creates a dramatic focal point, especially when captured from the hip, upstairs library lounge. You'll also love the comfy "record room" where you can sink into the plush sofas, play your favorite classic LPs, and gather with friends and family to catch up.

The hotel's event team will help you plan your menu (cake included!), and arrange overnight accommodations for your guests so that they can wake up to a day full of fun ways to spend their time: a swim in the infinity pool, a workout in the fitness center, and a leisurely stroll to explore this picturesque and very pedestrian-friendly neighborhood. Meanwhile, you and your new spouse can hit the snooze button and linger in your complimentary guest room a little while longer, before heading over to the hotel's new SALT restaurant for a taste of their innovative California cuisine. "Table for two, please!"

CEREMONY CAPACITY: The hotel holds 150 seated guests indoors and 250 seated outdoors.

EVENT/RECEPTION CAPACITY: The hotel accommodates 150 seated or 300 standing indoors and 150 seated or 350 standing outdoors.

MEETING CAPACITY: Meeting spaces seat up to 150 guests.

PRICES: WHAT'S THIS GOING TO COST?

Package Prices: $99/person and up
  • Package prices vary depending on the day of the week, time of day, and guest count.

Service Charge or Gratuity: 23%

AVAILABILITY: Year-round, daily.

SERVICES/AMENITIES:

Catering: in-house
Kitchen Facilities: n/a
Tables & Chairs: provided
Linens, Silver, etc.: provided
Restrooms: wheelchair accessible
Dance Floor: portable provided
Bride's Dressing Area: yes
AV/Meeting Equipment: CBA

Parking: valet available
Accommodations: 164 guest rooms
Outdoor Night Lighting: CBA
Outdoor Cooking Facilities: BBQ CBA
Cleanup: provided
View: pool area, panorama of marina

RESTRICTIONS:

Alcohol: in-house
Smoking: designated areas only
Music: amplified OK with restrictions

Wheelchair Access: yes
Insurance: not required

The Annenberg Community Beach House

415 Pacific Coast Highway, Santa Monica

310/458-4934

www.annenbergbeachhouse.com
beachhouseevents.mailbox@smgov.net

Historic Estate

- Rehearsal Dinners
- Ceremonies
- Wedding Receptions
- Private Parties
- Corporate Events
- Meetings
- Film Shoots
- Accommodations

Occupying five desirable oceanfront acres along Santa Monica State Beach and boasting nearly endless event possibilities, Annenberg Community Beach House is unlike any other venue in Southern California. Initially created by William Randolph Hearst for actress Marion Davies in the mid-1920s, the one-time private estate was a popular destination for Hollywood's elite, who flocked to this "Gold Coast" gem to attend the starlet's legendary parties.

The original 100-room mansion no longer stands, but in its footprint is the sleek, modern Pool House, whose towering concrete pillars pay homage to the Grecian columns of its predecessor. Here, you'll find the Sand & Sea Room, named for the grand hotel once housed in the mansion. Overlooking the historic tile-edged pool, this room features floor-to-ceiling windows and an incredible View Deck that provides an unobstructed panorama of the beach and ocean beyond.

Adjacent to the Pool House is the Event House, another fabulous option for a cozy indoor wedding. With its rich wood flooring and walls of windows letting in ample natural light and Pacific views, the house's Garden Terrace Room is a wonderful blank slate that easily transforms to accommodate any theme or color palette.

At the north end of the property, you'll find the Marion Davies Guest House. This divine Georgian Revival home is the work of renowned architect Julia Morgan, who helped Hearst design his iconic San Simeon "castle". Formerly an exclusive retreat for Ms. Davies' friends and family, it's the last remaining structure from the expansive estate and it showcases a bevy of charming vintage details: a delicately spindled staircase, carved fireplace, Art Deco chandeliers and light fixtures, and a bathroom with exquisite tilework depicting curling waves and a dramatic sailing ship. Many couples choose to wed on the home's gracious porch, where soaring columns support a peaked portico crowned with an inset porthole window. Guests look on from the sunken garden, which also works well for a breezy cocktail hour or a small al fresco reception.

Two outdoor spaces (used in conjunction with an indoor space) are available solely during the off-season, though with Santa Monica's near-perfect year-round weather there really is no "off-season". The more petite of these is the Splash Pad, whose beachside setting and swaying palms make it a lovely place to exchange vows or host an intimate reception. Larger celebrations take place in the adjacent Courtyard, notable for its striking views of the sand and surf. These open-air venues are truly stunning during and after sunset, especially with the added glow of market lights and lanterns.

Picturing a ceremony on Santa Monica's famously perfect beach? Not a problem—the city allows permit-free gatherings for groups under 150, and the Beach House's prime spot means you and your guests are only a few steps from your reception. History, glamour, and convenience...what's not to love?!

CEREMONY CAPACITY: The site seats 100 guests indoors and 150 outdoors.

EVENT/RECEPTION CAPACITY: The venue accommodates 120 seated or 150 standing guests indoors and 150 seated or standing outdoors.

MEETING CAPACITY: Meeting spaces seat up to 150 guests.

PRICES: WHAT'S THIS GOING TO COST?

Rental Fee: *$3,000–10,000/event*
- The rental fee varies depending on the day of the week, time of day, time of year, and space reserved.

Ceremony Fee: *$2,500–5,000/event*
- The ceremony fee varies depending on the day of the week, time of day, time of year, and space reserved.

AVAILABILITY: Year-round: Monday–Friday, 7am–10pm; Saturday and Sunday, 7am–11pm. Summer months (Memorial Day–Labor Day) are limited to 7pm–11pm.

SERVICES/AMENITIES:

Catering: preferred list
Kitchen Facilities: limited
Tables & Chairs: provided
Linens, Silver, etc.: outside caterer
Restrooms: wheelchair accessible
Dance Floor: yes
Dressing Areas: CBA
AV/Meeting Equipment: provided

Parking: limited large public lot
Accommodations: no guest rooms
Outdoor Night Lighting: CBA
Outdoor Cooking Facilities: none
Cleanup: provided
View: ocean panorama

RESTRICTIONS:

Alcohol: in-house, beer and wine only
Smoking: not allowed
Music: amplified OK indoors with restrictions

Wheelchair Access: yes
Insurance: required

Overwhelmed? Use the search criteria on www.HereComesTheGuide.com to narrow down your choices.

The Victorian

2640 Main Street, Santa Monica
310/392-4956
www.thevictorian.com
info@thevictorian.com

Special Event Location

●	Rehearsal Dinners	●	Corporate Events
●	Ceremonies	●	Meetings
●	Wedding Receptions	●	Film Shoots
●	Private Parties		Accommodations

Santa Monica is famous for trendy boutiques and bistros, oceanview resorts and powder-sand beaches…it's probably the last place you would expect to find a historic Victorian home and garden. Yet tucked inside Heritage Square on Santa Monica's Main Street, a pale yellow shingled mansion lends a turn-of-the-century gentility to the lively seaside town. This unexpected juxtaposition of old-fashioned glamour in a contemporary coastal milieu makes The Victorian a delightfully intriguing venue for formal banquets, family get-togethers and all sorts of parties—bridal couples in particular are drawn to the home's heirloom look and storied elegance.

Originally built near the Hotel Miramar in 1892 as the residence of one the neighborhood's founding families, the two-story building was moved to its current location in 1973. Heritage Square is a prime pocket of nostalgic architecture, with the California Heritage Museum and its sprawling lawn on one side and The Victorian on the other. Completely and carefully renovated, The Victorian has had its main rooms enlarged and added an exclusive speakeasy for a total of 15,000 square feet of event space including the landscaped grounds.

A brick path leading to the front door (and lined with candles and twinkle lights at night) curves among oak trees, blooming flowers and outdoor seating. As you enter, you're greeted by a polished oak bar, a congenial spot for cocktails, as are the home's two patios. Throughout, the décor is characteristic of the late 19th century—a mixture of fine antique furnishings, classical artwork and candles.

Couples often exchange vows upstairs in a lovely room with a built-in bar for champagne toasts and a covered veranda for pre-ceremony mingling. Open-air ceremonies are held on the Heritage Museum lawn or even on the beach, a short walk from here.

There's plenty of room both indoors and out for a sit-down reception or elegant buffet. The intimate main dining room features an octagonal enclave framed by tall windows at one corner, perfect for the bride and groom's table or to showcase the wedding cake. A line of French doors opens to a terrace, where guests sit among trees that seem to grow right up from the wooden floor and through the canopy. The terrace is enclosed for warmth and comfort, and guests are soothed by the sound of a nearby waterfall.

The Victorian boasts an experienced staff that will help you make the most of this unique property. They've even put together an inclusive wedding package that covers: meal service by their in-house caterer; beer, wine, champagne and soft bar; rental fee; on-site parking; a spacious dance floor; tables, linens and Chiavari chairs; and setup and breakdown—in other words, an easy and stress-free way to entertain.

The quaint home and its tranquil garden are awash in vintage charm, yet the salty tang in the air reminds visitors that the rolling waves are just one block away. With plenty of lodging options close by, your out-of-town guests will be thrilled with the opportunity to explore the local scene. Whether you fancy a cozy gathering or a lavish gala, the hospitality offered by The Victorian will lend your celebration the romantic sophistication of a bygone era.

CEREMONY CAPACITY: The Main Room holds 200 seated guests, the Museum Lawn up to 400, and the Upstairs Room up to 130 seated. A beach ceremony is also an option.

EVENT/RECEPTION CAPACITY: Indoors, the house accommodates 24–200 seated or 40–450 standing. Outdoors, the lawn holds 300 seated or 400 standing guests.

MEETING CAPACITY: Several spaces hold 30–200 seated guests.

PRICES: WHAT'S THIS GOING TO COST?

Package Prices: $156/person and up
- Package prices vary depending on the guest count and menu selection.
- Packages include: the site rental, sit-down dinner, dance floor, linens, Chiavari chairs, valet parking, and 3-hour bar service.

Service Charge or Gratuity: 20%

Additional Info:
- Other special events begin at approximately $80/person for seated or cocktail-style receptions. An extra fee and a food & beverage minimum apply to events on Saturday nights. An outside coordinator is required.
- Full-day meeting packages start at approximately $75/person including breakfast buffet, lunch, afternoon snack, and unlimited nonalcoholic beverage service.

AVAILABILITY: Year-round, daily, anytime.

SERVICES/AMENITIES:

Catering: in-house
Kitchen Facilities: n/a
Tables & Chairs: provided
Linens, Silver, etc.: provided
Restrooms: wheelchair accessible 1st floor only
Dance Floor: provided
Bride's Dressing Area: provided
AV/Meeting Equipment: CBA

Parking: 100-car lot with attendant, valet CBA
Accommodations: no guest rooms
Outdoor Night Lighting: yes
Outdoor Cooking Facilities: no
Cleanup: provided
View: no
Kosher: outside kosher caterer with approval

RESTRICTIONS:

Alcohol: available
Smoking: outdoors only
Music: amplified OK indoors until 1:30am

Wheelchair Access: main floor only
Insurance: liability required
Other: no rice or sparklers

Inn of the Seventh Ray

Restaurant

128 Old Topanga Canyon Road, Topanga
310/455-1311
www.innoftheseventhray.com/weddings
holly@innoftheseventhray.com

● Rehearsal Dinners	● Corporate Events
● Ceremonies	● Meetings
● Wedding Receptions	● Film Shoots
● Private Parties	Accommodations

Looking for a unique garden setting for your special celebration? Consider the Inn of the Seventh Ray, voted L.A.'s most romantic restaurant for 20 years. Combining its natural surroundings with market-driven menus featuring fresh organic foods and wines, the Inn is one of California's original culinary agents for change, serving up much more than standard fare for four decades.

Minutes from the city in the heart of Topanga Canyon, the Inn hugs the bank of a gently flowing creek and is surrounded by greenery. Huge oak and pine trees grow through and over the restaurant's two terraces, filtering sunlight and creating a sense of intimacy. Looking at this bucolic setting, it's hard to believe that when owners Lucy and Ralph Yaney found it in 1973, it was a defunct auto junkyard. Undaunted, they walked over piles of old tires to the center of the site, where they felt an intense energy. The feeling was so strong they immediately decided to buy the property, even though they had absolutely no idea what they would do with it. Over the next couple of years, they developed an interest in natural food and a desire to do something that would benefit society, and although neither one had any experience running a restaurant, they opened the Inn of the Seventh Ray.

The name comes from the seventh ray of the colorful spectrum you see when light passes through a prism—it's the violet ray, signifying change. And since getting married constitutes a significant change in most people's lives, it seems perfectly fitting that the Inn hosts weddings. Ceremonies are held in the Fountain Courtyard, a brick-and-stone terrace with an elevated, wisteria-covered gazebo. After they exchange vows, the bride and groom join their guests seated below for the reception. The courtyard is enclosed by a wild mix of canyon foliage on three sides and the Garden Room on the fourth. Tables are arranged around a white fountain, and beneath a lattice wood trellis laced with honeysuckle. Although the Garden Room is generally used just for the bar, it's also a quasi-rustic setting for indoor receptions, with a glass ceiling, latticed walls, tall plants, and a fireplace.

The Creekside Patio, not surprisingly, sits just above the creek and stretches along it for about a hundred feet. A narrow version of the Fountain Courtyard, it's framed by sycamores, and bordered by bushes and a low brick wall. Just behind the patio is the Church Room, the Inn's original structure. Once a gospel church, it's also rumored to have been Aimée Semple MacPherson's private mountain retreat in the '30s. Now a dining room, this ivy-covered building still feels a little like a country chapel, with its steeply peaked, open-beamed ceiling and arched stained-glass windows.

A series of clear, UV-rated, octagonal tents are placed over the patios. Open on the sides in summer and heated during winter months, they give diners access to everything around them and permit outdoor celebrations any time of year. Meals are pesticide- and additive-free, and the food is 80–95% organic, including the free-range meat and poultry. Fish is wild, and fresh seasonal vegetables come from local organic farms. The restaurant has a staunchly loyal clientele whose allegiance is spiritual as well as gastronomical: The Inn's unique bookstore is stocked with books that inspire, and the gazebo—purported to have a special energy—is considered a charmed spot for ceremonies. The soul-satisfying union of uplifting garden atmosphere and high-quality food puts the Inn of the Seventh Ray in a class by itself.

CEREMONY CAPACITY: The Fountain Courtyard and Creekside Patio combined hold up to 250 guests.

EVENT/RECEPTION CAPACITY: Indoors, the Inn accommodates up to 48 guests. Outdoor areas hold 2–250 seated or standing guests.

MEETING CAPACITY: Meeting space is available for 250 seated guests.

PRICES: WHAT'S THIS GOING TO COST?

Rental Fee: $800–7,500/event
- The rental fee varies depending on the day of the week, time of day, time of year, and guest count.

Meals (when priced separately): $41/person and up
- Meals start at $41/person for a brunch buffet and $63/person for a plated dinner with full service.

Service Charge or Gratuity: 20%

AVAILABILITY: Year-round.

SERVICES/AMENITIES:

Catering: in-house
Kitchen Facilities: n/a
Tables & Chairs: provided
Linens, Silver, etc.: provided
Restrooms: wheelchair accessible
Dance Floor: patio
Bride's Dressing Area: yes
AV/Meeting Equipment: microphone available

Parking: valet
Accommodations: nearby bed & breakfast inns
Outdoor Night Lighting: yes
Outdoor Cooking Facilities: n/a
Cleanup: provided in fees
View: Topanga Creek and mountains
Other: event coordination

RESTRICTIONS:

Alcohol: BWC provided or BYO
Smoking: designated area outdoors
Music: amplified OK with volume limits

Wheelchair Access: yes
Insurance: not required
Other: no rice, confetti, or taper candles

San Gabriel Valley

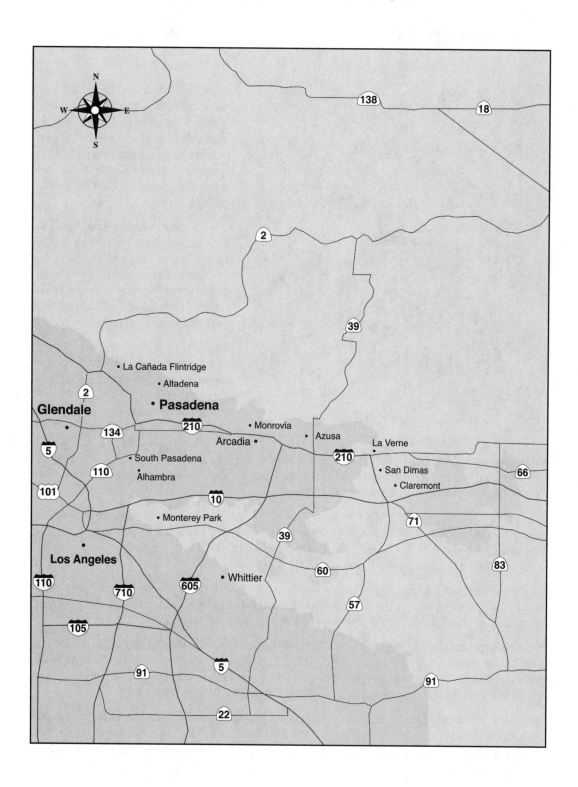

Descanso Gardens

1418 Descanso Drive, La Cañada Flintridge
818/949-4206
www.descansogardens.org
hhorne@descansogardens.org

Historic Home and Gardens

Rehearsal Dinners	● Corporate Events
● Ceremonies	● Meetings
● Wedding Receptions	● Film Shoots
● Private Parties	Accommodations

As you drive down the quiet, oak-lined residential street that leads to the Gardens, you get your first taste of this facility's peaceful seclusion. Living up to its name (*descanso* means "rest" in Spanish), Descanso Gardens is indeed a tranquil, verdant oasis at the foot of the arid San Gabriel Mountains.

Once a large private estate, the Gardens occupy over 150 acres, offering a wide variety of enchanting sites for weddings. One favorite is a quintessential California setting—a broad, open lawn under wide-spreading coast live oaks that convey a rustic simplicity.

Another option is the Magnolia Lawn. A wall of lattice entwined with crabapple vines and ruby-red buds marks the entrance, and guests pass beneath a pretty archway before taking their seats facing a pair of mature magnolia trees. The trees serve as a natural altar for the bride and groom, while their creamy white flowers evoke a feminine grace. The surrounding greenery is punctuated by seasonal surprises—think cheery tulips in spring and perfumed paperwhites in winter—that enhance the picturesque environs.

If you're exchanging vows with a few family and friends looking on, then consider the serene Japanese Garden. Your guests cluster along the bank of a koi-filled stream as you share your first kiss in front of the Full Moon Tea House. An orange footbridge and springtime show of pink cherry blossoms create a colorful, exotic milieu for photos.

And who can resist the romance of Descanso's five-acre rose garden? It boasts hundreds of rosebushes! Couples can wed at the wrought-iron Rose Garden gazebo, and continue their outdoor celebration in a timber-and-stone pavilion bordered by fragrant blooms.

Seated receptions can also be held in the classic Boddy House, poised at the edge of the oak forest. Larger gatherings convene in Van de Kamp Hall, which is situated near the Garden's main entrance. This Craftsman-style building boasts a lofty open-beamed ceiling and French doors that open onto a lovely and expansive tiled courtyard flanked by flowerbeds.

With its shade-dappled lawns, brilliant flowers, majestic camellia forests and secluded woodland clearings, Descanso Gardens is just the right wedding spot for any nature-loving couple. But whether you get married here or not, a visit to the gardens is a tonic to urban stresses and—dare we suggest it—frayed prenuptial nerves. You can breathe easy in this serene setting, or, as they say in Spanish, *aquí puede usted descansar.*

CEREMONY CAPACITY: Various outdoor locations hold up to 300 seated guests.

EVENT/RECEPTION CAPACITY: Van de Kamp Hall and the Rose Garden Pavilion each accommodate up to 170 seated guests. The Boddy House seats 50 guests indoors or 100 guests outdoors.

MEETING CAPACITY: Van de Kamp Hall seats 250 theater-style or 125 conference-style; classrooms Maple and Birch each hold 50 seated theater- or conference-style, and Minka Room seats 20.

PRICES: WHAT'S THIS GOING TO COST?

Rental Fee: $7,000/event and up
- This price is for a ceremony and reception. The fee for a reception only starts at $5,500. Discounted rates are available on Friday and Sunday.

Ceremony Fee: $4,000/event and up
- This price is for a ceremony only. Discounted rates are available on Friday and Saturday.

Package Prices: $80/person and up
- Packages are for catering only and do not include labor, service charge, and tax.

Additional Info: For meetings, the rental fee ranges $425–2,500 depending on the room reserved, guest count, day of the week, and time frame.

AVAILABILITY: Indoors year-round, daily, except Christmas. Business meetings, 8am–4pm or 5pm–10pm; wedding ceremonies 5pm–7pm. Evening receptions, 5pm–10pm. At Van de Kamp Hall, the time can be extended until 11pm on Fridays and Saturdays for an additional fee.

SERVICES/AMENITIES:

Catering: in-house
Kitchen Facilities: n/a
Tables & Chairs: provided
Linens, Silver, etc.: provided
Restrooms: wheelchair accessible
Dance Floor: provided
Bride's Dressing Area: yes
AV/Meeting Equipment: PA system, 2 microphones

Parking: two large complimentary lots
Accommodations: no guest rooms
Outdoor Night Lighting: yes
Outdoor Cooking Facilities: n/a
Cleanup: provided
View: rose garden, stream and koi pond, lawns, woods, estate home

RESTRICTIONS:

Alcohol: in-house
Smoking: not allowed
Music: amplified OK with restrictions

Wheelchair Access: yes
Insurance: liability required

Castle Green

Historic Landmark

99 South Raymond Avenue, Pasadena
626/793-0359
www.castlegreen.com
events@castlegreen.com

Rehearsal Dinners	● Corporate Events
● Ceremonies	Meetings
● Wedding Receptions	● Film Shoots
● Private Parties	Accommodations

Once you've seen Castle Green it's impossible to forget it. This one-of-a-kind landmark, which was built in 1898 during the Victorian era, has been faithfully restored in every detail and is now a Nationally Registered Historic Monument and Officially Designated Pasadena Treasure. And since they only host one event per day, when you have your wedding here you'll enjoy exclusive access to this unique venue.

The Castle's stunning Moorish Colonial style showcases a mixture of European and Middle Eastern architectural elements, such as wrought-iron balconies and towers capped with red domes. Its extensive grounds are equally impressive and include a koi pond, arched walkways and verandas, magnificent trees, and expansive lawns for outdoor ceremonies and lawn games.

Interior spaces are appointed with original antiques and plush velvet drapes—décor that evokes a bygone, more gracious time. The ground floor is a fabulous setting for an event, starting in the Lobby with its grand marble staircase and crystal chandelier. The Salon and several beautiful smaller rooms are available for your cocktail reception, followed by dinner and dancing in the Ballroom. Verandas and lawns provide opportunities for guests to mingle and relax throughout your big day. Needless to say, you and your photographer will find plenty of wonderful photo ops indoors and out.

When you book the Castle, you're not only reserving a gorgeous venue, you're also getting the benefit of an experienced team that can create a stress-free, joyful experience for you. They specialize in helping couples planning long-distance weddings, as well as those doing short-term planning (wanting to get married in a few months!). The Castle's flexibility extends to weddings with special ethnic or cultural culinary needs, too: One of their preferred caterers has a restaurant partnership, making it possible to serve any type of food. Plus, there's no food & beverage minimum and you can bring your own alcohol with no corkage fee.

While weddings are extremely popular here, Castle Green is also an intriguing venue for many other types of events: corporate galas, holiday parties, and fundraisers to name a few. This historic gem will captivate you with both its visual delights and personalized service, so arrange for a tour—you'll quickly see why it's one of Pasadena's favorite places to celebrate.

CEREMONY CAPACITY: The Ballroom holds 200 seated guests with a dance floor. The Garden seats 300.

EVENT/RECEPTION CAPACITY: The Ballroom holds 200 seated or 300 standing guests; the Garden/Veranda 300 seated or 400 standing. The Grand Salon accommodates up to 300 standing, and the ground floor up to 500 standing for a cocktail reception.

MEETING CAPACITY: Meetings do not take place at this facility.

PRICES: WHAT'S THIS GOING TO COST?

Rental Fee: $4,500–9,000/event
- The rental fee is $6,500 on Friday and Sunday, $9,000 on Saturday, $4,500 Monday through Thursday evenings, and $5,500 for December weekdays.
- The fee includes fully furnished cocktail areas, twenty 60" rounds, 200 gold Chiavari chairs, sweetheart/cake/cocktail tables, 4 bars, a grand piano, and complimentary rehearsal time.

Packages: $100–150/person
- Pricing includes: food & beverage from your choice of 4 preferred, full-service caterers; setup, servers, bartenders, cleanup, labor, and rentals.

Additional Info: There is no food & beverage minimum or cake-cutting fee. You may provide your own alcohol with no corkage fee.

AVAILABILITY: Year-round, daily. Weddings usually take place Fridays, Saturdays, and Sundays. Only one event is booked per day.

SERVICES/AMENITIES:

Catering: select from approved list
Kitchen Facilities: no
Tables & Chairs: provided indoors
Linens, Silver, etc.: through caterer
Restrooms: wheelchair accessible
Dance Floor: provided indoors, CBA outdoors
Bride's and Groom's Dressing Area: yes
AV/Meeting Equipment: BYO
Other: wood fireplace in The Salon, 2 grand pianos, 50" TV, children's room

Parking: large lot nearby, $6/car; or guest-provided valet
Accommodations: no guest rooms; discounts at nearby hotels
Outdoor Night Lighting: limited to bridge & veranda
Outdoor Cooking Facilities: yes
Cleanup: caterer
View: garden

RESTRICTIONS:

Alcohol: BYO, but caterer must serve; no corkage fee
Smoking: outdoors only in designated areas
Music: amplified OK indoors with volume limits and outdoors with City of Pasadena rules

Wheelchair Access: limited
Insurance: liability required from caterer and host
Other: no sparklers, rice, or birdseed; open-flame candles require permit; decorations restricted; children must be supervised

---

Want to know WHAT TO ASK a potential location or vendor? Check out our Questions to Ask starting on page 21.

The Grand Ballroom
at the Pasadena Convention Center

300 East Green Street, Pasadena
626/817-5635

www.pasadenacenter.com
lcotton@pasadenacenter.com

Historic Theatre & Convention Center

● Rehearsal Dinners	● Corporate Events
● Ceremonies	● Meetings
● Wedding Receptions	● Film Shoots
● Private Parties	Accommodations

The Pasadena Convention Center is a spectacular boutique venue for galas, weddings and special events. It offers a wide variety of event sites, so, brides, whatever style of celebration you have in mind they can make it happen!

Guests are impressed as soon as they arrive: As they walk across the 22,000-square-foot plaza, which spreads out along the front of the historic Civic Auditorium, they're treated to a wonderful view of the San Gabriel Mountains in the distance and City Hall as the backdrop. The plaza's beautiful tiled surface is perfect for a ceremony, an al fresco cocktail reception, or a convenient valet drop-off before moving inside for the main festivities.

The 25,000-square-foot Grand Ballroom—the largest one in the San Gabriel Valley—can be divided into 10 separate sections to comfortably accommodate an intimate gathering of 100 or a party for over 1,000 guests. Its neutral, modern interior is a blank canvas on which you can paint your own vision. The ballroom is also equipped with state-of-the-art audio and lighting systems and provides internet and WiFi access. Another plus: it opens to an 11,000-square-foot lobby with a sparkling terrazzo floor and artistic, freeform chandeliers. This foyer is ideal for cocktails and hors d'oeuvres, and can be turned into an inviting lounge area.

Weddings may be held in the main conference building's lower level, which houses another chic, contemporary event space. Done in soft grays and off-white, it complements almost any color scheme. Hang swags of fabric from the ceiling for an element of softness and movement, or add whimsical string lighting for a dramatic effect. Brides enjoy tossing their bouquet over the sleek metal railing on the upper level.

On the second floor of the Civic Auditorium you'll find the elegant Gold Room, featuring a rosette ceiling and elaborate moldings. It's a lovely choice for a smaller wedding ceremony and reception.

Recently restored, the Historic Exhibition Hall/Ballroom boasts a 30-foot ceiling, tall arched windows, and chandeliers original to the building. With over 17,000 square feet, it can easily host a large affair.

The Pasadena Convention Center's in-house culinary professionals are happy to customize your menu. They specialize in California cuisine with a focus on fresh, locally grown ingredients. The center has also implemented a host of "go green" initiatives, which should please environmentally conscious couples.

In addition to being a unique place for your event, the Center is a great destination for your guests! The facility is close to the Burbank and Los Angeles airports and just blocks from Old Pasadena, a historic area filled with shops, boutiques, restaurants, clubs, and hotels, all within walking distance. Museums, golf and live theater are nearby as well.

CEREMONY AND EVENT/RECEPTION CAPACITY: Several flexible indoor and outdoor event spaces accommodate more intimate gatherings to large extravaganzas for over 1,000 guests. With a dance floor and banquet-style seating, the Gold Room accommodates 150; the Lower Level Conference Building and Historic Exhibition Hall C, 500 each; and the Grand Ballroom 1,000 (2 sections are ideal for 150 each). Without a dance floor, the capacities for these spaces are greater. Please contact the catering department for more details.

MEETING CAPACITY: The Exhibition Hall seats 5,400 guests. Small to large events may be held in several flexible meeting spaces.

PRICES: WHAT'S THIS GOING TO COST?

Rental Fee:
  • The rental fee varies depending on the space(s) reserved.

Service Charge or Gratuity: *23%*

AVAILABILITY: Year-round, daily.

SERVICES/AMENITIES:

Catering: in-house, or BYO with approval
Kitchen Facilities: n/a
Tables & Chairs: provided
Linens, Silver, etc.: provided, specialty linens available for additional fee
Restrooms: wheelchair accessible
Dance Floor: yes
Bride's & Groom's Dressing Area: yes
AV/Meeting Equipment: CBA

Parking: large lot, valet CBA
Accommodations: no guest rooms; premium hotels nearby
Outdoor Night Lighting: yes
Outdoor Cooking Facilities: CBA
Cleanup: provided
View: cityscape, mountains
Other: event coordination

RESTRICTIONS:

Alcohol: in-house, no BYO
Smoking: outside, in designated areas only
Music: amplified OK

Wheelchair Access: yes
Insurance: liability required

The Langham Huntington, Pasadena

Hotel

1401 South Oak Knoll Avenue, Pasadena

626/585-6244

www.langhamhotels.com/pasadena
tllax.weddings@langhamhotels.com

- Rehearsal Dinners
- Ceremonies
- Wedding Receptions
- Private Parties
- Corporate Events
- Meetings
- Film Shoots
- Accommodations

How do you define elegance? One possible answer is The Langham Huntington, Pasadena. Since its unveiling in 1914, this legendary hotel has been a favorite for high-profile events, celebrity soirées and discerning world travelers. Lavishly renovated in the early '90s by Ritz-Carlton, the Huntington legacy continues to flourish under its new owner, Langham Hotels Group, one of the oldest and most prestigious hoteliers in the world.

Couples planning their once-in-a-lifetime event might begin in the Horseshoe Garden behind the hotel. Originally the main entrance, today it's the most striking vantage point from which to appreciate the Huntington's imposing architecture: The building's stone façade and balustrades strike a classical pose against the contour of the San Gabriel foothills, which echo the hotel's timeless grandeur. Center stage is a broad stone landing with twin staircases that sweep down toward a sprawling manicured lawn. This spectacular park-like enclave, dotted with colorful blooms, swaying palm trees and lush greenery, invites you to dream large for your wedding ceremony—make a fairytale entrance in a horse-drawn carriage, a classic Rolls Royce, or even atop a beribboned elephant!

In contrast, the sequestered Japanese Garden has a quiet, almost mystical beauty. A step-down waterfall pond is spanned by a curved footbridge, a charming spot for an intimate ceremony. Here, whispered endearments mingle with the sound of trickling water, evoking an aura of enchantment. Overlooking the garden's border, the weathered wooden trestle of the old Picture Bridge lends a turn-of-the-century nod to the serene setting.

Yet there's nothing understated about the hotel's posh interior. A stroll along marbled hallways takes you past priceless artwork and antiquities—Chinese porcelain, portraits from the era of Gainsborough, and hand-painted ceiling murals, for example. Several glass-walled corridors frame a view of the Courtyard, an outdoor haven where blossoming pear trees fringe a tranquil pond. Relaxed yet refined, the Courtyard is the just the place for a chic cocktail hour.

Next, host an impeccably serviced reception in one of the hotel's sumptuous ballrooms. The historic Georgian Ballroom feels palatial, with its soaring arched ceiling, stained-glass windows, and gorgeous pear-shaped chandeliers, each one fashioned of thousands of brilliant crystals and ringed with candelabra-style lights. Or consider the storied Viennese Ballroom, featuring a vaulted ceiling edged in gold and a glittering constellation of crystal chandeliers designed by the same atelier that crafted the chandeliers in the palace of King Ludwig II of Bavaria. If you prefer the natural glow of stars and moonlight, then stage your festivities on the Viennese Terrace, an open-air expanse that takes advantage of Pasadena's warm summer nights. The hotel's newest addition is the super-sized

Huntington Ballroom that lets you fête 650 guests in swanky style. Many a high-society gala has graced these ballrooms over the decades, and it takes no imagination at all to envision the gleam of silver and fine china, the swirl of satin gowns and the lighthearted laughter that will accompany your own celebration at such an incomparable establishment.

Add to this cornucopia of luxury even more delights! The award-winning Chuan Spa pampers with signature treatments inspired by traditional Chinese medicine and cutting-edge skincare technology. Then there's the outstanding dining offered by the Royce Wood-fired Steakhouse and the Terrace, as well as afternoon tea in the Lobby Lounge. And, of course, the plush accommodations provide serene havens for your guests. Yes, The Langham Huntington, Pasadena does indeed seem like the quintessential definition of elegance.

CEREMONY CAPACITY: The hotel holds up to 300 seated guests indoors, and 800 seated outdoors.

EVENT/RECEPTION CAPACITY: The hotel accommodates 650 seated or 1,400 standing indoors or outdoors.

MEETING CAPACITY: Meeting spaces seat 1,000 guests.

PRICES: WHAT'S THIS GOING TO COST?

Ceremony Fee: $3,500–7,500/event
  • The ceremony fee varies depending on the time of year and space reserved.

Package Prices: $150/person and up
  • Package prices vary depending on the day of the week, space reserved, and package chosen.

Service Charge or Gratuity: 22%

AVAILABILITY: Year-round, daily. Event curfew is 10pm outdoors, 2am indoors.

SERVICES/AMENITIES:

Catering: in-house or BYO with approval
Kitchen Facilities: n/a
Tables & Chairs: provided
Linens, Silver, etc.: provided
Restrooms: wheelchair accessible
Dance Floor: portable provided
Bride's & Groom's Dressing Area: CBA
AV/Meeting Equipment: CBA
Other: in-house wedding cake, spa services, event coordination, WiFi, fitness center, nearby golf, and bike-riding

Parking: valet required
Accommodations: 379 guestrooms
Outdoor Night Lighting: CBA
Outdoor Cooking Facilities: BBQ CBA
Cleanup: provided
View: garden patio; panorama of hills, landscaped grounds, mountains, garden, fountain, waterfall

RESTRICTIONS:

Alcohol: in-house
Smoking: outdoors in designated areas
Music: amplified OK indoors

Wheelchair Access: yes
Insurance: required for vendors only

San Dimas Canyon Golf Course

Golf Club

2100 Terrebonne Avenue, San Dimas
909/599-7459
www.countryclubreceptions.com
privateeventdirector@sandimasgc.com

● Rehearsal Dinners	● Corporate Events
● Ceremonies	● Meetings
● Wedding Receptions	● Film Shoots
● Private Parties	Accommodations

Set in a beautiful location at the base of the San Gabriel Mountains, San Dimas Canyon Golf Course has many attributes that make it popular for weddings.

First, you have two ceremony options to choose from: The tranquil Gazebo site next to the Canyon View Room, and the vintage Clock site near the Oak Tree Courtyard. Both overlook the golf course and distant mountains and, since each one is conveniently adjacent to a reception space, it's easy to have a seamless celebration.

Indoor events are held in the newly renovated Canyon View Room, which features a hardwood floor, neutral color scheme, elegant sconces and crystal chandeliers, plus floor-to-ceiling windows. The room opens to an expansive veranda that's outfitted with a fire pit and lounge furniture, and provides sweeping views of the rolling green fairways.

If you prefer to dine and dance outdoors, the Oak Tree Courtyard is perfect. Oak tree branches form a canopy overhead, and bistro lights strung across the courtyard add a romantic glow in the evening. During your party, you and your guests will also be treated to a fabulous panorama of the golf course and surrounding San Gabriel mountains.

Needless to say, with a property as photogenic as this one, great wedding pix are practically guaranteed. Between the landscaped grounds and the tree-covered golf course studded with lakes, there's an abundance of gorgeous backdrops.

The flexible staff will work with you to create a wedding that suits your style and budget, and is happy to recommend vendors for the additional services you may need. Reception menus are varied, your choices range from simple to elaborate, and you can even get your wedding cake made in-house! Yes, San Dimas Canyon Golf Course really does offer so many of the things that will make your big day a complete success.

CEREMONY CAPACITY: Ceremony spaces hold 200 seated guests outdoors.

EVENT/RECEPTION CAPACITY: The site accommodates 200 seated or 250 standing guests indoors, and 120 seated or standing outdoors.

MEETING CAPACITY: Meeting spaces can seat up to 200 guests.

PRICES: WHAT'S THIS GOING TO COST?

Package Prices: *$45/person and up*
- Pricing varies based on food, beverage, and rental inclusions. Food & beverage minimums will apply. Menus and packages can be customized to fit your needs and budget. Pricing does not include additional site fees, mandatory service charge, gratuity, and current sales tax.

AVAILABILITY: Year-round, daily.

SERVICES/AMENITIES:

Catering: in-house
Kitchen Facilities: not available to outside caterers
Tables & Chairs: provided
Linens, Silver, etc.: provided
Restrooms: wheelchair accessible
Dance Floor: provided
Bride's & Groom's Dressing Area: yes
AV/Meeting Equipment: some provided

Parking: large lot
Accommodations: no guest rooms
Outdoor Night Lighting: provided
Outdoor Cooking Facilities: no
Cleanup: provided
View: canyon, forest, garden, fairways, hills, landscaped grounds; panorama of mountains and valley
Other: in-house wedding cake, event coordination

RESTRICTIONS:

Alcohol: in-house
Smoking: designated areas only
Music: amplified OK

Wheelchair Access: yes
Insurance: not required

Beach Cities/Palos Verdes/Long Beach

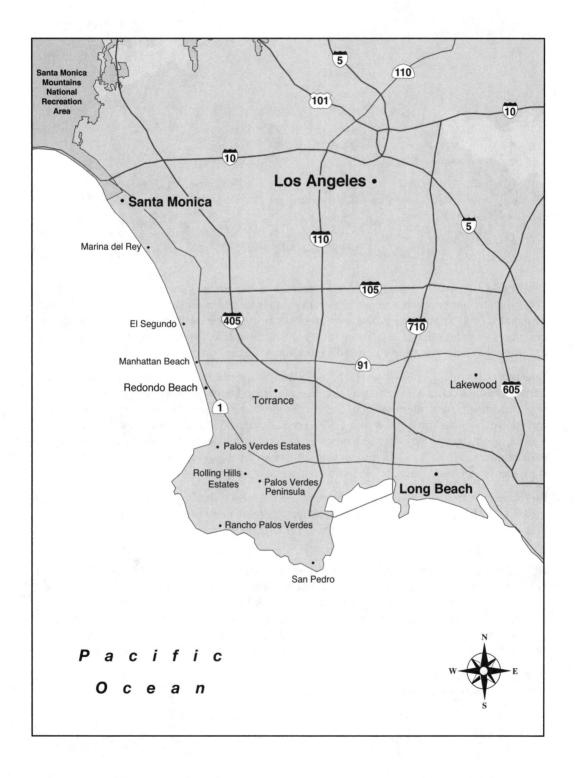

Lakewood Country Club

Country Club

3101 Carson Street, Lakewood
562/421-0550 x21
www.countryclubreceptions.com
srprivateeventmanager@lakewoodgolf.net

● Rehearsal Dinners	● Corporate Events
● Ceremonies	● Meetings
● Wedding Receptions	● Film Shoots
● Private Parties	Accommodations

Lakewood Country Club is both a delightful and convenient venue for gathering family and friends. Though mere minutes from a major airport, the club is tucked away on a quiet residential street, surrounded by 11 verdant acres of golf greens. Built in 1930 when golf was still an elite sport, the club now welcomes the public. Though hints remain throughout the property of its gracious past, Lakewood has been completely updated to accommodate the contemporary bride.

Lakewood's historic Spanish-style clubhouse adjoins a sprawling garden lawn encircled by lush foliage. Outdoor ceremonies are lovely on this manicured expanse, with flowering borders and trees providing natural adornment. An archway or the décor of your choice sets the stage for your walk down the aisle. You'll begin your grand entrance from the spacious bridal suite on the second floor of the clubhouse, where you've prepared in comfort and style. A musical cue is your signal to descend an exterior wrought-iron and stone staircase to the garden below. If you prefer a lake view, the first-tee box offers a more intimate space in a gorgeous setting.

Following the ceremony, you and your new spouse will be whisked away to pose for photos amid the beautiful lakes and greenery. Meanwhile, guests are invited inside the foyer for cocktails and hors d'oeuvres. This vintage-influenced interior courtyard leads to three separate, and quite different, room options for your reception.

Host an impressive gala in the spacious Avalon Ballroom, where your nearest and dearest can celebrate beneath ornate brass chandeliers. Tall windows overlook the golf course, and the view of the emerald fairways is like an artfully rendered landscape painting. More modest affairs are held in the Hacienda Room, a wonderfully airy and light-filled space, thanks to an open-beamed cathedral ceiling. For something cozier, the marvelous Fireside Room retains many details of the original building, including a decorative hearth—place flickering candles on it for a romantic glow.

With its rustic atmosphere, attention to detail, and competitively priced wedding packages, the Lakewood Country Club deftly answers the needs of today's brides.

CEREMONY, EVENT/RECEPTION & MEETING CAPACITY: The location holds up to 300 guests, indoors or outdoors. Reception spaces each accommodate 20–250 people.

PRICES: WHAT'S THIS GOING TO COST?

Package Prices: $52/person and up
- Pricing varies based on food, beverage, and rental inclusions. Food & beverage minimums will apply. Menus and packages can be customized to fit your needs and budget. Pricing does not include additional site fees, mandatory service charge, gratuity, and current sales tax.

AVAILABILITY: Year-round, daily.

SERVICES/AMENITIES:

Catering: in-house
Kitchen Facilities: n/a
Tables & Chairs: provided
Linens, Silver, etc.: provided
Restrooms: wheelchair accessible
Dance Floor: provided
Bride's Dressing Area: yes
AV/Meeting Equipment: CBA

Parking: large complimentary lot
Accommodations: no guest rooms
Outdoor Night Lighting: yes
Outdoor Cooking Facilities: BBQ
Cleanup: provided
View: fairways, lake, landscaped grounds
Other: house centerpieces and wedding cake are included

RESTRICTIONS:

Alcohol: in-house
Smoking: outside only
Music: amplified OK

Wheelchair Access: yes
Insurance: not required

The wedding vendors on our website are the best in the business. How do we know? Read page 425.

Aquarium of the Pacific

100 Aquarium Way, Long Beach
562/951-1663

www.aquariumofpacific.org
aopcatering@longbeachcc.com

Aquarium and Event Facility

- Rehearsal Dinners
- Ceremonies
- Wedding Receptions
- Private Parties
- Corporate Events
- Meetings
- Film Shoots
- Accommodations

You're exchanging vows in a place like no other: Behind you, slivers of light filter down through a soaring expanse of liquid turquoise, illuminating tall flowing sea plants and the iridescent sea creatures that are your audience. As your senses take in the enveloping hush and the gentle sway of the blue water, you feel at once serene and enlivened.

Such is the magical effect of the brilliant three-story kelp exhibit, the ceremony site of choice at the Aquarium of the Pacific in Long Beach. Receptions can be held in this area as well, or in many other spaces at the facility. Smaller parties, rehearsal dinners, and bridal showers often take place upstairs at the Veranda Roof Top, a popular spot where gorgeous sunsets are a regular occurrence. Here, the scent of the ocean is carried on the breeze, along with the calls of exotic birds from nearby Lorikeet Forest, an outdoor aviary that mimics the lush coastal lowlands of Australia.

Larger events unfold in the Great Hall, a generous space featuring multiple skylights and an enormous suspended blue whale that presides majestically over the festivities. A state-of-the-art sound and video system can be used to show your wedding footage, pictures, and videos. Automated screens—which cover the skylights at the touch of a button—project images around the room for all to see.

The Hall can be "designed" to create any mood you desire, from low-key to theatrical. For example, have your reception bathed in dramatic blue and gold light, punctuated by dozens of golden stars projected onto the dance floor. This dazzling setup captures the essence of a starry night reflected on a dark blue sea.

The Aquarium's first major expansion, Pacific Visions, represents the aquarium of the future. Housed in a stunning two-story glass biomorphic building, it features a state-of-the-art immersive theater, interactive art installations, engaging multimedia displays, and live animal exhibits. The Art Gallery, one of three galleries in this new venue, provides a wonderful space for receptions. Here you'll find high-resolution projections of colorful coral reefs and fascinating plankton as backdrops, as well as intricate glass sculptures hanging from the ceiling—there's even a virtual waterfall in the adjoining Orientation Gallery.

Depending on the arrangements you've made with the Aquarium, guests can wander among exhibits and marvel at the wonders of the deep. Host a unique cocktail hour where your family and friends become totally immersed in the enchantment of the sea as they watch playful otters or are simply mesmerized by the beautiful tropical coral reefs and habitats that surround them.

Located adjacent to Rainbow Harbor in downtown Long Beach, the Aquarium is truly a one-of-a-kind event venue with incredible marine views and spectacular exhibits. For ocean lovers or couples looking for a singular environment for their celebration, this is a magnificent place. It will transport you and your guests to an underwater fantasy come to life.

CEREMONY CAPACITY: The site holds 200 seated guests indoors in front of the Blue Cavern exhibit.

EVENT/RECEPTION & MEETING CAPACITY: The venue can accommodate up to 450 seated or 3,000 standing when the entire property is utilized.

PRICES: WHAT'S THIS GOING TO COST?

Package Prices: $93/person and up
  • There is a 150-guest minimum. Pricing for smaller groups varies; custom menus are available.

Service Charge or Gratuity: 22%

AVAILABILITY: Year-round, daily. The Veranda is available during the day and evening. Events inside the Aquarium begin at 7pm.

SERVICES/AMENITIES:

Catering: in-house
Kitchen Facilities: n/a
Tables & Chairs: some provided, CBA
Linens, Silver, etc.: some provided, CBA
Restrooms: wheelchair accessible
Dance Area: yes
Bride's & Groom's Dressing Area: yes
AV/Meeting Equipment: CBA

Parking: garage nearby
Accommodations: no guest rooms
Outdoor Night Lighting: CBA
Outdoor Cooking Facilities: barbecue CBA
Cleanup: provided
View: cityscape, coastline, harbor
Other: picnic area

RESTRICTIONS:

Alcohol: in-house
Smoking: permitted in designated areas
Music: amplified OK with restrictions

Wheelchair Access: yes
Insurance: liability required, coverage is offered

El Dorado Park Golf Course

Golf Course

2400 N. Studebaker Road, Long Beach
562/795-7751 X3
www.countryclubreceptions.com
privateeventmanager@eldoradoparkgc.com

● Rehearsal Dinners	● Corporate Events
● Ceremonies	● Meetings
● Wedding Receptions	● Film Shoots
● Private Parties	Accommodations

Set in the quiet El Dorado Park neighborhood of Long Beach, this historic golf course—once the site of the Queen Mary Open and now home to the prestigious Long Beach Open—is a favorite event location for locals and visitors alike. The lovely public park that surrounds the landscaped course frames it with even more trees, pretty paths and picturesque waterways—all ideal for beautiful day-of portraits of the bride and groom.

Couples can exchange vows outdoors on the Garden Ceremony Lawn overlooking the 18th green and gorgeous views of the course. Towering trees act as green "umbrellas," providing natural shade.

Cocktail receptions and dinner dances are held just a few steps away in the airy, white Garden Pavilion, a dramatic tented venue. Set apart from the clubhouse, it features a private Garden Patio entrance and a high, peaked ceiling with elegant draping; at night, chandeliers and twinkle lights contribute to a magical, fairy-tale atmosphere.

The space is incredibly flexible, which helps explain its widespread appeal. In addition to wedding receptions, this affordable and immensely popular setting accommodates corporate events, bar and bat mitzvahs, quinceañeras, sweet sixteen parties, anniversary celebrations—even auctions, mini-festivals and tournaments! El Dorado will provide all of your tables, chairs, linens, glassware, flatware and more. However, you can also bring in lounge furniture, decorations, special uplighting and floral arrangements to personalize the environment and create an ambiance that suits your party style.

Require more space? Inside the clubhouse, you'll find additional options. The handsome restaurant treats diners to floor-to-ceiling windows that showcase patio and golf course vistas, while the private dining room with coffered ceilings, mood lighting, and stained-glass accents is ideal for rehearsal dinners or smaller functions. When schedules permit, both can be used to expand and enhance your function.

El Dorado's on-site Private Event Team and experienced staff will make sure your every expectation is met. Come see why those who have hosted their important celebrations here call their experiences "unforgettable."

CEREMONY CAPACITY: The venue can accommodate up to 400 outdoors.

EVENT/RECEPTION & MEETING CAPACITY: The facility holds 90 seated or 150 standing indoors and 350 seated or 400 standing outdoors.

MEETING CAPACITY: Meeting spaces seat 350 guests.

PRICES: WHAT'S THIS GOING TO COST?

Package Prices: $47/person and up
- Pricing varies based on food, beverage, and rental inclusions. Food & beverage minimums will apply. Menus and packages can be customized to fit your needs and budget. Pricing does not include additional site fees, mandatory service charge, gratuity, and current sales tax.

AVAILABILITY: Year-round, daily, anytime.

SERVICES/AMENITIES:

Catering: in-house or BYO
Kitchen Facilities: n/a
Tables & Chairs: provided
Linens, Silver, etc.: provided
Restrooms: wheelchair accessible
Dance Floor: portable provided
Bride's Dressing Area: CBA
AV/Meeting Equipment: CBA

Parking: large lot, on-street
Accommodations: no guest rooms
Outdoor Night Lighting: provided
Outdoor Cooking Facilities: BBQ CBA
Cleanup: provided
View: forest, garden; panorama of fairways and park

RESTRICTIONS:

Alcohol: full in-house bar
Smoking: designated areas only
Music: amplified OK with restrictions

Wheelchair Access: yes
Insurance: not required

Queen Mary

1126 Queens Highway, Long Beach
562/499-1749
www.queenmary.com
weddings@queenmary.com

- Rehearsal Dinners
- Ceremonies
- Wedding Receptions
- Private Parties
- Corporate Events
- Meetings
- Film Shoots
- Accommodations

You and your guests will share a truly memorable experience when you celebrate in a place that's like no other: aboard the iconic *Queen Mary*.

Completed in 1936, this legendary ship raised the bar for transatlantic travel with unparalleled luxury and elegance. Her storied past includes hosting royalty, high society, and Hollywood stars, as well as playing a key role in the British navy's WWII victory. Now permanently docked in Long Beach Harbor, this ocean liner-turned hotel attraction will take your breath away and transport you to another era—without ever setting sail.

Surrounded by a panorama of the marina, ocean, downtown Long Beach, and an occasional pod of dolphins, you'll find it hard to resist an al fresco ceremony at the Gazebo or Verandah Deck. After saying "I do", linger over cocktails to soak up the lovely harbor views as the sunset colors the sky, before heading inside for your reception. (For those who prefer a more traditional setting for exchanging vows, the refined Royal Wedding Chapel is perfect!)

Inside, the *Queen Mary* is a treasure trove of museum-quality Art Deco design. Their 14 unique salons can accommodate 50–700 guests, and boast a wealth of exotic woods, inlaid marquetry, original light fixtures, and handcrafted textiles. We don't have room to describe them all, but here are a few outstanding examples…

The Queen Salon is a melding of dark, gleaming wood and warm golden touches, from graceful sconces to gold onyx fireplaces, including a floor-to-ceiling showstopper etched with a Deco tableau of flora and fauna. If you're planning a gala, the 9,000-square-foot Grand Salon is grandeur at its best. Here you'll find spectacular artwork, gilded surfaces, and burnished wood columns accented with gleaming chrome—a stunning combination of extravagance with a sleek, timeless flair.

For something quite different, check out the Royal Salon & King's View. A favorite of British monarchs and American politicians, this former first-class smoking lounge features artwork from the ship's ocean liner days and an after-dinner cocktail area with a wall of windows overlooking the harbor and city. And if you love a swanky supper club atmosphere, go straight from your Verandah Deck ceremony to the Verandah Grill. It's got plenty of sexy curves, lots of windows overlooking the city lights, a sunken dance floor, and an exuberant (and very famous) mural titled "Entertainment"! Need to take a break from dancing? Just walk out to the deck and enjoy the soft ocean breeze.

The choices here may seem endless, but that's where the event staff comes in. They'll be on hand to help you every step of the way, from taking you on a full tour and recommending vendors, to selecting décor and customizing the catering team's seasonal menus. They're also happy to arrange your rehearsal dinner, onboard accommodations, and much more. So expect to be pampered—this is the *Queen Mary* after all!

CEREMONY CAPACITY: The Royal Wedding Chapel seats 150, the Sun Deck Gazebo 100, and the Verandah Deck 350.

EVENT/RECEPTION CAPACITY: The ship has 14 rooms that can accommodate 20–1,500 seated guests. With a tent in the Queen Mary Park, receptions of up to 2,000 may be held (the tent requires a minimum of 800 guests, plus additional rental fees and permits).

MEETING CAPACITY: There is 45,000 square feet of meeting space and 50,000 square feet of exhibit space. Up to 500 seated guests can be accommodated.

PRICES: WHAT'S THIS GOING TO COST?

Package Prices: $60/person and up

Ceremony Fee:
  • There is an additional charge for a ceremony.

Service Charge or Gratuity: 22%

AVAILABILITY: Year-round, daily, including holidays.

SERVICES/AMENITIES:

Catering: in-house
Kitchen Facilities: n/a
Tables & Chairs: provided
Linens, Silver, etc.: provided
Restrooms: wheelchair accessible
Dance Floor: provided
Bride's Dressing Area: in Chapel only
AV/Meeting Equipment: full range, extra charge

Parking: hosted and non-hosted parking available
Accommodations: 346 guest rooms
Outdoor Night Lighting: CBA
Outdoor Cooking Facilities: no
Cleanup: provided
View: Long Beach Harbor and city skyline
Other: event coordination and wedding planning services

RESTRICTIONS:

Alcohol: in-house, no BYO
Smoking: on deck only
Music: amplified OK

Wheelchair Access: limited (no wheelchair access to Verandah Deck)
Insurance: not required
Other: security optional

Recreation Park 18 Golf Course

Golf Club

5001 Deukmejian Drive, Long Beach
562/494-5000 X233
www.countryclubreceptions.com
privateeventdirector@recreationparkgc.com

● Rehearsal Dinners		● Corporate Events	
● Ceremonies		● Meetings	
● Wedding Receptions		● Film Shoots	
● Private Parties		Accommodations	

From its earliest days, Recreation Park 18 Golf Course has been *the* place for Long Beach residents to get away from it all. Back in 1909, as a beautiful-but-rugged country club, it attracted golfers who were willing to take a train from town and then hike to the course; later a horse-and-buggy shuttle was added, making the trip much more convenient.

Today, even with a wide boulevard circling the grounds, you still get that sense of leaving the city behind once you enter this full-service park. As you drive in you first notice the lawn bowlers enjoying their genteel pastime. Then you pass a long row of tennis courts, and turn up a hill where the white Spanish Colonial clubhouse, with its columned front porch and red-tile roof, basks in the peaceful views of the surrounding property. Built in 1926 by the Bixby family, this historic landmark was deeded to the city of Long Beach in 1980 for one dollar, in what has to be one of the better real estate deals of the century.

Only one wedding is held in the clubhouse at a time, and couples will appreciate having two dressing areas that provide plenty of room for everyone to get ready. You'll especially love the renovated upstairs suite, which is air-conditioned and outfitted with an 8-person vanity, lounge area, and 3-way mirror. It's also filled with natural light, making it easy for your photographer to snap some great photos. Another perk: both dressing areas are available throughout your event.

Begin your celebration in the circular Rose Garden, a delightful ceremony spot featuring a 75-foot garden walkway that leads to a beautiful gazebo bordered by rosebushes. Afterwards, guests will follow a short path to an intimate hedged patio festooned with market lights to enjoy cocktails and hors d'oeuvres. At the appointed time, three sets of French doors just off the patio open to reveal the grandly proportioned Main Ballroom.

Here, original architectural details like a soaring ceiling, dark wood crossbeams, and period chandeliers evoke the lifestyle of the wealthy in the 1920s. A gilded *trompe l'oeil* balcony accentuates the room's height and lends a European ambiance. Above it, artisan stained-glass windows set off a subtle interplay of light, as the rays from the setting sun softly stream in while tiny runner lights begin to glitter just below the beams. A large built-in dance floor in front of a massive decorative fireplace provides ample room for a band or DJ.

Since the entire place is yours to enjoy, take advantage of the adjacent parlor for quiet conversation by a cozy hearth...as a retreat for the bridal party...or as a separate children's room. You can also step out onto the front porch to savor the night air. At the end of the evening, when the festivities have wound down and you drive back through the park's entrance, you'll find it hard to believe you were so close to the city all this time.

CEREMONY CAPACITY: The Rose Garden holds 250 seated guests; indoor spaces seat up to 200 guests.

EVENT/RECEPTION & MEETING CAPACITY: The Rose Garden holds up to 300 seated or 350 standing guests; the Main Ballroom accommodates 188 seated with a dance floor or 200 standing.

PRICES: WHAT'S THIS GOING TO COST?

Package Prices: $47/person and up
- Pricing varies based on food, beverage, and rental inclusions. Food & beverage minimums will apply. Menus and packages can be customized to fit your needs and budget. Pricing does not include additional site fees, mandatory service charge, gratuity, and current sales tax.

AVAILABILITY: Year-round, daily, 6am–1am.

SERVICES/AMENITIES:

Catering: provided
Kitchen Facilities: n/a
Tables & Chairs: provided
Linens, Silver, etc.: provided
Restrooms: wheelchair accessible
Dance Floor: provided
Dressing Area: yes
AV/Meeting Equipment: projector and screen, more CBA

Parking: large lot and on street
Accommodations: no guest rooms
Outdoor Night Lighting: yes
Outdoor Cooking Facilities: BBQ CBA
Cleanup: provided
View: park, fairways, landscaped grounds, rose garden

RESTRICTIONS:

Alcohol: provided
Smoking: outside only
Music: amplified OK indoors; 10pm noise curfew for outdoor events

Wheelchair Access: yes
Insurance: not required

Want to find more venues and services? Check out our informative website, www.HereComesTheGuide.com.

181

Skylinks at Long Beach

Golf Club

4800 East Wardlow Road, Long Beach
562/421-3388 x205
www.countryclubreceptions.com
privateeventmanager@skylinksgc.com

● Rehearsal Dinners		● Corporate Events
● Ceremonies		● Meetings
● Wedding Receptions		● Film Shoots
● Private Parties		Accommodations

The sky's the limit at Skylinks Golf Course when it comes to satisfying every wish, dream and special request for your wedding. You want doves released after the ceremony? No problem. Tents set up outside? Consider it done! In fact, it's hard to find a more accommodating staff than the one at Long Beach's premier public golf course.

While you're thinking up ways to let your creativity run wild, you'll be pleased to know that the event spaces here—whether in the clubhouse or on the golf course itself—are easy to customize. They've hosted all kinds of celebrations, from a casual cocktail reception to the most formal plated dinner and everything in between!

Their ceremony site is a thing of beauty. Couples say "I do" beneath a white, trellised arch set against a striking backdrop: a free-form rock waterfall and cascading pools, surrounded by a lush landscape of palm trees, flowering bushes and other greenery. As vows are exchanged, guests look on from their lawn seating, arranged in rows on either side of a petal-strewn aisle.

Receptions are held in the expansive Sky Room, whose vaulted ceiling makes it feel even more spacious. A wall of windows overlooks the property's signature waterfall, which is dramatically lit up at night. Just outside the Sky Room, a comfortable patio is yours to enjoy as well, with the nearby greens and the glorious waterfall balancing nature and artistry.

However, if you happen to have a guest list of 200 or more, consider having your festivities in a custom-designed tent on the driving range. In most cases, you can still have your ceremony in front of the gorgeous waterfall just a few yards away. Tenting the grass is also popular for corporate parties and fundraisers.

Providing numerous choices and flexibility, the Skylinks banquet staff functions like an attentive concierge—diligently translating what you imagine into the wedding you've always wanted.

CEREMONY CAPACITY: The Waterfall Lawn accommodates up to 200 seated guests.

EVENT/RECEPTION CAPACITY: The Sky Room accommodates up to 160 seated guests or 200 if the patio is included. Outdoors, the site holds 500 seated.

MEETING CAPACITY: Several spaces seat up to 160 guests.

PRICES: WHAT'S THIS GOING TO COST?

Package Prices: *$49/person and up*
- Pricing varies based on food, beverage, and rental inclusions. Food & beverage minimums will apply. Menus and packages can be customized to fit your needs and budget. Pricing does not include additional site fees, mandatory service charge, gratuity, and current sales tax.

AVAILABILITY: Year-round, daily, 6am–1am.

SERVICES/AMENITIES:

Catering: in-house

Kitchen Facilities: n/a

Tables & Chairs: provided

Linens, Silver, etc.: provided

Restrooms: wheelchair accessible

Dance Floor: yes

Dressing Area: yes

AV/Meeting Equipment: some provided, more CBA

Parking: large lot

Accommodations: hotels nearby, discounts CBA

Outdoor Night Lighting: provided

Outdoor Cooking Facilities: CBA

Cleanup: provided

View: waterfall, garden, pond, fairways

Other: some coordination

RESTRICTIONS:

Alcohol: in-house

Smoking: outdoors only

Music: amplified OK

Wheelchair Access: yes

Insurance: not required

Verandas Beach House

401 Rosecrans Avenue, Manhattan Beach
310/546-7805
www.verandasbh.com
info@verandasmb.com

Special Events Facility

•	Rehearsal Dinners	•	Corporate Events
•	Ceremonies	•	Meetings
•	Wedding Receptions	•	Film Shoots
•	Private Parties		Accommodations

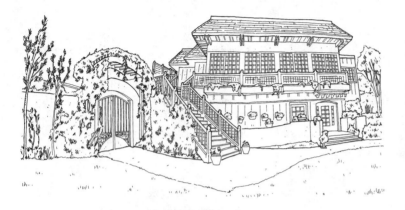

We love beach chic for a Southern California wedding, and that's exactly what this two-story, confection of a Manhattan Beach venue serves up—along with fabulous service and outstanding cuisine. Tucked away in a private garden just a short walk from the sandy shore (where beach ceremonies are an option), Verandas Beach House and its coastal ambiance will make you feel as if the honeymoon has already begun.

An ornate wrought-iron gate invites you behind the high white walls and into a fragrant little oasis, complete with manicured lawn and pathways, trellises, two petite waterfalls an exquisite koi pond full of flowering water plants and jewel-bright fish. Sunlit and dazzling by day, trimmed in twinkling lights at night, it's an entrancing setting for a wedding ceremony or a garden party.

A grand staircase, ideal for dramatic entrances and group photos, leads from the garden to the patio lounge upstairs. Furnished with comfortable outdoor sofas, it's perfect for chilling and chatting al fresco. Then, when you step inside, you'll think you've been swept away to some faraway sundrenched place: Design details like soft seashell colorations against crisp white contrasts, luxurious fabrics, and surprising textures suggest the sand and the sea.

Sip a champagne cocktail or another signature libation in the enticing white wainscoted vestibule with its driftwood accents and marble bar, then step into a capacious chamber with handsome French hardwood flooring and a beautiful lounge area with expansive windows that frame an ocean view. A wonderful environment for exchanging vows, a cocktail reception, dining or dancing, it will elevate any event and infuse it with a fresh, easy elegance.

From here, another stunning staircase (there's an elevator as well) descends to more lovely spaces, but you might want to pause on the landing—which is large enough to seat a string quartet and a super spot for photos—to bask in the opulent atmosphere. Downstairs the "swept away" experience continues. The exquisitely appointed bride's room and restrooms have a gracious spa-like ambiance, but the real show-stopper is the large skylit banquet room in which flashes of white play against sophisticated neutral shades, sumptuous textures and coastal details to create a rich yet contemporary tone.

The final element that makes this luxurious beach house an extraordinary event site is *New York Food Company,* renowned for their talented catering team and brilliantly presented cuisine. These creative professionals will have you and your guests believing, for an enchanted moment in time, that you're the very fortunate residents of your own seaside estate.

CEREMONY CAPACITY: Verandas Beach House holds up to 250 seated, indoors or outdoors.

EVENT/RECEPTION & MEETING CAPACITY: The entire facility can accommodate up to 250.

PRICES: WHAT'S THIS GOING TO COST?

Rental Fee: $2,000–8,000/event
- The rental fee varies depending on the day of the week and time of day.
- During the off-season (November 1st–May 30th), the price ranges $2,000–6,000.

Ceremony Fee: $1,700–4,000/event
- A garden ceremony runs $1,700 and a beach ceremony costs $4,000.

Meals (when priced separately): $77/person and up
- Catering pricing includes exclusive use of the property, a personal event coordinator, and complimentary parking. Pricing for beverages starts at $19/person.

Additional Info: For business functions Monday–Thursday, 8am–5pm: Breakfast meetings start at $15/person, luncheon meetings at $18/person. A $2,000 room rental fee and an $850 food minimum apply for events taking place Monday–Thursday, 8am–5pm.

AVAILABILITY: Weddings take place year-round, daily, 11am–4pm or 6pm–11pm. Additional hours can be accommodated for an extra fee.

SERVICES/AMENITIES:

Catering: provided by *New York Food Company*
Kitchen Facilities: n/a
Tables & Chairs: provided
Linens, Silver, etc.: provided
Restrooms: wheelchair accessible
Dance Floor: provided
Bride's Dressing Area: yes
AV/Meeting Equipment: CBA, extra fee

Parking: attended lot
Accommodations: no guest rooms
Outdoor Night Lighting: yes
Outdoor Cooking Facilities: no
Cleanup: provided
View: ocean and garden
Other: event design and coordination; sound system

RESTRICTIONS:

Alcohol: in-house or BYO
Smoking: outside only
Music: amplified OK indoors

Wheelchair Access: yes
Insurance: required for all vendors

La Venta Inn

796 Via Del Monte, Palos Verdes Estates

310/373-0123

www.laventa.com
info@laventa.com

Banquet Facility with Garden

● Rehearsal Dinners	● Corporate Events
● Ceremonies	● Meetings
● Wedding Receptions	● Film Shoots
● Private Parties	Accommodations

Early South Bay developers designed La Venta Inn as an exclusive retreat to entertain prospective land buyers, and it occupies a prime spot on a hill overlooking the sweep of the Palos Verdes Peninsula.

Built in the 1920s, its Spanish-style architecture is set off by a distinctive tower, red-tiled roofs and, in front, a courtyard with a bubbling fountain enclosed by a bougainvillea-covered arbor. At one time, La Venta Inn was used as a personal residence, and it has all the warmth and convenience of a private estate.

Inside, the rooms are spacious and airy, with wood floors and cream-colored walls that evoke vintage elegance and provide a neutral backdrop for decorations. The large main ballroom has a lofty open-beamed ceiling, antique wrought-iron chandeliers, and a handsome fireplace with a carved stone mantelpiece. French doors open onto a Palos Verdes stone patio that spans the length of the house, commanding stunning views of the entire L.A. Basin and Santa Monica Bay below. Two steps lead down onto a broad semicircle of lawn surrounded by flowering shrubs and palm trees, and there's a natural stone ceremony area at the lawn's edge with the sweep of the coastline as a dramatic backdrop. The developers chose this site well—it has a view that makes you want to stay here long after your celebration.

CEREMONY CAPACITY: La Venta Inn can accommodate up to 250 guests.

EVENT/RECEPTION CAPACITY: La Venta Inn holds 250 seated or standing guests.

MEETING CAPACITY: The venue seats up to 125 theater-style.

PRICES: WHAT'S THIS GOING TO COST?

Rental Fee: $4,000–11,000/event
 • The rental fee varies depending on the day of the week and event duration.
 • During the off-season (November 1st–May 30th), the rental fee ranges $2,500–8,000.

Ceremony Fee: $2,500/event

Meals (when priced separately): $78/person and up
 • Catering pricing includes exclusive use of the property, a personal event coordinator, and complimentary parking. Beverage pricing starts at $19/person.

AVAILABILITY: For weddings: Year-round, daily, 10am–3pm or 5pm–10pm. Functions are in 5-hour blocks, with 2 events per day. Additional hours and all-day events can be accommodated for an extra fee.

For business functions: Meeting space is available Monday–Thursday in blocks of 4, 6, or 8 hours.

SERVICES/AMENITIES:

Catering: provided by *New York Food Company*
Kitchen Facilities: n/a
Tables & Chairs: provided
Linens, Silver, etc.: provided
Restrooms: wheelchair accessible
Dance Floor: provided
Bride's & Groom's Dressing Area: yes
AV/Meeting Equipment: full range, extra fee

Parking: valet or attended parking provided
Accommodations: no guest rooms
Outdoor Night Lighting: yes
Outdoor Cooking Facilities: no
Cleanup: provided
View: Santa Monica Bay, L.A. Basin and coastal vistas
Other: event coordinator, state-of-the-art sound system

RESTRICTIONS:

Alcohol: in-house, or BYO
Smoking: outdoors only
Music: vendors require approval

Wheelchair Access: limited access; call for details
Insurance: required for all vendors

South Coast Botanic Garden

Garden

26300 Crenshaw Boulevard, Palos Verdes Peninsula
424/452-0920
www.southcoastbotanicgarden.org
eventsteam@southcoastbotanicgarden.org

● Rehearsal Dinners		● Corporate Events	
● Ceremonies		● Meetings	
● Wedding Receptions		● Film Shoots	
● Private Parties		Accommodations	

Gardenias, lilies, iris, honeysuckle, and more than 1,600 rosebushes are only a tiny part of the spectacular floral display at South Coast Botanic Garden. And flowers are just one of the attractions here: With 87 acres of over 150,000 plants and trees—accompanied by arbors, ponds, fountains, meadows, and terraces of every shape and size—this horticultural wonderland is unquestionably one of the most scenic outdoor wedding sites in Los Angeles County.

Whatever the event, your guests will enjoy congregating in the trellised Cornish Courtyard, named after one of the early supporters of this flowering paradise. The small kiosks here are a great place to look for your botanically inspired party favors, or for guests to select their own mementos of a celebration they won't want to forget.

From the courtyard, a cart path and walkways lead to a series of garden environments of surprising variety and dimension. The spacious Upper Meadow boasts two pergolas and broad lawns with sightlines that draw your attention to a lacy gazebo set like a gemstone in a flowery surround with sweeping views of the rest of the property. This area is roomy enough for any kind of large-scale entertaining—picnics to garden parties to swank nighttime affairs—tented or *en plein air*. The Lower Meadow has another gazebo and a much more intimate feel.

Their newest venue, the formal Rose Garden, is both a stunning showcase for the rose (hybrids, tea, grandiflora, and English varieties are displayed in abundance), and an exquisite setting for a wedding. Guests enter via two symmetrical staircases and walk along undulating pathways that guide them through what feels like a magical, secret garden, where a pair of cabana structures provide shaded seating for guests. The versatile Celebration Lawn, which features a grand pergola with a raised plaza that serves as a stage, is ideal for a ceremony, cocktail hour, or reception.

This is one location where there are no walls and every short walk takes you to extraordinary places…so why not explore more of the many possibilities? The cactus garden is lovely for a twilight photoshoot, while the amphitheater—beautifully bordered by star jasmine, flowering cherries, white camellias, and angel's trumpets—provides a stage and will suit any kind of production. The Koi Pond Patio, which comes complete with koi pond, stone lanterns, and plantings reminiscent of a Japanese garden, is perfect for more intimate gatherings.

Of course there are nonstop photo ops throughout the grounds, like the Living Wall, an enchanting oasis full of flowers and butterflies. But you'll also find lots of practical amenities like an assembly hall, prep kitchen for the caterers, classrooms, and plenty of complimentary parking. With its endless array of bloom-filled event options, as well as a supportive staff that aims to please, South Coast Botanic Garden is a venue that feels as good as it looks.

CEREMONY CAPACITY: The facility holds 300 seated guests indoors and 1,000 seated outdoors.

EVENT/RECEPTION CAPACITY: Several event spaces can accommodate 250 seated or 500 standing indoors and 1,000 seated or 2,000 standing outdoors.

MEETING CAPACITY: The facility seats 300 guests indoors.

PRICES: WHAT'S THIS GOING TO COST?

Rental Fee: $1,500/event and up
  • The rental fee varies depending on the day of the week, time of day, space reserved, and guest count.

AVAILABILITY: Year-round, daily, 8am–10pm.

SERVICES/AMENITIES:

Catering: select from preferred list

Kitchen Facilities: prep only

Tables & Chairs: rented through exclusive vendor

Linens, Silver, etc.: rented through preferred vendor

Restrooms: wheelchair accessible

Dance Floor: rented through exclusive vendor

Bride's Dressing Area: yes

AV/Meeting Equipment: CBA

Parking: large lot

Accommodations: no guest rooms

Outdoor Night Lighting: rented through exclusive vendor

Outdoor Cooking Facilities: rented through exclusive vendor or caterer

Cleanup: renter or caterer

View: garden, forest, fountain, courtyard, landscaped grounds, pond, meadow

Other: picnic area, gazebo

RESTRICTIONS:

Alcohol: BYO licensed bartender

Smoking: designated areas only

Music: amplified OK with restrictions

Wheelchair Access: limited

Insurance: liability required

This is important! Tell locations you're reading HERE COMES THE GUIDE and ask if our information is still current.

189

Los Verdes Golf Course

Golf Club

7000 West Los Verdes Drive, Rancho Palos Verdes
310/377-7888 x41

www.countryclubreceptions.com
directorofevents@losverdesgc.com

●	Rehearsal Dinners	●	Corporate Events
●	Ceremonies	●	Meetings
●	Wedding Receptions	●	Film Shoots
●	Private Parties		Accommodations

"The promise of paradise fulfilled" is how one author describes Rancho Palos Verdes, a chic community nestled on a picturesque peninsula. In this coastal Eden, dream homes built on rugged bluffs enjoy panoramas of lush hillsides, crashing surf and spectacular sunsets. Grazing cattle and family farms once inhabited this beautiful 13-square-mile neighborhood, but in 1913 banker Frank Vanderlip began transforming it into a "fashionable and exclusive residential colony." He envisioned an enclave in harmony with its natural surroundings, and during the few minutes it takes to drive through Rancho Palos Verdes you realize how well Vanderlip succeeded.

One of the most striking sites belongs to Los Verdes Golf Course, a private event venue perched on the crest of a gentle slope. If you fantasize about a wedding with the ocean as your backdrop, but are daunted by sky-high prices, then meet the accommodating folks at Los Verdes—they call the regulars by name and welcome newcomers like they're old friends. On-site event experts offer advice, such as design tips for the reception or the most romantic spots for memorable photographs. They'll also connect you with reputable local vendors, who have worked together for years and also know their way around Los Verdes—all of which ensures that your event will come off without a hitch.

And as for getting hitched…Los Verdes has a truly inspiring spot for a wedding ceremony. A circular driveway leads to a pair of wrought-iron gates that open onto the Catalina Terrace, which is flanked by towering pines on one side and glass doors leading to the newly renovated Vista Ballroom on the other. Overlooking the golf greens, the Terrace will seduce your guests with a sweeping view of rolling fairways dotted with blossoms and evergreens, and the azure Pacific beyond. In fact, Los Verdes Golf Course boasts an ocean view from every hole, and couples can wed right on the scenic 10th tee. At any of the ceremony sites, wedding guests are treated to a captivating scene—stretching from Malibu to Catalina Island—of tranquil ocean, soaring seabirds, and graceful sailboats.

Amidst all this beauty, everyone will want to stay outdoors a little bit longer, so hors d'oeuvres can be set up under the shade of the Terrace's awning. When it's time for the reception, guests flow into the Vista Ballroom, where two walls of floor-to-ceiling windows keep that gorgeous view at hand. Adjoining the Vista is a smaller meeting space that can be sectioned off for restless kids and their toys.

If you're planning a corporate golf tournament or theme party, consider taking over the entire country club. Whatever your celebration requires, Los Verdes delivers with fine cuisine, reasonable prices, and lovely surroundings.

CEREMONY CAPACITY: The Ceremony Terrace seats 150, and the 10th tee 370.

EVENT/RECEPTION CAPACITY: The Vista Ballroom accommodates 370 seated or standing guests; the Catalina Terrace 120 seated or 350 standing.

MEETING CAPACITY: The Vista Ballroom holds 370 seated theater-style or 200 classroom-style.

PRICES: WHAT'S THIS GOING TO COST?

Package Prices: $69/person and up
- Pricing varies based on food, beverage, and rental inclusions. Food & beverage minimums will apply. Menus and packages can be customized to fit your needs and budget. Pricing does not include additional site fees, mandatory service charge, gratuity, and current sales tax.

AVAILABILITY: Year-round, daily.

SERVICES/AMENITIES:

Catering: in-house or BYO
Kitchen Facilities: fully equipped
Tables & Chairs: provided
Linens, Silver, etc.: provided
Restrooms: wheelchair accessible
Dance Floor: provided
Bride's & Groom's Dressing Area: yes
AV/Meeting Equipment: CBA
Other: ceremony coordination

Parking: large lots, no fee
Accommodations: no guest rooms
Outdoor Night Lighting: yes
Outdoor Cooking Facilities: CBA
Cleanup: provided
View: panorama of ocean, Catalina Island, and Malibu; golf fairways
Kosher: off-site kosher caterer allowed

RESTRICTIONS:

Alcohol: in-house
Smoking: outdoors only
Music: amplified OK indoors or outdoors

Wheelchair Access: yes
Insurance: not required
Other: no glitter, birdseed, rice, or confetti

Terranea Resort

Oceanfront Resort & Spa

100 Terranea Way, Rancho Palos Verdes
844/391-5689
www.terranea.com
catering@terranea.com

- Rehearsal Dinners
- Ceremonies
- Wedding Receptions
- Private Parties
- Corporate Events
- Meetings
- Film Shoots
- Accommodations

Prepare to fall in love … with this magnificent 102-acre coastal resort, situated on a bluff overlooking the sea at the very tip of the stunning Palos Verdes Peninsula. If you're searching for an earthly paradise, you're bound to find it here, where every meandering path transports you to new and varied delights. Built on land that once served as the exotic setting for numerous films and TV shows, this vast oceanside sanctuary is designed to capture hearts and instill indelible memories. In fact, just checking this venue out is a treat you won't want to miss.

Terranea Resort is definitely the location for postcard-perfect celebrations. Promontories with jaw-dropping vistas abound on grounds landscaped to showcase native vegetation and ecology. Catalina Point, with its hilltop trellis, broad lawn, and sightlines all the way to its namesake island, is ideal for open-air vows. The nearby Ocean Lawn also boasts views that will set your heart racing. If your guest list numbers in the high hundreds, scenic Palos Verdes Meadows offers a vast expanse for a ceremony or an affair *en plein air* with a backdrop that features the Point Vicente lighthouse, the sky-blue-meets-sea-blue horizon and a glorious sunset.

Inside Terranea's seven-story central complex, the choices are similarly compelling. You can't help but be dazzled by this wonderland of possibilities! There are multiple ballrooms of varying dimensions, all grand, impressive, and splendidly appointed. Whether your choice is the casual grace of the Catalina Ballroom, the warmth and sophistication of the Marineland Ballroom, or the elegance and scale of the Palos Verdes Grand Ballroom, your selection can be personalized to create just the right frame for your special occasion. All are teamed with Terranea's lovely terraces, allowing seamless transitions from indoor pleasures to al fresco cocktails and dining. Up on the sixth floor, the same refined sensibility and service can be yours in a series of suites with oceanview balconies—some ample enough to accommodate a small ceremony—that work well for welcome receptions, rehearsal dinners, post-wedding brunches and countless other social or business events. A legion of handsome Point Rooms on the second floor may also be combined with the Mediterranean-inspired Point Terrace and Lawn for a sun-splashed or star-lit gathering with a garden and seascape surround.

Once the festivities are over, let the leisure begin. Indulge in soothing treatments at their signature spa mere steps from the ocean's edge … sample the fabulous fare at any of the six restaurants—including several with celebrity status … savor unhurried walks along the shoreline … play a round of golf on their award-winning 9-hole, par-3 course, The Links. A host of gorgeous accommodations, ranging from luxurious guest rooms and suites to beautifully outfitted freestanding casitas and villas, will entice you to extend your stay. And with so many divine opportunities for pampering, relaxing, and alone time, Terranea is *the* place for a romantic honeymoon. But we warn you: Book early. This resort made *Conde Nast Traveler's* Gold List as one of the Best Places on Earth for a reason. Once you see it, you'll know why.

CEREMONY CAPACITY: The resort seats 900 theater-style outdoors and over 1,500 indoors.

EVENT/RECEPTION & MEETING CAPACITY: The resort can accommodate 700 for an outdoor dinner buffet and over 850 for an indoor plated or buffet dinner.

PRICES: WHAT'S THIS GOING TO COST?

Rental Fee: $250–10,000/event
  • The rental fee varies depending on the day of the week, time of day, and space reserved.

Meals (when priced separately): $70–200/person

Service Charge or Gratuity: 24%

AVAILABILITY: Year-round, daily.

SERVICES/AMENITIES:

Catering: in-house
Kitchen Facilities: n/a
Tables & Chairs: provided
Linens, Silver, etc.: provided
Restrooms: wheelchair accessible
Dance Floor: portable provided
Bride's Dressing Area: yes
AV/Meeting Equipment: CBA
Other: grand piano

Parking: valet required
Accommodations: 582 guest rooms, suites, bungalows, casitas, and villas
Outdoor Night Lighting: CBA
Outdoor Cooking Facilities: BBQ CBA
Cleanup: renter
View: panorama of Pacific Ocean, coastline, beach cove, bluffs, and Catalina Islands

RESTRICTIONS:

Alcohol: in-house
Smoking: designated areas only
Music: amplified OK indoors

Wheelchair Access: yes
Insurance: not required

Bluewater Grill

Restaurant

665 North Harbor Drive, Redondo Beach
310/318-3474
www.bluewatergrill.com
vdye@bluewatergrill.com

● Rehearsal Dinners	● Corporate Events
● Ceremonies	● Meetings
● Wedding Receptions	● Film Shoots
● Private Parties	Accommodations

Bluewater Grill isn't just a local favorite—it's also a hotspot for rehearsal dinners, wedding receptions and lots of private parties. The reason for its popularity is obvious to anyone who dines here: It offers a picturesque waterfront location and the kind of food that keeps people coming back again and again.

Sitting right at the edge of King Harbor, the restaurant overlooks the water. Guests seated inside or out on the deck are treated to a fantastic, up-close view of hundreds of colorful boats either passing by or bobbing at their moorings. The ambiance in the main dining room is comfortably casual, with vintage photos of fishermen and their prize catches adorning the walls, teak floors, and polished brass fixtures throughout. But if you're planning a special celebration, you'll want to reserve one of their two private dining rooms.

Both versatile rooms offer harbor vistas and can accommodate a wide range of events, from a birthday bash to a business meeting. The intimate Captain's Cabin is ideal for a rehearsal dinner or small reception. Its unique interior features an abundance of wood in the barrel ceiling and wainscoting, as well as floor-to-ceiling windows that let in lots of natural light along with a harbor view. On cool evenings, a fireplace at one end adds a warm glow. The room works equally well for an informal gathering or a sophisticated soirée.

The Avalon Room upstairs hosts larger groups, and this is where most wedding receptions take place. Wraparound windows and a high, peaked ceiling lend this space an open, airy quality. It's easy to transform this room into whatever style you have in mind: Go festive with vibrant table settings and balloons floating overhead, or host an elegant sit-down dinner with custom linens and stunning centerpieces. No matter what ambiance you create inside, you'll always be able to look out onto the harbor scene and, if you're lucky, a glorious sunset.

The on-site Event Coordinator will help you plan your celebration from start to finish. And although this eatery specializes in fresh, sustainable fish, their banquet menus offer a wide range of dishes that will satisfy everyone in your group.

Bluewater Grill is within walking distance of many Redondo Beach hotels and beaches, making it convenient not just for events but for a great lunch or dinner out while you and your guests are staying in town. Drop by, relax with an exotic martini, and enjoy a quintessential beach city experience at one of the area's best loved restaurants.

CEREMONY & MEETING CAPACITY: The restaurant can accommodate 100 seated guests.

EVENT/RECEPTION CAPACITY: The Captain's Cabin holds 60–70 seated or 80 standing guests, and the Avalon Room holds 100–120 seated or 150 standing.

PRICES: WHAT'S THIS GOING TO COST?

Rental Fee:
- There are no separate fees, but a food & beverage minimum will apply based on the date and time of the event.

Meals (when priced separately): $40/person and up
- Meals start at $40/person for luncheon and $50/person for dinner.

Service Charge or Gratuity: 20%

AVAILABILITY: Year-round, daily, 11am–11pm.

SERVICES/AMENITIES:

Catering: in-house
Kitchen Facilities: n/a
Tables & Chairs: provided
Linens, Silver, etc.: provided
Restrooms: wheelchair accessible
Dance Floor: portable provided
Bride's Dressing Area: no
AV/Meeting Equipment: some provided

Parking: large lot, valet required
Accommodations: no guest rooms
Outdoor Night Lighting: yes
Outdoor Cooking Facilities: none
Cleanup: provided
View: harbor, marina, coastline
Other: wedding coordinator

RESTRICTIONS:

Alcohol: in-house
Smoking: outdoors only
Music: amplified OK indoors

Wheelchair Access: yes
Insurance: not required

Chart House Redondo Beach

Oceanfront Restaurant

231 Yacht Club Way, Redondo Beach
310/798-7666
www.chart-house.com
chrecsm@ldry.com

● Rehearsal Dinners	● Corporate Events
● Ceremonies	● Meetings
● Wedding Receptions	● Film Shoots
● Private Parties	Accommodations

This is a true story: The Chart House of Redondo Beach can trace its origins to a 1960s surf-safari. That's right—legendary longboarders Buzzy Bent and Joey Cabell surfed their way down the West Coast on an enviable twofold mission: to find the best surf in California and a stellar restaurant location. When the duo reached the Redondo Beach breakwaters, they knew they'd hit pay dirt—they had not only discovered a surfing paradise, but also a building with unsurpassed ocean views and beach access.

After an extensive remodel by the noted architect Kendrick Bangs Kellog, the Chart House opened in 1969 and has enjoyed renown as both an exceptional restaurant and event venue for decades.

Built on sturdy piers, the Chart House is a contemporary, low-profile, cream stucco building with a red-tile hipped roof. Huge beams and pillars define the restaurant's newly renovated, smartly dressed interior, while a ribbon of tinted windows around the perimeter heightens the sense of space and provides guests with a breathtaking seascape. Diners enjoy a rare 180-degree view of the Pacific Ocean from anywhere in the house. During winter's high tides, a window seat is a giddy ride, as the surf thunders and splashes against the glass. On chillier days, a fireplace in the restaurant's lounge area adds warmth and comfort.

If you're having a large event, reserve the entire restaurant so guests can mingle freely and enjoy the facility's amenities: an upscale circular bar with chic lighting fixtures, all new furnishings, and a variety of artwork.

Smaller-scale parties can raise their glasses for a toast in the Sunset Room, a private space offering an expansive view of the north coast. This room can be completely separated from the rest of the dining area by simply closing its glass doors.

The Chart House is one of the only places in the South Bay where you can get married on the beach, and weddings here are conducted with ease. As you might imagine, sunset is often the preferred hour for ceremonies, with couples exchanging vows barefoot, right on the sand. It's a glorious tableau, with the sun's last shimmering light preserving the moment in a golden glow.

CEREMONY CAPACITY: Indoors, overlooking the ocean, the site seats up to 100 guests. Outdoors, the beach holds up to 300 seated.

EVENT/RECEPTION & MEETING CAPACITY: For daytime receptions when the restaurant is closed, the venue can accommodate up to 275 seated indoors. Evening receptions are held in a private room that seats up to 90 guests (75 with a dance floor) or up to 100 for a rehearsal dinner or other nighttime special event.

PRICES: WHAT'S THIS GOING TO COST?

Ceremony Fee: Beach ceremony packages range $2,200–2,600.

Package Prices: $850/event
• For an indoor ceremony, add $18/person to the package price.

Meals (when priced separately): $41–85/person
• Plated entrées range $41–85/person and buffets range $53–65/person.

Additional Info: A food & beverage minimum may apply to specific times, days, and rooms.

AVAILABILITY: Year-round, daily, 11am–4pm, 5pm–10pm or 6pm–11pm.

SERVICES/AMENITIES:

Catering: in-house, no BYO
Kitchen Facilities: n/a
Tables & Chairs: provided
Linens, Silver, etc.: provided
Restrooms: wheelchair accessible
Dance Floor: provided, extra fee
Bride's Dressing Area: CBA
AV/Meeting Equipment: CBA

Parking: included during the day; valet only at night, $6/car
Accommodations: no guest rooms
Outdoor Night Lighting: yes
Outdoor Cooking Facilities: no
Cleanup: provided
View: 180-degree ocean view, coastline vistas, Redondo Beach Harbor and sailboats
Other: event coordination

RESTRICTIONS:

Alcohol: in-house, no BYO
Smoking: designated area only
Music: amplified OK

Wheelchair Access: yes
Insurance: not required

Overwhelmed? Use the search criteria on www.HereComesTheGuide.com to narrow down your choices.

197

The Portofino Hotel & Marina

Hotel & Marina

260 Portofino Way, Redondo Beach

310/798-5874

www.hotelportofino.com
weddings@hotelportofino.com

- Rehearsal Dinners
- Ceremonies
- Wedding Receptions
- Private Parties
- Corporate Events
- Meetings
- Film Shoots
- Accommodations

If Redondo Beach, with its sunshine and balmy ocean breezes epitomizes the Southern California lifestyle, then the Portofino Hotel & Marina is the perfect place to enjoy it. Set on a lush private peninsula, it offers guests a chance to relax, let loose, and embrace the "endless summer" experience.

The venue has the unassuming intimacy of a boutique hotel, and its casual, nautical-chic ambiance makes you feel immediately at home. The inviting lobby is actually dubbed "the Living Room," although we don't know too many people who have a three-story atrium in their house—or such an astounding view! Tall, multipaned windows overlook King Harbor, where kayaks and yachts regularly make their way out to sea. There's no sign of land, only rippling sapphire-blue water, so you have the impression of floating on some elaborate houseboat. It's a remarkably soothing vision, and between the soft jazz playing on the sound system and the cocktail you're served from the bar tucked discreetly in one corner, you might want to lounge in the comfortable Living Room chairs indefinitely.

But there's a celebration afoot, beginning with a Seaside Lawn ceremony. It's surprising how many guests this intimate area can accommodate, but up to 200 of your friends and family can watch you exchange vows under an archway or gazebo with the water as the backdrop and the refreshing scent of sea spray in the air.

A short stroll from the hotel proper takes you to the Pavilion, a crisp contemporary building with two distinctive ballrooms for receptions. The sophisticated Bayside Ballroom has a 180-degree view of the ocean, and at night the twinkling stars and the lights of the Palos Verdes Peninsula cast a dreamy shimmer on the water. Next door, the Pacific Ballroom features floor-to-ceiling windows that take in the action of the lagoon and the cityscape beyond. Your guests can flow onto the terrace for cocktails overlooking the ocean.

Your Portofino wedding package includes a room for your wedding night so that you can snuggle under the covers and savor your ocean view a while longer. With first-class service, a long list of amenities and a spectacular setting, it's no wonder The Portofino Hotel & Marina has become one of California's most desirable spots for weddings, vacations and romantic getaways.

CEREMONY CAPACITY: The Pacific or Bayside Ballrooms each hold 250 seated. Outdoors, the Seaside Lawn holds 200 seated.

EVENT/RECEPTION CAPACITY: The Bayside Ballroom accommodates 250 seated or 350 standing. The Pacific Ballroom holds 140 seated or 250 standing.

MEETING CAPACITY: The Pacific or Bayside Ballrooms seat 200–300, depending on the configuration.

PRICES: WHAT'S THIS GOING TO COST?

Ceremony Fee: *$1,900-2,400/event*

Package Prices: *$99–175/person*
- Wedding packages include a custom wedding cake and an oceanside room for the bridal couple.

Service Charge or Gratuity: *24%*

Additional Info: Special discounted room rates for overnight hotel accommodations are available.

AVAILABILITY: Year-round, daily, 11am–4pm and 6pm–midnight.

SERVICES/AMENITIES:

Catering: in-house
Kitchen Facilities: n/a
Tables & Chairs: provided
Linens, Silver, etc.: provided
Restrooms: wheelchair accessible
Dance Floor: provided
Bride's Dressing Area: provided
AV/Meeting Equipment: full range AV, extra fee

Parking: large lots, $15/car valet or self-parking
Accommodations: 161 guest rooms
Outdoor Night Lighting: access only
Outdoor Cooking Facilities: n/a
Cleanup: provided
View: ocean and coastline
Other: event coordination

RESTRICTIONS:

Alcohol: in-house
Smoking: outdoors only
Music: amplified indoors with restrictions

Wheelchair Access: yes
Insurance: not required
Other: no rice, birdseed, or smoke/fog machines

The Redondo Beach Historic Library

309 Esplanade, Redondo Beach

310/937-6844

www.rbhistoriclibrary.com
info@rbhistoriclibrary.com

Book lovers that we are, it was a foregone conclusion that the Redondo Beach Historic Library would capture our hearts. Whether you're a bibliophile or not, however, the library is bound to appeal to you and all who walk through its impressive double wooden doors. Local architect Lovell Pemberton built the library in 1930, positioning it to command a view of both the Pacific and the sprawling lawn of Veterans' Park.

Combining both Spanish and Dutch colonial styles, the library is a handsome three-story ivory stucco building with arched windows, a red-tile roof and straight-edged gables peaking on its north and south wings. Ornamental ironwork on the windows and Art Deco moldings on the front façade spice up the architectural mix still further. Shading the library is its gorgeous companion—a giant Moreton Bay Fig, itself a registered landmark.

Guests stepping out onto the library's main floor will undoubtedly be a little in awe of the expansive, illumined space that greets them. With windows set in almost every wall and skylights opening up the ceiling, the main floor is radiant in light—ideal for large celebrations. Cream-colored walls offset by a dusky burgundy-and-blue carpeting impart a simple elegance. Overhead, arches and dark wood beams echo the Spanish motif. Although renovated throughout, some of the library's original amenities remain, namely the circular brass lamps suspended from the ceiling and the wooden bookshelves bracketing three walls—an excellent showcase for memorabilia, pictures, votive candles or flowers.

Most couples say their vows during sunset's lavish light, in front of a quartet of ocean-facing windows on the main floor. Other possible ceremony sites include the long stretch of lawn directly behind the library or on the Veterans' Park concert green, situated on the building's north side. If it's a more intimate fête you're hosting—perhaps a communion or baby shower—then you'll want to reserve one of the library's smaller spaces: either the overflow room or the third-floor mezzanine, which also affords a glorious ocean view.

Since its opening in 1996 as an event venue, the library has proved to be one of the most popular event facilities in Redondo Beach, booking almost every weekend. Call to make an appointment to visit this site, and chances are you'll sign their dance card too.

CEREMONY CAPACITY: The outdoor ceremony area holds 250 seated, the indoor ceremony area 120–160 seated.

EVENT/RECEPTION CAPACITY: The site accommodates up to 250 seated or standing guests indoors.

MEETING CAPACITY: The main room seats 250.

PRICES: WHAT'S THIS GOING TO COST?

Package Prices: *$18,000/event and up*
- All-inclusive wedding packages cover so many items and are very cost effective. They start at $18,000 for 100 guests and include: event manager plus all service and culinary staff; valet parking; DJ/MC; tray-passed or stationary hors d'oeuvres; gourmet buffet or seated meal; hosted beer, wine, soft drinks, and champagne toast; wedding cake; and more.

AVAILABILITY: Year-round, daily, anytime.

SERVICES/AMENITIES:

Catering: by *Spectrum Catering*, no BYO
Kitchen Facilities: n/a
Tables & Chairs: provided, including Chiavari chairs & lounge furniture
Linens, Silver, etc.: provided
Restrooms: wheelchair accessible
Dance Floor: provided
Bride's Dressing Area: yes
AV/Meeting Equipment: CBA, extra charge

Parking: valet included in package
Accommodations: no guest rooms
Outdoor Night Lighting: access lighting only
Outdoor Cooking Facilities: CBA
Cleanup: provided
View: Pacific Ocean, Redondo Beach Pier, Palos Verdes Peninsula, and nearby park
Other: event coordination, themed events

RESTRICTIONS:

Alcohol: in-house, no BYO
Smoking: outside only
Music: amplified OK

Wheelchair Access: yes
Insurance: not required
Other: no confetti or glitter

Harlyne J. Norris Pavilion

Event Facility

501 Indian Peak Road, Rolling Hills Estates

310/544-0403 X264

www.palosverdesperformingarts.com
rentals@pvperformingarts.com

- ● Rehearsal Dinners
- ● Ceremonies
- ● Wedding Receptions
- ● Private Parties
- ● Corporate Events
- ● Meetings
- ● Film Shoots
- Accommodations

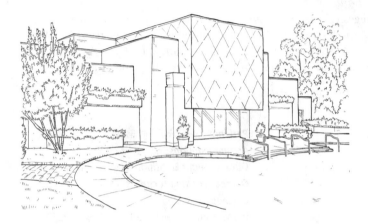

It's showtime! If you're planning a sensational wedding, glamorous gala, or fabulous party, we think a truly great place to take a bow is the Harlyne J. Norris Pavilion. Part of an impressive performing arts complex, this dramatic venue is perfectly suited to its stylish Palos Verdes Peninsula setting.

The Pavilion's picturesque circular parking court, with its sparkling fountain and lush green border of sun-dappled jacaranda and pine trees, is great for photos (especially in front of the theater marquee, personalized for your event), but the real magic begins after you step through the wide glass entry doors …

… and into the skylit Lobby, where a soaring ceiling and chic black granite bar make it ideal for welcoming guests, cocktail intermissions, and mixers of all kinds. Romantic al fresco ceremonies take place on the elegant West Terrace. Designed with a tranquil stone fountain, Roman colonnades, and greenery all around, this graceful and serene courtyard is the quintessential spot to tie the knot—plus, bistro lights and uplighting add a festive glow at night. It also pairs well with the adjoining Ballroom, conveniently accessible through floor-to-ceiling glass doors.

Undeniably the star of the show, this highly customizable space is an absolute stunner. Auditorium-sized, it's large enough to host even the most elaborate party production. Rich cherrywood walls, 14-foot paneled doors, spectacular domed chandeliers, a built-in stage, 12 rows of retractable stadium seating, and magnificent theater lighting—including uplights, pin spots, patterned and custom wall gobos—maximize your options. And despite the room's grand dimensions, you can easily create a dreamy ambiance that's both intimate and sophisticated. Naturally, the audio system is state-of-the-art, too—there's a sound and lighting booth (technician required), and the acoustics are out of this world.

As if that weren't enough, you'll also find a mirrored dance studio, two dressing rooms fit for a leading lady and her entourage, and an expert planning staff ready to usher you through everything from choosing a caterer to selecting how best to use the variety of spaces in ways that will make your event a hit.

No wonder this venue consistently garners five-star reviews: "The Norris Pavilion is a hidden gem!" exclaims one bride. "I couldn't have imagined having my wedding reception anywhere else."

"Hosting our wedding reception at the Norris Pavilion was amazing! We could not have had a better experience!" says another. "Every one of our guests commented on how beautiful and spacious it was. We all had a great time!

CEREMONY CAPACITY: The outdoor ceremony area holds 180 seated, the indoor ceremony area 230 seated.

EVENT/RECEPTION CAPACITY: The Ballroom accommodates up to 230 seated or 400 standing guests, the West Terrace up to 180 seated or 150 standing.

MEETING CAPACITY: Meeting spaces vary; please inquire for details.

PRICES: WHAT'S THIS GOING TO COST?

Rental Fee: $1,500–10,500/event
- The rental fee varies depending on they day of the week and type of event.
- A security fee is additional and varies depending on the guest count.

AVAILABILITY: Year-round, daily, until midnight.

SERVICES/AMENITIES:

Catering: select from preferred list; or BYO with approval, extra fee
Kitchen Facilities: fully equipped, non-preferred caterers have limited access (contact Director of Rentals for details)
Tables & Chairs: provided
Linens, Silver, etc.: some provided
Restrooms: wheelchair accessible
Dance Floor: portable provided
Bride's & Groom's Dressing Areas: yes
AV/Meeting Equipment: CBA, extra fee

Parking: garage or lot nearby
Accommodations: no guest rooms
Outdoor Night Lighting: bistro or colored uplights CBA, extra fee
Outdoor Cooking Facilities: no
Cleanup: caterer
View: fountain, garden, patio; panorama of hills

RESTRICTIONS:

Alcohol: BYO, licensed server required for cash bar
Smoking: outside only
Music: amplified OK with restrictions

Wheelchair Access: yes
Insurance: not required

DoubleTree by Hilton San Pedro
Port of Los Angeles

Waterfront Hotel

2800 Via Cabrillo Marina, San Pedro

310/514-3344

sanpedro.doubletree.com
whitney.neal@hilton.com

● Rehearsal Dinners	● Corporate Events
● Ceremonies	● Meetings
● Wedding Receptions	● Film Shoots
● Private Parties	● Accommodations

Having your wedding at the DoubleTree by Hilton San Pedro, a remarkable Los Angeles waterfront destination, is pretty much guaranteed to be a dream come true: Situated right on the Cabrillo Marina, and offering a variety of beautiful indoor and outdoor venues, this alluring location is your ticket to a great time.

Although the hotel is well equipped to handle any type of social or corporate event, they absolutely delight in weddings. Options for amazing ceremonies and receptions abound, so all you have to do is pick the ones that best fit your celebration. Your event is customizable, and you can choose from an array of packages and enhancements to suit your particular needs and budget.

Given the sunny coastal surround, our favorite sites, of course, are the hotel's outdoor courtyard, plaza, and terrace. At the gorgeous Marina View Courtyard, you can tie the knot *and* dance and dine on a broad, paved piazza framed by flowers, palms, and other lush greenery. Sailboats and yachts bob on the sun-sequined waters behind you, and market lights and Parisian-style streetlamps amp up the romance after sunset. On the opposite side of the building you'll find the equally stunning and even more spacious Rose Terrace, where slightly elevated platforms create natural stages for the wedding couple or entertainers while providing marina and hillside views.

For a slightly more cloistered outdoor setting, consider the appropriately named Intimate Madeo Plaza. Long, elegant, and lit by Old World-style sconces and strings of bistro lights, it's large enough for a ceremony on one end (complete with a substantial aisle for a grand entrance) and a party on the other.

All of these *plein air* settings can be used on their own or partnered with indoor spaces. The Rose Terrace pairs well with the adjacent Marina Room for drinks and hors d'oeuvres and the Bosanko Room for dinner. The much larger Madeo Ballroom located upstairs and the smaller Madeo Room on the first floor just beneath it may be used individually or in tandem with the other galleries and courtyards. Additional rooms of varying sizes can all be easily customized for your affair.

One of the things we especially like about the DoubleTree by Hilton San Pedro is that extending your festivities is a breeze. Are you considering a rehearsal dinner, wedding breakfast or brunch, shower, or cocktail cruise? You can host all of your wedding-related events here. Planning to stay overnight? There are special accommodations for you and your new spouse, plus lodging for all your guests. Everyone will enjoy the on-site restaurant, pool, full bar, and other amenities, not to mention the complimentary transport to nearby points of interest, as well as a shuttle to the beach and back. In fact, once the main event is over, it's the perfect opportunity for family and friends to spend some quality time together with a mini-vacation at this incredibly hospitable hotel.

CEREMONY CAPACITY: The hotel holds 320 seated guests indoors, or 500 seated outdoors.

EVENT/RECEPTION CAPACITY: The hotel can accommodate up to 320 seated or standing indoors, and 300 seated or 350 standing outdoors.

MEETING CAPACITY: Meeting spaces seat up to 350 guests.

PRICES: WHAT'S THIS GOING TO COST?

Ceremony Fee: $1,200/event and up
 • The fee is for a ceremony in The Courtyard.

Package Prices: $55–95/person
 • Packages include the meal; alcohol is additional. A cash bar is $125 (plus tax) per bar or you may host in accordance with your budget.

Service Charge or Gratuity: 21%

AVAILABILITY: Year-round, daily, 10am–3:30pm and 6pm–midnight.

SERVICES/AMENITIES:

Catering: in-house, ethnic caterers are allowed on Friday and Sunday
Kitchen Facilities: fully equipped
Tables & Chairs: provided
Linens, Silver, etc.: provided, extra fee may apply
Restrooms: wheelchair accessible
Dance Floor: portable provided
Dressing Areas: CBA
AV/Meeting Equipment: provided, extra fee may apply

Parking: large complimentary lot
Accommodations: 226 guest rooms
Outdoor Night Lighting: market lights, streetlamps, bistro lights, and sconces
Outdoor Cooking Facilities: no
Cleanup: provided
View: fountain, garden, landscaped grounds, pool area; a beautiful marina filled with colorful boats and yachts

RESTRICTIONS:

Alcohol: in-house
Smoking: designated areas only
Music: amplified OK with restrictions

Wheelchair Access: yes
Insurance: not required

Want to know WHAT TO ASK a potential location or vendor? Check out our Questions to Ask starting on page 21.

Michael's Tuscany Room

470 West 7th Street, San Pedro
310/519-7100
www.michaelstuscanyroom.com
michaeltuscanyroom@att.net

Special Event Venue

● Rehearsal Dinners	● Corporate Events
● Ceremonies	● Meetings
● Wedding Receptions	● Film Shoots
● Private Parties	Accommodations

Exciting things are happening in San Pedro these days. Thanks to a spruced up waterfront and a resurgent downtown, locals and tourists alike are flocking to this vibrant area where the First Thursday art walk brings a party atmosphere to the newly created cultural district. Right in the midst of this dynamic neighborhood, supporting unique mom-and-pop stores as well as hip art galleries, is Michael's Tuscany Room, a beautiful and very romantic wedding and event venue.

Wrought-iron gates and slender trees adorn the outside of the building, where three sets of French doors are topped with magnificent stained-glass windows. Step inside and you feel like you've been transported to an upscale, yet rustic, country home somewhere in Tuscany.

As you take in this soaring, 30-foot-high space, your eye is drawn up to the open-beamed ceiling with its pyramid-shaped skylights and mix of ornate Old World chandeliers. Once one of Mr. Cutri's warehouses, the room has been lovingly refashioned to capture the charms of his homeland. The walls are sandblasted weathered brick, punctuated with rows of French doors in a rich dark wood. There's a decorative balcony that runs the length of both sides of the room, creating the illusion of being in an outdoor courtyard. Faux windows and flower boxes brim with colorful blooms, and the fancy wrought-iron railing is laced with green, cascading vines.

Near the back of the room is a gracious, curving staircase that leads up to the mezzanine. Entwined with mini lights, it's perfect for the bride making her grand entrance for a ceremony at the base of the stairs.

Afterwards, guests mingle on the main floor and up on the mezzanine, as they raise a glass of bubbly and toast to *amore*. Dinner is served at tables set around the central dance floor. The mezzanine, which is decorated with a bucolic countryside mural and fireplace, can also be used for additional guest seating, your band/DJ, or as a photo booth area

As captivating as this place is, it's not just a feast for the eyes. With an owner whose first love was the culinary arts (which he studied in Tuscany), you'd expect a lot of care to go into the cuisine and you won't be disappointed. A truly mouth-watering array of dishes—most with an Italian influence—is offered, but menus can also be customized for your particular event and budget.

CEREMONY CAPACITY: The site holds 150 indoors for a non-traditional yet lovely ceremony with guests seated at their table.

EVENT/RECEPTION CAPACITY: The facility can accommodate 250 seated or 300 standing guests indoors.

MEETING CAPACITY: Meetings of up to 150 can take place Monday–Thursday. There is a food minimum; please contact the venue for details.

PRICES: WHAT'S THIS GOING TO COST?

Rental Fee:
• A $300 rental fee is required only if the time reserved exceeds the standard hours.

Package Prices: *$32/person and up*
• Luncheon wedding packages start at $32/person and dinner packages start at $42/person.

Service Charge or Gratuity: *20%*

AVAILABILITY: Year-round. Lunch: 11am–3pm, daily; Dinner: Sunday–Thursday, 5–10pm and Friday–Saturday 6–11pm. Additional hours can be arranged; rental fee will apply.

SERVICES/AMENITIES:

Catering: in-house
Kitchen Facilities: n/a
Tables & Chairs: provided
Linens, Silver, etc.: provided
Restrooms: wheelchair accessible
Dance Floor: provided
Bride's Dressing Area: CBA
AV/Meeting Equipment: BYO

Parking: large lot, on street
Accommodations: no guest rooms
Outdoor Night Lighting: access only
Outdoor Cooking Facilities: no
Cleanup: provided
View: no
Other: in-house event coordination assistance

RESTRICTIONS:

Alcohol: beer and liquor in-house, or BYO wine or champagne with corkage fee
Smoking: outdoors only
Music: amplified OK with restrictions

Wheelchair Access: yes
Insurance: not required

Torrance Cultural Arts Center

Arts Center

3330 Civic Center Drive, Torrance
310/781-7150
www.arts.torranceca.gov
tcac@torranceca.gov

● Rehearsal Dinners	● Corporate Events
● Ceremonies	● Meetings
● Wedding Receptions	● Film Shoots
● Private Parties	Accommodations

Since its 1991 inauguration, the Torrance Cultural Arts Center has become a mecca for all types of events, including thousands of bridal showers, wedding receptions, parties and dinners. With its many different event venues, this unique complex easily sparks the imagination of many a bride or event planner. The spacious facilities spread out in a series of lofty buildings joined together by open spaces, such as a sweeping entry plaza, a large courtyard and a serene Japanese Garden.

The most popular reception room is the Toyota Meeting Hall. This room has high ceilings and a bright foyer for pre-dinner gatherings. An entire wall of glass doors opens onto the Torino Festival Plaza, an inner courtyard that accommodates tented seating or simply affords diners a place to mingle in the fresh air. A fully equipped professional kitchen is accessible to any licensed caterer.

The Ken Miller Recreation Center offers two event spaces with a shared kitchen connected by an open lobby. The Auditorium benefits from lots of natural light, and its stage will accommodate a DJ or small band with ease. The adjoining Assembly Room features hardwood floors and track lighting.

Couples getting married here often like to have their ceremony in the natural environment of the Pine Wind Japanese Garden, which contains two waterfalls, a small stream and a pond. As you enter this diminutive world (it holds approximately 60 people), you're greeted by the sound of rushing water. The wide modern fountain by the entrance releases a continuous sheet of falling water; the more romantic rock-lined waterfall in the garden's center serves as a beautiful backdrop for a ceremony or formal photo shoot. Guests may sit on redwood risers in the small amphitheater, or stand above the garden on an overlooking walkway. Afterward, they'll enjoy wandering along a circular pathway of stepping stones leading through a landscape of dainty bonsai, maple trees and bamboo.

Adjacent to the garden, the Garden Room provides a more intimate space for a bridal shower, or preparation for a wedding party holding their ceremony at the center. A custom wall divider and two separate entrances allow flexibility in the room setup, and guests will appreciate the view of the Pine Wind Japanese Garden through large picture windows.

With an easy, accessible location, free parking, competitive rental rates, and a professional staff, the Torrance Cultural Arts Center promises to make your event a success.

CEREMONY CAPACITY: The Pine Wind Japanese Garden holds 60 seated guests, the Toyota Meeting Hall 300 seated, and the outdoor Torino Festival Plaza 530 seated.

EVENT/RECEPTION CAPACITY: Indoors, the center accommodates up to 300 seated or 350 standing; outdoors, up to 300 seated or 600 standing.

MEETING CAPACITY: Indoor facilities can seat up to 502 guests theater-style, and 100 conference-style or classroom-style.

PRICES: WHAT'S THIS GOING TO COST?

Rental Fee
- The rental fee varies depending on the space reserved and event duration.
- The rate for weddings is $81–205/hour. Setup and staff charges are additional.

Additional Info: For events where alcohol is served, 2 Torrance police officers are required at an additional hourly fee, as is an additional $500 deposit and alcohol insurance. Liability insurance is required for all events.

AVAILABILITY: Year-round, daily, until midnight.

SERVICES/AMENITIES:

Catering: Toyota Meeting Hall requires licensed caterer; BYO for Ken Miller Recreation Center

Kitchen Facilities: 2 available

Tables & Chairs: provided

Linens, Silver, etc.: caterer or renter

Restrooms: wheelchair accessible

Dance Floor: varies per space

Bride's & Groom's Dressing Areas: CBA

AV/Meeting Equipment: full range

Parking: large complimentary lot

Accommodations: no guest rooms

Outdoor Night Lighting: some, call for details

Outdoor Cooking Facilities: through caterer

Cleanup: caterer and renter

View: Torino Festival Plaza and Pine Wind Japanese Garden

Other: grand piano, PA system, video projector, free WiFi

RESTRICTIONS:

Alcohol: BYO BWC only; licensed and insured server required

Smoking: outside only

Music: amplified OK

Wheelchair Access: yes

Insurance: liability required

Other: no birdseed, rice, glitter, confetti, or open flames

Orange County

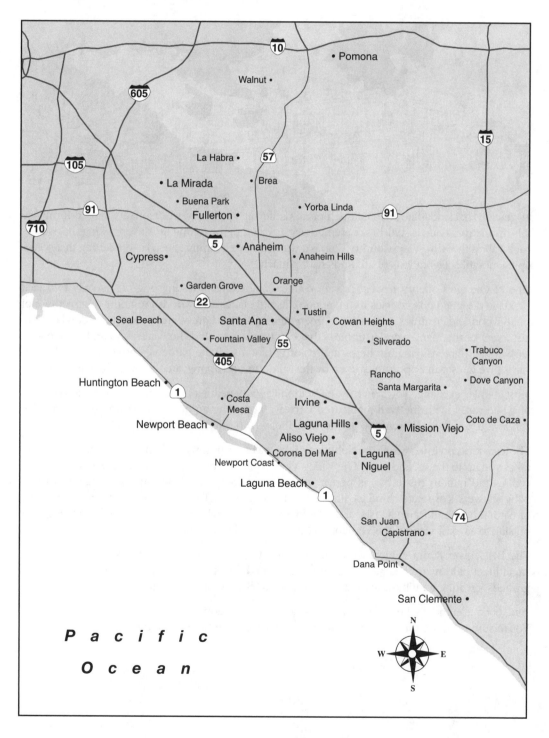

Aliso Viejo Country Club

Country Club

33 Santa Barbara, Aliso Viejo
949/609-3305
www.alisogolf.com
Kira.Columna@clubcorp.com

● Rehearsal Dinners	● Corporate Events
● Ceremonies	● Meetings
● Wedding Receptions	● Film Shoots
● Private Parties	Accommodations

Its gracious hacienda-like architecture hints at California's past, but in personality and performance this distinctive venue is stylishly contemporary. Located in the rolling hills overlooking the Saddleback Valley, the Aliso Viejo Country Club is a warm and welcoming special event setting that serves up memorable celebrations of all kinds with panache.

One of Orange County's newest private country clubs (and boasting one of the only two Jack Nicklaus-designed golf courses in the region), its little lakes and woods are home to a plethora of small woodland creatures. Kingfishers, green herons, snowy egrets, and western meadowlarks are just a few of the many wonderful birds that can be seen around the waterways and well-tended fairways and greens. Fragrant herbs and colorful blooms fill the gardens, and terraces and courtyards give guests an opportunity to enjoy the outdoors and appreciate the beautiful surroundings.

Most couples exchange vows on the Celebration Lawn beneath a handsome arbor framed by beds of white roses, with the well-manicured fairways providing an applause-worthy backdrop. You can also upgrade to a ceremony on the 10th Tee, which offers a lake view.

The festivities continues inside the clubhouse, where a handsome wrought-iron staircase (or elevator) takes you up to the second floor. The Valley View Dining Room, designed with a vaulted, beamed ceiling and built-in rustic bar, is perfect for a wide variety of receptions: weddings, brunches, baby showers, corporate shindigs, and anniversary dinners. Two walls of windows let in plenty of natural light and frame a vista of the Saddleback Valley, while a pair of balconies invite guests outside to savor a view of the verdant golf course and distant mountains.

The Bell Tower Room, which serves as an elegant lounge, has French doors that open onto a small Juliet balcony in the clubhouse tower. Its arched, brick window openings look out over the grounds, creating an ultra-romantic frame for photos of the bride and groom.

And, of course, there's the golf course itself—a stunning location for those joyful wedding pictures. You're sure to be wearing big smiles because your wedding here is the best. one. ever.

CEREMONY & EVENT/RECEPTION CAPACITY: The facility accommodates 180 seated or 250 standing guests indoors or outdoors.

MEETING CAPACITY: Meeting spaces seat 200 indoors.

PRICES: WHAT'S THIS GOING TO COST?

Packages: $74/person and up
- Packages include 6 hours of event time, ceremony (on the Celebration Lawn) and reception, setup and breakdown, and more. Tax and service charge are additional.
- There is a $1,500 fee for a ceremony upgrade on the 10th Tee.

Service Charge: 21%

AVAILABILITY: Year-round, daily, 6am–midnight.

SERVICES/AMENITIES:

Catering: in-house
Kitchen Facilities: n/a
Tables & Chairs: provided
Linens, Silver, etc.: provided
Restrooms: wheelchair accessible
Dance Floor: provided
Bride's Dressing Area: yes
AV/Meeting Equipment: CBA

Parking: large complimentary lot
Accommodations: no guest rooms
Outdoor Night Lighting: CBA
Outdoor Cooking Facilities: BBQ CBA
Cleanup: provided
View: cityscape, courtyard, fairways, hills, mountains, landscaped grounds
Other: event coordination

RESTRICTIONS:

Alcohol: in-house
Smoking: designated areas only
Music: amplified OK with restrictions

Wheelchair Access: yes
Insurance: not required

THE RANCH Events Center

1025 East Ball Road, Anaheim

714/817-4207

theranch.com/events-center/weddings
sales@theranch.com

- Rehearsal Dinners
- Ceremonies
- Wedding Receptions
- Private Parties
- Corporate Events
- Meetings
- Film Shoots
- Accommodations

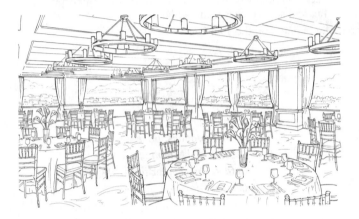

A little bit country and quite a bit uptown-chic, this private events center is unlike anything else you'll find in or around Orange County. Occupying the entire top floor of the glossy Extron Electronics building, it's the sister venue to the award-winning THE RANCH Restaurant & Saloon (located just downstairs on the ground floor), and was purposely designed to host one-of-a-kind celebrations.

You'll start your big day in The Suites, two adjoining dressing spaces that boast luxe furniture, private changing rooms, and lounge areas. Natural light streams in through oversized windows (your photographer will appreciate this!), and gilded crystal chandeliers add more than a hint of glamour. Once your final touches have been made and you've taken a last glance in the full-length mirror, it's showtime.

The Hospitality Suite is a popular choice for ceremonies, with its warm-toned wood walls, crackling fireplace, and huge windows that look out across the city. An attached terrace can serve as an airy spot for welcome or post-ceremony cocktails. You might also opt for an exclusive, supper-club feel in The Dining Room, where built-in alder wood cabinetry displays some of THE RANCH'S finely curated wine collection. Both of these spaces, plus several other charming, smaller private rooms, are also available for intimate receptions.

After your vows, greet guests and sip cocktails in the spacious prefunction area before moving into The Great Room, the gorgeous main reception hall. With its classic cream-and-taupe palette, it complements a broad range of décor. Wraparound windows let everyone take in panoramic views that include the city, as well as the lush green hills of north county and the San Gabriel Mountains. At around 9:30pm, you and your guests are in for a special treat: a bird's-eye-front row seat to Disneyland Resort's spectacular fireworks.

Executive Chef Michael Rossi is renowned across the southland for his work at THE RANCH Events Center. Together with his brother, accomplished pastry chef David Rossi, they'll create a menu that's sure to delight, with seasonally driven fare inspired by the restaurant's own local farm. Chef Rossi is also a certified sommelier, so you're guaranteed a perfect wine pairing with each offering.

If the party's wrapping up but you're not quite done celebrating, just hop into the elevator and head down to the Saloon. Here, you can sidle up to the 47-foot Longhorn Bar for a local beer or handcrafted cocktail, then hit the sunken dance floor and two-step the night away to live country music bands and DJs. Yee-haw!

CEREMONY CAPACITY: The venue can seat up to 180 indoors.

EVENT/RECEPTION CAPACITY: The facility accommodates 220 seated or 350 standing guests indoors.

MEETING CAPACITY: Meeting spaces seat 264 guests indoors.

PRICES: WHAT'S THIS GOING TO COST?

Ceremony Fee: *$1,500/event and up*
  • The ceremony fee varies depending on the package chosen.

Food & Beverage Minimum: *$5,000/event and up*
  • The food & beverage minimum varies depending on the space reserved.

Meals (when priced separately): *$80–165/person*

Service Charge or Gratuity: *21%*

AVAILABILITY: Year-round: weekdays after 4pm, weekends 10am–2am.

SERVICES/AMENITIES:

Catering: in-house
Kitchen Facilities: n/a
Tables & Chairs: provided
Linens, Silver, etc.: provided
Restrooms: wheelchair accessible
Dance Floor: yes, extra fee may apply
Dressing Areas: yes
AV/Meeting Equipment: yes, extra fee may apply

Parking: large lot, valet available
Accommodations: no guest rooms
Outdoor Night Lighting: CBA
Outdoor Cooking Facilities: no
Cleanup: provided
View: garden/patio; 6th-floor city panorama including landscaped grounds, Disneyland fireworks, and mountains
Other: event coordination

RESTRICTIONS:

Alcohol: in-house
Smoking: outside only
Music: amplified OK indoors

Wheelchair Access: yes
Insurance: not required

The wedding vendors on our website are the best in the business. How do we know? Read page 425.

Brea Community Center

695 East Madison Way, Brea
714/990-7140
www.breafacilities.com
tiannan@ci.brea.ca.us

● Rehearsal Dinners	● Corporate Events
● Ceremonies	● Meetings
● Wedding Receptions	Film Shoots
● Private Parties	Accommodations

Tucked in the northeast corner of Orange County, the town of Brea is an attractive option for out-of-town visitors: It's just a quick jaunt from both LAX and John Wayne airports, and offers easy access to beaches, shopping, entertainment, and amusement parks. Brea Community Center is the jewel of this close-knit community—beautiful, affordable, and convenient, it checks all of the most essential boxes. And once you add in the kind and conscientious staff, you've got a party-planning combo that's tough to beat.

The Arts Garden plays host to lovely outdoor ceremonies, and it's absolutely fantastic. Completely secluded from public access, it's got a private, "secret garden" feel, with winding pathways, lush landscaping, and an elevated gazebo topped with graceful shade sails. Following your vows, you'll move to your cocktail hour into the bright, cheerful Art Studio, where a wall of windows overlooks the Garden and fills the room with natural light.

While you're toasting the occasion and mingling with your guests, the Community Center's staff will be transforming the Arts Garden into an open-air celebration space, where you can dine and dance beneath twinkling market lights in your own urban oasis. Don't forget to snap a photo (or three, or four) in front of the gorgeous vine wall—it's totally unique and definitely share-worthy.

Indoor weddings are held in the Community Hall, which boasts blonde hardwood flooring, cool, modern light fixtures hung from the recessed ceiling, and a wall of glass doors that open onto a private landscaped patio. The room can be divided into smaller sections to accommodate intimate events, and the spacious, terraced prefunction area is a wonderful spot for welcome cocktails. You'll also find all the necessary event essentials, including a large catering kitchen, free WiFi, and state-of-the-art audiovisual equipment.

Expecting to have little ones in attendance? You can make this an extra-special day for them, too! Just a few doors down from the Community Hall is the KidWatch Room, a wonderful childcare area stocked with toys, games, kid-friendly DVDs, and an outdoor playground. If you opt to take advantage of this awesome perk, your rental contract will include trained, caring staff for the duration of your event. The teens on your guest list won't be left out either—set them up in The Zone, a super-cool, supervised spot decked out with board games, five web-accessible PCs, a pool table, an enclosed outdoor patio, and a big-screen TV hooked up to three different video game systems. Wow—a place that makes both parents *and* kids happy? Score!

CEREMONY CAPACITY: The venue can seat up to 300 outdoors.

EVENT/RECEPTION CAPACITY: The facility accommodates 320 seated or 450 standing guests indoors and 180 seated or 300 standing outdoors.

MEETING CAPACITY: Meeting spaces seat 450 guests.

PRICES: WHAT'S THIS GOING TO COST?

Rental Fee: *$139–$332/hour*
- The rental fee varies depending on the space reserved and type of event.
- The fee includes tables, chairs, event staff, and free parking.

AVAILABILITY: Year-round, daily, 9am–12am.

SERVICES/AMENITIES:

Catering: BYO
Kitchen Facilities: fully equipped
Tables & Chairs: provided
Linens, Silver, etc.: BYO
Restrooms: wheelchair accessible
Dance Floor: BYO
Dressing Areas: yes
AV/Meeting Equipment: yes, extra fee may apply

Parking: large lot
Accommodations: no guest rooms
Outdoor Night Lighting: provided
Outdoor Cooking Facilities: BBQ CBA
Cleanup: renter
View: garden patio/courtyard

RESTRICTIONS:

Alcohol: BYO
Smoking: designated areas only
Music: amplified OK

Wheelchair Access: yes
Insurance: required

Los Coyotes Country Club

Country Club

8888 Los Coyotes Drive, Buena Park

714/994-7750

www.countryclubreceptions.com
eventdirector@loscoyotescc.com

● Rehearsal Dinners	● Corporate Events
● Ceremonies	● Meetings
● Wedding Receptions	Film Shoots
● Private Parties	Accommodations

The two things people ooh and aah the most about at Los Coyotes Country Club are the food and the facility's good looks. The Executive Chef, along with his culinary team, has given this site a reputation for consistently serving gourmet meals. And the club's Mission-style architecture—with its tiled roofs, arched colonnades and beautiful vantage atop a small hill—is a bragging point among regulars.

But there's a third thing to tout here, and it may be just as important as the other two: the view. It's particularly striking from the grand flagstone-paved terrace along one side of the clubhouse. Here, you look out over a putting green and beyond toward three long verdant fairways, each separated from the others by lines of mature trees. And while you're gazing off at those fairways—even though you know there are millions of people and all the trappings of modern civilization within a few miles of where you stand—you'd swear the green earth goes on forever. The sense of being away from the Southland's pressure-cooker environment is both palpable and soothing.

The terrace, part of which is shaded under an archway, adjoins a spacious ballroom featuring an 18-foot-high ceiling, six-lamp chandeliers, and beautiful wall sconces. The terrace-facing side of the ballroom, as well as another side that looks out onto a small manmade lake, are lined with picture windows and French doors. The room can be divided into three sections, but most couples decide to reserve the entire space. They love this ballroom's drama—it looks impressive (because of its height) and inviting (thanks to its big, sun-loving windows) at the same time.

Los Coyotes' lush setting inspires many al fresco ceremonies and offers two options for exchanging vows: The Lakeside Ceremony Site, bordered by a tranquil lake on one side and a large putting green on another, provides the quintessential golf course experience. The Terrace affords the convenience of saying "I do" and then stepping right into the ballroom for the reception. During those rare times when the weather is inclement, or for smaller parties seeking an indoor setting, the Cypress Palm Room, with its French door-framed view of the lake, is popular.

Located down the hall from the ballroom, the bride's dressing room is a posh extension of Los Coyotes' stylish décor. It's nicely appointed with an oversized oak-trimmed vanity mirror, a sink, a large closet and a wall mirror.

Even the drive up to Los Coyotes has appealing touches: The curving road sweeps through a well-landscaped neighborhood of large ranch-style houses, and the tall palms along the median strip evoke an almost resort-like feel. When you reach the club, the banquet room's dramatic porte-cochère entrance only reinforces that feeling of refinement. Ah, if a day can unfold so agreeably just getting to Los Coyotes, you can be confident it will continue that way long after you've arrived.

CEREMONY CAPACITY: The Lakeside site and the Terrace hold up to 300 seated guests. Indoors, the Cypress Palm Room seats up to 150.

EVENT/RECEPTION & MEETING CAPACITY: The Ballroom holds 350 seated with a dance floor or 500 standing guests. Outdoors, the Terrace accommodates up to 150 seated or 400 standing.

PRICES: WHAT'S THIS GOING TO COST?

Package Prices: $78/person and up
  • Pricing varies based on food, beverage, and rental inclusions. Food & beverage minimums will apply. Menus and packages can be customized to fit your needs and budget. Pricing does not include additional site fees, mandatory service charge, gratuity, and current sales tax.

AVAILABILITY: Year-round, daily.

SERVICES/AMENITIES:

Catering: in-house
Kitchen Facilities: n/a
Tables & Chairs: provided
Linens, Silver, etc.: provided
Restrooms: wheelchair accessible
Dance Floor: provided
Bride's Dressing Area: yes
AV/Meeting Equipment: CBA

Parking: large lot, valet required for over 70 guests
Accommodations: no guest rooms
Outdoor Night Lighting: yes
Outdoor Cooking Facilities: CBA
Cleanup: provided
View: fairways, trees, lake

RESTRICTIONS:

Alcohol: in-house
Smoking: outdoors only
Music: amplified OK

Wheelchair Access: yes
Insurance: not required
Other: no open flames or confetti, no affixing anything to the walls or ceiling

Five Crowns Restaurant

Restaurant & Garden

3801 East Coast Highway, Corona del Mar
949/760-1115 or 949/760-0331

www.lawrysonline.com/five-crowns
arobbins@lawrysonline.com

- Rehearsal Dinners
- Ceremonies
- Wedding Receptions
- Private Parties
- Corporate Events
- Meetings
- Film Shoots
- Accommodations

If you're familiar with Orange County's fine dining scene, chances are you've heard of Five Crowns. Established in 1965 in upscale Corona del Mar—one of Southern California's most idyllic coastal villages—the Tudor-style culinary landmark is a recreation of England's oldest country inn, Ye Olde Bell (est. 1135 A.D.). In this pocket of seaside affluence, it's also an icon of patrician respectability, award-winning cuisine, and premier vintages, owned by the Frank and Van De Kamp families of Lawry's Restaurants fame.

Known for serving up some of the best prime rib in town, as well as contemporary renditions of fresh seafood, roasted fowl, and succulent lamb, Five Crowns has hosted legions of discriminating local diners and such illustrious guests as Elizabeth Taylor and past President Richard Nixon.

What you may not know is that this revered dining establishment is also a classic setting for weddings, receptions, rehearsal dinners and other singular celebrations. With its rich wood paneling, ceiling beams, antique maritime memorabilia and cozy nooks, the venue exudes an Old World ambiance.

The most popular area for saying your vows in this historic site is the patio and garden, off the restaurant's sunlit greenhouse. A traditional trellis, adorned with flowers and herbs, lends just the right amount of formality to the intimate setting.

Depending on the size of your party, guests will enjoy pre- and post-ceremony hospitality in the greenhouse and brick-lined patio, the main Crown Nelson Room, or The Brighton Room, named for the pleasure palace George IV of England built in 1782. In all of these areas, service is provided by a friendly and very professional staff. Many couples opt to capture memories of the day at the front entrance of the restaurant, where an antique red British telephone booth is a recognizable landmark on the East Coast Highway.

Before and after the merrymaking, out-of-town guests can enjoy accommodations in many four- and five-star hotels along the coast, or at the newly restored Crystal Cove Cottages, just a mile down the road in the Crystal Cove State Park Historic District. You might consider a post-celebration treat of your own: a romantic moonlit walk with your new spouse along this stretch of pristine coastline.

CEREMONY CAPACITY: The capacity varies depending on the time of day and space reserved. For ceremonies, the venue can accommodate up to 150 seated guests.

EVENT/RECEPTION CAPACITY: The main event space seats 150. With a buyout, the restaurant accommodates 200 seated or standing.

MEETING CAPACITY: The restaurant holds 150 seated guests.

PRICES: WHAT'S THIS GOING TO COST?

Packages: $2,000/event and up
- The ceremony-only package includes setup of ceremony tables, up to 50 ceremony chairs, and use of the space for 4 hours max (including load-in and load-out).

Food & Beverage Minimum: $500/event and up
- The food & beverage minimum varies depending on the time of day, space reserved, and guest count.

Meals (when priced separately): $40–88/person
- Kids meals are $34/child (12 years old or younger).

Additional Info: There is no ceremony fee when a reception is booked to follow. Prices are subject to a 2% service charge, 7.75% Sales tax, and server gratuity.

AVAILABILITY: Year-round, daily, anytime.

SERVICES/AMENITIES:

Catering: in-house
Kitchen Facilities: n/a
Tables & Chairs: provided
Linens, Silver, etc.: provided
Restrooms: wheelchair accessible
Dance Floor: CBA
Bride's & Groom's Dressing Area: yes
AV/Meeting Equipment: CBA

Parking: valet required
Accommodations: no guest rooms
Outdoor Night Lighting: provided
Outdoor Cooking Facilities: no
Cleanup: provided
View: garden courtyard
Other: event coordination

RESTRICTIONS:

Alcohol: in-house
Smoking: not allowed
Music: amplified OK with restrictions

Wheelchair Access: yes
Insurance: not required

Center Club Orange County

Private Club

650 Town Center Drive, Costa Mesa
714/438-3860 Catering
www.center-club.com
chris.hartley@clubcorp.com

● Rehearsal Dinners	● Corporate Events
● Ceremonies	● Meetings
● Wedding Receptions	● Film Shoots
● Private Parties	Accommodations

If you want your wedding or special event to take center stage, then definitely consider the Center Club Orange County. Talk about centrally located! This prestigious member of the Club-Corp family is located in the center of Orange County, in the center of South Coast Metro at the base of the award-winning Center Tower adjacent to the glamorous Segerstrom Center for the Arts. Occupying the garden level of a performing arts complex, the swank business club has been an in-demand event site for more than 30 years, and it's now going to attract even more fans thanks to its brand new look.

A recent $3.1 million renovation has taken the Center Club from elegantly traditional to magnificently contemporary. Grand social and professional affairs will be right at home here, in a place that's chic, sophisticated and ultra-upscale.

From the moment you step into the pleasingly posh lobby, you'll be swept away by an arts-inspired setting. Waltz down the lustrous, handsomely appointed hall—there's a musical score subtly worked into its walls—toward the Symphony Ballroom. No ordinary rectangular box, this stunning space has an architectural splendor that allows for intimacy without sacrificing scale. That "far corner of the room" syndrome does not exist here. Three adjoining chambers create the ballroom's dynamic arrowhead shape, and when they're all used together they offer sightlines from the central "prow" that make the whole room visible and enticingly accessible in spite of its lavish dimensions. In addition, the three chambers can function independently as the Mozart, Chopin and Beethoven Rooms—each totally alluring in its own right.

The Chopin Room, for example, has a spacious outdoor terrace that's perfect for ceremonies or cocktails. It features sculptural details like the "green wall" planted with ferns, the Four Lines Oblique Gyratory-Square IV structure by George Rickey, and towering eucalyptus trees for a look that's sleek and streamlined, yet serene. The Mozart and Beethoven Rooms, like the Chopin, have floor-to-ceiling windows, although these look out onto a palatial water garden (designed by leading Modernist movement landscape architect, Peter Walker) that radiates tranquility and a grand museum feel. All three rooms are decorated in tasteful shades of pewter, bronze and dove-gray that allow their beautiful bones—high ceilings, crown moldings and impressive soffits—to shine. Nothing has been overlooked—even the furnishings are works of art, sculpted and finished to echo and enhance a design perspective that bespeaks luxury and taste.

Of course, as you'd expect from a world-class event venue like this one, a variety of other options is also available for your partying pleasure: The traditional Zen, and high-tech Earth, Wind, and

Fire rooms provide private boardroom and dining opportunities. If more space is required, the sumptuous Encore Lounge with its clubby leather and hardwood accents; the VIP Lounge; and a spectacular Founders Room further expand your choices. Top it off with Center Club Orange County's impeccable service, culinary expertise and unparalleled farm-to-table cuisine, and you'll have a recipe for a smashing success.

CEREMONY CAPACITY: The Mozart Room seats 130 guests, and the Symphony Ballroom Patio seats 200.

EVENT/RECEPTION & MEETING CAPACITY: The Symphony Ballroom holds 250 seated or 350 standing, the Beethoven Room 130 seated or 200 standing, the Mozart Room 60 seated or 100 standing, and the Chopin Room 20 seated or 30 standing.

PRICES: WHAT'S THIS GOING TO COST?

Ceremony Fee: $1,200/event
• The ceremony fee covers covers setup, chairs, runner, rehearsal, and sound system.

Package Prices: $100/person and up
• Package prices vary depending on the day of week.
• All wedding packages include valet parking, service charge, and sales tax. Saturday packages start at $130/person.

Additional Info: Food & beverage minimums apply.

AVAILABILITY: Year-round, daily, 7am–2am in 5-hour blocks. Additional hours are available for a fee.

SERVICES/AMENITIES:

Catering: in-house or BYO
Kitchen Facilities: prep access
Tables & Chairs: provided
Linens, Silver, etc.: provided
Restrooms: wheelchair accessible
Dance Floor: provided, extra charge
Bride's & Groom's Dressing Areas: yes
AV/Meeting Equipment: yes

Parking: valet included in packages
Accommodations: no guest rooms
Outdoor Night Lighting: yes
Outdoor Cooking Facilities: n/a
Cleanup: provided
View: water and sculpture gardens
Other: chocolate fountain, ice sculptures

RESTRICTIONS:

Alcohol: in-house, no BYO
Smoking: outside only
Music: amplified OK

Wheelchair Access: yes
Insurance: not required

Want to find more venues and services? Check out our informative website, www.HereComesTheGuide.com.

223

Chart House Dana Point

Waterfront Restaurant

34442 Green Lantern Street, Dana Point
949/493-1183
www.chart-house.com/locations/dana-point
mmcquillan@ldry.com

● Rehearsal Dinners	● Corporate Events
● Ceremonies	● Meetings
● Wedding Receptions	● Film Shoots
● Private Parties	Accommodations

If ever there was a "Wait, there's more!" venue in Here Comes The Guide, Dana Point's Chart House has to be one of them. Start with the restaurant's show-stopping vista, a sensational hillside view of Dana Point Harbor, its long breakwater and the Pacific beyond. High palisades rise to the east, topped with luxurious homes, then drop down to an inviting, leafy shoreside park. Boats of all kinds are constantly arriving and departing, and two sleek twin-masted sailing ships moor at the bottom of the hill. This is easily one of the best sea views in Orange County. So naturally the long, carefully manicured ceremony lawn that overlooks it is one of the most dramatic wedding sites in all of the Southland.

With a panorama this incredible, it would be a shame to limit the lawn to ceremonies. Fortunately, it doubles as a spot for "California luau" dinners, which feature tiki torches and buffet food. News about the appealingly informal parties has gotten around—some nearby upscale resorts often send wedding parties here for their rehearsal dinners. They know that casual dining overlooking a great view is just the thing to soothe pre-wedding jitters.

There's more! Chart House, a modernistic building of three interconnected circular spaces called "pods," is the design of architect Kendrick Bangs Kellogg, a student of the great Frank Lloyd Wright. Completed in the late 1970s, the building beautifully melds rough-textured concrete, redwood, steel and glass into a memorable configuration. It's very much in the style of Wright, with its creative use of curves and materials, as well as its exterior palette of rust-red wood and light blue steel.

Inside, a harmonious medley of light gray concrete, 62 miles of bent redwood formed into concentric circles on the ceilings, and seeming acres of windows create a striking interior. Almost every seat in the house has a view. All of the booths in the restaurant's three pods have plush leather cushions and backrests with subdued, but playful, abstract patterns. Pod 1 has a built-in dance floor and stage—perfect for a head table—plus the magnificent harbor view. (Delicate cornflowerblue mood lights are suspended from its coiled redwood ceiling—a sweet little touch.) Pod 2 has a grand staircase descending from the restaurant's entry tower, as well as a wine cellar and dining booths. Pod 3, which affords direct access to the patio, has a long bar and an intriguing Art Deco/1950s look.

Still more! Besides a terrific location and singular architectural style, Chart House has another great thing going for it: an experienced kitchen staff that has garnered a devoted clientele over almost three decades. That kitchen is one of the reasons why Chart House attracts dozens of daytime wedding receptions each year. Couples also like having the whole venue to themselves throughout their event.

From the road, Chart House is almost hidden. You see its signature view before you see its redwood entry tower, and you see the tower before you see the restaurant itself. That slow unfolding of delights is this place's greatest strength and its greatest charm.

CEREMONY CAPACITY: The facility accommodates 220 seated guests outdoors.

EVENT/RECEPTION & MEETING CAPACITY: The site holds 200 seated or standing guests indoors and 80 seated or standing outdoors.

PRICES: WHAT'S THIS GOING TO COST?

Ceremony Fee: $10/person

Package Prices: $750–1,500/event

Meals (when priced separately): $42–90/person
• Plated meals and buffets are available.

Additional Info: Food & beverage minimums may apply to specific times, days, and rooms.

AVAILABILITY: Year-round, daily, 11am–4pm and 5–10pm.

SERVICES/AMENITIES:

Catering: in-house, no BYO
Kitchen Facilities: n/a
Tables & Chairs: provided
Linens, Silver, etc.: provided
Restrooms: wheelchair accessible
Dance Floor: provided
Bride's & Groom's Dressing Area: no
AV/Meeting Equipment: some provided, BYO

Parking: on street or large lot, valet required
Accommodations: no guest rooms
Outdoor Night Lighting: CBA
Outdoor Cooking Facilities: no
Cleanup: provided
View: coastline, Dana Point harbor, landscaped grounds
Other: event coordination

RESTRICTIONS:

Alcohol: in-house, no BYO
Smoking: not allowed
Music: amplified OK with restrictions

Wheelchair Access: yes
Insurance: not required

Laguna Cliffs Marriott Resort & Spa

Resort & Spa

25135 Park Lantern, Dana Point
949/661-5000
www.lagunacliffs.com
weddings@lagunacliffs.com

- ● Rehearsal Dinners
- ● Ceremonies
- ● Wedding Receptions
- ● Private Parties
- ● Corporate Events
- ● Meetings
- ● Film Shoots
- ● Accommodations

Just south of Laguna Beach lies a picturesque curve of coastline with white sandy beaches and balmy breezes wafting in from the Pacific. At the tip of this idyllic cove is Dana Point, a historic headland named for 19th-century seafaring adventurer and author Richard Henry Dana, who dubbed it "California's most romantic spot."

If romantic celebrations are on your agenda, then you'll love the Laguna Cliffs Marriott, a AAA Four Diamond luxury retreat overlooking the Pacific. The upscale resort's oceanview setting, which encompasses acres of emerald-green parks, a bustling marina and the boundless blue sea, creates the perfect backdrop for weddings and receptions.

The Laguna Cliffs takes full advantage of its breathtaking location by offering three beautiful outdoor venues for wedding ceremonies. The secluded Del Mar Lawn embraces a layered view of mountains, sea, and a section of shore known as "the California Riviera." The Vue Lawn treats guests to a colorful parade of yachts and sailboats against an ocean panorama. A third enclave, the Laguna Brick, captures glorious sunsets unfurling across the watery horizon. The resort's ceremony packages include the setup of full wedding regalia—a custom floral arch or pedestal arrangements, and a rose-petal aisle.

Gala receptions are staged in one of two newly renovated ballrooms, each illuminated by novel pendant fixtures. A color palette that calls to mind the sea and sun-kissed sand, gold Chiavari chairs, and the soft flickering of votive candles contribute to an ambiance of sophisticated coastal elegance. Equally impressive is the award-winning catering that puts a new spin on California cuisine.

The resort staff takes your event as seriously as you do. A dedicated team of Wedding Professionals ensures that every detail is just the way you envision it. Wedding packages come with upgrades such as cake cutting, a luxurious bridal suite, and a "Couple's Spa Massage" to soothe any pre-wedding jitters. Speaking of spa, this one is an award-winning favorite in the O.C. and has been named by *Spa Finder* magazine "Best Spa" and "Best Spa for Romance." The Bridal Beauty Packages are fabulous, and they'll customize a skin care regimen so you look more gorgeous than ever.

You and your guests will also appreciate the newly renovated guest rooms, updated with the latest amenities. Thoughtful comforts like plush feathertop beds, duvets and spa robes encourage relaxation. With a host of on-site diversions, including a state-of-the-art fitness center, the spa and two oceanview pools, Laguna Cliffs Marriott truly is an ideal destination.

The Director of Catering Sales told us, "We strive to create a customized event experience that reflects each couple's personal vision." We think you'll agree that Laguna Cliffs is a most hospitable ambassador for the Southern California lifestyle.

CEREMONY CAPACITY: The hotel holds up to 600 seated indoors or outdoors on the lawn. Smaller spaces are also available.

EVENT/RECEPTION CAPACITY: Indoor spaces accommodate 30–600 seated or 40–900 standing. Outdoors, the site holds 250–500 seated or 350–900 standing.

MEETING CAPACITY: Several rooms seat up to 1,000 guests theater-style.

PRICES: WHAT'S THIS GOING TO COST?

Ceremony fee: $4,500 and up
- The ceremony package includes an oceanview location, fresh floral arch or 2 pedestal arrangements, aisle runner or petals, rehearsal time, two dressing rooms for the wedding couple, and a couple's spa massage at the Spa at Laguna Cliffs.

Package Prices: $140/person and up
- Packages include butler-passed hors d'oeuvres, 1-hour hosted bar, 3-course plated meal, custom-designed wedding cake, wine service throughout the meal, champagne toast, gold Chiavari chairs, and complimentary oceanview guest room for the wedding couple.

Service Charge or Gratuity: 25%

AVAILABILITY: Year-round, daily, until midnight indoors.

SERVICES/AMENITIES:

Catering: in-house or BYO with approval
Kitchen Facilities: service area
Tables & Chairs: provided
Linens, Silver, etc.: provided
Restrooms: wheelchair accessible
Dance Floor: provided
Dressing Area: yes
AV/Meeting Equipment: AV equip. provided

Parking: valet
Accommodations: 378 guest rooms
Outdoor Night Lighting: yes
Outdoor Cooking Facilities: BBQ and fire pits
Cleanup: provided
View: Pacific Ocean, Dana Point Harbor, mountains, coastline
Other: on-site wedding concierge

RESTRICTIONS:

Alcohol: in-house, or BYO wine with corkage
Smoking: outdoors only
Music: amplified OK

Wheelchair Access: yes
Insurance: not required

Dove Canyon Golf Club

Golf Club

22682 Golf Club Drive, Dove Canyon

949/858-2800 x155

www.dovecanyongc.com
svaughn@dovecanyongc.com

● Rehearsal Dinners	● Corporate Events
● Ceremonies	● Meetings
● Wedding Receptions	● Film Shoots
● Private Parties	Accommodations

If you have a very private and elegant setting in mind for your special event, the clubhouse at Dove Canyon will exceed your expectations. Its prime location—in a secluded gated community at the edge of a canyon in the hills of southern Orange County—is matched by its design, style and ambiance.

The clubhouse pays homage to the architecture of Frank Lloyd Wright in its soaring wood-beamed cathedral ceiling lit by skylights, earth-tone slate floors, rich Honduran mahogany paneling, and carved plaster columns. When you hold your special event here you have exclusive use of the entire second floor of the facility. Ceremonies are held in the sunken lounge where a floor-to-ceiling window suspends you right over the canyon, or on the picturesque outdoor terrace below.

Nestled against a wooded hillside that's tamed only by the occasional box hedge, the terrace meets a free-form pond, ringed by seasonal flowers and natural rock formations. The pond gives way to a waterfall that flows out of sight into the canyon below. The canyon vista is your backdrop—a panorama that extends as far as the eye can see. After the ceremony, you and your photographer will be whisked away in a limo golf cart for some photos in front of the waterfall, while everyone else gets to know each other over cocktails and hors d'oeuvres. Take your time—your guests will be busy enjoying the splendor of the clubhouse.

The clubhouse Lobby and adjacent Main Dining Room easily accommodate large events and also work well for intimate gatherings. Cozy sitting areas in the Lobby are flanked by double-sided fireplaces, and the sunken lounge demonstrates its versatility. Thanks to tinted glass, it stays cool even on the brightest day, making it a great spot not only for a small ceremony, but for dancing or showcasing the cake, too.

The Main Dining Room itself is a marvelously conceived space. One wall of floor-to-ceiling windows overlooks the 18th fairway and frames that gorgeous canyon view. Fireplaces blaze at both ends, and a skylight in the peaked ceiling adds more natural light. The warm feeling in the room is enhanced even further by abundant wood detailing and a plush, burgundy and brushed-gold carpet. Adjustable lighting allows you to control the mood, and with candles on the tables and fireplace mantels, romance will definitely be in the air.

Three other rooms are available for rehearsal dinners, showers or brunches. Like the rest of the facility, they benefit from the warmth of wood, natural light and terrific canyon views. In addition to a remarkably beautiful clubhouse and setting, Dove Canyon is very flexible: If none of their packages suits you, they'll customize one for you. As we said, this golf club will exceed your expectations.

CEREMONY CAPACITY: Indoors, the Sunken Lounge holds up to 250 seated. Outdoors, the Terrace seats up to 280.

EVENT/RECEPTION: The Main Dining Room accommodates 280 seated or 500 standing guests.

MEETING CAPACITY: Meeting spaces seat 250.

PRICES: WHAT'S THIS GOING TO COST?

Ceremony Fee: $2,500–4,500/event
- The ceremony fee varies depending on the day of the week and package chosen.
- The ceremony package includes: the outdoor Canyon Terrace or indoor Sunken Lounge, both with breathtaking views of the 18th fairway & lakes; white wooden garden chairs; white aisle runner; choice of ceremony backdrop (arch, pillars, or gazebo); a large bridal suite; and a scheduled ceremony rehearsal.

Package Prices: $65–200/person
- Package prices vary depending on the package chosen and include: 5 hours of event time plus an additional 30 minutes for the ceremony; professional bartender and service staff; a custom menu tasting; hors d'oeuvres; bone satin floor-length linens and coffee station; place card and standing cocktail tables with standard linens; all glassware, silverware & china; dance floor; and much more.
- Additional upgrades (Chiavari chairs, skylight draping, speciality linens, valet parking) are available.

Service Charge or Gratuity: 20%.

AVAILABILITY: Year-round. Weekdays, 6am–12:30am; weekends, 11am–4pm or 6pm–11pm. Clients can purchase additional time beyond the 5-hour block included in the packages.

SERVICES/AMENITIES:

Catering: in-house, no BYO
Kitchen Facilities: n/a
Tables & Chairs: provided
Linens, Silver, etc.: provided
Restrooms: wheelchair accessible
Dance Floor: provided
Bride's Dressing Area: yes
AV/Meeting Equipment: provided

Parking: large lot, valet optional
Accommodations: no guest rooms
Outdoor Night Lighting: yes
Outdoor Cooking Facilities: BBQ
Cleanup: provided
View: fairways, lake, hills, fountain, waterfall, canyon
Other: wedding cake, grand piano

RESTRICTIONS:

Alcohol: in-house
Smoking: outdoors only
Music: amplified OK

Wheelchair Access: yes
Insurance: liability required

Coyote Hills Golf Course

Golf Club

1440 East Bastanchury Road, Fullerton

714/672-6800 x5

www.countryclubreceptions.com
privateeventdirector@coyotehillsgc.com

● Rehearsal Dinners	● Corporate Events
● Ceremonies	● Meetings
● Wedding Receptions	● Film Shoots
● Private Parties	Accommodations

Since opening its doors in 1996, Coyote Hills Golf Course has generated considerable public interest, and it's not just the links that have attracted a following: The versatile clubhouse and lovely setting have become popular for all types of events. While fundraisers, theme parties, anniversary celebrations and golf tournaments (naturally) are frequently hosted here, weddings are definitely a specialty.

A long walkway leads to their unique ceremony site, which is custom-built and quite breathtaking. Guests take their seats beneath a wisteria-draped wooden pergola that frames a two-tiered waterfall. It's here that the couple exchanges vows, surrounded by a landscape filled with flowers, trees and an abundance of greenery. This area also lends itself to intimate events and, of course, makes a gorgeous backdrop for photos.

Receptions are held on the upper level of the clubhouse in a pair of banquet rooms that can be used individually or combined, depending on the size of the celebration. The Vista Falls Room, tastefully designed with exquisitely styled Japanese lamps and a lofty ceiling paneled in polished maple, has an elegant simplicity. Plenty of floor-to-ceiling windows take advantage of the inspiring landscape spread out below: acres of green hummocks, footbridges, sand traps, and a gently flowing creek. The room also overlooks a lake and two waterfalls. One of them, the amazing two-tiered water cascade at the ceremony site, is especially captivating at night when illuminated. Four sets of double doors open out onto a long terrace that runs the length of the room. Here, you can sit and enjoy the sunshine or sweet evening air and listen to the music of the falls.

Another benefit of the Vista Falls Room is that the clubhouse bar, located next door in the facility's restaurant, may be available for your event. Airy and inviting, the restaurant is a big octagonal space accented with tropical plants that stand out against creamy walls. Sunlight pours in through an eight-sided skylight, and large picture windows offer a panoramic view of the fairways.

If you're planning a small meeting, reception or indoor ceremony, reserve the Vista Pointe Room, separated from the Vista Falls Room by a movable airwall. Laid out in an interesting octagonal shape like the restaurant, it shares the same patio as the Vista Falls Room as well as the view of the fairways and waterfalls through plenty of windows.

During our visit, we couldn't help but notice the serene, satisfied faces of the venue's patrons, inside the clubhouse or out on the links. Hold your event at Coyote Hills Golf Course and we bet you'll acquire that look of satisfaction, too.

CEREMONY CAPACITY: The outdoor ceremony site seats up to 300 and the Vista Pointe Room seats up to 75.

EVENT/RECEPTION CAPACITY: The Vista Falls and Vista Pointe Rooms combined hold 300 seated, 275 with a dance floor.

MEETING CAPACITY: The Vista Pointe Room holds 100 seated theater-style or 70 conference-style; the Vista Falls Room seats 220 theater-style or 120 conference-style. When combined, the two rooms accommodate 400 seated theatre-style or 200 conference-style.

PRICES: WHAT'S THIS GOING TO COST?

Package Prices: $68/person and up
- Pricing varies based on food, beverage, and rental inclusions. Food & beverage minimums will apply. Menus and packages can be customized to fit your needs and budget. Pricing does not include additional site fees, mandatory service charge, gratuity, and current sales tax.

AVAILABILITY: Special events and business functions, year-round, daily, 7am–1am.

SERVICES/AMENITIES:

Catering: in-house or BYO
Kitchen Facilities: fully equipped
Tables & Chairs: provided
Linens, Silver, etc.: provided
Restrooms: wheelchair accessible
Dance Floor: provided
Bride's & Groom's Dressing Areas: yes
AV/Meeting Equipment: CBA, WiFi included

Parking: large lot
Accommodations: no guest rooms
Outdoor Night Lighting: on Terrace
Outdoor Cooking Facilities: no
Cleanup: provided
View: waterfall, lake, and golf course

RESTRICTIONS:

Alcohol: in-house
Smoking: on Terrace only
Music: amplified OK indoors

Wheelchair Access: yes
Insurance: may be required
Other: no rice, confetti, glitter, sparklers, or attached decorations

---

This is important! Tell locations you're reading HERE COMES THE GUIDE and ask if our information is still current.

Muckenthaler Mansion

Historic Mansion

1201 West Malvern, Fullerton
714/447-9190 Colette's Catering and Events
www.colettesevents.com
sara@colettesevents.com

● Rehearsal Dinners	● Corporate Events
● Ceremonies	● Meetings
● Wedding Receptions	● Film Shoots
● Private Parties	Accommodations

With its broad lawns and period architecture, Fullerton's Muckenthaler Mansion might be the backdrop for one of the fictitious revelries in an F. Scott Fitzgerald novel. On its gracious grounds a bride can easily imagine herself as the dreamy heroine from *The Great Gatsby* as she glides across the velvety green expanse atop a wooded knoll. The fantasy continues inside, where turn-of-the-century photos document life in a gentler era.

Built in 1924 as the dream home of Walter and Adella Muckenthaler, the stunning Italian Renaissance-style structure stands on nine landscaped acres overlooking a quiet residential neighborhood. In 1965, Adella and her son donated the estate to the City of Fullerton for use as a cultural center for touring art exhibits. Thus, whatever artwork is on display at the mansion contributes a unique aesthetic to special events.

Prior to tying the knot, the bride can prepare and unwind in a dressing room featuring its own private entrance and bathroom. Guests await the bride's entrance in the estate's rose garden, and they're sure to "ooh and aah" as she floats into view surrounded by a flurry of colorful blooms. She meets her husband-to-be by the gazebo set amidst a palm-fringed Italian garden.

After the ceremony, many couples serve cocktails inside the mansion, where almost every room is a gallery filled with art from around the globe. Of particular note is the octagonal solarium, warmed by light flowing in through expansive windows. Meanwhile, the wedding party poses in the mansion's foyer, where a wrought-iron spiral staircase imported from Italy makes a perfect photographic centerpiece.

The Muckenthaler has numerous enclaves for receptions. Al fresco options include: the Center Circle Courtyard, lit by necklaces of twinkling lights; the Adella and Northwest Lawns for larger parties; and the charming Palm Court for daytime events. In the evening you can fête your guests in a fancy tent, or let the starlit sky create the ambiance.

For indoor festivities guests enjoy mingling in the wooden-floored atrium with its ornate tiled fireplace. Dinner and dancing often unfold in the main gallery, where a baby grand piano is on hand for musical entertainment. When it's time to toss the bouquet the bride stands on the mansion's front porch and flings her flowers to the bridal hopefuls waiting below on the lawn.

In addition to its extraordinary setting, the two-story mansion offers exclusive catering and full bar services by *Colette's*. Known for fabulous cuisine, magnificent cakes and impeccable service, the Fullerton caterer offers complete dinner packages, customized international menus, and creative reception ideas for 20 to 1,000.

The Muckenthaler Mansion is one of North Orange County's most picturesque event venues, and a great place to "write" the first chapter of your new life together.

CEREMONY CAPACITY: The Italian Garden seats up to 240 guests and the Adella Lawn up to 400 guests. Other areas of the property can accommodate 600.

EVENT/RECEPTION CAPACITY: Indoor spaces hold up to 130 seated or 200 standing guests. Various outdoor areas hold 500 seated or 700 standing.

MEETING CAPACITY: Spaces accommodate 8–120 seated guests.

PRICES: WHAT'S THIS GOING TO COST?

Rental Fee: $1,750–4,750/event
   • The rental fee varies depending on the day of the week and guest count.

Ceremony Fee: $950/event and up

Package Prices: $73–120/person
   • Prices are for catering packages that include a wedding cake or fabulous dessert.

AVAILABILITY: Year-round, daily, 7am–10pm.

SERVICES/AMENITIES:

Catering: in-house, no BYO
Kitchen Facilities: n/a
Tables & Chairs: provided
Linens, Silver, etc.: provided
Restrooms: wheelchair accessible
Dance Floor: CBA
Bride's & Groom's Dressing Areas: yes
AV/Meeting Equipment: CBA, extra charge

Parking: large lot, valet optional
Accommodations: no guest rooms
Outdoor Night Lighting: provided
Outdoor Cooking Facilities: BBQ CBA
Cleanup: provided
View: garden, park, cityscape, landscaped grounds
Other: event coordination

RESTRICTIONS:

Alcohol: in-house
Smoking: outdoors only
Music: amplified OK

Wheelchair Access: yes
Insurance: not required
Other: no rice, confetti, or birdseed

Summit House

Restaurant

2000 East Bastanchury Road, Fullerton

714/671-3092

www.summithouseweddings.com
events@summithouse.com

● Rehearsal Dinners	● Corporate Events
● Ceremonies	● Meetings
● Wedding Receptions	● Film Shoots
● Private Parties	Accommodations

Perched on one of the highest points in North Orange County and encircled by 12 acres of Fullerton's Vista Park, the Summit House is one of the most romantic wedding locations in Southern California. No matter where you stand on the grounds, a spectacular panorama inspires you: To the north loom the San Gabriel and San Bernardino mountains; to the east are the Santa Anas; to the south and west are the Laguna Hills and the sparkling Pacific. As night falls and the lights begin twinkling in the valley below, you can easily imagine yourself adrift on a sea of stars.

Equally inspiring is the Summit House Restaurant itself. Built in the tradition of an English country manor, its classic Old World architecture has the appearance and appeal of a much older, wiser structure. Lush sycamores shade the manicured lawns and rose gardens surrounding the building, and it all creates a beautiful setting for the ceremony.

The bride and her party can spend the day preparing in the Summit House's newly completed bridal suite. When she's ready, it's just a short stroll to the wedding gazebo, decorated according to her wishes. As she and her groom exchange vows, they can look out over all their guests seated in the open-air amphitheater carved into the hillside.

After the ceremony, guests may wander around the park or sip champagne on the outside patios before they slip into the Grand Summit Ballroom for the reception. With delicate cream-colored walls, coffered ceilings and pewter chandeliers, the spacious ballroom seats a crowd comfortably. Light flows in through enormous bay windows and oversized French doors, and let's not forget the panoramic view! If your guest list requires more room, a movable wall rolls aside, giving you access to the equally attractive Queen's Room and adjoining patio.

To ensure that your big day is glitch-free, the Summit House provides both a catering and a ceremony coordinator. And what amazing food and service! No wonder this facility has such a great reputation. Truth is, the Summit House will go the whole nine yards to accommodate your wildest wish, whether you want to arrive in a roaring cavalcade of Harleys, as one couple did, or simply leave the old-fashioned way in a horse and buggy. And included in every wedding package is an invitation for the newlyweds to return on their first anniversary to celebrate the special occasion all over again and relive their magical memories, compliments of the Summit House.

CEREMONY CAPACITY: The Gazebo Amphitheater in Vista Park holds up to 250 seated or 500 standing guests.

EVENT/RECEPTION & MEETING CAPACITY: The Grand Summit Ballroom holds 250 seated, 300 with the patio, and 300 standing guests.

PRICES: WHAT'S THIS GOING TO COST?

Ceremony Fee: $850–1,200/event
- The fee includes: coordination of the wedding rehearsal and the ceremony, white wooden padded rental chairs, and post-ceremony cleanup. Use of the gazebo requires an additional $750 charge for park rental, and a refundable $150 damage deposit.

Package Prices: $97–133/person
- The price includes a meal.

Meals (when priced separately): $52–63/person
- Pricing is for dinner.

Service Charge or Gratuity: 22%

AVAILABILITY: Year-round, daily, 11am–midnight.

SERVICES/AMENITIES:

Catering: in-house, no BYO
Kitchen Facilities: n/a
Tables & Chairs: provided
Linens, Silver, etc.: provided
Restrooms: wheelchair accessible
Dance Floor: provided
Bride's Dressing Area: yes
AV/Meeting Equipment: podium with microphone, 8' screen, projector

Parking: large lot, complimentary evening valet
Accommodations: no guest rooms
Outdoor Night Lighting: yes
Outdoor Cooking Facilities: no
Cleanup: provided
View: surrounding valleys; San Gabriel, Santa Ana, and San Bernardino Mountains
Other: event coordination

RESTRICTIONS:

Alcohol: in-house, or WC corkage $25/bottle
Smoking: outside only
Music: amplified OK indoors with volume limits

Wheelchair Access: yes
Insurance: not required

Hyatt Regency Huntington Beach
Resort and Spa

Waterfront Hotel

21500 Pacific Coast Highway, Huntington Beach

714/845-4652

huntingtonbeach.regency.hyatt.com
nancy.monte-frye@hyatt.com

- Rehearsal Dinners
- Ceremonies
- Wedding Receptions
- Private Parties
- Corporate Events
- Meetings
- Film Shoots
- Accommodations

Romance abounds at the Hyatt Regency Huntington Beach Resort & Spa, where your choice of gorgeous venues ranges from perfectly manicured lawns to ballrooms with stunning coastal views. And, whether you envision a simple gathering or an elaborate formal affair, your wedding at this oceanview resort will be treated as a one-of-a-kind event.

Celebrations unfold with grace and elegance in the sumptuously appointed Conference Center, where the dramatic King Triton Fountain and porte-cochère greet guests upon arrival. The Grand Conference Lobby, with its cathedral-high ceiling and second-story balcony surround, has a sweeping inner courtyard feel. Festivities can easily begin here, or guests can proceed to any one of the property's numerous ballrooms, courtyards, and terraces. The Lighthouse Courtyard is particularly enchanting for your outdoor ceremony or event. It's a wide lawn, surrounded by stately palms, that leads from the shimmering Mermaid Fountain to the resort's fabulous white Lighthouse Tower and Bridge. The ocean view is spectacular and uninterrupted here, but that's no surprise—this is a world full of unparalleled Pacific vistas.

Coast and sea also captivate from the striking Huntington Ballroom Foyer and Terrace—a delightful spot for cocktails and hors d'oeuvres, where delicate ocean breezes and the sound of the surf drift in through the open archways. A sculpted balustrade and handsome wrought-iron sconces give it a romantically Mediterranean feel. Also opening onto the terrace is the Grand Ballroom, which accommodates up to 2,000 and has its own Grand Foyer. Both ballrooms feature beautiful design elements that reflect the resort's breezy Andalusian style, like regal columns, soaring ceilings crossed with artfully carved and scrolled beams, seashell-shaped sconces, and hand-blown glass chandeliers. The effect is an ambiance that's majestic, yet intimate, whether the rooms are divided into smaller sections or used in their splendid entirety. The Mariner's Ballroom downstairs shares the same subtle allure. Whether partitioned by gauzy draperies or open to seat 600, it feels very private, comfortable and secluded.

The Hyatt Regency Huntington Beach Resort and Spa is a venue where you can entertain on an opulent scale and still feel totally at home…it's a setting that's both luxurious and relaxed. You may get lost just exploring the grounds, checking out the ballrooms, courtyards, and galleries, but you probably won't want to leave. Fortunately you won't have to. The resort has 517 spacious guest rooms, 57 plush suites, a 20,000-square-foot spa, shops, a multitude of services, and an experienced and attentive staff. All you and your guests have to do is settle in, celebrate, unwind, and stay for as long as you like.

CEREMONY, EVENT/RECEPTION & MEETING CAPACITY: The site holds 2,000 seated or standing guests indoors, and 400 seated or standing outdoors.

PRICES: WHAT'S THIS GOING TO COST?

Rental Fee: $1,300/event and up
- The rental fee varies depending on the day of the week, time of day, time of year, space reserved, and guest count.

Package Prices: $105/person and up
- Wedding packages start at $105/person for luncheon and $138/person for dinner.

Service Charge or Gratuity: 25%

AVAILABILITY: Year-round, daily.

SERVICES/AMENITIES:

Catering: in-house or BYO
Kitchen Facilities: n/a
Tables & Chairs: provided
Linens, Silver, etc.: provided
Restrooms: wheelchair accessible
Dance Floor: portable provided
Bride's Dressing Area: yes
AV/Meeting Equipment: some provided

Parking: valet required
Accommodations: 517 guest rooms
Outdoor Night Lighting: yes
Outdoor Cooking Facilities: no
Cleanup: provided
View: fountain, garden, courtyard, landscaped grounds, coastline, ocean/bay
Other: spa services, event coordination

RESTRICTIONS:

Alcohol: in-house
Smoking: not allowed
Music: amplified OK with restrictions

Wheelchair Access: yes
Insurance: required for vendors

Kimpton Shorebreak Resort

Waterfront Resort

500 Pacific Coast Highway, Huntington Beach
714/965-4462
www.shorebreakhotel.com/huntington-beach-wedding-venues
Kyra.Rydlund@shorebreakresort.com

● Rehearsal Dinners	● Corporate Events
● Ceremonies	● Meetings
● Wedding Receptions	● Film Shoots
● Private Parties	● Accommodations

If you're looking for the coolest setting for a California coastal wedding in Orange County, you have to check out this completely reinvented venue in the heart of Surf City, USA. It delivers amazing oceanside views with an energetic Huntington Beach downtown surround and 10,000 square feet of terrific indoor/outdoor event space.

The 3,000-square-foot Epic Ballroom (divisible into thirds), its adjoining Foyer, and the adjacent Deck are all truly epic. Polished and beautifully conceived with every imaginable feature, these spaces are also FUN. The resort's new Bungalow Room and wraparound Bungalow Porch are great for parties of up to 100 guests.

As for the cuisine, their culinary team serves up a host of tasty beach-inspired hors d'oeuvres, hand-crafted cocktails, and traditional favorites with a contemporary spin, relying on locally sourced ingredients and a generous serving of "beachy good vibes".

Of course, in addition to the experience-enhancing design, the best part of staging an event in a Kimpton resort like Shorebreak is the personalized service from the warm, welcoming staff and all of the on-site amenities. And don't forget there are 157 rooms and 39 suites here so guests can easily extend their stay. With the comforting sound of waves within earshot and the enticements of Main Street, Huntington Beach at their feet, this is the ultimate destination for anyone wanting to celebrate or play in true Southern California style.

CEREMONY CAPACITY: The facility holds 150 seated guests, indoors or outdoors.

EVENT/RECEPTION & MEETING CAPACITY: The hotel can accommodate 150 seated or 200 standing guests indoors and 100 seated or 150 standing outdoors.

PRICES: WHAT'S THIS GOING TO COST?

Rental Fee: *$1,000/event and up*
- The rental fee varies depending on the space reserved and guest count.
- A discount is available for small weddings of 60 or less.

Ceremony Fee: *$1,000/event*
- A wedding coordinator is required for all on-site ceremonies.

Meals (when priced separately): *$75/person and up*

AVAILABILITY: Year-round, daily. Business functions: 8am–5pm or 6pm–11pm.

SERVICES/AMENITIES:

Catering: in-house
Kitchen Facilities: n/a
Tables & Chairs: provided
Linens, Silver, etc.: provided
Restrooms: wheelchair accessible
Dance Floor: portable provided
Bride's Dressing Area: yes
AV/Meeting Equipment: provided, extra charge

Parking: valet and self in garage, extra charge
Accommodations: 157 guest rooms
Outdoor Night Lighting: provided, extra charge
Outdoor Cooking Facilities: none
Cleanup: provided
View: cityscape, garden patio, ocean
Other: event coordination

RESTRICTIONS:

Alcohol: in-house
Smoking: not allowed
Music: amplified OK indoors with restrictions

Wheelchair Access: yes
Insurance: liability required

Overwhelmed? Use the search criteria on www.HereComesTheGuide.com to narrow down your choices.

239

Old World Event Venues and Catering

Special Event Facility

7561 Center Avenue, #49, Huntington Beach
714/893-0112
www.oldworld.ws/banquet-hall-facilities-rental-rates
banquets@oldworld.ws

- ● Rehearsal Dinners
- ● Ceremonies
- ● Wedding Receptions
- ● Private Parties
- ● Corporate Events
- ● Meetings
- ● Film Shoots
- ☐ Accommodations

Part of Old World German Restaurant, this unique private event space is nestled in Old World Village, a charming re-creation of a tiny European hamlet. Located just off 405 and less than 20 minutes from the beach, its an appealing option for both local and out-of-town guests, offering them the experience of traveling to a quaint Bavarian town—without leaving Huntington Beach! And just think of the wonderful photos you'll capture among the cobblestone streets, iron gas lamps, and tile-roofed shops whose walls are adorned with intricate, hand-painted designs.

Outdoor ceremonies take place in the spacious Garden on the steps of a sweet, white gazebo. Featuring latticework detailing, a shake-shingle roof, and a dainty cupola, it's the perfect spot to exchange vows, and it also serves as a sheltered location to showcase your cake during the reception.

If you'd like to continue the celebration outside, the Garden won't disappoint. As the ceremony area is cleared to become your al fresco dance floor, your guests can sip cocktails beneath graceful shade sails, surrounded by towering pines and native trees that are hung with string lights and lanterns for a romantic, after-sunset glow.

The super-fun Festival Hall plays host to indoor affairs. Modeled after a classic German beer hall, this rustic space was built with revelry in mind—its got two stages, shiny brick flooring, wrought-iron railings, and ample room for dancing. The walls are festooned with fanciful European signage and props, and market lights are draped across the open-raftered ceiling. A special perk: When you opt for a party in the hall, you can extend the festivities until 1am!

If you're planning a small event or rehearsal dinner, consider the Jaeger Room. This intimate, newly renovated space boasts accents of wrought iron and warm wood, and has a large attached courtyard.

You're welcome to bring in your own caterer, but before you do you'll definitely want to check out the great work done by the on-site restaurant. Though they specialize in traditional German fare (their sausages have been voted "Best in California"!), the culinary team can also create just about anything you can imagine, including Hawaiian, Italian, or Texas BBQ buffets.

Old World has its own patisserie, *Euro Bakery,* that's been an area favorite for years (they deliver off-site, too…did somebody say "cupcakes"?) and, as if you needed more reasons to love this place, it's one of the more affordable venues in this part of Orange County. We can't think of a better reason to celebrate. *Prost!*

CEREMONY CAPACITY: The facility seats 400 guests indoors or 300 outdoors.

EVENT/RECEPTION & MEETING CAPACITY: The site can accommodate 400 seated or 600 standing guests indoors and 300 seated or 500 standing outdoors.

PRICES: WHAT'S THIS GOING TO COST?

Rental Fee: $550–3,200/event

Ceremony Fee: $250/event and up

Packages: $25–100/person
  • Packages include the venue rental, food, service charge, and tax.

Food & Beverage Minimum: $500/event and up

Meals (when priced separately): $13–30/person

Service Charge or Gratuity: 18%

Additional Info: Pricing varies depending on the day of the week, time of day, time of year, guest count, space reserved, event duration, and package chosen. Security and damage deposits are extra.

AVAILABILITY: Year-round, daily, 6am–midnight.

SERVICES/AMENITIES:

Catering: in-house, BYO
Kitchen Facilities: n/a
Tables & Chairs: provided
Linens, Silver, etc.: provided
Restrooms: wheelchair accessible
Dance Floor: patio or deck
Dressing Areas: no
AV/Meeting Equipment: some provided

Parking: on street
Accommodations: no guest rooms
Outdoor Night Lighting: CBA
Outdoor Cooking Facilities: none
Cleanup: provided
View: garden patio/courtyard
Other: in-house wedding cake, event coordination (additional fee)

RESTRICTIONS:

Alcohol: in-house
Smoking: outdoors only
Music: amplified OK

Wheelchair Access: yes
Insurance: liability required

Red Horse Barn
At Huntington Central Park

18381 Goldenwest Street, Huntington Beach
949/395-2606

www.theredhorsebarn.com
redhorsebarn@hcpec.com

Equestrian Ranch & Event Location

● Rehearsal Dinners	● Corporate Events
● Ceremonies	● Meetings
● Wedding Receptions	● Film Shoots
● Private Parties	Accommodations

You don't need to be more comfortable in boots than high heels to fall head-over-heels for this very special wedding and event venue. Situated on a gentle rise at the Huntington Central Park Equestrian Center (HCPEC), The Red Horse Barn has a graceful, storybook charm that's as right for a rustic farmhouse gathering as it is for a chic Derby Day.

With its sense of seclusion and unhurried vibe, this site is definitely a breath of fresh air. The property's white paddock fences, expansive terrace, broad lawns, and meticulous landscaping lend an immediate air of sophistication to the scene. The showcase-quality, ultra-elegant 10-horse stable—complete with handsome thoroughbreds—celebrates the high-end equestrian lifestyle. It's perfect for all kinds of functions, from fancy fundraisers to company shindigs, but naturally our top choice for this location is weddings.

Bride and groom will both be well cared for here. The groom's getaway can also be used for meetings, wedding showers and private parties. It features a tastefully appointed great room and bath with polished wood floors, beamed ceilings, fireplace seating, and attractive wood, suede and natural hemp furnishings. The spacious bride's suite has the same flexibility and appealing mix of restful areas and comfortable, yet stylish, design. It strikes a somewhat more feminine note with lovely cream-colored accents and a full modern kitchen with granite countertops and a long breakfast bar. Both also have exactly the kind of porches you'd wish for: sweet, shady places just right for guests to sit back and relax with a tumbler of ice-cold lemonade or a glass of bourbon and branch.

For the wedding ceremony, we suggest tying the knot under the garden- and fountain-framed gazebo, though the back lawn is another inviting option. The capacious gazebo terrace is ideal for games, activities, and cocktail receptions, too, not to mention dining and dancing under the sun or stars. Add your own fanciful touches to customize this artfully arranged blank canvas. We like the idea of rustic décor and accessories here, but The Red Horse Barn's bright breezy spirit can easily accommodate any vision, be it vintage or glam.

Horse fanciers will also be happy knowing that the HCPEC's 25 acres are home to nearly 400 horses, numerous stables, and miles of public trails. Photo ops abound in various scenic natural environments, as well as at the picturesque but more formal event complex. Equine aficionado or not, you couldn't find a more vibrant setting. The Pacific with its myriad coastal delights is just two miles away, but you won't miss it in this pleasing equestrian enclave. We think The Red Horse Barn might just be the best-kept secret in Huntington Beach.

CEREMONY, EVENT/RECEPTION & MEETING CAPACITY: The site accommodates 20 seated or standing guests indoors and 250 seated or standing outdoors.

PRICES: WHAT'S THIS GOING TO COST?

Rental Fee: $4,500–6,000/event
  • The rental fee varies depending on the time of year and guest count.

Package Prices: $10,000/event and up
  • All-inclusive wedding packages start at $10,000 for up to 100 guests (additional guests are $90 each) and include: standard rentals, catering, hosted bar package, day-of coordination, bridal party florals, custom-designed wedding cake, and professional DJ/MC.
  • The venue rental fee and gratuities are additional.

AVAILABILITY: Year-round, daily, anytime. Call for details.

SERVICES/AMENITIES:

Catering: through caterer
Kitchen Facilities: limited
Tables & Chairs: through caterer or BYO
Linens, Silver, etc.: through caterer or BYO
Restrooms: wheelchair accessible
Dance Floor: CBA
Bride's Dressing Area: yes
AV/Meeting Equipment: BYO

Parking: garage or lot nearby
Accommodations: no guest rooms
Outdoor Night Lighting: CBA
Outdoor Cooking Facilities: BBQ CBA
Cleanup: caterer or renter
View: landscaped grounds, horse barn, equestrian center
Other: photography opportunities with horses

RESTRICTIONS:

Alcohol: select from preferred list
Smoking: designated areas only
Music: amplified OK outdoors

Wheelchair Access: yes
Insurance: required for vendors
Other: no birdseed, rice, confetti, or bubbles

SeaCliff Country Club

6501 Palm Avenue, Huntington Beach

714/536-8866

www.countryclubreceptions.com
directorofevents@seacliffcc.net

Country Club

- Rehearsal Dinners
- Ceremonies
- Wedding Receptions
- Private Parties
- Corporate Events
- Meetings
- Film Shoots
- Accommodations

Situated less than a mile from the shore, dependably sun-kissed and cooled by ocean breezes, the sophisticated SeaCliff Country Club is a special place—and it's the only private club available for nonmember events in Huntington Beach.

A profusion of colorful foliage and a stream spilling over stones in a rock garden highlight the lovely entrance. While valets are greeting your guests as they arrive in SeaCliff's gracious circular driveway, you and your attendants will have full use of the bridal suite, where you can get ready and calm jittery nerves with some snacks and a bit of bubbly.

When it's time for the ceremony, everyone gathers at the Oval Terrace, the club's beautiful outdoor site. You'll walk down a petal-strewn aisle to your choice of archway (Cinderella, bamboo, or four Greek columns) adorned with flowers, and exchange vows against a stunning backdrop: a panorama of SeaCliff's lake and 18-hole golf course. Photos snapped here can't help but be gorgeous!

The club's two reception spaces offer very different atmospheres. If your guest list is long or you prefer a formal ambiance, the SeaCliff Ballroom is ideal. With its own entrance, exit, restrooms, and secluded courtyard, it provides complete privacy. More intimate gatherings are held in the versatile Pacific Dining Room and Lounge, which even includes an ebony grand piano. The dining and lounge areas are informally separated by a granite-topped bar, so it's easy for guests to mingle over cocktails on the lounge side and then walk right over to the other side for dinner. Both areas also feature a wall of glass overlooking the Oval Terrace, and double doors that open to the outdoors and give guests an opportunity to enjoy the fresh air and view of the golf course and lake.

The neutral décor in both rooms will complement whatever color scheme you choose, and you can enhance any of their turnkey reception packages with full room draping, chandeliers, or a chocolate fountain.

Adding to the attractions of this upscale venue are those that surround it in mellow Surf City USA. After your festivities wind down, you'll have miles of uninterrupted beach to stroll along, a historic pier to explore, and a colorful oceanfront boardwalk to visit.

CEREMONY CAPACITY: The Oval Terrace accommodates up to 250 seated guests. Indoors, banquet rooms hold up to 250 seated.

EVENT/RECEPTION & MEETING CAPACITY: Indoors, the SeaCliff Ballroom holds up to 270 seated or 300 standing guests and the Pacific Room up to 150 seated or 200 standing. Outdoors, the Oval Terrace holds up to 250 seated or 300 standing.

PRICES: WHAT'S THIS GOING TO COST?

Package Prices: $70/person and up
  • Pricing varies based on food, beverage, and rental inclusions. Food & beverage minimums will apply. Menus and packages can be customized to fit your needs and budget. Pricing does not include additional site fees, mandatory service charge, gratuity, and current sales tax.

AVAILABILITY: Year-round. Weddings take place in a 6-hour block for a ceremony and reception or a 5-hour block for a reception only. Additional event time may be purchased.

SERVICES/AMENITIES:

Catering: in-house
Kitchen Facilities: n/a
Tables & Chairs: provided
Linens, Silver, etc.: provided
Restrooms: wheelchair accessible
Dance Floor: provided
Bride's Dressing Area: yes
AV/Meeting Equipment: CBA
Other: event coordination, grand piano, WiFi, fire pits, lounge furniture

Parking: valet required for groups of 50 or more
Accommodations: no guest rooms
Outdoor Night Lighting: access only
Outdoor Cooking Facilities: BBQ CBA
Cleanup: provided
View: landscaped grounds, trees, hills, lake/water feature

RESTRICTIONS:

Alcohol: in-house
Smoking: outside only
Music: amplified OK with restrictions

Wheelchair Access: yes
Insurance: not required

La Mirada Golf Course

Golf Club

15501 East Alicante Road, La Mirada
562/943-7123 x2

www.countryclubreceptions.com
privateeventdirector@lamiradagc.com

● Rehearsal Dinners	● Corporate Events
● Ceremonies	● Meetings
● Wedding Receptions	● Film Shoots
● Private Parties	○ Accommodations

Tucked away in a quiet neighborhood, La Mirada Golf Course is one of the most popular in Southern California. It may also be one of the Southland's most wedding-friendly venues. What's the attraction? Affordable prices, no need to be a member (it's a public course), the biggest dance floor in town, and an accommodating staff that knows how to soothe anxieties and keep things flowing smoothly. Even though this course is in high demand, the banquet facility is completely private: Brides never have to worry about curious golfers wandering through their celebration.

Every wedding here is individualized. The bride meets with the private event staff for a food tasting well before the wedding day. Because the city of La Mirada is an ethnic crossroads, the facility has extensive experience dealing with different religious and cultural needs. They're also very flexible about time, and late evening celebrations aren't a problem—they're relatively far from the nearest neighboring houses, meaning no worries about disturbing anyone.

Many couples start with an outdoor ceremony at the beautiful lakeside gazebo. Afterwards, festivities move to the clubhouse's newly renovated ballroom, where windows on three sides let in plenty of natural light. The wood floor is ideal for dancing, while contemporary crystal chandeliers and a wall of decorative silver metal paneling add extra sparkle. The ballroom opens to a spacious terrace that offers a panoramic view of the golf course fairways that seem to go on for miles.

Maybe the best way to think of La Mirada is to remember what was going through Goldilocks' mind when she was testing porridge at the Bear residence. Goldie wasn't looking for too big or too cool; she was looking for Just Right. This place has so many "just right" things going for it that it may just be right for you.

CEREMONY CAPACITY: The site seats up to 200.

EVENT/RECEPTION & MEETING CAPACITY: The ballroom seats up to 250 guests with a dance floor, or up to 400 without one.

PRICES: WHAT'S THIS GOING TO COST?

Package Prices: $30/person and up
- Pricing varies based on food, beverage, and rental inclusions. Food & beverage minimums will apply. Menus and packages can be customized to fit your needs and budget. Pricing does not include additional site fees, mandatory service charge, gratuity, and current sales tax.

AVAILABILITY: Year-round, daily.

SERVICES/AMENITIES:

Catering: in-house
Kitchen Facilities: n/a
Tables & Chairs: provided
Linens, Silver, etc.: provided
Restrooms: wheelchair accessible
Dance Floor: provided
Bride's Dressing Area: CBA
AV/Meeting Equipment: CBA

Parking: large lot and on street
Accommodations: no guest rooms
Outdoor Night Lighting: yes
Outdoor Cooking Facilities: BBQ
Cleanup: provided
View: fairways, lake, garden, landscaped grounds
Other: wedding cake, florals, chair covers, clergy referrals available

RESTRICTIONS:

Alcohol: in-house
Smoking: outside only
Music: amplified OK indoors

Wheelchair Access: yes
Insurance: not required

Want to know WHAT TO ASK a potential location or vendor? Check out our Questions to Ask starting on page 21.

247

Occasions at Laguna Village

577 South Coast Highway, Laguna Beach
866/321-9876 or 949/939-7979
www.occasionsatlagunavillage.com
lagunaoccasions@aol.com

Waterfront Special Event Facility

●	Rehearsal Dinners	●	Corporate Events
●	Ceremonies	●	Meetings
●	Wedding Receptions	●	Film Shoots
●	Private Parties		Accommodations

Refreshing breezes, a white sand beach, crashing waves and a beautiful sunset accompany your ceremony…you and your guests dine and dance beneath the stars…. It all sounds pretty fabulous, doesn't it! Well, if you've always wanted a seaside celebration but have been daunted by all the effort involved, why not have your event at the Occasions at Laguna Village? At this unique facility you can enjoy all the things you love about being near the ocean without having to lift a finger!

Of course, the main attraction here is the location: on top of a bluff with a 180-degree view of Laguna Beach, the adjacent coastline and the Pacific. A staircase leads from the street-level parking lot down to the venue, a spacious outdoor area with a built-in checkerboard dance floor bordered by a well-tended lawn. Though the site is not actually on the beach, if it were any closer, you might consider wearing a bathing suit!

The most popular ceremony spot is a circular platform near the cliff's edge at one end of the lawn. Although the setting doesn't require it, you can put up a wedding arch or a set of faux Roman columns if you like. Since this site faces due west, your guests can watch the sun sink behind the two of you while you say your vows. Another option is getting married at the other end of the lawn in an airy white gazebo.

Guests are seated on the dance floor during the ceremony; afterwards they stroll over to the lawn to enjoy cocktails and hors d'oeuvres, while tables are set up around the dance floor for the reception. In the evening, street lamps and twinkle lights augment the glow of candlelit tables, as the waves below murmur a soothing accompaniment.

Aside from its stellar location, the thing that makes the Occasions at Laguna Village so special is the outstanding service you'll receive. If you're a fan of "one-stop shopping," this is the place for you. They can provide anything and everything else you might desire, including catering, linens, flowers, entertainment, lighting, market umbrellas, and potted palms. So if you think that the words "effortless" and "seaside celebration" can't possibly appear in the same sentence, look into the Occasions at Laguna Village. Here, you'll be able to have the oceanfront party of your dreams without getting sand in your shoes.

CEREMONY CAPACITY: The facility holds up to 175 seated guests outdoors.

EVENT/RECEPTION & MEETING CAPACITY: The venue seats up to 175 guests.

PRICES: WHAT'S THIS GOING TO COST?

Rental Fee: *$1,500–4,800/event*

Package Prices:

• Elopement packages start at $2,995 and include: on-site wedding coordinator and professional DJ; ceremony forum with Roman pillars; lighted gazebo with padded white folding chairs, white aisle runner, and off-white market umbrellas; water station; gift & guest book tables; bridal dressing room; and beautiful oceanfront terrace for post-ceremony mingling and photos.

Meals (when priced separately): *$50/person and up*

AVAILABILITY: Year-round, daily, 9am–10pm in 4-hour time blocks; overtime can be arranged at an additional cost.

SERVICES/AMENITIES:

Catering: in-house, no BYO

Kitchen Facilities: n/a

Tables & Chairs: provided

Linens, Silver, etc.: provided

Restrooms: wheelchair accessible

Dance Floor: provided

Bride's Dressing Area: no

AV/Meeting Equipment: CBA, extra charge

Parking: valet and shuttle required

Accommodations: no guest rooms

Outdoor Night Lighting: yes

Outdoor Cooking Facilities: CBA

Cleanup: provided

View: panorama of ocean and cityscape

Other: event coordination

RESTRICTIONS:

Alcohol: in-house, no BYO

Smoking: outside only

Music: amplified OK with volume limits, 10pm music curfew

Wheelchair Access: yes

Insurance: required for vendors only

Other: no rice, confetti, or birdseed

La Casa del Camino

Historic Boutique Hotel

1289 South Coast Highway, Laguna Beach
949/505-5088
www.lacasadelcamino.com
lindseya@lacasadelcamino.com

●	Rehearsal Dinners	●	Corporate Events
●	Ceremonies	●	Meetings
●	Wedding Receptions	●	Film Shoots
●	Private Parties	▲	Accommodations

Even in a town as picturesque as Laguna Beach, the utterly charming La Casa del Camino is in a class by itself. With an alluring mix of waterfront location, early Spanish Mediterranean architecture and expansive views of the Pacific Ocean, this landmark boutique hotel is a standout choice for a romantic wedding celebration.

Built in 1929 and distinguished by its red-tiled roof, classic archways and wooden balconies, this beachside gem provides a tantalizing peek at a time when it was a favorite getaway for Hollywood stars and starlets. Combine that historic cachet with what today's La Casa del Camino has to offer—the hip energy of its wildly popular K'ya Bistro Bar and its open-air rooftop retreat with unparalleled ocean vistas—and you get the quintessential Laguna Beach experience.

The first thing that greets you here is the beautiful lobby, a welcoming Spanish Mediterranean-style space with high plaster ceilings accented with wooden crossbeams. There's a baby grand piano off to the right, while on the left you'll find an adobe-style fireplace topped with a tiled niche displaying flickering candles that cast a warm glow. This large-yet-cozy setting is perfect for hosting friends and family for cocktails, dinner or dancing.

But without doubt, the *pièce de résistance* at La Casa del Camino is its Rooftop Lounge. The only one like it in Laguna Beach, it serves up a 360-degree panorama with head-on ocean views. This sprawling, wraparound deck and full-service bar is a spectacular wedding site: You can make a dramatic entrance through a tile-roofed private portal and exchange vows in front of an infinite expanse of sparkling blue water. Your nearest and dearest gather around you in V-shaped, theater-style seating, giving everyone a great vantage for watching the ceremony. Afterwards, invite everyone to enjoy an al fresco toast and bask in the cool marine breezes before sitting down at beautifully appointed tables. Then dine in the company of the surrounding sea and sky.

And if one perfect day is just not enough, you might want to consider reserving the entire hotel for a weekend. Their Spanish-style guest rooms are done in rich, warm tones and feature intricately hand-carved wood furnishings, while the ten Surf Suites offer a more contemporary "beach" vibe. Each one-of-a-kind suite has been branded by a different surf company—like Rip Curl, Roxy, Quiksilver, and Billabong—and incorporates design elements and colors selected by that company. Your out-of-town guests will love spending an extra day or two here, so that they can truly savor their time with you at this wonderful home-away-from-home.

CEREMONY & EVENT/RECEPTION CAPACITY: The hotel holds 120 seated or standing guests indoors and outdoors.

MEETING CAPACITY: Indoor meeting spaces hold 25 guests theater-style.

PRICES: WHAT'S THIS GOING TO COST?

Rental Fee: up to $4,500
  • The rental fee varies depending on the time of year and guest count.

Meals (when priced separately): $69–95/person

Service Charge or Gratuity: 21%

AVAILABILITY: Year-round, daily, 8am–10pm.

SERVICES/AMENITIES:

Catering: in-house
Kitchen Facilities: n/a
Tables & Chairs: provided
Linens, Silver, etc.: provided
Restrooms: wheelchair accessible
Dance Floor: CBA
Bride's Dressing Area: CBA
AV/Meeting Equipment: CBA
Other: coordination

Parking: on street, valet optional
Accommodations: 37 guest rooms + Beach Cottage (sleeps 8)
Outdoor Night Lighting: yes
Outdoor Cooking Facilities: none
Cleanup: provided
View: landscaped grounds; panorama of coastline, hills, and ocean

RESTRICTIONS:

Alcohol: in-house
Smoking: not allowed
Music: non-percussion acoustic or amplified (recorded only) with volume restrictions

Wheelchair Access: yes
Insurance: not required

seven 7 seven

777 Laguna Canyon Road, Laguna Beach
949/494-6044
www.777lagunabeach.com
weddings@777lagunabeach.com

- Rehearsal Dinners
- Ceremonies
- Wedding Receptions
- Private Parties
- Corporate Events
- Meetings
- Film Shoots
- Accommodations

If your idea of bliss is strolling through serene European gardens adorned with statuary, but your fiancé would rather hit a pop-up tour of downtown graffiti, is this marriage doomed? No way! And neither is your wedding, because there's a perfect venue that will make you both happy.

Nestled amid the sweeping natural beauty of Laguna Canyon and just a couple of minutes from the sandy beach, SEVEN 7 SEVEN is an ideal blend of Old World charm and bold modern art. It's set against a panorama of rugged, sage-covered hills dotted with the occasional mansion, and has the feel of a Mediterranean piazza/garden oasis. Formerly known as "Tivoli Too", this long-time favorite has passed the torch to new owners who've maintained and enhanced its unique qualities while adding a few exciting twists in keeping with Laguna Beach's reputation as a dynamic, creative hub. (FYI: This has been the home of the annual Art-A-Fair festival for more than 50 years!)

Wrought-iron gates beneath a tiled-roof pavilion open to the huge brick-and-flagstone courtyard, bordered by the picturesque verandas of SEVEN 7 SEVEN's restaurant (open only during July and August), bar, and craftsman-style bridal cottage—all of which offer irresistible photo ops. At one end of this expansive outdoor haven is the utterly romantic open-air "chapel". Its raised, circular, stone stage features a breathtakingly lush backdrop made up of a profusion of native trees, flowering shrubs, lacy ferns, succulents, and pots of fragrant blooms. The scene is pure paradise, complete with three gentle streams merging into a cascading waterfall.

Your guests take their seats to live piano music, while a classic statue of a winged angel watches over your ceremony from atop her pedestal. Celebrate your "I do"s with a champagne toast followed by cocktails and tray-passed hors d'oeuvres at the cake gazebo. For larger groups, half of the guests can mingle at the bar while the other half catches up with friends and family in the reception tent. Meanwhile, it's time to have fun with those all-important wedding photos!

After posing for some dreamy portraits in front of the waterfall, embrace your edgy side with images that incorporate the striking murals around the property, like a fantastic diorama bursting with myriad shapes, patterns, swirls, dots, and neon colors…or a surrealistic giant bluebird in a kaleidoscopic dreamscape…or a three-dimensional installation with a close-up of a woman's face behind a luscious pink rose.

Then, it's time to rejoin your guests for dinner and dancing. SEVEN 7 SEVEN's in-house catering focuses on fresh, healthy ingredients with an extensive choice of menu options—including a sublime tiered carrot cake. Their packages are virtually all-inclusive, with two coordinators to make sure you have an amazing event. So yes, this really is the perfect venue—refined, elegant and cool, plus they take care of just about everything.

CEREMONY CAPACITY: The courtyard can seat up to 250 guests.

EVENT/RECEPTION CAPACITY: The venue holds 250 seated or 300 standing guests indoors, and 300 seated or standing outdoors.

MEETING CAPACITY: Meeting spaces accommodate 250 guests.

PRICES: WHAT'S THIS GOING TO COST?

Packages: $145/person and up
- All-inclusive, full-service packages include: the ceremony space (with fresh florals and a live pianist) and a rehearsal prior to the event; 2 tray-passed appetizers during your formal pictures; use of bridal rooms; an array of sit-down or buffet-style menus; choice of a wide variety of linen colors, silverware, and servers; a tray of homemade wedding cookies and a coffee bar; free-flowing beer, wine, and champagne; wedding cake; and 2 wedding coordinators to assist with planning and running your event from beginning to end.

Additional Info: Package pricing varies depending on the day of the week, time of day, time of year, space reserved, guest count, event duration, and package chosen.

AVAILABILITY: Year-round, daily.

SERVICES/AMENITIES:

Catering: in-house, preferred list
Kitchen Facilities: fully equipped
Tables & Chairs: provided
Linens, Silver, etc.: provided
Restrooms: wheelchair accessible
Dance Floor: yes
Dressing Areas: yes
AV/Meeting Equipment: some provided

Parking: large lot, street, garage, or nearby lot
Accommodations: no guest rooms
Outdoor Night Lighting: yes
Outdoor Cooking Facilities: BBQ CBA
Cleanup: provided
View: fountain/water feature, garden patio/courtyard, waterfall
Other: in-house wedding cake and florals; picnic area; event coordination

RESTRICTIONS:

Alcohol: in-house
Smoking: not allowed
Music: amplified indoors OK

Wheelchair Access: yes
Insurance: not required

[seven-degrees]

891 Laguna Canyon Road, Laguna Beach
949/376-1555
www.seven-degrees.com
tabatha@seven-degrees.com

Special Events Venue

● Rehearsal Dinners		● Corporate Events	
● Ceremonies		● Meetings	
● Wedding Receptions		● Film Shoots	
● Private Parties		Accommodations	

Attracted by the balmy weather, azure ocean, and *la dolce vita* of a small seaside town, scores of artists settled in Laguna Beach in the early 20th century. In fact, the first art museum in California was founded here in 1918. Since then the city has established itself as a major player in the art world, hosting numerous galleries and summer art festivals, proud and indulgent of its boho-chic artist population.

Perhaps the most remarkable addition to the city's art community is [seven-degrees], a "multi-purpose idea lab for the promotion of artistic endeavor, invention and exhibition".

Nestled in Laguna Canyon a few blocks from the ocean, this uber-modern glass, steel and granite facility is a visual marvel. The all-glass façade, whose asymmetry and angular lines defy conventional architecture, reflects the surrounding canyon walls while revealing the artwork displayed inside.

When you have an event here, you immediately become part of the art scene. Enter through the gallery, where you and your guests can peruse the exhibition du jour. Then pass by the studios of the artists, which are often open for viewing works in progress. Before the festivities begin, mingle with family and friends in the courtyard between buildings or ascend to the Hillside Terrace, a tentable rooftop patio with multiple uses. Ceremonies are often held here, but the space is also perfect for an outdoor cocktail reception. In addition to canyon views, there are meandering trails with bamboo railings, leading to a series of overlooks built into the canyon walls. A gentle waterfall and lush plantings among the rocks make this setting an unexpected oasis.

Nature takes a back seat to your own creativity in the Media Lounge. Unadorned, it's a simple, 4,500-square-foot oblong room with gray concrete walls and floors. But with the help of experienced in-house coordinators, the latest in lighting technology, and a phalanx of on-site audiovisual equipment, you'll be able to transform the space into anything you like. Past metamorphoses include a Rococo-style ballroom with gilded mirrors and jacquard textiles; a midsummer night's dream with a forest's worth of potted plants and flowers; and a postmodern discothéque thumping with sound and light. Live webcasting is available, and you can even project an image of yourselves (or anyone else!) on internal or external surfaces. Your guests will be part of an unforgettable multimedia experience, limited only by your imagination (and your budget). [seven-degrees] is a true original in the world of event venues, a place inspired by and dedicated to art. Whether you're planning a wedding, a corporate party or any other celebration here, you'll enjoy being an honored artist-in-residence for the day.

CEREMONY CAPACITY: The Hillside Terrace holds up to 200 seated or 250 with some standing guests.

EVENT/RECEPTION & MEETING CAPACITY: The Media Lounge holds up to 250 seated or 388 standing.

PRICES: WHAT'S THIS GOING TO COST?

Packages:
  • Full-service packages are available; call for details.

Meals (when priced separately): *$49/person and up*

AVAILABILITY: Year-round, daily, until 1am. Events take place in 5-hour blocks and weddings take place in 5.5-hour blocks.

SERVICES/AMENITIES:

Catering: in-house or BYO with approval
Kitchen Facilities: full commercial kitchen
Tables & Chairs: included for 200 with wedding portfolio
Linens, Silver, etc.: white linens included with wedding portfolio
Restrooms: wheelchair accessible
Dance Floor: no
Bride's Dressing Area: yes
AV/Meeting Equipment: yes

Parking: large lot
Accommodations: no guest rooms
Outdoor Night Lighting: full specialty lighting
Outdoor Cooking Facilities: CBA
Cleanup: provided, extra fee
View: terraced hillside garden
Other: event coordination

RESTRICTIONS:

Alcohol: in-house, no BYO
Smoking: outdoors only
Music: amplified OK

Wheelchair Access: yes
Insurance: only required for outside vendors

The wedding vendors on our website are the best in the business. How do we know? Read page 425.

255

SEVEN4ONE

741 South Coast Highway, Laguna Beach
949/494-6200
www.seven4one.com
guestrelations@seven4one.com

- Rehearsal Dinners
- Ceremonies
- Wedding Receptions
- Private Parties
- Corporate Events
- Meetings
- Film Shoots
- Accommodations

Chic … private … a treasure hidden in plain sight … You're missing something fabulous if you haven't been tipped off about this ultra-private wedding and special event venue.

Secreted away in the very midst of sun-splashed Laguna Beach, it's just steps from the sandy shore and surf. No signage clutters the simple but stylish exterior, and passersby would never guess that this façade of smoky windows, reclaimed wood and cascading greenery conceals the luxurious accommodations and inspiring event spaces of a boutique hotel available exclusively for you and your guests.

Here, you get the kind of seclusion that celebrities long for, but you don't need to be a movie star or win the lottery to have total access to everything the hotel has to offer: 8 handsome, contemporary guest rooms and 2 suites; 3 extraordinary event areas; a concierge staff and team of wedding professionals—including a personal chef, an in-house mixologist, and a Wedding Coordinator—devoted to you and your party. In fact, customization is key at Seven4one, and their event experts are quite keen on matching their exceptional talents for food and entertaining with your particular desires.

A celebration here is going to feel quite magical. Whether you and your company decide to stay for a night, a weekend or longer, you'll be in your very own world, a two-story palace of a place in a million-dollar setting. It's all rather dreamy—no rush, no interruptions, impeccable service—your big day can unfold in a natural way without the stress of time limits or unexpected intrusions.

While you and your entourage relax in your suites and rooms, guests can congregate downstairs in the lobby or the sleek martini lounge. Or, they might stroll into the spacious open-air interior courtyard. This favorite group environment is the ideal stage for a ceremony, a reception or both. Surrounded above by the second-floor balcony, it features a beautiful "living" wall of cascading greenery and reclaimed wood and is easily transformed through lighting and props to suit any vision. A retractable roof makes it weatherproof, but this is Laguna Beach so most of the time you can be sure that the canopy of sky is going to remain bright blue by day and moon- and star-lit once the sun goes down.

And speaking of sunsets, the place to enjoy them is the hotel's second-floor sundeck, which is often used for cocktails or smaller ceremonies. When there's no party in progress, it's a divine escape from the hubbub of entertaining as well as the perfect Pacific-facing perch for taking in the property's sweeping vistas of sea, sky and gorgeous California coast.

The most appealing aspect of Seven4one is that once the main event is over, you and your guests won't have to tear yourselves away. You'll all have plenty of time to press the pause button, unwind, settle in, and savor this remarkable slice of the good life a little longer.

CEREMONY CAPACITY: The facility seats up to 110 guests.

EVENT/RECEPTION CAPACITY: The facility can accommodate 140 with mixed seating and interactive dining, or for a cocktail-style reception. Formal seating capacity at traditional rounds or banquet tables is 100.

MEETING CAPACITY: Meeting spaces seat 110.

PRICES: WHAT'S THIS GOING TO COST?

Rental Fee: $7,000-13,000/event
- The rental fee varies depending on the day of the week and time of year.
- Saturday or weekend wedding packages require a buyout of Seven4one's 10 guest rooms for an additional fee. You may opt to have your guests cover the cost of their own rooms.

Meals (when priced separately): $64/person and up
- Customized menus include taxes, gratuities, staffing, event insurance, and day-of wedding coordination.
- Food & beverage minimums apply.

Additional Info: An optional Beach Wedding Ceremony is available. For midweek, one-night events, and other options such as accommodations-only, please inquire.

AVAILABILITY: Year-round with an 11pm event curfew, but overnight event guests are free to continue the party after 11pm.

SERVICES/AMENITIES:

Catering: in-house
Kitchen Facilities: n/a
Tables & Chairs: included
Linens, Silver, etc.: included
Restrooms: wheelchair accessible
Dance Floor: provided
Dressing Area: yes
AV/Meeting Equipment: CBA
Other: day-of coordination

Parking: valet required (included in wedding packages)
Accommodations: 10 guest rooms
Outdoor Night Lighting: included
Outdoor Cooking Facilities: no
Cleanup: provided
View: cityscape, coastline, garden, hills, mountains, ocean panorama

RESTRICTIONS:

Alcohol: in-house
Smoking: designated areas only
Music: amplified OK indoors with restrictions

Wheelchair Access: limited
Insurance: included

Surf & Sand Resort

Waterfront Resort

1555 South Coast Highway, Laguna Beach
855/923-7450
www.surfandsandresort.com/weddings
surfweddings@jcresorts.com

- Rehearsal Dinners
- Ceremonies
- Wedding Receptions
- Private Parties
- Corporate Events
- Meetings
- Film Shoots
- Accommodations

Surf & Sand Resort is renowned for both its prime location in Laguna Beach and its proximity to the ocean. The high-rise hotel sits so close to the water that it puts you quite literally—and hypnotically—right above the crashing surf. If you haven't seen it yet, check out the Mediterranean-style Conference Center, a separate event venue that adds to Surf & Sand's reputation as a place where you can have it all—a corporate gala, an executive meeting or a lovely wedding.

"Conference Center" doesn't do justice to the banquet rooms—the Pelican and Sand Dollar—which are decorated in a Mediterranean beach-luxe style that could grace the pages of *Architectural Digest*. Each one is a handsome and tasteful mix of blond hardwoods, airy hues of sand and cream, coffered ceilings, lots of whitewashed wood-shuttered windows, neoclassical appointments and unique works of art.

Ceremonies at Surf & Sand take place on the Catalina Terrace and on the Ocean Terrace, where you'll have a breathtaking view of Catalina Island while the breaking waves resound just below your feet. After the wedding, guests head off to the largest reception space, the Pelican Room, which has a graceful foyer and a terrace with a view of the hotel and the ocean. Perfectly suited for mid-sized groups, the Sand Dollar Room is complemented by a series of archways forming a patio covered with vinery. And just outside the Sand Castle Room, you'll find a babbling fountain and a peek of the ocean below.

After your event, stay a while longer, or better yet, have your honeymoon here. All of Surf & Sand's luxurious accommodations have seaview balconies, all with commanding views of the Pacific Ocean. While there are plenty of nearby places to go sightseeing or shopping (Laguna Beach boutiques and galleries are within walking distance), you may just want to pamper yourself at the resort's AquaTerra Spa or sink back in your poolside deck chair or beach chair on the sand and enjoy the sun's warmth. With its seabreeze air plus ocean and sunset vistas, Surf & Sand is an exhilarating locale for any celebration.

CEREMONY CAPACITY: The Ocean Terrace seats 80 guests, the Catalina Terrace seats 180; South Beach can accommodate up to 50 standing.

EVENT/RECEPTION CAPACITY: With dance floor, the Pelican Room holds 180 seated, the Sand Dollar Room 80 seated, the Sand Castle Room 60 seated.

MEETING CAPACITY: Please contact the facility for detailed information regarding meetings.

PRICES: WHAT'S THIS GOING TO COST?

Ceremony Fee: $1,000–4,500/event
   • The ceremony fee varies depending on the time of year and space reserved.

Meals (when priced separately): $89/person and up

AVAILABILITY: Year-round, daily.

SERVICES/AMENITIES:

Catering: in-house, no BYO
Kitchen Facilities: n/a
Tables & Chairs: provided
Linens, Silver, etc.: provided
Restrooms: wheelchair accessible
Dance Floor: provided
Bride's Dressing Area: yes
AV/Meeting Equipment: full range

Parking: valet, nominal fee
Accommodations: 167 guest rooms
Outdoor Night Lighting: access only
Outdoor Cooking Facilities: no
Cleanup: provided
View: Pacific Ocean, coastal hills, Catalina Island, sunsets

RESTRICTIONS:

Alcohol: in-house, no BYO
Smoking: not allowed
Music: amplified OK

Wheelchair Access: limited
Insurance: not required

Terra Laguna Beach

650 Laguna Canyon Road, Laguna Beach
949/494-9650
www.terralagunabeach.com
jessica@terralagunabeach.com

Special Events Venue

- Rehearsal Dinners
- Ceremonies
- Wedding Receptions
- Private Parties
- Corporate Events
- Meetings
- Film Shoots
- Accommodations

Sandy coves, scenic hills, and a clifftop location make Laguna Beach one of California's must-see coastal villages. Known for its natural beauty and creative ambiance, this Orange County gem hosts a variety of wildly popular art festivals, most prominently "The Pageant of the Masters"—a mesmerizing piece of performance art that transforms some of the world's most famous paintings into a series of unforgettable live tableaux. Odds are, if you've attended one of these events you probably dined at Tivoli Terrace, the on-site local favorite that recently completed its own transformation into the new and exciting Terra Laguna Beach.

Just minutes from the ocean, this romantic event venue is like a mixed media work of art. Nestled into a hillside within the festival grounds, it blends historic mid-century architecture with a cool, sophisticated, urban vibe. Its expansive two-level design offers options for every aspect of your wedding, from September through June when the crowds are gone and the focus is on you.

A sleek, glass-sided staircase leads up to a garden veranda, a lovely spot for exchanging vows. Driftwood-toned open beams and a surround of tall trees create an arbor-like chapel for your ceremony, with a lush backdrop of greenery, succulents, flowering plants, and the rugged canyon.

Outdoor receptions and more intimate gatherings like rehearsal dinners and engagement parties are held downstairs in an atrium-style venue. The focal point here is Terra's *pièce de résistance,* an enormous wing-like "roof" that's suspended over the space and looks like its about to take flight. Built in 1957 and hidden from view for decades, this architectural standout has been fully restored and delivers the same futuristic impact that it did more than a half-century ago. In a stroke of brilliance (literally!), they've lined it with strings of bistro lights, creating a glittering canopy for your cocktail hour, dinner, and dancing. Guests are also treated to panoramic vistas of the festival grounds, hills, and canyon.

Celebrations in this unique setting are accompanied by topnotch cuisine. Based on fresh, ethically sourced ingredients, it's all artfully prepared and presented by executive chef Matt Pike. Plus, their friendly, experienced staff can help you customize your menu and add signature cocktails. And, with Terra Laguna Beach's packages, they'll be there every step of the way so you can actually feel like a pampered guest at your own wedding.

CEREMONY CAPACITY: The venue accommodates 150 seated guests.

EVENT/RECEPTION CAPACITY: The facility can hold 180 seated or 200 standing guests indoors, and 200 standing outdoors.

MEETING CAPACITY: Meeting spaces hold up to 200 guests.

PRICES: WHAT'S THIS GOING TO COST?

Rental Fee: $4,000–7,500/event
- The rental fee varies depending on: the day of the week, time of day, time of year, space reserved, guest count, event duration, and package chosen.
- Rental includes 5.5 hours of event time, excluding setup and cleanup. Additional hours can be secured for $1,700/hr.

Package Prices:
- Full-service packages are available; call for details.

Meals (when priced separately): $69/person and up

AVAILABILITY: Year-round, daily, 6am–11pm.

SERVICES/AMENITIES:

Catering: in-house, preferred list
Kitchen Facilities: fully equipped
Tables & Chairs: provided
Linens, Silver, etc.: provided
Restrooms: wheelchair accessible
Dance Floor: yes
Dressing Areas: bride's yes, groom's CBA
AV/Meeting Equipment: yes

Parking: large lot, on street, garage, nearby lot; valet available
Accommodations: no guest rooms
Outdoor Night Lighting: yes
Outdoor Cooking Facilities: n/a
Cleanup: provided
View: canyon, garden patio/courtyard
Other: in-house wedding cake and florals, event coordination

RESTRICTIONS:

Alcohol: in-house
Smoking: not allowed
Music: amplified outdoors OK

Wheelchair Access: no
Insurance: not required

The Hills Hotel

25205 La Paz Road, Laguna Hills
949/586-5000

www.thelagunahillshotel.com
tfattahi@thelagunahillshotel.com

Ballroom & Hotel

- Rehearsal Dinners
- Ceremonies
- Wedding Receptions
- Private Parties
- Corporate Events
- Meetings
- Film Shoots
- Accommodations

Modern, trendy, and conveniently located, The Hills Hotel is perfect for an Orange County destination wedding. At this upscale boutique hotel, you have everything you need in one place: a variety of versatile event spaces, accommodations for all your guests, and plenty of local attractions and activities to keep everyone entertained.

A grand staircase (or elevator) takes you up to the third floor where celebrations unfold. You'll have exclusive use of the entire level, and can choreograph your event in whatever way works best for you.

The festivities typically start with guests mingling on the Mezzanine at the top of the stairs, but the fun really begins with a cocktail hour in the adjoining Crystal Lounge. Here, drinks and delectable appetizers are served at a long, marble-topped bar, and guests can relax on white tufted benches or step outside for a little fresh air on the attached patio, which gets some extra sparkle from white star lights strung overhead.

Dining and dancing take place in the Crystal Ballroom, highlighted by six glittering crystal chandeliers that cast a warm glow on the shimmering, pearlescent walls. LED lights in the ceiling can be set to a range of colors, allowing you to create the mood you desire. The ballroom opens to The Veranda, an atrium-style corridor illuminated by its own set of seven crystal chandeliers plus a wall of windows. This space is ideal for a luxurious buffet setup during your dinner reception.

The hotel offers more event spaces on the first floor. For an elegant ceremony, reserve The Garnet Gallery. Decorated in regal hues of maroon and purple and enhanced by gold frames artistically arranged on the walls, it provides a classic, yet modern, ambiance. If you're planning an intimate ceremony or a rehearsal dinner, the Platinum Room is an excellent choice. It's done in all-white with silver accents, and affords a view of the pool.

Two beautifully curated wedding reception packages (Crystal and Diamond) feature a long list of amenities: customizable menus; complimentary bride & groom entrées; wedding cake; Chiavari chairs; menu and escort cards; dance floor; gorgeous floral centerpieces; and much more. As newlyweds, you'll also receive a complimentary room (with a sweet gift of champagne and chocolate-covered strawberries)…and the next morning you'll enjoy a complimentary breakfast in bed or in the Hills Restaurant.

Guests staying the weekend will be happy they did! They can take a dip in the pool, listen to live music in the hotel's Emerald Lounge, or explore the area. Hills Hotel is close to beaches, art galleries, shopping, and fine dining, not to mention Disneyland, Knott's Berry Farm, Mission Viejo Lake, and Laguna Niguel Regional Park.

Weddings, birthdays, quinceañeras, bar mitzvahs, and other special occasions and meetings are all equally at home at The Hills Hotel. No matter what event you have in mind, their highly experienced team is dedicated to making it a memorable one!

CEREMONY CAPACITY: The Crystal Ballroom holds a maximum of 400 guests (seated theater-style); Garnet Gallery can accommodate 140 seated, and the Platinum Room seats 80.

EVENT/RECEPTION CAPACITY: The Crystal Ballroom seats 280, the Garnet Gallery 90, and the Platinum Room up to 50.

MEETING CAPACITY: Meeting spaces accommodate 50–400 depending on the room and the seating setup (theater, classroom, conference, etc.).

PRICES: WHAT'S THIS GOING TO COST?

Package Prices: $84/person and up

Service Charge or Gratuity: 22% (tax is additional)

AVAILABILITY: Year-round, daily. Events must end by midnight.

SERVICES/AMENITIES:

Catering: in-house or BYO, licensed and insured

Kitchen Facilities: n/a

Tables & Chairs: Chiavari chair upgrade included in ceremony & reception package

Linens, Silver, etc.: floor-length satin linens and tableware included in reception package

Restrooms: wheelchair accessible, available upstairs and downstairs

Dance Floor: included in reception package

Bride's Dressing Area: included in ceremony package

AV/Meeting Equipment: CBA through Catering Dept.

Parking: self-parking

Accommodations: 147 guest rooms and 2 suites

Outdoor Night Lighting: no

Outdoor Cooking Facilities: no

Cleanup: included in ceremony and reception package

View: panorama of hills and mountains

RESTRICTIONS:

Alcohol: in-house

Smoking: 20 feet away from any outdoor terrace or entrance

Music: restrictions apply; inquire for DJ policy and other details

Wheelchair Access: yes

Insurance: required

Want to find more venues and services? Check out our informative website, www.HereComesTheGuide.com.

Electra Cruises

Yachts

3439 Via Oporto, Newport Beach

800/952-9955

www.electracruises.com
info@electracruises.com

- Rehearsal Dinners
- Ceremonies
- Wedding Receptions
- Private Parties
- Corporate Events
- Meetings

Film Shoots

Accommodations

When it comes to choosing a place to get married, few conjure up romance quite like a wedding at sea. Whether you set sail under the California sun or beneath a starry night sky, you get to leave the rest of the world behind as you celebrate with the glorious Pacific Ocean as your backdrop.

Their affordable wedding packages offer so much more than just the yacht, food, and beverages. From suggesting innovative invitation ideas (think messages in bottles or custom-designed wedding passports), to weaving your color palette into great fabrics, linens, and florals, to planning the actual wedding-day itinerary, menus, and to-die-for displays, they'll put together an event with that special touch.

This high level of service is matched by their elegant fleet of five luxurious private yachts. Between them they can easily accommodate an intimate gathering of your closest friends to a party of 300 guests. Vintage romance is a hallmark of the *Electra*, a 100-foot, all wood classic fantail yacht. At 83 feet, the New Orleans-style paddle wheeler *Newport Princess* is a charming, Old World Mississippi riverboat with a lot of character. *Athena* is a modern 110-foot motor yacht decked in marble with a Greek motif. The 125-foot *Destiny* features an abundance of glass and ultra-modern décor. Electra Cruises' newest and largest yacht is the 140-foot *Eternity*, which is ADA-approved and outfitted with an elevator. All of their yachts have multiple levels, a main salon with full bar, baby grand piano, leather couches and spectacular views.

With Electra Cruises, you won't have to settle for just another event. They'll customize your big day, make your guests say "Wow!" and do it all at a reasonable price. For an exceptional wedding, reception or commitment ceremony, you can count on these dedicated professionals. Give them a call to arrange a complimentary event consultation and see what they can do for YOU.

CEREMONY CAPACITY: *Electra's* top deck holds 100 seated guests. The *Athena* and *Destiny* each hold 150, the *Newport Princess* up to 150, and the *Eternity* can accommodate 300 guests.

EVENT/RECEPTION & MEETING CAPACITY: The *Electra* holds up to 100 guests, maximum. The *Athena* and *Destiny* each hold 150, the *Newport Princess* 150, and the *Eternity* up to 300 guests.

PRICES: WHAT'S THIS GOING TO COST?

Package Prices: *$95/person and up*
- Packages include the yacht charter, a captain to perform the ceremony, service staff, DJ, photographer, event coordinator, catering, wedding cake, bar service, rentals, and florals.

AVAILABILITY: Year-round, daily including holidays, anytime.

SERVICES/AMENITIES:

Catering: in-house
Kitchen Facilities: full galley
Tables & Chairs: provided
Linens, Silver, etc.: provided
Restrooms: wheelchair accessible
Dance Floor: available upon request
Bride's & Groom's Dressing Area: yes
AV/Meeting Equipment: full range CBA

Parking: parking structure
Outdoor Night Lighting: yes
Outdoor Cooking Facilities: no
Cleanup: provided
View: Pacific Ocean; Newport Harbor and city skyline
Other: full event coordination

RESTRICTIONS:

Alcohol: in-house, no BYO
Smoking: outside areas
Music: amplified OK

Wheelchair Access: yes
Insurance: not required
Other: no sparklers, floating lanterns, or candles

Environmental Nature Center

Community Center

1601 East 16th Street, Newport Beach
949/645-8489

encenter.org
heather@encenter.org

● Rehearsal Dinners	● Corporate Events
● Ceremonies	● Meetings
● Wedding Receptions	● Film Shoots
● Private Parties	Accommodations

Building a beautiful future together? How about starting it out with a fabulous eco-friendly celebration at the Environmental Nature Center. This award-winning venue has a dreamy 8,500-square-foot facility with halls, patios, and native gardens planted in the midst of its gorgeous 3.5-acre natural setting. The first building in Orange County to achieve Leadership in Energy and Environmental Design (LEED) Platinum Certification, it features energy-conserving climate control, water efficient systems and fixtures, and the imaginative use of recycled and recyclable materials throughout.

Begin your party in the Center's airy Museum, where guests can marvel at the effortless integration of "green" building solutions into stylish contemporary design. The ENC actually produces more energy than it consumes, and a computer monitor in the hallway displays its usage levels. Guests will find plenty of interactive exhibits to explore and discuss, as they meet and greet one another before stepping out though the glass foldaway doors and onto the broad Garden Patio.

Flanked on one side by a catering prep kitchen and patio, library/lounge with private powder room for the bride and her attendants, and a butterfly garden…and on the other side by the pale desert shades and dramatic shapes of its California native gardens, this is a stunning outdoor venue—day or night—for your scrumptious seasonal, earth-friendly reception. It's also great for dancing under sunny skies or beneath a nighttime canopy of stars and the facility's softly luminous solar-powered lanterns. At the foot of the patio, a small amphitheater with built-in bench seating frames a large open fire pit that's ideal for an elegant version of a favorite campfire activity—that's right, how about toasting the good times with champagne and s'mores?

Wondering about indoor options? Follow the paw prints in the sand-textured walkway to the Oak and Sycamore Rooms, two cozy chambers separated by a movable airwall that can be used individually or combined into one large space. Well-equipped for just about any function, the rooms have picture windows, high ceilings, handsome honey-colored cabinets (composed of recycled materials like wheat chaff and sunflower seed), and AV and internet capability. Center staff can help by providing all kinds of exciting biodegradable and reusable decorating options.

For a surprisingly affordable celebration with the tiniest possible carbon footprint, consider a picnic wedding and reception. You can tie the knot in a picturesque way in the little garden amphitheater or at the end of the small garden stream. Then hold your reception amid berries and blossoms on picnic tables under the trees before releasing guests to wander off along the ENC's many enchanting paths. Whether your affair is large or small, you can be sure that you're doing the world a big favor when you have it here. And you're helping the local community, too, since your event fees are also recycled: Most of them go to supporting the Center's operating costs and programs, and a big portion of your bill is tax deductible, too.

CEREMONY, EVENT/RECEPTION & MEETING CAPACITY: The site holds 125 seated or 245 standing guests indoors or outdoors.

PRICES: WHAT'S THIS GOING TO COST?

Rental Fee: $4,000–6,000/event
• The rental fee includes a membership.

AVAILABILITY: Year round, daily.

SERVICES/AMENITIES:

Catering: BYO
Kitchen Facilities: limited
Tables & Chairs: some provided
Linens, Silver, etc.: CBA
Restrooms: wheelchair accessible
Dance Floor: provided
Bride's & Groom's Dressing Area: CBA
AV/Meeting Equipment: provided

Parking: large lot
Accommodations: no guest rooms
Outdoor Night Lighting: yes; string lights over the patio
Outdoor Cooking Facilities: no
Cleanup: renter or caterer
View: creek, forest, courtyard, waterfall
Other: picnic area, fire ring and wood

RESTRICTIONS:

Alcohol: select from preferred vendor list
Smoking: not allowed
Music: amplified OK with restrictions

Wheelchair Access: yes
Insurance: liability required

Harborside Grand Ballroom
Located in the Historic Balboa Pavilion

400 Main Street, Newport Beach
949/673-4633
www.harborside-banquets.com
vicki@harborside-pavilion.com, corey@harborside-pavilion.com

Waterfront Events Facility

● Rehearsal Dinners	● Corporate Events
● Ceremonies	● Meetings
● Wedding Receptions	● Film Shoots
● Private Parties	Accommodations

Few beach towns on the West Coast can rival Balboa, annexed to Newport Beach on a peninsula between the Pacific Ocean and Newport Bay. Everything about this small community is in perfect balance and proportion. The compact downtown is thriving, but not colonized by chain stores. The neighborhoods range from neatly trimmed cottages to the understated houses of the wealthy. The beach is wide, the municipal pier has a great burger shack and there's a classic bayside strand of amusement parlors, harbor tours and quaint shops that evoke all the heady sights and smells of life at the beach.

At the heart of town is the historic Balboa Pavilion, a majestic Victorian structure overlooking Newport Harbor that was built in 1905 at the foot of Main Street. From the water, the distinctive shape of this two-story building's steeply sloped roof has always made the Pavilion an instantly recognizable landmark.

The Harborside Grand Ballroom, which is on the second floor of the Pavilion, has the best views of the bay in the harbor. Originally designed as America's answer to the palatial dance halls of early 20th-century Europe, the room is about 140 feet wide and has a huge dance floor and two bars. Floor-to-ceiling windows line every inch of the ballroom on three sides, framing sweeping views out to Newport Bay. Just outside the larger of the bars there's a glass-protected terrace—perfect for catching a breath of fresh air. The elegant, wide staircase that climbs from the front entryway to the ballroom makes a beautiful stage for a photogenic entrance.

When you reserve the ballroom, the experienced Harborside staff will assist you with every aspect of your event, from customizing your menu to helping you choose the right linens. They're also skilled at bringing to life whatever celebration you have in mind, be it a formal black-tie affair, a contemporary beach-themed wedding or a rousing casino night. As the Banquet Manager says, "There isn't anything we can't do."

The Harborside Grand Ballroom is unquestionably one of the best waterfront locations in Newport Beach. But for all its majesty, this splendid event space never upstages the bride and groom—it quietly serves as a memorable backdrop.

CEREMONY CAPACITY: The venue holds up to 250 guests for a ceremony in conjunction with a reception.

EVENT/RECEPTION & MEETING CAPACITY: Harborside has two ballrooms, the Catalina and the Lido rooms. Each has a capacity of 250 guests; when used together as the Grand Ballroom they can accommodate a total of 500 guests.

PRICES: WHAT'S THIS GOING TO COST?

Rental Fee: *$500–1,250/event*
   • The rental fee varies depending on the day of the week.

Meals (when priced separately): *$30–75/person*

AVAILABILITY: Year-round, daily, 8am–11pm.

SERVICES/AMENITIES:

Catering: in-house, or select from list of approved ethnic caterers
Kitchen Facilities: n/a
Tables & Chairs: provided
Linens, Silver, etc.: provided
Restrooms: wheelchair accessible
Dance Floor: yes
Bride's & Groom's Dressing Area: yes
AV/Meeting Equipment: limited, please inquire

Parking: self-parking or valet, extra charge
Accommodations: no guest rooms
Outdoor Night Lighting: yes
Outdoor Cooking Facilities: no
Cleanup: provided, extra fee
View: Newport Harbor
Other: full event coordination, WiFi available

RESTRICTIONS:

Alcohol: in-house, no BYO
Smoking: outside only
Music: amplified OK indoors

Wheelchair Access: yes
Insurance: certificate required for vendors
Other: no rice, birdseed, fog machines or glitter

Hornblower Cruises & Events

Yachts

Hornblower South: 2431 West Coast Highway, Newport Beach
Hornblower North: 2527 West Coast Highway, Newport Beach
949/650-2412
www.hornblower.com/newport-beach/weddings
nb@hornblower.com

● Rehearsal Dinners		● Corporate Events	
● Ceremonies		● Meetings	
● Wedding Receptions		● Film Shoots	
● Private Parties		Accommodations	

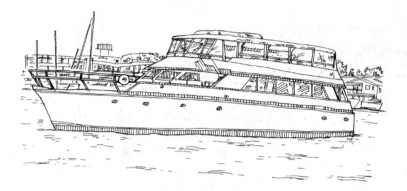

When your friends ask where you plan to get married, you say you're not sure yet but you know it will be on a boat. Actually, what you want is more of a yacht—something sleek and classy that glides through the water like a graceful swan.

You see yourself and your beloved on the sun deck, refreshed by the gentle breeze. As the captain pronounces you husband and wife, you gaze out at the glittering sea and feel at one with the world. If this vision speaks to you, we suggest you pay a visit to Hornblower Cruises & Events, an award-winning yacht charter company where making dreams come true is a way of life.

Each vessel in their fleet of luxury yachts has its own style and personality. Among them—they offer the largest selection in Southern California—is the state-of-the-art *Endless Dreams*. Unlike most big event vessels, which are floating party barges, this one offers the true sophistication of a yacht along with a capacity for 450 guests. The interior is custom-designed with high ceilings and lots of warm wood, granite, and stainless steel throughout the spacious Grand Salon and Entertainment Deck. Amenities include a built-in dance floor, raised DJ platform, and two plasma TVs. There's an outdoor balcony for ceremonies, and a huge bow and Sky Deck for savoring the fresh air. With features you won't find on any other boat on the West Coast, *Endless Dreams* makes other vessels this size pale in comparison.

The impressive *Icon* is sumptuously appointed with rare exotic woods, granite, marble, "Ultra" glass murals, and designer wall and fabric coverings. Interior amenities include a large main salon with a baby grand piano, marble fireplace, entertainment center, and bar. Guests enjoy outdoor viewing areas from the large bow, aft deck, or by strolling the "walk-around" decks. The enclosed upper deck seats up to 130 with a full-service bar, and it also makes a great space for dancing.

Mojo has long been one of the most popular charter vessels in Southern California. An elegant, 100-foot custom-designed Ditmar-Donaldson motor yacht, she's outfitted with an airy enclosed upper deck available for dining, a plush main salon including a full bar, three contemporary staterooms, and a generous forward open bow.

Hornblower Cruises & Events, Newport Beach is more than just the sum of its boats. It's also a full-service event company that offers several budget-friendly packages and the personal assistance of a professional event planner. From entertainment to floral design, Hornblower can help you pull it all together without breaking the bank. (Spectacular sunsets and glittering starscapes come with no extra charge!) If you're looking to put a nautical spin on romance, then let Hornblower Cruises & Events show you the way.

CEREMONY & EVENT/RECEPTION CAPACITY: Hornblower Cruises and Events, Newport Beach accommodates up to 400 seated or 550 standing guests.

MEETING CAPACITY: They can accommodate 10–550 people for business functions, seated conference or theater-style.

PRICES: WHAT'S THIS GOING TO COST?

Package Prices: $78/person and up
- Wedding packages include boat rental, food, cake, nonalcoholic beverages, and a ceremony by the captain.
- Intimate weddings start at $550 for up to 20 guests. There is an additional cost for dinner cruise tickets, which range $75–99/person. Packages include: dockside ceremony, performed by the ship's captain; bouquet for bride & boutonnière for groom; a champagne toast with two commemorative flutes; 4-course seated meal; wedding cake; and more!

Additional Info: Hourly boat rental rates and à la carte services can also be arranged.

AVAILABILITY: Year-round, daily, anytime.

SERVICES/AMENITIES:

Catering: in-house, or BYO depending on the vessel
Kitchen Facilities: n/a
Tables & Chairs: provided
Linens, Silver, etc.: provided
Restrooms: wheelchair accessibility varies
Dance Floor: available
Dressing Areas: yes
AV/Meeting Equipment: CBA

Parking: self-parking, shuttle or valet
Accommodations: no guest rooms
Outdoor Night Lighting: yes
Outdoor Cooking Facilities: no
Cleanup: provided and/or caterer
View: Pacific Ocean and coastal skyline
Other: full event coordination, licensed officiant

RESTRICTIONS:

Alcohol: in-house; BYO varies per vessel
Smoking: on decks only
Music: multiple entertainment options are available

Wheelchair Access: varies per vessel
Insurance: not required

This is important! Tell locations you're reading HERE COMES THE GUIDE and ask if our information is still current.

271

Newport Dunes Waterfront Resort & Marina

Waterfront Resort

1131 Back Bay Drive, Newport Beach
949/999-3124
www.newportdunes.com
sales@newportdunes.com

- Rehearsal Dinners
- Ceremonies
- Wedding Receptions
- Private Parties
- Corporate Events
- Meetings
- Film Shoots
- Accommodations

There's nothing pretentious about the Newport Dunes Waterfront Resort, where weddings and special events are, quite simply, a blast. Nestled on a picturesque lagoon at the entrance to the Back Bay Nature Preserve and the Newport Bay Conservancy, this 110-acre retreat offers 50,000 square feet of function space including 10 exciting indoor and outdoor venues … along with planning assistance, catering, accommodations, and loads of fun at extraordinarily affordable prices.

One reason this resort is so popular is that *Coast Magazine* named its Pavilions the top beach location for events in Orange County. Here, you can have your ceremony, reception, business gala, picnic, barbecue, or any other celebration, right on the beach. That means watersports, volleyball, bonfires and actual sand between your toes are all part of the scene at this much-loved venue. Another reason for its popularity is the wide range of settings to choose from—all of which can be reimagined in a multitude of ways with the help of the experienced and accessible staff.

Take, for example, those Pavilions: Cabana-like structures built over cement pads on the beach, they're easily transformed with tables, twinkle lights, tiki torches and more into magical environments. The Gazebo is, as the name suggests, outdoors and tailored for weddings—especially if your guest list is on the slightly longer side. This romantic spot has the same beachy endowments that the Pavilions possess, and its garden-style gazebo roofed in Spanish tile, ceremony lawn and white picket fence make it even more charming. A special parking lot nearby is convenient for food trucks, carriages, limos, fancy motorcycles, classic cars—and other playful party additions on wheels.

For events on a grand scale—giant weddings or fundraisers, super-sized corporate extravaganzas, and festivals—the Bayside Pavilion can accommodate happy guests by the hundreds. It's a 14,000-square-foot structure that's open-air for half the year and tented November to March (although you can add a tent during warmer months, too). Another option for parties numbering in the hundreds is the Marina Terrace, an expansive grass area on the other side of the lagoon.

Both sites offer maximum flexibility for your multifaceted affair, and include plenty of room on the beach plus lagoon, harbor and Back Bay views.

Want to celebrate indoors? The attractive Bay View Room, which is perfect for more intimate events, features multiple sets of French doors that open to a lush garden and frame lovely views of the lagoon. For larger groups, the spectacular Back Bay Bistro is the place. An outdoor deck, a vast wall of windows that look out over the picturesque Back Bay and Marina, and a retractable roof make it a stunning space. It also provides private salons for cozier get-togethers, as well as a banquet menu that includes delicious and delightfully fresh American, Mediterranean, Hispanic, Asian and other fusions of favorite cuisines.

When the festivities are over, no need to leave. There's a host of comfy beach cottages and bungalows at the resort, and the Hyatt Newport Beach is right across the street. So stay and enjoy the destination, the activities, and the lifestyle that have made the region famous.

CEREMONY CAPACITY: The resort holds 650 seated guests outdoors.

EVENT/RECEPTION & MEETING CAPACITY: The resort accommodates 650 seated or 1,000 standing guests indoors and 450 seated or 800 standing outdoors.

PRICES: WHAT'S THIS GOING TO COST?

Rental Fee: $1,200–5,500/event
  • The rental fee varies depending on the day the of week, the time of year, and the space reserved.

Meals (when priced separately): $70–115/person

Service Charge or Gratuity: 22%

AVAILABILITY: Year-round, daily, 6am–10pm for outdoor venues or 6am–11pm for indoor venues.

SERVICES/AMENITIES:

Catering: in-house or BYO
Kitchen Facilities: not available to outside caterers
Tables & Chairs: provided
Linens, Silver, etc.: provided with in-house catering
Restrooms: wheelchair accessible
Dance Floor: portable provided with in-house catering
Bride's Dressing Area: CBA
AV/Meeting Equipment: CBA

Parking: large lot
Accommodations: 18 guest rooms
Outdoor Night Lighting: CBA
Outdoor Cooking Facilities: no
Cleanup: provided with in-house catering
View: panorama of waterfront, coastline, cityscape, marina, and Newport Beach Nature Preserve
Other: event coordination, extra fee

RESTRICTIONS:

Alcohol: in-house
Smoking: designated areas only
Music: amplified OK with restrictions

Wheelchair Access: yes
Insurance: required for outside caterers

Beachcomber Cafe at Crystal Cove

Waterfront Restaurant

15 Crystal Cove, Newport Coast
949/644-8759
www.thebeachcombercafe.com
catering@thebeachcombercafe.com

● Rehearsal Dinners	● Corporate Events
● Ceremonies	● Meetings
● Wedding Receptions	● Film Shoots
● Private Parties	● Accommodations

Want to treat yourself and your guests to a quintessential Southern California "endless summer" experience? Well, raise the martini flag—as well as your expectations of a really great time—and invite them to an event staged right on the beach at historic Crystal Cove Park, one of the Newport coast's most celebrated sites. This is the place for the classic Southern California beach wedding or party at its best. We're talking anything from gowns and tuxedos to bikinis and board shorts—whatever you envision, it will look amazing with the foaming surf and the scintillating sun close at hand.

Run by *Beachcomber Catering*, experts in coastal entertaining, festivities here unfold in with energy and ease. There are adorable and affordable settings for every kind of affair. A host of tiny cottages and event sites dot the property, all offering varying degrees of privacy and communal activity.

The Beaches Cottage, with its sand-strewn terrace and white picket fence a mere 20 yards from the Pacific, is about as picturesque as you can get. This was the set for the Bette Midler movie, *Beaches*, as well as a long list of other films over the decades. Exchange vows on the inviting blanket of sand out front, then pop around the fence for cocktails, dinner, cake, and a big dose of charm.

The park-like Commons has cute and quirky surfside event areas, as well as marvelous ocean and creek views—Trancos Creek meets the sea here. Not far from the Commons, the Beach Promenade provides a gorgeous sandy stretch for a ceremony, cocktail hour and dining. Imagine a clambake…a luau…a fiesta with mariachis or a romantic tiki-lit banquet with the sea murmuring nearby. Wine tasting, food stations, cracked crab and buckets of ice-cold beer, lobster steamed to perfection, sushi platters, margaritas and mini-ahi tacos, surf and turf extravaganzas—your options are practically unlimited. The dedicated *Beachcomber Catering* team will turn your vision into reality by delivering excellent service, incorporating fresh local products, and customizing every aspect of your event.

Of course you might want to hang out above it all. If that's the case, plan to party up at the Cultural Center Cottage with its expansive deck—it's a heavenly perch designed with elegant entertaining in mind and overlooking exhilarating views of the ocean.

Whatever venue you ultimately choose, we're certain that when your celebration is over you (and some of your guests!) may not want to leave this seductive seaside location. No worries. Just slip off your sandals and stay awhile at one of the many cottages at your disposal. Then take a little time to unwind and explore the coast. You'll soon discover what's made Crystal Cove a popular destination since the 1930s, and why people who arrive as visitors soon turn into devoted fans.

CEREMONY & EVENT/RECEPTION CAPACITY: The site can accommodate up to 200 seated or standing guests outdoors.

MEETING CAPACITY: Meeting spaces hold up to 30 seated guests.

PRICES: WHAT'S THIS GOING TO COST?

Meals (when priced separately): $52–95/person

Service Charge or Gratuity: 22%

Additional Info: The state site permit fee ranges $750–2,750 depending on the venue selected.

AVAILABILITY: Year-round, daily, 8am–9pm.

SERVICES/AMENITIES:

Catering: in-house, or BYO ethnic caterer with approval

Kitchen Facilities: fully equipped

Tables & Chairs: provided

Linens, Silver, etc.: provided

Restrooms: wheelchair accessible

Dance Area: provided

Bride's Dressing Area: yes

AV/Meeting Equipment: CBA

Parking: large lot

Accommodations: 24 cottages

Outdoor Night Lighting: CBA

Outdoor Cooking Facilities: BBQ on site

Cleanup: provided

View: Pacific Ocean

Other: in-house florals, off-premise catering

RESTRICTIONS:

Alcohol: full in-house bar

Smoking: designated areas only

Music: amplified OK outdoors with restrictions

Wheelchair Access: yes

Insurance: not required

Marbella Country Club

Country Club

30800 Golf Club Drive, San Juan Capistrano
949/248-3700 x307
www.countryclubreceptions.com
events@marbellacc.net

● Rehearsal Dinners	● Corporate Events
● Ceremonies	● Meetings
● Wedding Receptions	● Film Shoots
● Private Parties	Accommodations

It may be nestled in the pastoral valley between the Pacific Ocean and the Saddleback Mountains, but the elegant Marbella Country Club embodies the spirit of the Mediterranean. Even if you're not jetting off to the coast of Italy for your honeymoon, you'll still get a taste of it when you celebrate your Big Day in this impressive setting.

After driving through the club's gated community, past manicured lawns and a flowerbed blooming with ivory roses, you reach the porte-cochère of the 50,000-square-foot clubhouse where valets await. Glittering like a baronial villa in the San Juan Capistrano sun, the majestic structure offers a genteel welcome with a tri-tier fountain ringed by palms and birds of paradise.

Upon arrival and during the cocktail hour, your guests will mingle in the handsome South Bar and around the fire pit of the spacious Valencia Terrace, enjoying mixed libations and delectable hors d'oeuvres.

Most couples say their vows on the Croquet Lawn, under a wrought-iron arch adorned with flowers and greenery that overlooks the championship golf course. Fragrant petals define a colorful aisle, where seating for up to 240 can be arranged. Although the bride and groom garner most of the attention, guests can't help but notice the border of roses and the stunning rock waterfall. Three stairways leading to this area provide numerous ways to choreograph your ceremony for sentimental impact.

After the knot is tied, Marbella's picturesque fairways and beautiful clubhouse architecture make spectacular backdrops for photos. While your photographer is capturing your first pictures as newlyweds, your guests stroll across the lawn to the Catalonia Terrace and luxuriously appointed Catalonia Grille for the reception. Here, they'll savor creative specialties prepared by the club's Certified Master Chef. If you like, place votive candles on the tables for a romantic touch.

From your sweetheart table you can watch your contented guests as they flow easily between the Catalonia Grille and the terrace through five sets of French doors. Après-dinner festivities continue on the dance floor.

When you have your wedding at the Marbella Country Club, it's the only event scheduled for the entire evening. So take your time and immerse yourself in the celebration, knowing it will be an unforgettable experience for all who attend.

CEREMONY CAPACITY: The Croquet Lawn seats up to 220 guests.

EVENT/RECEPTION CAPACITY: The Terrace holds up to 220 seated or 240 standing guests.

MEETING CAPACITY: Indoor spaces accommodate up to 190 seated guests.

PRICES: WHAT'S THIS GOING TO COST?

Package Prices: $88/person and up
- Pricing varies based on food, beverage, and rental inclusions. Food & beverage minimums will apply. Menus and packages can be customized to fit your needs and budget. Pricing does not include additional site fees, mandatory service charge, gratuity, and current sales tax.

AVAILABILITY: Year-round, daily, 7am–midnight.

SERVICES/AMENITIES:

Catering: in-house
Kitchen Facilities: n/a
Tables & Chairs: provided
Linens, Silver, etc.: provided
Restrooms: wheelchair accessible
Dance Floor: provided
Bride's Dressing Area: yes
AV/Meeting Equipment: provided

Parking: large lot, valet provided
Accommodations: no guest rooms
Outdoor Night Lighting: yes
Outdoor Cooking Facilities: BBQ
Cleanup: provided
View: fairways, garden, landscaped grounds
Other: grand piano

RESTRICTIONS:

Alcohol: in-house
Smoking: outdoors only
Music: amplified OK indoors, and outdoors with restrictions

Wheelchair Access: limited
Insurance: required

The Hacienda

1725 College Avenue, Santa Ana
714/558-1304
www.the-hacienda.com
weddings@the-hacienda.com

- ● Rehearsal Dinners
- ● Ceremonies
- ● Wedding Receptions
- ● Private Parties
- ● Corporate Events
- ● Meetings
- ● Film Shoots
- Accommodations

As soon as you walk through the front gates of The Hacienda, you travel back in time to a more peaceful and romantic era. Once part of an orange and avocado ranch from the early 1900s, this whitewashed adobe and its charming courtyard is now one of Orange County's most popular wedding locations.

Two settings are available for both ceremonies and receptions. If you'd like to celebrate outdoors, the flagstone courtyard is ideal. Ivy-covered balconies, an abundance of potted flowers, and a three-tiered fountain in the center give the space an Old World atmosphere. Off to one side is a wooden arbor, hung with stained-glass panels and entwined with vines, that serves as an altar for ceremonies. When a couple exchanges vows here, candelabras provide old-fashioned warmth and sparkle. For courtyard weddings, the bride's dressing room is the old master bedroom in the main hacienda, appointed with antiques and giant mirrors. From here she can step out onto her balcony to survey her guests below.

Indoor events are hosted in the Taos Room, a beautiful ballroom in the building adjacent to the main hacienda. It has a Southwest flavor, with its 200-year-old decorative doors carved from Mexican mesquite wood, oversized fireplace, antiques and original artwork. A 20-foot ceiling with skylights and a row of French doors that open to the courtyard provide natural light. At the far end, a flight of Spanish tile stairs—perfect for making a grand entrance—leads up to the bride's dressing room. Large mirrors, lots of space, and roses stenciled above the doors and windows make brides feel quite comfortable.

The Hacienda is owned by June Neptune, an experienced wedding maven with a bride-friendly philosophy. "Weddings should be stress-free and fun," she says. Her all-inclusive packages really simplify the planning process, covering everything from floral decorations and live music for the ceremony, to appetizers, drinks, dinner and even the wedding cake. Another built-in benefit is assistance from June's staff of wedding coordinators, who will help you plan your event and make sure it comes off just as you envisioned it.

CEREMONY CAPACITY: The Taos Courtyard holds 180 seated, 300 if combined with the Taos Room. The Inner Courtyard seats up to 120 guests.

EVENT/RECEPTION CAPACITY: The Hacienda holds 400 guests.

MEETING CAPACITY: Event spaces accommodate 30–400 seated guests.

PRICES: WHAT'S THIS GOING TO COST?

Package Prices: $60/person and up
- The brunch package starts at $60/person. Afternoon/evening packages start at $85/person for Fridays, Saturdays, and Sundays.
- Wedding packages include: event coordinators; live music; fresh flowers, tables and chairs; linens; food service; passed hors d'oeuvres; cake; and unlimited beer, wine and champagne.

Service Charge or Gratuity: 20%

AVAILABILITY: Year-round, daily, until 11pm.

SERVICES/AMENITIES:

Catering: in-house, no BYO
Kitchen Facilities: n/a
Tables & Chairs: provided
Linens, Silver, etc.: provided
Restrooms: wheelchair accessible
Dance Floor: flagstone patio or tile floor
Bride's & Groom's Dressing Areas: yes
AV/Meeting Equipment: podium, PA system, microphones; other CBA

Parking: several lots nearby
Accommodations: no guest rooms
Outdoor Night Lighting: yes
Outdoor Cooking Facilities: no
Cleanup: provided
View: garden, fountains, and courtyard
Other: event coordination

RESTRICTIONS:

Alcohol: in-house, no BYO
Smoking: not allowed
Music: amplified OK

Wheelchair Access: yes
Insurance: not required
Other: no rice, birdseed, or confetti; children must be supervised

---

Overwhelmed? Use the search criteria on www.HereComesTheGuide.com to narrow down your choices.

279

Heritage Museum of Orange County

Museum and Garden

3101 West Harvard Street, Santa Ana
714/540-0404 x223

www.heritagemuseumoc.org
weddings@heritagemuseumoc.org

Rehearsal Dinners		● Corporate Events	
● Ceremonies		● Meetings	
● Wedding Receptions		● Film Shoots	
● Private Parties		Accommodations	

The heart of this museum is the old H. Clay Kellogg House, a lovingly restored 1898 Victorian that sits amid ten acres of historic gardens and turn-of-the-century buildings. Created to preserve Orange County's cultural heritage, the museum takes you back to the early 1900s: While you're ambling along its jasmine-covered walkways, or through its orange groves and rose garden, you'll think you've stepped back in time onto a country estate. Another benefit of this location is that there are no noise ordinances and on select evenings you can party until midnight—a rarity for Orange County outdoor venues!

Heritage Museum of Orange County has recreated a gracious past, and weddings are often inspired by the setting's peaceful Victorian ambiance. Although you can't host your wedding inside, a stroll around the Kellogg House—outfitted with the utmost in Victoriana—is enough to set the mood. The spacious lawns lend themselves to a number of possibilities for parties and receptions, and the gazebo is popular for ceremonies.

The flexible and experienced Heritage Museum staff are happy to accommodate your special needs in every way they can. All proceeds from weddings and receptions go to support the museum's nonprofit programs, which provide "hands-on" historical enrichment for visitors. A portion of the proceeds are also tax deductible. Not only is Heritage Museum a lovely place to host your wedding, you'll have the satisfaction of benefiting a wonderful cultural resource.

CEREMONY CAPACITY: The Gazebo Lawn and the front of the Kellogg House hold a maximum of 300 guests.

EVENT/RECEPTION CAPACITY: The Rose Garden Lawn accommodates 400 seated guests or 600 standing. A shaded pavilion seats 150.

MEETING CAPACITY: The shaded pavilion holds 150 seated conference-style or 300 theater-style. The meeting room seats 20 conference-style or 40 theater-style. Audiovisual equipment is not provided by the museum.

PRICES: WHAT'S THIS GOING TO COST?

Rental Fee: *$3,300–4,900/event*
- The rental fee varies depending on the day of the week and time of year.
- The fee is for a ceremony & reception and includes a tax-deductible, nonrefundable $1,500 deposit. A refundable $1,000 security deposit is additional.

Package Prices: *$46/person and up*
- Packages are based on a 100-guest minimum and include: standard rentals, setup & break-down, hors d'oeuvres, salad, entrée, some beverages, and more!
- Sales tax, service charge, and gratuity are additional.

Additional Info: Bar packages are also available for an extra fee.

AVAILABILITY: Year-round, Monday–Thursday, 4pm–10pm; Friday and Saturday, 10am–midnight; Sunday, 10am–10pm.

SERVICES/AMENITIES:

Catering: provided by the exclusive caterer, *Country Garden Caterers*
Kitchen Facilities: n/a
Tables & Chairs: through exclusive vendor
Linens, Silver, etc.: through caterer
Restrooms: wheelchair accessible
Dance Floor: patio
Bride's Dressing Area: yes
AV/Meeting Equipment: BYO

Parking: ample free
Accommodations: no guest rooms
Outdoor Night Lighting: yes
Outdoor Cooking Facilities: no
Cleanup: caterer or renter
View: rose garden, citrus grove, gazebo, historic homes, blacksmith shop, fountains, wetlands

RESTRICTIONS:

Alcohol: provided by the exclusive caterer, *Country Garden Caterers*
Smoking: designated areas only
Music: amplified OK
Wheelchair Access: yes

Insurance: certificate required through WedSafe
Other: no rice, birdseed, synthetic rose petals or confetti; no nails, tacks, staples, glue or tape; no sparklers or other pyrotechnics; restrictions on open flames

Old Ranch Country Club

Country Club

3901 Lampson Avenue, Seal Beach
562/596-4425

www.oldranchweddings.com
kmesinas@oldranch.com

● Rehearsal Dinners	● Corporate Events
● Ceremonies	● Meetings
● Wedding Receptions	● Film Shoots
● Private Parties	Accommodations

The Old Ranch Country Club enjoys a reputation for being a place that's easy to get to and easy to work with. With its comfortable clubhouse, it's also a place where guests feel right at home.

Situated at the northern edge of Orange County, Old Ranch is within a short drive to three airports and several major freeways, making it convenient for local or out-of-state travelers en route to your celebration.

Although Old Ranch has been a members-only venue since its inception in 1967, their banquet facilities are available to nonmembers for special events. As you enter, you're greeted by a huge mural of blue skies, trees and rolling hills—a tableau that mimics the club's pastoral surroundings. Framed by a stone arch, it provides a dramatic backdrop for photos, as well as a conversation piece for guests socializing here before heading into the spacious reception salon.

Once you're in the salon, prepare to be delighted by what you see. A wall of floor-to-ceiling Nana windows open like an accordion to an outdoor terrace with an expansive view of the golf course and lake, complete with a fountain. This modern 6,000-square-foot banquet space is large enough to accommodate both a wedding and reception. However, it's also divisible into four sections that can be used individually or in combination, depending on the size of your event. With its casual-yet-refined sensibility, the club atmosphere invites guests to relax with a glass of chilled Chardonnay as they drink in the landscape. Speaking of the landscape, there are a number of photogenic spots overlooking the fairways for some before- or after-ceremony pictures.

Perhaps the club's most popular area is its gorgeous bridal courtyard, designed especially for outdoor ceremonies. Ringed by flowers, palm trees and other greenery, it has a lush, almost tropical feel. As friends and family look on from their lawn seating, they have a breathtaking view of the lake and golf course in the background.

Old Ranch is not only conveniently located for your special event, it's also only a short drive to the beach for some fun in the California sun. The beach we're referring to is Seal Beach, a haven for those in search of a laid-back, small town atmosphere. Replete with suntanned surfers, a treelined Main Street and a colorful past, the town is packed with seaside delights and history. Between this appealing country club and its friendly coastal neighbor, you'll find all the elements you need for a wonderful weekend wedding.

CEREMONY CAPACITY: Outdoors, the Bridal Courtyard seats up to 400 guests.

EVENT/RECEPTION & MEETING CAPACITY: The Salon holds 400 seated or 500 standing guests. This room can be split into four smaller rooms, each holding 60–100 guests.

PRICES: WHAT'S THIS GOING TO COST?

Packages: $68–165/person

AVAILABILITY: Year-round: Monday–Thursday, 6am–11:30pm; Friday–Sunday, 6am–midnight; extra hours may be available.

SERVICES/AMENITIES:

Catering: in-house, BYO with extra fee

Kitchen Facilities: n/a

Tables & Chairs: provided

Linens, Silver, etc.: provided

Restrooms: wheelchair accessible

Dance Floor: provided

Dressing Areas: yes

AV/Meeting Equipment: CBA, extra charge

Parking: large lighted lot

Accommodations: no guest rooms, hotel across the street and local hotels will shuttle

Outdoor Night Lighting: in the Bridal Courtyard

Outdoor Cooking Facilities: no

Cleanup: provided

View: golf course, lake, fountain, distant mountains

RESTRICTIONS:

Alcohol: in-house, or BYO wine with corkage fee

Smoking: outside only

Music: amplified OK

Wheelchair Access: yes

Insurance: provided

Rancho Las Lomas

19191 Lawrence Canyon, Silverado
949/888-3080

www.rancholaslomas.com
info@rancholaslomas.com

- Rehearsal Dinners
- Ceremonies
- Wedding Receptions
- Private Parties
- Corporate Events
- Meetings
- Film Shoots
- Accommodations

Nestled among the rolling hills of South Orange County, the 32-acre Rancho Las Lomas is a testimony to the charms of early California. Surrounded by orange groves and flowering shrubs, the hacienda-style buildings of the ranch sit under the cooling shade of towering oak and sycamore trees, and are connected by terracotta walkways and bridges. Guests can take enchanted strolls through the grounds—redolent of orange blossoms and lush with botanical garden-quality flora—and peek into the large ornamental birdcages that house a collection of rare tropical birds and exotic animals.

On a plateau at the top of a gentle slope is the Grand Salon, a spacious light-filled room with a big stone fireplace as its stunning centerpiece. The combination of white stucco walls, beamed ceiling, terracotta floor and wood-framed windows makes the Salon ideal for all types of gatherings. And with the adjoining patio, adorned with a sparkling blue-tile reflecting pool, you can easily have an indoor/outdoor reception.

Smaller affairs are often held in Rick's Cafe, a four-level Casablanca-style villa built into the hillside just beyond the Grand Salon patio. An oak bar, a rough-hewn beamed ceiling, stone fireplace, and an eclectic mix of Victorian antiques in its many inviting conversation nooks, create an intimate atmosphere for parties.

The venue's newest space is La Terraza, an open-air cobblestone terrace bordered by California Oaks and native cactus. Large enough for hosting weddings, concerts, gala fundraisers, and corporate retreats, it's the perfect place for dining under the stars. It's also a charming spot for saying "I do": Here, the bride begins her grand entrance at the top of a hill, descending a wide, rustic wood staircase until she reaches her guests seated below. When glowing candles are placed on the stairs, the scene is positively romantic.

Wedding ceremonies also take place in the Teatro, an open-air theater with a marble stage, stone patio and bubbling fountains. The cozy Casa Bonita next door, which has full-length mirrors plus a makeup area and parlor with fireplace, is one of the loveliest bride's dressing rooms we've seen.

Everything at Rancho Las Lomas has been carefully conceived and realized, from its blossoming foliage to the abundance of hand-painted tile. If you're looking for a simply sensational setting, this is it.

CEREMONY CAPACITY: The Teatro/Chapel seats 350 guests; La Terraza seats 400.

EVENT/RECEPTION CAPACITY: Outdoor areas accommodate up to 500 guests. Indoors, the facility holds up to 200 seated or 300–500 standing for a cocktail reception.

MEETING CAPACITY: The Grand Salon holds 300 guests seated theater-style.

PRICES: WHAT'S THIS GOING TO COST?

Rental Fee: $3,500–9,500/event
- The nonrefundable fee includes use of both indoor and outdoor facilities for a specific time frame, along with the following: bistro lighting in the Teatro, access to the Wildlife Foundation, 200 fruitwood Chiavari chairs (with choice of white, ivory, or black cushion), and a variety of banquet and cocktail tables.

Package Prices: $175/person and up

AVAILABILITY: Year-round, daily, 9am–midnight.

SERVICES/AMENITIES:

Catering: in-house
Kitchen Facilities: n/a
Tables & Chairs: provided for up to 200 guests
Linens, Silver, etc.: through caterer
Restrooms: wheelchair accessible
Dance Floor: provided, additional fee
Bride's & Groom's Dressing Areas: yes
AV/Meeting Equipment: provided, extra fee

Parking: valet required, additional fee
Accommodations: no guest rooms
Outdoor Night Lighting: provided
Outdoor Cooking Facilities: n/a
Cleanup: caterer
View: 100-year-old Sequoias, rose gardens, Cleveland National Forest

RESTRICTIONS:

Alcohol: in-house, no BYO
Smoking: allowed in designated areas
Music: amplified OK indoors until midnight and outdoors until 10pm

Wheelchair Access: yes
Insurance: may be required
Other: no rice, confetti, or sparklers

Tustin Ranch Golf Club

Golf Club

12442 Tustin Ranch Road, Tustin

714/734-2116

www.countryclubreceptions.com
events@tustinranchgolf.com

● Rehearsal Dinners	● Corporate Events
● Ceremonies	● Meetings
● Wedding Receptions	● Film Shoots
● Private Parties	Accommodations

Expect the unexpected at Tustin Ranch Golf Club. Not only is this venue a rare find—a public golf course with a graceful palm-lined entrance, cascading waterfalls, lakes, and lush year-round greenery—nothing can top the sense of well-being that comes with planning a special event here. The high-end yet utterly carefree feel is a delight, but an even bigger part of the appeal is the facility's imaginative and engaging event staff, who come up with so many creative ways to roll out the red carpet.

The special treatment begins on arrival with a welcome at the sun-drenched Front Courtyard, where your guests can congregate under big red umbrellas with a refreshing libation. Brides, make sure to check out your dressing room! You might not anticipate this level of chic in a golf course setting, but there it is, perfectly outfitted in champagne and rose gold with luxurious seating and accents—just the place to prepare in style for a ceremony on the Lakeview Patio. You'll make a stunning appearance at the top of the clubhouse stairway before descending regally to tie the knot under a flower-draped arbor backed by a sparkling lake and fountain.

After the ceremony, take a short walk past a handsome putting green set up for fun. Miniature hazards and golf balls customized with names or logos make this a great way to relax post-ceremony. Meanwhile, cocktails are served on the adjacent Greenside Patio, a multi-tiered sundeck that allows for several levels of entertaining. The broad stone patio enhanced by mood lighting is a superlative spot for functions large and small, and it's ideal for drinking, dining, or dancing under the sun or stars.

Sit-down receptions generally unfold in the Main Clubhouse, where a soaring beamed ceiling; soft, neutral tones; and floor-to-ceiling windows create a light, airy ambiance. The spacious Augusta Room and the somewhat smaller Broadmoor Room (which has a full bar) can be used separately or together, depending on the size of your gathering. Both boast panoramic views of the property's captivating surroundings. The highly customizable Cypress and Doral Rooms, as well as the Player's Lounge, offer additional options for banquets, luncheons, meetings, and more when you have a shorter guest list. And for those who just want to slip away to catch up and chill, the Pine Tree Patio provides outdoor seating with bistro lighting and views of the 18th hole.

Of course, the best way to slip away here—whether for photos, a quick break, or simply a bit of fun—is by golf cart. They offer one designed specifically for newlyweds that's just the ticket if you plan on posing in front of those marvelous water features and manicured fairways. No wonder so many couples rave about Tustin Ranch Golf Club and its outstanding staff. "I would recommend using this venue to everyone," says a bride, "and I think my guests would do the same." "It was amazing," adds another. "If I could, I'd get married there all over again."

CEREMONY CAPACITY: The facility holds 250 seated guests indoors and 350 seated outdoors.

EVENT/RECEPTION CAPACITY: The site can accommodate 220 seated or 250 standing indoors and 200 seated or 275 standing outdoors.

MEETING CAPACITY: Meeting spaces hold 400 seated guests.

PRICES: WHAT'S THIS GOING TO COST?

Package Prices: $83/person and up
- Pricing varies based on food, beverage, and rental inclusions. Food & beverage minimums will apply. Menus and packages can be customized to fit your needs and budget. Pricing does not include additional site fees, mandatory service charge, gratuity, and current sales tax.

AVAILABILITY: Year-round, daily, anytime.

SERVICES/AMENITIES:

Catering: in-house
Kitchen Facilities: n/a
Tables & Chairs: provided
Linens, Silver, etc.: provided
Restrooms: wheelchair accessible
Dance Floor: portable provided
Bride's & Groom's Dressing Areas: yes
AV/Meeting Equipment: available, extra fee may apply

Parking: large complimentary lot
Accommodations: no guest rooms
Outdoor Night Lighting: CBA, uplighting under the palm trees
Outdoor Cooking Facilities: BBQ CBA
Cleanup: caterer
View: fountain, garden patio; panorama of fairways

RESTRICTIONS:

Alcohol: in-house
Smoking: designated areas only
Music: amplified OK indoors with restrictions

Wheelchair Access: yes
Insurance: liability required

Want to know WHAT TO ASK a potential location or vendor? Check out our Questions to Ask starting on page 21.

Black Gold Golf Club

Golf Club

1 Black Gold Drive, Yorba Linda
714/961-0253 x118

blackgoldgolf.com
CYoung@blackgoldgolf.com

- Rehearsal Dinners
- Ceremonies
- Wedding Receptions
- Private Parties
- Corporate Events
- Meetings

Film Shoots
Accommodations

Tucked away in the quiet foothills of Yorba Linda, Black Gold Golf Club occupies a spot that showcases the best views in Orange County: gently sloping mountains to the east, the wide valley floor spread out below, and the sparkling Pacific beyond. On a clear day you can even see Catalina Island in the distance.

The entire venue has been designed with entertaining in mind, from the 20,000-square-foot Craftsman-inspired clubhouse to the secluded, charming ceremony site. Meticulously manicured fairways (this property is consistently voted one of Southern California's best public courses), stunning lakes, and a serene waterfall set the scene for beautiful photos. Your guests are sure to appreciate the convenient, plentiful parking and close proximity to a wide range of accommodations.

Your ceremony will be memorable at The Falls, a completely private area next to a cascading waterfall and surrounded by spectacular vistas in every direction. Vows are exchanged under a pretty white arbor, which can be draped with flowers or hung with lights, fabric, lanterns—whatever accents you choose to complement your theme.

With floor-to-ceiling windows that look out over the lush 18th green, the clubhouse's Lakeview and Valleyview Rooms can serve as intimate reception halls on their own, but may also be combined to create one grand space for larger, more lavish affairs. During the cocktail hour, your guests can mingle on the adjoining patio and enjoy watching you cruise around below in a golf cart, posing for photos on the course as the sun begins to set behind the twinkling lights of the valley.

Couples love the personalized attention they receive from the staff here, who are quick to respond to questions and are known for going "above and beyond" what's expected. They're seasoned pros, and will walk you through the planning process with reassuring ease. Most importantly, they'll be present on the wedding day to act as vendor liaisons, coordinate the timing of events, and take care of last-minute needs. All you and your partner will need to do is show up, say "I do," and have the time of your lives.

CEREMONY CAPACITY: The site holds 200 seated guests indoors and 250 seated outdoors.

EVENT/RECEPTION CAPACITY: The site accommodates 200 seated or 300 standing indoors.

MEETING CAPACITY: Meeting spaces seat 200 guests.

PRICES: WHAT'S THIS GOING TO COST?

Meals (when priced separately): $40/person and up

AVAILABILITY: Year-round, daily.

SERVICES/AMENITIES:

Catering: in-house, or BYO with approval
Kitchen Facilities: fully equipped
Tables & Chairs: provided
Linens, Silver, etc.: provided
Restrooms: wheelchair accessible
Dance Floor: portable provided
Bride's Dressing Area: yes
AV/Meeting Equipment: available, extra fee

Parking: large lot
Accommodations: no guest rooms
Outdoor Night Lighting: yes
Outdoor Cooking Facilities: no
Cleanup: provided
View: landscaped grounds, lake, cityscape; panorama of waterfall, canyon, hills, fairways, and greens
Other: event coordination, in-house wedding cake, complimentary golf

RESTRICTIONS:

Alcohol: in-house
Smoking: outdoors only
Music: amplified OK

Wheelchair Access: yes
Insurance: not required

San Bernardino Mountains/
Lake Arrowhead

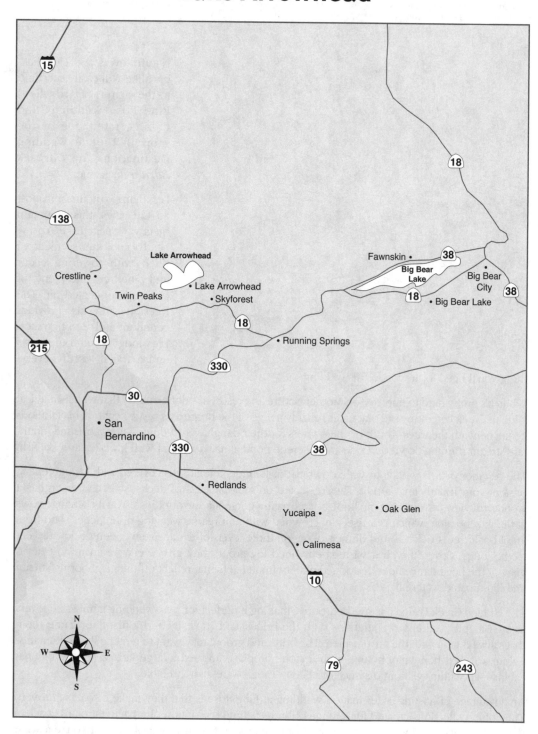

Arrowhead Pine Rose Weddings and Cabins

Resort

25994 State Highway 189, Lake Arrowhead

909/337-2341

www.pineroseweddings.com
events@pinerosecabins.com

● Rehearsal Dinners	● Corporate Events
● Ceremonies	● Meetings
● Wedding Receptions	● Film Shoots
● Private Parties	● Accommodations

Nature lovers and city slickers alike will easily succumb to the charms of Arrowhead Pine Rose Weddings and Cabins, rated one of the "Top 10 Unique Wedding Destinations" by *Harper's Bazaar* magazine.

Less than two hours from most So Cal cities, this mountain "getaway" near Lake Arrowhead occupies ten scenic acres filled with towering cedar and pine trees and plenty of clean, pine-scented air. The forested setting also provides ceremony and reception sites, plus lodging for your guests and a friendly staff—everything you'll need for a wonderful wedding.

While it's pretty hard to improve on Mother Nature, the resort has done exactly that with its magical Hidden Creek ceremony site that takes full advantage of the property's rustic beauty. This fabulous venue beneath the trees—built by the owners for their daughter's wedding—has a pristine mountain stream running down one side and a serene pond at its base filled with lily pads and koi fish.

The ceremony starts with your walk down the aisle under a log trellis covered with lush greenery, past all your friends and family. They're seated on multiple tiers of decks, so each person has a wonderful view of you tying the knot, as well as the gorgeous surroundings. You'll exchange vows at the gazebo altar, which is artistically crowned with an organic weaving of branches shed from an old oak tree. Cocktails and dinner follow on three levels of expansive wooden decks adjacent to the lodge. Covered with a wisteria-entwined log arbor, they give everyone an unobstructed view of the huge dance floor, festooned with twinkle lights that reflect off the neighboring stream and illuminated waterfall.

The Hidden Creek Lodge has five bedrooms, making it perfect for post-wedding family sleepovers as well as pre-wedding preparations with the bridesmaids upstairs and a first-floor game room that's always a hit with the groomsmen. The bride and groom may want to rent the Rustic Romance Cabin, an ideal honeymoon suite with a stone fireplace and extra-large Jacuzzi tub. Additional cabins—all within walking distance of Hidden Creek—are also available.

An advantage of hosting a destination wedding at Pine Rose is that they make it so easy for you. They offer collections created for a range of budgets (and the option of a payment plan), a selection of screened local vendors to choose from, and menu tastings. What's more, if you're a wine connoisseur or craft beer aficionado, you'll love the fact that you can bring in your choice of alcoholic beverages. The staff here really has thought of everything so that you can have a stress-free experience in this fairy-tale place in the woods.

CEREMONY CAPACITY: The site holds 40 seated guests indoors and 175 seated outdoors.

EVENT/RECEPTION CAPACITY: The resort can accommodate 40 seated or 50 standing guests indoors and 175 seated or standing outdoors.

MEETING CAPACITY: Meeting spaces seat up to 40 guests indoors and 175 outdoors.

PRICES: WHAT'S THIS GOING TO COST?

Package Prices: $15,000–30,000/event
- Package prices vary depending on the guest count.
- All packages include: exclusive use of the wedding site from 1pm on the day of the wedding to 10am the following day; 1 night's lodging for up to 14 wedding guests at Hidden Creek Lodge; ceremony chair placement and takedown; reception table setup and takedown; ceremony and reception coordination; catering (can accommodate special dietary restrictions), custom wedding cake or dessert bar, linens, bartender and bar setup, professional DJ, and large dance floor.

AVAILABILITY: Weddings for 41 or more guests are held from the first weekend in May to the last weekend in October; for 40 guests or fewer, November–April. Elopements for 2 are available year-round.

SERVICES/AMENITIES:

Catering: in-house (plated service for the bride & groom, as well as disabled or elderly guests)
Kitchen Facilities: yes
Tables & Chairs: provided
Linens, Silver, etc.: provided
Restrooms: wheelchair accessible
Dance Floor: provided
Bride's Dressing Area: bridal suite
AV/Meeting Equipment: provided
Other: event coordination, WiFi, pool, hot tub, state-of-the-art sound system, cake, gazebo, honeymoon cabin with hot tub on site

Parking: on-site parking attendants provided for weddings over 100
Accommodations: 16 cabins and 4 lodges sleep up to 135
Outdoor Night Lighting: market lighting
Outdoor Cooking Facilities: no
Cleanup: provided for weddings
View: creek, forest, pond, meadow, waterfall, log swings, log bridges

RESTRICTIONS:

Alcohol: bar packages available, or BYO with Pine Rose's certified bartender (no corkage fee)
Smoking: designated areas only
Music: OK with restrictions

Wheelchair Access: yes
Insurance: liability required

Lake Arrowhead Resort & Spa
An Autograph Collection by Marriott

Resort Hotel

27984 Highway 189, Lake Arrowhead
909/336-1511 x662
www.lakearrowheadresort.com
djohnson@lakearrowheadresort.com

● Rehearsal Dinners	● Corporate Events
● Ceremonies	● Meetings
● Wedding Receptions	● Film Shoots
● Private Parties	● Accommodations

The picturesque lake region high up in the richly forested San Bernardino Mountains is a favorite Southland destination, attracting skiers, boaters, nature lovers, and engaged couples longing to tie the knot amid unspoiled surroundings. The premier venue for year-round weddings and social events in this scenic landscape is the Lake Arrowhead Resort and Spa. The full-service AAA Four Diamond Resort occupies a prime location along the lakeshore. What's more, it has numerous possibilities for large and small celebrations that showcase the area's seasonal charms.

The wood deck in the resort's Lakeside Lawn is a spectacular spot to exchange vows, especially in the springtime when butterflies, songbirds, and blooming foliage are sweet accompaniments. Towering pines flank each side of the deck, and the blue water and tree-covered mountains form a panoramic backdrop. The adjacent diamond-shaped lawn can be set theater-style for the ceremony or used for receptions. In the summer, why not stage casual festivities right on the resort's private beach, and maybe even say "I do" with the warm sand between your toes? A favorite choice for indoor affairs, especially during winter months, is the Arrowhead Ballroom, whose grandeur and well-appointed detailing make for a stunning reception. Another option is the Lakeview Terrace Room, furnished with warm tones and picture windows that frame a scintillating winterscape or the burnished autumn scenery. Glass doors open out to a terrace, so your guests can enjoy an up-close vista of the shimmering lake and savor the crisp mountain air.

The Lake Arrowhead Resort can host weddings and receptions for 30 to 300 guests, and has plenty of upscale guest accommodations, too: 162 ultra-contemporary, lodge-style rooms and 11 luxurious suites with balconies or patios. Newlyweds can wallow in romance in a spacious Lakeview Suite, outfitted with a fireplace, plush bed linens and an oversize soaking tub. But what makes the resort unique to the area is its staff's ability to provide full-service coordination and catering for large gatherings. Smaller parties here are no less special: Day-after brunches or rehearsal dinners convene in the resort's fine dining restaurant, BIN189. The refined, yet relaxed, ambiance—replete with water views, a top-flight wine list and acclaimed gourmet menus—ensures a sense of occasion. The Magnum, a cozy private dining room enclosed by glass walls lined with wine bottles, is a sophisticated choice for intimate get-togethers.

Whether you've come to the resort for your wedding, honeymoon, or to relive the memories on your anniversary, be sure to experience the Spa of the Pines. With certified practitioners and nature-inspired treatments, the spa offers supreme nurturing and indulgence.

If you've got a long guest list and a penchant for the pristine alpine environment of Lake Arrowhead, look no further.

CEREMONY CAPACITY: The Lakeside Lawn holds 300 seated. Indoor ceremonies take place in various banquet rooms that can seat 30–300.

EVENT/RECEPTION CAPACITY: Indoor areas accommodate up to 300 seated or 450 standing. Outdoor seating ranges 80–300.

MEETING CAPACITY: Several spaces seat 16–450 guests.

PRICES: WHAT'S THIS GOING TO COST?

Ceremony Fee: $1,500–2,500/event
- The ceremony fee varies depending on the day of week and time of year.
- The fee for the Lakeside Lawn area includes rehearsal and ceremony coordination, white garden chairs, gift and guest book tables, wedding arch, directional signage, signature "Spa of the Pines" water station.

Package Prices: $95–175/person
- Package prices vary depending on the package chosen
- Wedding packages start at $95/person for dinner and include: champagne and sparkling cider toast, butler-passed hors d'oeuvres (included with dinner package), 3-course meal and wedding cake. A complimentary guest room for the bride and groom is provided with more than 50 guests, and group discounts for overnight wedding guests can be arranged.

AVAILABILITY: Year-round, daily.

SERVICES/AMENITIES:

Catering: in-house, no BYO

Kitchen Facilities: n/a

Tables & Chairs: provided

Linens, Silver, etc.: provided

Restrooms: wheelchair accessible

Dance Floor: provided

Bride's Dressing Area: yes

AV/Meeting Equipment: full range

Parking: ample on-site or valet

Accommodations: 173 guest rooms

Outdoor Night Lighting: some, more CBA

Outdoor Cooking Facilities: BBQs CBA

Cleanup: provided

View: lake, mountains and pine trees

Other: health spa, event coordination, on-site restaurant BIN189

RESTRICTIONS:

Alcohol: in-house, no BYO

Smoking: designated areas only

Music: moderately amplified OK indoors until 1am, outdoors until 9pm

Wheelchair Access: yes

Insurance: not required

Other: no rice, birdseed, or confetti

Riverside/Inland Empire

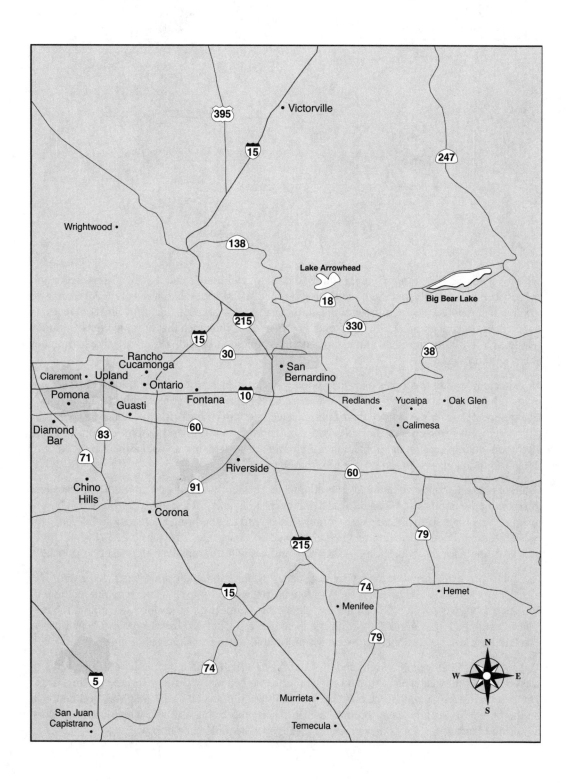

Los Serranos Golf and Country Club

Golf Club

15656 Yorba Avenue, Chino Hills
909/325-6943
www.losserranoscountryclub.com
jkramer@jcresorts.com

● Rehearsal Dinners	● Corporate Events
● Ceremonies	● Meetings
● Wedding Receptions	● Film Shoots
● Private Parties	Accommodations

When you enter Los Serranos Country Club's impressive clubhouse, you may hear the three grand bells in its bell tower ring out the hours. The red-tile roof and adobe-like walls of the Mission-style tower and clubhouse are a reminder of the club's history: It sits on 300 beautiful acres of what was once a Spanish land grant. During California's pioneer days, the ranch that occupied these grounds served as a haven for travelers, and its time-honored tradition of taking care of visitors continues at Los Serranos today.

As expected, wedding couples are exceptionally well taken care of. When brides who've been married here are asked what they like best about Los Serranos, they consistently cite its flexibility and service. For example, while a lot of places have fixed time blocks for weddings, Los Serranos is fine with whatever time of day suits you. You can follow the Inland Empire custom of a late afternoon wedding, when the light and temperature are perfect, but if you'd rather tie the knot in the morning, midday or in the evening, no problem!

Catering is another area where the club is adaptable. Los Serranos' culinary staff does an excellent job catering the hundreds of weddings and golf events that take place every year, but if you have a menu that requires special ethnic dishes, they're happy to let you bring in an outside caterer. "Our willingness to accommodate different needs is based on a core rule," says the course's Events Director. "We're here for the brides. This is their day and we will try to make it the best one possible."

Flexibility also extends to this facility's event spaces, which can handle almost any size group. The heart of Los Serranos' clubhouse is the Montebello Ballroom. By itself it can accommodate up to 300 guests, but when you roll back the oak doors that connect it to the club's restaurant, the two venues combined hold up to 550—with the bonus of a full-service bar at one end. Small party? The ballroom can be sectioned to create a comfortable space for 80 guests or less.

The Montebello Ballroom is bright and airy thanks to a high, coffered ceiling and three walls of glass that offer a lovely view of the room's veranda, the ceremony garden, and the driving range. The courtyard-like garden is enclosed by the veranda on one side and a long, hedge-lined wall on the other. Guests are seated on the lawn in the center, facing a classic white gazebo. Palms, flowering plants, roses, and other greenery create a photogenic backdrop.

By the way, if your reception is very small, ask about hosting it on the ceremony garden's veranda. On occasion, it's possible to have exclusive use of that area for an al fresco party. Guests enjoy its fresh air, verdant landscaping, and the soothing sounds of a pair of fountains in the background.

The golf club dates back to 1925, and over the years it has become a seasoned event facility known for its attentiveness in serving the needs of brides and grooms. If you have your celebration here, we expect that you, too, will add your voice to the chorus of compliments Los Serranos Country Club receives.

CEREMONY CAPACITY: The site seats 400 guests outdoors.

EVENT/RECEPTION & MEETING CAPACITY: The club holds 550 seated or standing guests indoors.

PRICES: WHAT'S THIS GOING TO COST?

Rental Fee: $500/event and up
- The rental fee varies depending on the day of the week, time of day, and type of event.

Package Prices: $45/person and up

Service Charge or Gratuity: 20%

AVAILABILITY: Year-round, daily, anytime.

SERVICES/AMENITIES:

Catering: in-house, or BYO with restrictions
Kitchen Facilities: limited
Tables & Chairs: provided
Linens, Silver, etc.: provided
Restrooms: wheelchair accessible
Dance Floor: portable provided
Bride's Dressing Area: yes
AV/Meeting Equipment: some provided, more CBA

Parking: large lot
Accommodations: no guest rooms
Outdoor Night Lighting: CBA
Outdoor Cooking Facilities: BBQ CBA
Cleanup: provided
View: fountain, garden, fairways, hills, land-scaped grounds
Other: coordination, in-house wedding cake and florals

RESTRICTIONS:

Alcohol: in-house only
Smoking: outdoors only
Music: amplified OK with restrictions

Wheelchair Access: yes
Insurance: not required

The wedding vendors on our website are the best in the business. How do we know? Read page 425.

DoubleTree by Hilton Claremont

Hotel

555 West Foothill Boulevard, Claremont
909/626-2411

www.doubletreeclaremont.com
jgutzwiller@doubletreeclaremont.com

- Rehearsal Dinners
- Ceremonies
- Wedding Receptions
- Private Parties
- Corporate Events
- Meetings
- Film Shoots
- Accommodations

In Claremont, a town many people call "The City of Trees," the DoubleTree stands out as an oasis within an oasis. Its 14-acre grounds, adorned with dozens of different species of flowers and trees as well as some beautiful sculptural elements, are a hub of social life—and weddings—in this westernmost part of the Inland Empire. Besides the earthy and exuberant subtropical feel of its landscaping, the 50-yearold local landmark also has plenty of architectural character. While owners through the years have expanded the facility and remodeled its interior, they've done so carefully, keeping the boutique-hotel vibe intact.

The heart of the DoubleTree is its courtyard, by far the favorite location for weddings. Brides love it both for its look and its privacy (it's closed to everyone but wedding party guests for the duration of the ceremony). The courtyard's focal point is a water feature at one end—a long slate-brick wall set into a high, arched alcove. Water runs gently down the stone, calling to mind the cooling Moorish fountains of old Spain. The water's sparkle and soothing sound are delights to the senses, and add a tranquil element to any gathering. Sometimes, when there's a breeze, swirls of mist dance away from the wall—an entrancing sight. A colorful fringe of ivy, palms and flowers frames the fountain, while overhead, bright cloth streamers span the courtyard and shade people from the afternoon sun.

Just steps from the courtyard, DoubleTree's two neighboring ballrooms are typically used in tandem: one for a cocktail reception and the other for the seated dinner. The hotel also regularly and seamlessly hosts small weddings in its inviting Cedar Room on the second floor. Guests often like to mingle outside on the room's arcaded veranda, where they can enjoy some people-watching in the courtyard below.

An independently operated on-site day spa is a welcome haven for the bride and her entourage to prep for the ceremony or wind down and relax. It's co-ed, so men in the wedding party can step in and have some fun, too. Also on the property, but detached from the main buildings, is "Piano Piano," a lounge that's perfect for bachelor, bachelorette or boy-girl parties. With its dozens of nightclub-style tables and booths, and a stage set with two pianos that professional players often use to engage in some uproarious musical duels, "Piano Piano" is a fine place to get noisy and happy. People can let off steam without worrying about the neighbors.

Getting married at the DoubleTree is like cocooning yourself in a beloved local institution that manages to be hip and traditional, efficient and hang-loose, formal and casual—all at the same time and all to the right degree. When you stand before that glistening slate fountain with your groom, surrounded by greenery, golden light and affectionate well wishers, you'll experience the world at that moment as being just about as right as it can possibly be.

CEREMONY CAPACITY: The hotel seats 375 guests indoors and 250 outdoors.

EVENT/RECEPTION CAPACITY: The hotel can accommodate 250 seated or 400 standing guests indoors and 100 seated or 300 standing outdoors.

MEETING CAPACITY: Meeting spaces hold up to 375 seated guests.

PRICES: WHAT'S THIS GOING TO COST?

Rental Fee: $0–8,015/event
  • The rental fee varies depending on the type of event, and is normally waived if the food & beverage minimum is met.

Meals (when priced separately): $40–80/person

Service Charge or Gratuity: 21%

AVAILABILITY: Year-round, daily, anytime.

SERVICES/AMENITIES:

Catering: in-house
Kitchen Facilities: n/a
Tables & Chairs: provided
Linens, Silver, etc.: provided
Restrooms: wheelchair accessible
Dance Floor: provided
Bride's Dressing Area: CBA
AV/Meeting Equipment: CBA

Parking: large lot
Accommodations: 195 guest rooms
Outdoor Night Lighting: CBA
Outdoor Cooking Facilities: BBQ CBA
Cleanup: provided
View: garden patio, waterfall

RESTRICTIONS:

Alcohol: in-house
Smoking: not allowed
Music: amplified OK indoors

Wheelchair Access: yes
Insurance: not required

Eagle Glen Golf Club

Golf Club

1800 Eagle Glen Parkway, Corona
951/278-2842 x204

eagleglengc.com
eventsales@eagleglengc.com

● Rehearsal Dinners	● Corporate Events
● Ceremonies	● Meetings
● Wedding Receptions	● Film Shoots
● Private Parties	Accommodations

One of the best things in life is pleasant surprises, and Eagle Glen Golf Club on Corona's lofty west side is full of them. The first time you lay eyes on its cupola-topped clubhouse with its impressive entrance of cinnamon-colored wood trusses, you may be amazed to find a place like this up here. The next surprise comes when you step into the soaring light-splashed lobby and see the quality of the architecture and design. But that's just a prelude to the final treat, first glimpsed through the lobby's glass doors and windows: the stunning view of the verdant golf course against a backdrop of chaparral-covered hills.

Eagle Glen ambles along the base of some very steep hills on the eastern edge of Cleveland National Forest. While you're on the golf course, you're in a private, human realm. But once you leave the greens and start heading up the hills, you enter a wild domain of untamed landscapes. Eagle Glen gives you the wonderful sensation of gazing over nature's might from an absolutely civilized vantage.

There are two outdoor ceremony options to choose from. The Lakeside site features a wrought-iron arbor, perched on a small rise above a reed-ringed pond with a fountain playing at its center. Surrounding it are close-cropped greens that flow up to the foot of the hills. A graceful low wooden bridge that spans the pond at its narrowest point is a splendid spot for photos. For a more dramatic setting, take a stroll over to the Mountainside site, which has a mountain vista. Here, you can get married beneath a wrought-iron gazebo, enclosed by a semicircle of sheltering pine trees.

Eagle Glen's spacious ballroom is managed by a seasoned catering staff that handles scores of weddings each year. Floor-to-ceiling windows and glass doors let in lots of natural light, and look out to the veranda and beyond. Here, guests can sit and savor picturesque views of the back nine's grand swath of lawn, as it tumbles toward the clubhouse from the edge of the national forest. In the afterglow of a lovely ceremony and great food, you and your guests will feel a sense of total satisfaction as the sun sets behind the mountains.

Perched just above the treelined streets of the surrounding community, and next to a national forest, Eagle Glen really is one of Corona's best-kept secrets. After experiencing this inviting venue's beautiful location and high-quality services, you and your guests will not be disappointed.

CEREMONY CAPACITY: The Club holds up to 500 seated guests outdoors and 340 indoors.

EVENT/RECEPTION & MEETING CAPACITY: Indoor spaces accommodate 340 seated or 600 standing guests.

PRICES: WHAT'S THIS GOING TO COST?

Meals (when priced separately): $10–85/person

Service Charge or Gratuity: 20%

AVAILABILITY: Year-round, daily, 6:30am–midnight.

SERVICES/AMENITIES:

Catering: in-house, no BYO
Kitchen Facilities: n/a
Tables & Chairs: provided
Linens, Silver, etc.: provided
Restrooms: wheelchair accessible
Dance Floor: yes
Bride's Dressing Area: yes
AV/Meeting Equipment: CBA

Parking: large lot
Accommodations: no guest rooms
Outdoor Night Lighting: access only
Outdoor Cooking Facilities: no
Cleanup: provided
View: fairways, mountains, canyon, lake, grounds
Other: event coordination, wedding cake

RESTRICTIONS:

Alcohol: in-house or BYO with corkage fee
Smoking: outside only
Music: amplified OK

Wheelchair Access: yes
Insurance: liability required

Fairview Green River

Golf Club

5215 Green River Road, Corona
951/739-5985
www.fairviewevents.com/fairview-green-river
GreenRiver@FairviewEvents.com

- Rehearsal Dinners
- Ceremonies
- Wedding Receptions
- Private Parties
- Corporate Events
- Meetings
- Film Shoots
- Accommodations

It seems like most of us look forward to getting away from the hustle and bustle of the city, and going to a tranquil setting where we can become one with ourselves and nature. Fairview Green River, located in the Santa Ana Canyons where Orange County meets the Inland Empire, is just such a place. The Santa Ana River wends its way through this 560-acre property, filled with rolling hills, trees and lakes. Over 50 species of birds—including the endangered golden eagle—call Green River home. If this sounds like a picture-perfect location for a wedding or special event, it is.

Because along with this venue's natural beauty, Fairview Green River will not only ensure that your celebration unfolds effortlessly, but will do it all for a reasonable price—their all-inclusive packages come with lots of perks!

But make no mistake: The venue may be a bargain, but Fairview Green River provides both a serene and sophisticated experience for your friends and family. Guests stroll into the Spanish Revival-style building under a gabled roof and green awning, and through a doorway flanked on both sides by huge urns. They mingle in the foyer, and enjoy cocktails served in an adjacent peach-hued room, where they can also sit at tables and chat. When it's time for the reception everyone gathers in the newly updated banquet room, an inviting space with subtle recessed lighting in a coffered ceiling. The neutral color scheme makes it easy to decorate the room to your taste: Do something simple, or if you really want to pull out all the stops, create an ethereal wonderland with yards of tulle and white fairy lights. Large picture windows frame views of the verdant fairways and ravines beyond.

Those of you who choose to get married here, too, will appreciate the three enchanting ceremony sites. One of them is a garden, bounded by a trellised fence and located on a sloped area right next to the immaculately groomed fairway. Two stone-edged steps lead to a platform where vows are exchanged. The second option, a recently added gazebo, provides a vista of the Santa Ana mountain range. (Don't be too surprised if a deer decides to join your party!) The newest site for exchanging vows is atop a green expanse of lawn with an up-close view of the nearby hills—quite the dramatic backdrop!

Wonderful photo opportunities abound, among them a burbling stone fountain and an arcaded cloister not far from the banquet room. Green River's appealing combination of skilled staff and gorgeous natural surroundings—plus a convenient location with easy access from multiple freeways—promises an unforgettable celebration.

CEREMONY CAPACITY: The club holds up to 400 seated guests outdoors.

EVENT/RECEPTION & MEETING CAPACITY: The Grand Ballroom holds 400 seated or 600 standing when used in its entirety. It can also be divided into 4 sections, each of which accommodates 60 seated guests. The Green River Room seats up to 170, and the Tri County Room seats up to 170.

PRICES: WHAT'S THIS GOING TO COST?

Ceremony Fee: $1,050/event
- The ceremony fee includes tax and service charge, sound system, and changing room.
- The ceremony fee is waived if you hold a Monday–Thursday wedding reception for 100 or more guests.

Package Prices: $40/person and up
- Completely customizable wedding packages include room rental fees, invitations, DJ, dinner, and more. For most packages, a champagne toast and wine with dinner are included. Tax and service charge are additional.

AVAILABILITY: Year-round, daily, anytime.

SERVICES/AMENITIES:

Catering: in-house
Kitchen Facilities: n/a
Tables & Chairs: provided
Linens, Silver, etc.: provided
Restrooms: wheelchair accessible
Dance Floor: yes
Bride's Dressing Area: CBA
AV/Meeting Equipment: CBA

Parking: ample on site
Accommodations: no guest rooms
Outdoor Night Lighting: yes
Outdoor Cooking Facilities: no
Cleanup: provided
View: forest, fairways, fountain, garden, hills, lake, landscaped grounds, mountains
Other: event coordination CBA

RESTRICTIONS:

Alcohol: in-house
Smoking: outside only
Music: amplified OK

Wheelchair Access: yes
Insurance: not required
Other: no open flames

Diamond Bar Center

Event Center

1600 Grand Avenue, Diamond Bar

909/839-7065

www.diamondbarca.gov
reservations@diamondbarca.gov

●	Rehearsal Dinners	●	Corporate Events
●	Ceremonies	●	Meetings
●	Wedding Receptions	●	Film Shoots
●	Private Parties		Accommodations

From the moment the Diamond Bar Center opened, it garnered raves and it's easy to see why. Designed to blend into its surroundings, this serenely modern venue is actually quite a standout. Taking a cue from iconic architect Frank Lloyd Wright's work, this city-owned facility incorporates natural materials, clean lines and large expanses of glass to both take advantage of and become part of its hilltop setting in Summitridge Park. Atop its lovely perch within the 26-acre recreation area (which abuts 250 additional acres of wild preserve), the Center affords sweeping vistas of tranquil gardens, hiking trails and city lights down below, making it feel like a deluxe retreat that's remarkably close to three major counties.

If you have your ceremony here, your day will probably start at the aptly named Wedding Oval. You'll make your entrance down a long, covered walkway, bordered by white iceberg roses as well as iris. From this site, you and your guests will be able to see the San Gabriel Valley and, depending upon the time of year, you might even catch a glimpse of snow on the mountains.

Continue to drink in the panoramic views while enjoying cocktails and hors d'oeuvres on the center's wraparound patio, or head inside to mingle in the foyer. Either way, you can keep the ballroom doors closed until you're ready for dinner…and the big "reveal." The soaring, two-story-tall ballroom seems even more spacious, thanks to its coffered ceiling and expansive windows. Organic stonework in shades of sandstone and dusky adobe adds visual drama to some of the walls. The large room has a raised center stage with a dropdown screen and everything you need to present an audiovisual show. It also features customized zone and accent lighting, which allows you to control the level of light inside so that everyone can see the city sparkle in the distance.

For a more intimate gathering, use just a section of the ballroom, or consider the similarly styled Pine Room or Sycamore Room, which has its own patio for that indoor/outdoor flow. Whichever space you choose, the entire facility provides an elegant, minimalist backdrop for you to decorate. Flexibility is key here, so you have enormous freedom to bring in your choice of professional catering services, flowers, decorations, etc., that best match your vision and your budget. But remember, the Diamond Bar Center is *very* popular and books up fast, so reserve early!

CEREMONY CAPACITY: The site seats 822 indoors or 250 outdoors.

EVENT/RECEPTION CAPACITY: The ballroom can accommodate up to 438 seated banquet-style and 822 seated theater-style.

MEETING CAPACITY: Facility meeting spaces hold 60–822 seated theater-style.

PRICES: WHAT'S THIS GOING TO COST?

Rental Fee: $130–700/hour
  • The rental fee varies depending on the day of the week, time of day, and space reserved.

AVAILABILITY: Year-round: Sunday–Thursday, 7:30am–midnight; Friday & Saturday, 7:30am–1am.

SERVICES/AMENITIES:

Catering: BYO
Kitchen Facilities: prep only
Tables & Chairs: provided
Linens, Silver, etc.: BYO
Restrooms: wheelchair accessible
Dance Floor: CBA, extra fee
Bride's Dressing Area: CBA, extra fee
AV/Meeting Equipment: CBA, extra fee

Parking: large lot
Accommodations: no guest rooms
Outdoor Night Lighting: access only
Outdoor Cooking Facilities: no
Cleanup: renter
View: garden, landscaped grounds; panorama of cityscape, mountains, and hills

RESTRICTIONS:

Alcohol: BYO
Smoking: designated areas only
Music: amplified OK indoors

Wheelchair Access: yes
Insurance: liability required

Want to find more venues and services? Check out our informative website, www.HereComesTheGuide.com.

The HomeStead

Private Estate

11951 Oak Glen Road, Oak Glen

909/790-8010

www.homesteadoakglen.com
info@homesteadoakglen.com

Rehearsal Dinners	● Corporate Events
● Ceremonies	● Meetings
● Wedding Receptions	● Film Shoots
● Private Parties	Accommodations

Surrounded by nature's beauty, this relaxed mountain retreat on 5.5 acres in scenic Oak Glen positively exudes timeless charm. Once part of the sprawling, century-old Wilshire apple orchard, the property boasts fabulous views of the San Bernardino Mountains, Lake Perris, and Wilshire Peak. It's no surprise that the current owners fell hard for this little piece of heaven, and created a romantic outdoor wedding venue that will make every nature lover, history buff, and vintage collector's heart flutter.

A sense of calm immediately envelops you amid the majestic oaks, towering sycamores, fragrant lilac fields—and, of course, heirloom apple trees. Many features of this historic venue have been retained but with a twist: An old buzz saw now rests amid delicate vines and wildflowers, while two of the original HomeStead buildings, the rustic Cabin and Cottage, have been turned into comfortable private suites for the couple and attendants to get ready.

The HomeStead's peaceful, courtyard ceremony site is graced with gorgeous old-growth trees whose spreading branches filter the sunlight, dappling the ground below. The wedding couple and party enter through what appear to be old barn doors, and step into an area that's like a magical clearing in the woods. Here, vows are exchanged on a terraced stage in front of the picturesque façade of a country chapel with the green foothills as a backdrop.

The photo ops throughout this locale are amazing, from lush lawns and woodsy paths to a waterfall spilling over boulders into a rock-strewn pool. You might even glimpse a deer or two grazing nearby since the area is a wildlife sanctuary. And the reception courtyard is no less photogenic: With wooden buildings and a weathered water tower lining the perimeter—plus unbelievable panoramas that go on forever—it feels like you're in the midst of a charming movie set with authentic décor and the warm golden glow of gas lamps and overhead café lights.

A raised sweetheart table gives you great sightlines to your guests partying on the dance floor. There's a bar to keep the libations flowing and, as the evening progresses, a fire ring is lit—the perfect opportunity to treat yourselves to s'mores!

Their attentive staff, all-inclusive packages, and in-house vendors mean that you can relax and enjoy the day. And, with only one event per day, their focus is on you. From coordination and customizing your menu and cake, to arranging the flowers, DJ, rehearsal, and décor (they have a treasure trove of antiques and unique items!), they're with you every step of the way. They even offer a few special extras, like a photo booth, late-night treats, and a daytime scavenger hunt for your younger guests. Most of all, they make you feel like family.

CEREMONY & EVENT/RECEPTION CAPACITY: Outdoor areas accommodate up to 200 seated or standing guests.

MEETING CAPACITY: The meeting space seats up to 200 guests.

PRICES: WHAT'S THIS GOING TO COST?

Packages: $15,100–24,900/event
  • Prices vary depending on the day of the week and guest count.

AVAILABILITY: May through mid-November: Sunday–Thursday, 10:15am–8pm; Friday and Saturday, 11:15am–10pm.

SERVICES/AMENITIES:

Catering: in-house, preferred list
Kitchen Facilities: prep only
Tables & Chairs: provided
Linens, Silver, etc.: provided
Restrooms: wheelchair accessible
Dance Floor: portable provided
Dressing Areas: yes
AV/Meeting Equipment: CBA, extra fee may apply

Parking: large lot
Accommodations: no guest rooms
Outdoor Night Lighting: yes
Outdoor Cooking Facilities: BBQ on site
Cleanup: provided
View: mountains, landscaped grounds, garden, forest/wooded area, courtyard
Other: in-house wedding cake, in-house florals, DJ, event coordination

RESTRICTIONS:

Alcohol: BYO
Smoking: designated areas only
Music: amplified OK outdoors

Wheelchair Access: yes
Insurance: not required

Serendipity

Private Estate

12865 Oak Glen Road, Oak Glen

844/749-5683

www.serendipitygardenweddings.com
info@serendipitygardenweddings.com

Rehearsal Dinners	● Corporate Events
● Ceremonies	● Meetings
● Wedding Receptions	● Film Shoots
● Private Parties	Accommodations

Designed specifically for weddings and located at the edge of a mountain canyon that overlooks an oak-sheltered creek, Serendipity is truly a stunning venue. Plus, this private estate is set at 4,200 feet in the San Bernardino Mountains—high enough to be 10 or 15 degrees cooler than the flats below, making it popular for summer weddings—something few outdoor wedding sites in the region can boast.

One of the best things about celebrating your big day here is that you have a variety of outdoor and indoor options to choose from, which means you can personalize your event to your taste.

The traditional ceremony site, built halfway down the canyon slope, is a showstopper with a glorious panorama of the Inland Empire's mountains and valleys, as well as the impressive granite peak of Mt. San Gorgonio. Guests are seated on a lawn facing this inspiring view, and the couple recite their vows on a simple wooden dais that's easily adorned. A second ceremony choice is Oak Grove, an intimate spot next to the new Barn. Encircled by trees hung with chandeliers, and lit by strings of bistro lights overhead, it's a sweet place to say "I do".

The cocktail hour is often hosted on the expansive terrace, where guests mingle over the wedding couple's signature cocktail and hand-passed hors d'oeuvres. From here they can take in the sweeping view of the valley to the south. For a more rustic garden vibe, serve cocktails in the Oak Grove.

Al fresco receptions are held in Serendipity's beautifully conceived outdoor dining and dancing area. Tables are arranged on this spacious stone-tiled "patio", and there's a permanent dance floor on one side (with the canyon as its dramatic backdrop) and a full bar with a blazing fireplace on the opposite side. Extra benefits include balmy evening air, gorgeous sunsets, romantic string lighting, and a star-filled sky.

If you prefer an indoor ceremony, cocktail hour, or reception, you'll love the Barn. It's rustic-chic perfection, with a warm, wood interior, soaring open-beamed ceiling, and huge faux-candle chandeliers. Soft white draping adds an elegant touch.

Serendipity now has a cozy new site for rehearsal dinners, too. It features a water wall plus custom-designed tables made of concrete tops supported by tree stumps, and affords panoramic views of the canyon and surrounding mountains.

When we asked Serendipity's owner how this unique, weddings-only facility in the highlands has worked out, she clearly enjoyed answering the question: "Each bride tells me, 'This is my little haven, my own piece of the mountain for a day.'"

CEREMONY & EVENT/RECEPTION CAPACITY: The facility holds 200 seated guests outdoors.

MEETING CAPACITY: Meetings spaces hold 200 seated at tables.

PRICES: WHAT'S THIS GOING TO COST?

Packages: $17,500/event and up
- Package prices vary depending on guest count and services selected.
- All-inclusive wedding packages cover catering, cake, flowers, a DJ, a golf cart shuttle for guests, bride's dressing area, and a horse-drawn carriage ride for the bride and groom to the ceremony site and reception area.
- Rehearsal dinners may be hosted on site in the new Serendipity Falls area as an additional upgrade.

Additional Info: A separate Bride's Cottage that's spacious enough for the bridal entourage is an upgrade available on the day of the wedding for an extra fee. It also comes with an adjacent Beauty Cottage that's fully equipped with vanities, outlets, mirrors, etc.

AVAILABILITY: Year-round, 9am–10pm.

SERVICES/AMENITIES:

Catering: in-house
Kitchen Facilities: n/a
Tables & Chairs: provided
Linens, Silver, etc.: provided
Restrooms: wheelchair accessible
Dance Floor: provided
Bride's & Groom's Dressing Area: yes
AV/Meeting Equipment: some provided
Other: coordination, grand piano

Parking: large lot
Accommodations: no guest rooms
Outdoor Night Lighting: yes
Outdoor Cooking Facilities: BBQ on site
Cleanup: provided
View: garden, waterfall, pond, fountain, landscaped grounds; panorama of mountains, canyon, cityscape, valley, hills, fields and barn

RESTRICTIONS:

Alcohol: BYO
Smoking: designated areas only
Music: amplified OK outdoors

Wheelchair Access: yes
Insurance: liability required

Mountain Meadows Golf Course

Golf Club

1875 Fairplex Drive, Pomona

909/623-3704 X3

www.countryclubreceptions.com
privateeventdirector@mountainmeadowsgc.com

● Rehearsal Dinners	● Corporate Events
● Ceremonies	● Meetings
● Wedding Receptions	● Film Shoots
● Private Parties	Accommodations

A curving boulevard whisks you swiftly up from the valley floor to this popular golf course. Its many jacaranda trees will be ablaze with lilac-colored blooms when you arrive, and if it's a clear day the San Gabriel Mountains will pop up bold and high—one of several pleasing sights that will capture your interest.

Like all savvy golfing venues, Mountain Meadows has set its ceremony site and banquet room overlooking the golf course to take advantage of the view, which is exceptionally beautiful here. In addition to the manicured fairways, the verdant vista includes a wide variety of trees, lush foliage, and rolling hills in the background.

Occupying the far end of the clubhouse, the banquet room features a number of elements that make it an inviting space: A wall of tall windows lets in a crystalline northern light and looks out past the adjacent patio to the action of the 10th and 18th holes. Overhead, gorgeous chandeliers hang from the vaulted, wood-beamed ceiling, which is accented by swags of satin draping laced with twinkle lights. The overall effect adds an elegant contrast to the room's rustic tone.

The banquet room opens to a large patio, shaded by a wooden trellis strung with bistro lights. It has a great view of the golf course, and is right next to an expansive ceremony site with a large, open gazebo. Couples saying "I do" here walk up a few steps and are elevated in full view of their family and friends, who are seated in white chairs on a manicured lawn. This ceremony area is spacious and flexible enough to accommodate other options, too: For example, if the gazebo isn't your style, you can create your own focal point with a *chuppah* or other type of arch, as well as spiral or stadium-style seating.

Photo ops abound, from the gazebo and its surroundings to the course's man-made lake. Or you can ride a golf cart up to a scenic overlook with a fantastic view of Mountain Meadows.

Finally, the on-site kitchen knows what it's doing. As is typical in the Inland Empire, with its rich variety of cultures, customs and ethnic groups, the banquet staff—who handle more than 100 weddings per year—are experts at seamlessly accommodating brides' different tastes and needs.

Mountain Meadows achieves something that looks easy only if you have a lot of experience doing it: balancing quality services and elegance with accessibility and affordability.

CEREMONY CAPACITY: The site holds up to 400 seated guests.

EVENT/RECEPTION CAPACITY: The banquet room accommodates up to 330 seated or 450 standing guests.

MEETING CAPACITY: The banquet room seats up to 500 guests.

PRICES: WHAT'S THIS GOING TO COST?

Package Prices: $55/person and up
   • Pricing varies based on food, beverage, and rental inclusions. Food & beverage minimums will apply. Menus and packages can be customized to fit your needs and budget. Pricing does not include additional site fees, mandatory service charge, gratuity, and current sales tax.

AVAILABILITY: Year-round, daily, 6am–2am.

SERVICES/AMENITIES:

Catering: in-house

Kitchen Facilities: no

Tables & Chairs: provided

Linens, Silver, etc.: provided

Restrooms: wheelchair accessible

Dance Floor: provided

Bride's Dressing Area: yes

AV/Meeting Equipment: some provided, more CBA

Parking: large lot

Accommodations: no guest rooms

Outdoor Night Lighting: CBA

Outdoor Cooking Facilities: no

Cleanup: provided

View: fairways, hills, mountains, grounds

RESTRICTIONS:

Alcohol: in-house

Smoking: outside only

Music: amplified OK

Wheelchair Access: yes

Insurance: not required

Christmas House

Historic Victorian Inn

9240 Archibald Avenue, Rancho Cucamonga
909/980-6450

christmashouseinn.com
contact@christmashouseinn.com

Rehearsal Dinners	● Corporate Events
● Ceremonies	Meetings
● Wedding Receptions	● Film Shoots
● Private Parties	● Accommodations

All the quaint pleasures we associate with a Victorian Christmas—old-fashioned elegance, warm family gatherings, and a childlike sense of wonder—are available year-round at the Christmas House Inn, a historic landmark that received its yuletide moniker thanks to the extravagant holiday parties hosted by its early owners.

Built in 1904, the three-story mansion is a charming example of the Queen Anne-style favored by late Victorian architects. It was renovated and restored in 1983 by its current owners, Janice and Jay Ilsley, and boasts all of the original stained-glass windows and gorgeous woodwork—the seven Victorian fireplace mantels are each made of a different wood, and accented with Italian tiles and beveled glass mirrors.

Brides and bridesmaids will definitely feel at home in the Celebration Suite, the comfortable upstairs dressing room replete with fireplace, lacy adornments, and an abundance of mirrors. The groom and his guys have their own space, too: The Butler's Quarters, created with a vintage English pub in mind, features rock walls, leather club chairs around a flatscreen TV, a game table with vintage poker chips, and a dart board in the wine cellar.

Outdoor ceremonies are set in The White Garden, a classic European walled garden lined with Indian Hill Laurel Trees and over 200 white rose bushes. The focal point is a French wire "Birdcage" gazebo, where the couple exchanges vows to the sound of a fountain trickling in the background.

Another option is to follow Victorian tradition and say "I do" in front of the parlor's hearth, decked with shimmering candles. As the accompanist plays the processional on the grand piano, glide down the carved, redwood burl staircase to say your vows before your family and friends, gathered close enough to hear every word. After the ceremony, guests may stroll through the house and grounds while savoring tray-passed hors d'oeuvres in the lovely rose garden, on the shady veranda, or in the the house itself.

When everyone returns to the garden for the reception, they'll find tables and chairs elegantly set with floor-length linens and gleaming glass and cutlery. Dinner is served beneath the leafy boughs of magnolia and guava trees strung with twinkle lights. The newlyweds share their first dance in the adjacent garden ballroom, complete with crystal chandeliers, multiple grand carved mirrors, and classic topiaries. (More intimate weddings of 30 to 50 guests may be held inside the house.)

Among the most endearing attractions of the Christmas House are the six distinctive guest rooms. The luxurious bridal suite comes with a fireplace, a private garden courtyard with hot tub, and a delicious breakfast the morning after. Add in the affordable packages that include gourmet catering and other extras, and this venue becomes simply irresistible.

The inn is quite popular, and it owes its success as much to the Ilsleys' service-oriented attitude as to the inviting surroundings and great amenities. "We want couples to feel like the Christmas House is their own home," reveals Janice, "especially on their wedding day."

CEREMONY & EVENT/RECEPTION CAPACITY: The Parlor holds up to 50 guests, the garden up to 150.

PRICES: WHAT'S THIS GOING TO COST?

Package Prices:
- Package prices vary depending on the space reserved and guest count.
- For indoor events, packages start at $5,700 for 30 guests and include exclusive use of the site, all rentals, catering and staff, wedding cake, and all setup and cleanup. For each person over 30 guests, pricing starts at $24/person.
- For garden events, packages range $13,725–16,700 for 100 guests and include everything that's in the indoor package plus many more amenities, including professional DJ services. For each person over 100 guests, pricing ranges $39–53/person.
- If you would like bar service, many options are available at an extra charge.

AVAILABILITY: Year-round, daily, 10am–10pm.

SERVICES/AMENITIES:

Catering: in-house
Kitchen Facilities: n/a
Tables & Chairs: provided
Linens, Silver, etc.: provided
Restrooms: limited accessibility
Dance Floor: provided for garden receptions
Bride's & Groom's Dressing Area: provided
AV/Meeting Equipment: n/a

Parking: valet included
Accommodations: 6 guest rooms
Outdoor Night Lighting: yes
Outdoor Cooking Facilities: no
Cleanup: provided
View: landscaped Victorian gardens
Other: event coordination, bar service

RESTRICTIONS:

Alcohol: in-house
Smoking: outside only
Music: amplified OK with volume restrictions until 10pm

Wheelchair Access: limited
Insurance: not required
Other: no rice, birdseed, or confetti

This is important! Tell locations you're reading HERE COMES THE GUIDE and ask if our information is still current.

315

Victoria Gardens Cultural Center

12505 Cultural Center Drive, Rancho Cucamonga
909/477-2773
www.vgculturalcenter.com
johnette.maddox@cityofrc.us

Cultural Center

● Rehearsal Dinners	● Corporate Events
● Ceremonies	● Meetings
● Wedding Receptions	● Film Shoots
● Private Parties	Accommodations

The delightfully imaginative Victoria Gardens Cultural Center has a motto: "Where Dreams Come to Life." But it could just as easily be "Let's Put on a Show," because that's what they do so dynamically at this outstanding venue.

The center, known primarily for its Lewis Family Playhouse, one of regional theater's rising stars, is a multifaceted performing arts mecca that includes several unique indoor and outdoor sites for special events. Here, they believe that every wedding is a story, and they love having the same creative wizards who put the magic into dozens of critically acclaimed theatrical productions each year help you tell yours.

The Cultural Center, comprised of the playhouse and Celebration Hall, is an architecturally colorful treat. The curved buildings, sporting hues of pink, desert rose and verdigris, form a semicircle around the Imagination Courtyard, a large, cobblestone space that lends itself to outdoor gatherings. Ringed by tall, feathery palms, it's open on one side to the Victoria Gardens shopping and entertainment plaza (a big plus during the holidays when the majestic Christmas tree is visible from here), and anchored on the other by the center's soaring, arched glass entrance. Topped with a backlit, stylized marquee, this façade makes a picturesque backdrop for an al fresco ceremony.

Many brides opt to have cocktails (or even dinner) out here and exchange vows in the more private Lobby, a whimsical stage set of the perfect little street, complete with storefronts and trees—it's like having your very own village! On one end of "town," there's a staircase to use either as a riser for your altar, or as a starting point for your dramatic descent to the main floor where you can say "I do," bathed in light filtering through that gorgeous glass entrance behind you.

The center gives you enormous flexibility in choosing how you want to use its spaces, but it's the way the staff works with a team of art and entertainment professionals to turn your vision into reality that makes this place so special. Want to add an animal to the proceedings? No problem.

They've wrangled camels, horses, an elephant—even albino peacocks—for various events. Unconventional entertainment? They can find everything from acrobats to belly dancers to gospel choirs. And with the help of some of L.A.'s most talented set decorators, lighting designers, seamstresses and hair/makeup artists, they will produce an affair to remember.

Nowhere is their creativity more rewarded than in the Celebration Hall Ballroom. A wonderful blank canvas, this huge space has polished concrete floors, cream-colored walls, windows on two sides and an adjacent Patio hugged by shrubbery. In it's natural state, it's a bright and airy spot for dinner and dancing with an indoor/outdoor flow. But say the word and they can transform it with elegant draping and dramatic lighting into a romantic oasis, a sophisticated supper club, or an exotic foreign locale. There's no charge for either the consultation or design, making this an incredible value. Plus, they do so much of the work in-house that you can also save on flowers, catering, and more for a one-of-a-kind event that's sure to win rave reviews.

CEREMONY CAPACITY: The site holds up to 250 seated guests indoors or 350 seated outdoors.

EVENT/RECEPTION & MEETING CAPACITY: The facility accommodates 250 seated or 350 standing indoors and 400 seated or 500 standing outdoors.

PRICES: WHAT'S THIS GOING TO COST?

Rental Fee: $3,500–8,000/event
 • The rental fee varies depending on guest count, event duration, and custom décor options.

Meals (when priced separately): $45-70/person
 • Meals are provided by their exclusive caterer.

AVAILABILITY: Year-round, daily until 1am.

SERVICES/AMENITIES:

Catering: exclusive caterer, no BYO
Kitchen Facilities: n/a
Tables & Chairs: provided
Linens, Silver, etc.: provided
Restrooms: wheelchair accessible
Dance Floor: upon request
Bride's Dressing Area: available with ceremony package
AV/Meeting Equipment: provided

Parking: large complimentary lot; garage nearby
Accommodations: no guest rooms
Outdoor Night Lighting: upon request
Outdoor Cooking Facilities: no
Cleanup: provided
View: garden courtyard, landscaped grounds
Other: custom décor services, specialty lighting, and more

RESTRICTIONS:

Alcohol: exclusive vendor
Smoking: not allowed
Music: amplified OK

Wheelchair Access: yes
Insurance: liability required

The Mitten Building

345 North Fifth Street, Suite A, Redlands
909/793-1294
www.mittenbuilding.com
mittenbuilding@gmail.com

Historic Event Faciity

- Rehearsal Dinners
- Ceremonies
- Wedding Receptions
- Private Parties
- Corporate Events
- Meetings
- Film Shoots
- Accommodations

Redlands is a city that has always had its own, unique character, which derives in part from its distinctive buildings: one of the best-preserved collections of late 19th and early 20th-century architecture in all of Southern California.

So, a building has to be pretty special to stand out here. And stand out is exactly what the Mitten Building does.

Built in 1890, the brick structure not only has a fine looking exterior, it impresses on the inside as well. With its exposed rafters, beams and joists, and its stairs and banisters flying up and down each floor, the interior is a tumult of wood, an almost giddy exposition of the carpenter's art. It's the kind of place people love, because they're endlessly fascinated by all its nooks, angles, and wondrous lines.

And it's perfect for couples who prefer a venue with character and history. The current owners have lovingly restored the Mitten, wisely retaining the things that give the building its wonderful patina of age: the weathered beams, the heavy freight door that opens along an overhead metal track, and the original swaths of paint on some surfaces. They cleaned but did not alter the Mitten's sturdy brick walls, knowing how crucial they are to the building's feel. The bricks vary in color from gray, dusty pink, and fiery red to nearly maroon, while their textures range from baby smooth to worn and rough. If a building can have the equivalent of a beautifully aged human face, these walls are that.

The multilevel interior invites people to move around, explore, and mingle. Typically, the downstairs is set up as a reception area. Wrought-iron chandeliers descend from the Mitten's 50-foot ceiling, and garlands entwined with twinkle lights run along every rail and banister, creating a festive ambiance. Big windows set into the thick north brick wall admit a mellow northern light—the kind artists adore because of the way it complements everything it falls on. The mezzanine above has a beautiful narrow-slat maple floor, and its slender iron support beams are each flanked by two shiny brass lamps. Couples often wed on the upper level, head downstairs for their reception, then come right back up to dance away the evening.

The recently refurbished basement level is now a bar featuring turn-of-the-century dark wood cabinetry with inlaid detailing. Reminiscent of a speakeasy, it fits right in with the 1890s period when the building was constructed. On request, this space also serves as a groom's pre-ceremony getaway.

The Mitten Building's newest addition is the Summerbell Ballroom, which has a decidedly modern feel. Colored LED uplights transform the walls, and pinpoint lights overhead showcase each table's centerpiece. There's also a granite-topped bar, a dance floor, and a lounge section with a leather couch and bar tables. An adjoining patio, overlooking a lushly landscaped garden, lends itself well to outdoor ceremonies.

Since its restoration, the building has become a favorite among locals (and out-of-towners in the know!). Everyone who celebrates here owes a debt of gratitude to the visionaries who looked at this building with affectionate eyes, saw its magnificent possibilities, and brought it to life as a splendid event site.

CEREMONY CAPACITY: The upper level holds up to 400 seated guests. The new courtyard space seats 100.

EVENT/RECEPTION & MEETING CAPACITY: The venue accommodates up to 700 seated or standing guests. The new Summerbell Ballroom and outdoor patio hold 30–225 seated or standing.

PRICES: WHAT'S THIS GOING TO COST?

Rental Fee: $500–8,000/event
- The rental fee varies depending on the day of the week, time of day, guest count, and services selected.

Meals (when priced separately): $19–45/person
- These prices are for the on-site caterer.

AVAILABILITY: Year-round, daily until 1am.

SERVICES/AMENITIES:

Catering: in-house
Kitchen Facilities: n/a
Tables & Chairs: provided
Linens, Silver, etc.: some provided, more CBA
Restrooms: wheelchair accessible
Dance Floor: CBA, extra fee
Bride's Dressing Area: yes
AV/Meeting Equipment: some provided, more CBA

Parking: large lot and garage nearby
Accommodations: no guest rooms
Outdoor Night Lighting: yes
Outdoor Cooking Facilities: BBQ CBA
Cleanup: provided
View: cityscape, garden patio
Other: coordination available for a fee

RESTRICTIONS:

Alcohol: in-house
Smoking: outside only
Music: amplified OK

Wheelchair Access: limited
Insurance: liability required

Canyon Crest Country Club

Country Club

975 Country Club Drive, Riverside
951/274-7905
www.canyoncrestcc.com
Andrea.Deputy@clubcorp.com

- Rehearsal Dinners
- Ceremonies
- Wedding Receptions
- Private Parties
- Corporate Events
- Meetings
- Film Shoots
- Accommodations

Everything works just right at Canyon Crest, a country club whose combined outdoor and indoor assets are appealing for all types of events, especially weddings.

A treelined boulevard sweeps its way to the club, making you feel like you've arrived at a capital "D" destination. The golf course, set along the contours of a natural bowl at the foot of desert mountains, has a touch of the exotic, with its subtropical assortment of palms, pines and eucalyptus. A fountain in the middle of a man-made lake jets water 50 feet into the air against a backdrop of nearby peaks.

But perhaps the best feature on the grounds is the ceremony site: A simple white stone arch—which you can decorate any way you like—sits at the edge of a knoll above the course, flanked by a lawn where guests assemble to witness vows. Overlooking the lake and fountain, fairways and scenery, this spot feels set apart from the country club's bustle.

The broad green canopy that shades the steps down from the parking lot to the clubhouse's gleaming glass doors imparts a decidedly upscale feel. Walk inside to the dining room, where an all-glass wall lets you gaze out on the vast and impressive green of the course—in fact, lush green is all you see. Three wide doors open onto an adjoining canopied terrace, which offers a splendid view of the fairways, lake and nearby highlands. Located just above the putting green, the tiled terrace is ideal for hosting pre- and post-wedding gatherings and cocktails, and it serves as an overflow space for dining. At dusk, lights strung overhead create an enchanting look.

Just off the terrace is a spacious room set aside for the bride and her bridesmaids. The room, which is perfect for hanging out and relaxing, happens to be located so that she and her entourage can discreetly peek out the windows to see who's arrived and what's going on.

The club's venue coordinator will assist with all your event needs, such as vendor selection, menu planning, the rehearsal, and day-of ceremony coordination. Their flexible culinary team can custom-design menus, offer recommendations based on their experience, and provide almost any style of food. Canyon Crest also accommodates rehearsal dinners, bridal showers and brunches. The club is private, so indoor music can go on forever. (Outdoor music has to shut down by 11pm.)

We think Canyon Crest's good looks and versatile kitchen, as well as its relaxed feel and flow, make it one of the Inland Empire's best contenders for a one-stop, affordable wedding venue.

CEREMONY CAPACITY: The site holds 160 seated guests outdoors.

EVENT/RECEPTION CAPACITY: The club can accommodate 160 seated or 200 standing guests indoors, and 100 outdoors (seated or standing).

MEETING CAPACITY: Meeting spaces hold up to 150 seated guests.

PRICES: WHAT'S THIS GOING TO COST?

Ceremony Fee: *$1,500/event*
- The ceremony package includes: white padded ceremony chairs, unity table with linen, pre-ceremony beverages, tax and service charge, and more.

Package Prices: *$65–110/person*
- Packages include the ceremony, standard rentals, 2-course plated dinner, custom wedding cake, tax and service charge, and more.

AVAILABILITY: Year-round, daily, anytime.

SERVICES/AMENITIES:

Catering: in-house
Kitchen Facilities: n/a
Tables & Chairs: provided
Linens, Silver, etc.: provided
Restrooms: wheelchair accessible
Dance Floor: portable provided
Bride's & Groom's Dressing Area: yes
AV/Meeting Equipment: provided
Other: groom's suite, complimentary WiFi

Parking: complimentary large lot
Accommodations: no guest rooms
Outdoor Night Lighting: provided
Outdoor Cooking Facilities: none
Cleanup: provided
View: canyon, fountain, golf course fairways, lake, landscaped grounds, pool area, panorama of mountains

RESTRICTIONS:

Alcohol: in-house
Smoking: OK in designated areas
Music: amplified OK indoors

Wheelchair Access: yes, except for the outdoor ceremony site
Insurance: not required

The Mission Inn Hotel & Spa

Historic Inn

3649 Mission Inn Avenue, Riverside
800/344-4225
www.missioninn.com
weddings@missioninn.com

● Rehearsal Dinners	● Corporate Events
● Ceremonies	● Meetings
● Wedding Receptions	● Film Shoots
● Private Parties	● Accommodations

Few places are as magical as the renowned Mission Inn Hotel & Spa. With its dazzling Spanish architecture and European charm, this extraordinary castle-like venue is *the* place for a fairytale wedding.

As you walk through its iconic bell-tower entrance, you're transported to a world of timeless romance. Beauty is everywhere in the form of fountains, statues, carved pillars, balconies, spiral staircases, and gardens—as well as in the unique event spaces.

Ceremonies are breathtaking in the St. Francis of Assisi Chapel, exquisitely embellished with seven jewel-toned Tiffany stained-glass windows and a gleaming, 18-karat gold leafed altar from the mid 1700s. When the chapel's huge wooden doors are opened and sunlight streams in, the bride is spotlighted in a special glow as she makes her entrance. Two courtyards are also available for outdoor weddings.

Large receptions are held in the Grand Parisian Ballroom, which resembles a baronial hall in an Old World castle. Sumptuous details include custom-woven wool carpeting inspired by the French Aubusson rugs of the 17th and 18th centuries, damask draperies framing the room's stained-glass windows, and eight spectacular crystal chandeliers suspended from the original beamed ceiling.

The Spanish Art Gallery is ideal for groups of up to 120. Richly appointed with regal 17th-century European décor and an elegant gold palette, it's a sophisticated space featuring an impressive marble staircase and a flowing ceiling canopy.

For an intimate celebration, reserve the charming Santa Barbara Room. Traditional wrought-iron and glass light fixtures create a cozy ambiance, while sheer drapes diffuse the light from tall windows overlooking both the picturesque interior courtyard of the Hotel and the Oriental Court.

The inn, which boasts two on-site chapels and a dozen reception sites, is sure to have settings that will suit your event. They've been hosting weddings and special occasions for over a century, and every one of them has been personalized by their dedicated staff who will help you realize your vision.

The Mission Inn Hotel & Spa is a place where generations of families celebrate weddings and start their own traditions. It's a place where the past and the present connect, as granddaughters pose for photos in the same spots where their mother and grandmother were photographed on their wedding day. It truly is the perfect place to give your future life together an auspicious beginning.

CEREMONY CAPACITY: The St. Francis of Assisi Chapel seats 150 guests, the St. Cecilia Chapel seats 12, and The Oriental Courtyard seats 170.

EVENT/RECEPTION CAPACITY: The hotel can accommodate 20–296 seated guests for a wedding reception or 20–350 standing guests for a cocktail reception.

MEETING CAPACITY: Indoor meeting facilities accommodate 10–310 guests.

PRICES: WHAT'S THIS GOING TO COST?

Package Prices: $2,000–3,500/event
- The Chapel Package includes an on-site special events coordinator, wedding-night accommodations for the newlyweds, and bride & groom preparation rooms for 2 hours.
- Reception dinner packages start at $75/person and include: a 2-course meal, cheese display, tray-passed champagne and cider during the cocktail hour, and champagne toast.

Service Charge or Gratuity: 23%

AVAILABILITY: Year-round, daily, 6am–midnight.

SERVICES/AMENITIES:

Catering: in-house, no BYO
Kitchen Facilities: n/a
Tables & Chairs: provided
Linens, Silver, etc.: provided
Restrooms: wheelchair accessible
Dance Floor: portable parquet provided
Bride's Dressing Area: provided with Chapel Package
AV/Meeting Equipment: full range, extra charge

Parking: on-site self & valet, additional charge
Accommodations: 238 guest rooms & suites
Outdoor Night Lighting: provided
Outdoor Cooking Facilities: no
Cleanup: provided
View: landscaped courtyards
Other: special events manager, 7,000-square-foot spa

RESTRICTIONS:

Alcohol: in-house, no BYO
Smoking: outside hotel only
Music: amplified OK indoors

Wheelchair Access: yes
Insurance: liability required for vendors
Other: no rice, birdseed, or confetti

Overwhelmed? Use the search criteria on www.HereComesTheGuide.com to narrow down your choices.

The Guest Ranch at Pacific Crest
in Wrightwood

Ranch

26000 Big Pines Highway, Wrightwood
760/249-5093

www.theguestranchpc.com
info@theguestranchpc.com

● Rehearsal Dinners	● Corporate Events
● Ceremonies	● Meetings
● Wedding Receptions	● Film Shoots
● Private Parties	Accommodations

In the late 1920s, Hollywood's playful elite were understandably drawn to Wrightwood, a sweet mountain town with brisk air, beautiful views and year-round outdoor diversions. Nestled in a valley between slopes blanketed with evergreen pines, it's an easy 90-minute journey from Los Angeles and the San Gabriel Valley along California State Highway 2, (or simply "The Two," for locals.)

The Guest Ranch at Pacific Crest in Wrightwood sits just off one of the prettiest stretches of "The Two" on 300 acres of forested wilderness that encompasses lawns, private hiking trails, and pristine wildlife habitat. Its design is inspired by the traditional dude ranch, with a rustic, wood-sided main cabin overlooking rocky seasonal riverbeds, weathered stone and wood bridges, and trickling creeks that flow into sparkling ponds. Weddings held here can't help but exude the same welcoming, down-home vibe of the town itself, which has retained its quiet alpine charm.

As guests arrive—they may be shuttled in from the nearby parking lot, or opt to take the short walk to the site—they're greeted by a huge expanse of grass at the base of the main cabin. (The cabin is used as the ranch's office, but has a cute area for bridal preparations, too.) The grass practically begs for lawn games, so many couples kick off the day with bocce ball, croquet, or horseshoes. Guests more interested in relaxing can simply mingle and chat, enjoying cocktails under the pines.

The centerpiece of the property is an extraordinary 250-year-old oak whose multiple trunks reach upward and outward, stretching toward the sky to create an enormous natural canopy and a most idyllic spot to say your vows. After the ceremony, guests cross a bridge over a small pond to a manicured lawn where the celebration continues. A large stage, just the right size for a bridal party or sweetheart table, overlooks the festivities. As twilight becomes evening, white globe lights placed throughout the trees, on bridges and along the fence line encircle the reception area in a twinkly glow. (Some couples have chosen to flip the sites, holding the ceremony on the stage and the reception under the oak; either setup works wonderfully.)

The expansive lawn area, which extends to the surrounding forest, is also where you'll find the aptly named Woodpecker Bar. It's located next to the pond in the shade of a towering pine tree with a trunk completely covered in woodpecker holes. The ranch provides your bar service, as well as a variety of flexible options for all budgets. There's ample room on the green for a tent in the event of rain, though it's unlikely you'd need it since weddings at the Ranch are held from May through October, when the weather is almost unfailingly sunny and mild.

In case you're thinking this place sounds like a great destination for a weekend wedding, it is. They provide a preferred lodging list, plus some serious fun right on the property! Their zipline company's Ziplines at Pacific Crest are not only located at the ranch, they offer a special wedding party discount package on rides during the wedding weekend.

But perhaps the loveliest thing about The Guest Ranch at Pacific Crest in Wrightwood is the people who work here. The employees have an enormous amount of pride in their venue, and it's evident in the care and commitment they show each couple.

CEREMONY, EVENT/RECEPTION & MEETING CAPACITY: The site holds 300 seated or standing guests outdoors.

PRICES: WHAT'S THIS GOING TO COST?

Package Prices: *$7,500/event and up*
   - Package prices vary depending on the package chosen, catering, and amenities.
   - Package pricing covers up to 60 guests. Tax, gratuities, and service charge are included.

AVAILABILITY: Weddings may be held May–October, Friday–Sunday. Other special events and Corporate Team Building take place year-round.

SERVICES/AMENITIES:

Catering: select from list

Kitchen Facilities: limited

Tables & Chairs: provided

Linens, Silver, etc.: linens provided; china service available with packages

Restrooms: wheelchair accessible

Dance Floor: yes

Bride's Dressing Area: yes

AV/Meeting Equipment: BYO

Other: picnic area, Ziplines at Pacific Crest, event coordination

Parking: large complimentary lot with shuttle

Accommodations: preferred lodging list for the town of Wrightwood

Outdoor Night Lighting: yes

Outdoor Cooking Facilities: no

Cleanup: provided

View: garden, landscaped grounds, waterfall with pond; panorama of fields, forest, and mountains

RESTRICTIONS:

Alcohol: in-house

Smoking: designated areas only

Music: amplified OK outdoors

Wheelchair Access: yes

Insurance: liability required

The Pavilion at Chapman Ranch

Golf Club

33725 Chapman Heights Road, Yucaipa
909/790-6522 x2

www.yucaipavalleygolf.com
info@yucaipavalleygolf.com

- Rehearsal Dinners
- Ceremonies
- Wedding Receptions
- Private Parties
- Corporate Events
- Meetings
- Film Shoots
- Accommodations

Overlooking the landscaped grounds of Yucaipa Valley Golf Course, The Pavilion at Chapman Ranch occupies a gorgeous spot in the serene town of Yucaipa. Here—midway between Los Angeles and Palm Springs—the valley's gentle foothills begin their ascent, gradually becoming the rugged peaks that crown the San Bernardino Mountains. Whether you're dreaming of a rustic outdoor wedding, a reception in an elegant hall, or something in between, you'll find lots to love here.

Exchange vows within full view of the stunning mountains at the property's "secret garden"-style ceremony space. Tucked away from the rest of the club's activities, this enclosed grassy expanse becomes your private sanctuary, complete with a flower-fringed gazebo and antique-inspired street lamps that add turn-of-the-century character. A scattering of trees are silhouetted against a vast canopy of blue sky, and as the sun dips below the horizon, a warm pastel glow kisses the mountainscape.

After your ceremony, the festivities move to the airy Pavilion, a brand new banquet space with a breezy terrace that that's just right for a cocktail hour. An adjacent lawn is perfect for party games or an al fresco lounge area. Guests move indoors for the reception, where walls of windows and glass doors frame a superb view of the surrounding golf greens and the mountains (which are often snow-capped long past winter). Wooden rafters overhead make draping the ceiling a snap, and are also helpful for displaying floral arrangements, specialty lighting, or fanciful décor.

A host of "bonus" amenities make the Pavilion at Chapman Ranch even more appealing: There's a fun, pub-style restaurant at the clubhouse next door that's great for a more casual affair, rehearsal dinner, or after-party. Your guests will appreciate the ample free parking, and there are two on-site bridal suites for your day-of preparations.

Along with its picturesque setting and stylish facilities, this venue is proud of being one of the most affordable in the region, offering a terrific value with your choice of four tiered packages, ranging from basic to grand. However, the Pavilion at Chapman's greatest asset may be its incredible staff. They're not only thoughtful and professional, they're also super flexible when it comes to choreographing your event or accommodating special menu requests. You're only limited by your own imagination, and from the very first meeting you'll be impressed by this team's dedication to ensuring your wedding fits your budget and your unique vision.

CEREMONY CAPACITY: The facility seats 200 guests indoors and 250 outdoors.

EVENT/RECEPTION CAPACITY: Indoors, the Banquet Hall holds a maximum of 140 seated or 200 standing; combined with the Terrace it seats up to 300 guests. Outdoors, the venue accommodates receptions of up to 1,000.

MEETING CAPACITY: Meeting spaces seat up to 160 guests.

PRICES: WHAT'S THIS GOING TO COST?

Rental Fee: $2,000/event and up
  • The rental fee may be reduced or waived depending on the food & beverage spend.

Package Prices: $39/person and up

Service Charge or Gratuity: 20%

AVAILABILITY: Year-round, daily, 6am–midnight.

SERVICES/AMENITIES:

Catering: in-house, select from list, or BYO (must be licensed and insured)
Kitchen Facilities: fully equipped
Tables & Chairs: provided, extra fee may apply
Linens, Silver, etc.: some provided; extra fee may apply
Restrooms: wheelchair accessible
Dance Floor: yes
Dressing Areas: yes
AV/Meeting Equipment: provided

Parking: large lot
Accommodations: no guest rooms
Outdoor Night Lighting: access only
Outdoor Cooking Facilities: BBQ CBA
Cleanup: provided
View: forest, garden patio, landscaped grounds, valley; panorama of mountains, hills and fairways
Other: event coordination available, extra fee

RESTRICTIONS:

Alcohol: full bar available in-house, or BYO wine or champagne with corkage fee
Smoking: outdoors only
Music: amplified OK with restrictions

Wheelchair Access: yes
Insurance: not required

Temecula Wine Country

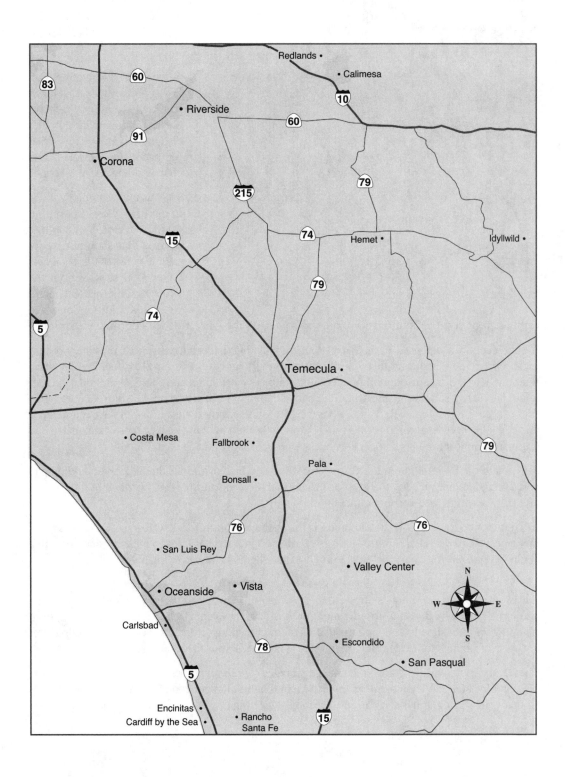

Callaway Vineyard and Winery

Winery

32720 Rancho California Road, Temecula
951/676-4001

www.callawaywinery.com
events@callawaywinery.com

● Rehearsal Dinners	● Corporate Events
● Ceremonies	● Meetings
● Wedding Receptions	Film Shoots
● Private Parties	Accommodations

50 years in the making, Callaway Vineyard & Winery has long been known for its award-winning wines, but it's also earned an equally stellar reputation as a modern and chic wedding & event venue.

Two unique ceremony locations, the West Lawn and Courtyard, sit atop a 1,600-foot plateau that showcases panoramic views of the Temecula Valley. Both sites overlook the winery's Cabernet Sauvignon vineyards, and the Courtyard can host your cocktail hour or reception, too—plus, it's the perfect dance floor under the stars!

Indoor receptions take place in the Barrel Room, an inviting space that delivers a truly wine-country experience. Guests enter by first passing through the temperature-controlled steel Fermentation Room, where they're surrounded by gleaming stainless steel tanks and the cool air and aroma of wine sparks their senses and gives them a tantalizing hint of what's to come. The Barrel Room—one of the largest in the Temecula Valley—has a high ceiling adorned with iron candlelit chandeliers, and walls lined with hundreds of barrels of actively fermenting wine. All of these elements create a romantic atmosphere for a special evening with your closest friends and family.

Adjacent to the Barrel Room is the Chardonnay Room, which overlooks the helicopter landing pad and Zinfandel vineyard. It's a cozy space that's ideal for cocktail parties, birthday bashes, bridal and baby showers, and corporate meetings.

Another option for an outdoor celebration is the sheltered Vineyard View Terrace, an extension of Meritage at Callaway's Restaurant. Here, you'll dine on impeccable farm-to-table cuisine beneath a ceiling of passionfruit vines and Edison-bulb market lights, while enjoying a view of the Cabernet Sauvignon vineyard.

Callaway's wedding & events staff are experts at making sure your big day unfolds just the way you envisioned it. A dynamic coordination team will tend to venue-related wedding details, from planning your timeline to enlisting the talents of an elite group of local vendors. They'll also offer a variety of options for designing a menu that will best fit your tastes and style.

There's one more perk you'll want to take advantage of: Callaway's prime location for appreciating breathtaking sunsets! Their team will assist you in scheduling your ceremony for the optimal time, so that your photographer can capture the magical setting of the vineyards at nightfall.

Remarkable views, great event spaces, fresh and diverse cuisine, and a detail-driven coordination team make Callaway a fabulous wedding venue. It's not surprising that for so many couples it's love at first sight!

CEREMONY CAPACITY: The site accommodates 350 guests indoors or outdoors.

EVENT/RECEPTION CAPACITY: Indoors, the facility holds 200 seated or 350 standing; outdoors 350 seated or standing.

MEETING CAPACITY: Meeting spaces seat 350 guests.

PRICES: WHAT'S THIS GOING TO COST?

Packages: $114–149/person
- Package prices vary depending on the time of year and package chosen.
- Packages include the venue rental, food, and alcohol.

Service Charge or Gratuity: 20%

AVAILABILITY: Year-round, daily, 8am–1am.

SERVICES/AMENITIES:

Catering: in-house
Kitchen Facilities: n/a
Tables & Chairs: provided
Linens, Silver, etc.: provided
Restrooms: wheelchair accessible
Dance Floor: provided
Dressing Areas: yes
AV/Meeting Equipment: CBA, extra fee

Parking: large lot
Accommodations: no guestrooms
Outdoor Night Lighting: decorative lights
Outdoor Cooking Facilities: no
Cleanup: provided
View: cityscape, garden, hills; panorama of mountains, valley, and vineyards
Other: event coordination

RESTRICTIONS:

Alcohol: in-house
Smoking: designated areas only
Music: amplified OK

Wheelchair Access: yes
Insurance: not required

CrossCreek Golf Club

Golf Club

43860 Glen Meadows Road, Temecula
951/506-3402 x4

www.crosscreekgolfclub.com
dgarner@crosscreekgolfclub.com

- Rehearsal Dinners
- Ceremonies
- Wedding Receptions
- Private Parties
- Corporate Events
- Meetings
- Film Shoots
- Accommodations

Naturally beautiful and secluded, this club is a rare find in increasingly popular Temecula Valley. Offering a tranquil ambiance and stellar views of the San Jacinto Mountains, CrossCreek feels blissfully removed from the tourist bustle. Factor in its fab location (an easy drive from Los Angeles, San Diego, and Orange Counties, and a stone's throw from some really wonderful wineries), and you've got all the elements of a perfect wedding weekend.

The festivities start off with a memorable treat for your guests—chauffeur service in the form of a golf cart! After a jaunt across the grounds, they'll arrive at your dreamy ceremony location. Here, the branches of an ancient oak stretch wide, creating an enchanting, shaded space to say "I do" as light filters through the grand tree's fluttering leaves.

Following your vows, it's back to the golf carts for a ride to the second half of your celebration. The spacious, grassy area adjacent to the clubhouse is skirted by mature olive, bay, and oak trees, and offers plenty of room for lawn games and cocktail-hour mingling. As the sun sets, strings of market lights illuminate the entire expanse in a romantic glow.

You can hold your event entirely outside, or gather in the wedding canopy, whose clear walls create a breezy indoor/outdoor feel. It provides a cool shelter on warmer days, and a great "Plan B" in the rare event of rain. The layout is completely up to you; some couples opt for open-air dining and a dance floor beneath the canopy, while others choose to dance under the stars.

CrossCreek is also one of the most affordable wedding spots in Temecula Valley. One simple package gets you all the basics—setup, cleanup, dance floor, bartender, and more—and includes use of the canopy (which saves you both money and peace of mind!). You're free to bring in the caterer of your choice, but you'll definitely want to check out staff favorite *BC Cafe & Catering*. With creative twists on American comfort food classics and an intimate knowledge of CrossCreek's unique layout, there's a reason this family-owned company has earned its "preferred" status.

Overnight guests are sure to appreciate the club's "stay and play" packages in partnership with nearby hotels, which include affordable, comfortable accommodations and a round or two of golf. We think a bridal party tournament is in order!

CEREMONY CAPACITY: The site seats 300 outdoors.

EVENT/RECEPTION CAPACITY: The venue can accommodate 300 seated or standing guests outdoors.

MEETING CAPACITY: Meeting spaces seat up to 300 guests.

PRICES: WHAT'S THIS GOING TO COST?

Package Prices: $82-98/person
- The standard package is $98/person and includes the ceremony and reception site, catering, canopy or market lights, all tables and chairs, fire pit, dance floor, and couches.
- When catering is not included in the package, the rate is $82/person.

Service Charge or Gratuity: 15%

AVAILABILITY: Year-round, daily.

SERVICES/AMENITIES:

Catering: in-house
Kitchen Facilities: n/a
Tables & Chairs: provided
Linens, Silver, etc.: some provided
Restrooms: wheelchair accessible
Dance Floor: portable provided
Bride's Dressing Area: yes
AV/Meeting Equipment: some provided

Parking: large lot
Accommodations: no guest rooms
Outdoor Night Lighting: provided
Outdoor Cooking Facilities: no
Cleanup: provided
View: hills, fairways, forest/wooded area, creek/river, garden patio/courtyard

RESTRICTIONS:

Alcohol: in-house
Smoking: outdoors only
Music: amplified OK outdoors

Wheelchair Access: yes
Insurance: not required

Want to know WHAT TO ASK a potential location or vendor? Check out our Questions to Ask starting on page 21.

Falkner Winery

Winery

40620 Calle Contento, Temecula
951/676-8231 x102

www.falknerwinery.com
weddings@FalknerWinery.com

● Rehearsal Dinners	Corporate Events
● Ceremonies	● Meetings
● Wedding Receptions	Film Shoots
● Private Parties	Accommodations

Perched on a quiet hilltop overlooking acres of rolling, vine-covered slopes, this wonderful family-owned winery is a Temecula Valley treasure. Its 1,500-foot elevation and "off the path" location ensure more than gorgeous views, though: You'll have no noise from busy roadways or tourist traffic—nothing but the sound of the breeze through trees and the gentle trickle of a Tuscan-inspired fountain.

The lush vineyard itself is by far the most popular spot for ceremonies, and for good reason. Here, you'll find towering cypress trees, bountiful white roses, and natural arches of jasmine that fill the air with their delicate fragrance. As you exchange vows beneath a wooden arch on an elevated stage, your guests will feel like they've been transported to a Mediterranean villa.

You also have the option to wed in the Garden, where large trees create a fully shaded glen that looks out across the mountains and vineyards. This site is also popular for receptions, and can be used in conjunction with the delightfully rustic tasting room, whose ivy-covered patio is the perfect place for cocktails. The Garden is absolutely lovely in the evening, with its twinkle-lit trees and romantic market lights strung high above the tables and dance floor.

Hand-carved doors featuring delicate grapevines lead to the Pinnacle Room, the winery's unforgettable space for indoor receptions. One entire curved wall is outfitted with tall windows, offering dramatic 180-degree views of the valley below. The room's columns, floor, and circular bar are all built from rich, oak wood,and there's an airy balcony where guests can step outside and admire the sunset.

For your day-of preparations, you'll settle into the pretty Bride's Suite, with its beamed ceiling, comfy furnishings, and huge mirror (it's practically begging you to twirl around in front of it!). The guys get their own hangout, too—a "man cave"-inspired VIP lounge, nestled in the inviting Barrel Room.

Your menu will be designed by Falkner's in-house Executive Chef. An avid foodie himself, he's always up on the latest trends, and is more than willing to accommodate special traditions or preferences. When paired with the vineyard's fantastic wines—80% of which have won local and national awards—you're guaranteed a dining experience your guests will be raving about long after the last slice of cake is cut.

Packages are completely customizable, and the owners take great joy in personalizing each wedding. Have a request that seems a little unorthodox? They can probably make it happen.

Weddings that begin after 5pm will have the entire venue to themselves (it's like having your own private winery), and the secluded location means you can dance outside until 11pm. Still have more celebrating to do? Move the party inside, and you can revel until 1 in the morning!

CEREMONY CAPACITY: The site holds 150 seated guests indoors and 215 outdoors.

EVENT/RECEPTION CAPACITY: The winery can accommodate 175 seated or 200 standing guests indoors, and 225 seated or 250 standing outdoors.

MEETING CAPACITY: Meeting spaces seat up to 50 guests.

PRICES: WHAT'S THIS GOING TO COST?

Package Prices: $134/person and up
   • Pricing varies depending on the day of the week, time of year, and guest count.
   • All-inclusive wedding packages for weekend events start at $134/person and include the venue rental, food, alcohol (wine, beer, and champagne), service charge, and more!

Service Charge or Gratuity: 22%

AVAILABILITY: Year-round, 4pm-1am

SERVICES/AMENITIES:

Catering: in-house

Kitchen Facilities: n/a

Tables & Chairs: provided

Linens, Silver, etc.: provided

Restrooms: wheelchair accessible

Dance Floor: provided

Bride's & Groom's Dressing Areas: yes

AV/Meeting Equipment: BYO

Other: event coordination

Parking: self-parking adjacent to the winery

Accommodations: no guest rooms

Outdoor Night Lighting: market lights, decorative spotlights, and wall lighting

Outdoor Cooking Facilities: no

Cleanup: provided

View: panorama of mountains, valleys, and vineyards; flowers; amazing sunsets

RESTRICTIONS:

Alcohol: in-house

Smoking: outdoors only

Music: amplified OK

Wheelchair Access: yes

Insurance: liability required

Lake Oak Meadows Weddings and Events

Private Waterfront Estate

36101 Glen Oaks Road, Temecula
951/676-6162

www.lakeoakmeadows.com
info@lakeoakmeadows.com

Rehearsal Dinners	● Corporate Events
● Ceremonies	● Meetings
● Wedding Receptions	● Film Shoots
● Private Parties	● Accommodations

In the heart of Temecula wine country is a private, ten-acre estate where rose bushes scent the air and a wonderful variety of trees form shady groves around a serene lake, known for its spectacular nighttime display: "Fountains of Fire and Water."

While this almost Eden-like oasis is terrific for concerts, retreats, memorials and reunions, it's utterly romantic for weddings. Couples recite their vows under a flower-adorned arch on a grassy peninsula that juts out into the lake. Ornate lamps and fragrant roses edge the ceremony space, and stately pepper trees form a sheltering backdrop. Just across the lake, a picturesque waterfall cascades down large rocks.

Guests enjoy post-ceremony cocktails under a shady arbor and on the adjoining lawn. Strings of twinkle lights dangle from the arbor and wrap around the trees, and the optional addition of delicate Japanese lanterns enhances the romantic atmosphere. At night, the illumination elicits many "oohs" and "ahhs," which multiply even more when the lake's fountains light up in their fiery dance.

Steps away from the arbor, the reception courtyard is a particularly comfortable setting as Temecula's famous late afternoon breeze begins to stir. Caterers love having a prep room close by—it makes keeping food coming fast and fresh a snap. The reception courtyard, which can be canopied, has lines of lights streaming above it and along the low wooden fence that borders it. With a bar tucked into one corner, there's plenty of room for tables and chairs. An area is available for serving hors d'oeuvres and wine, and your guests can mingle around fire pits under a canopy of grapevines and trees. The adjacent reception lounge is where your DJ sets up, and its majestic fireplace and chandelier create a welcoming ambiance for your guests to dance the night away.

Conveniences abound in the Bridal Suite, including air conditioning, full-length mirrors, mirrored makeup seating, a kitchenette, refrigerator, and shower. Outside, there's a private patio enclosed by wood lattice walls covered with fragrant jasmine vines. A popular tradition here is for the bride to emerge from her dressing room, walk across a small bridge with a rock waterfall, and step into a horse-drawn carriage that takes her to the lakeside ceremony site.

The Groom's Suite is equally enticing to the guys, with its rustic cabin feel, fireplace, TV, and pool table.

A grassy knoll behind the lake is a favorite spot for photos. Pepper and black gum trees shade this pleasant green rise, which is bordered by a quaint split-rail fence that zigzags between the lawn and flowerbeds.

Lake Oak Meadows Weddings and Events has a distinct "ranch feel," but with all the rough edges smoothed away. What remains is a beautiful, amenity-rich venue that immediately captures the fancy of almost everyone. After you take a quick stroll from the parking lot down the terraced stairway and get your first dazzling lake view, you'll see why this location is worth considering for any event.

CEREMONY CAPACITY: The site can accommodate up to 450 seated guests outdoors.

EVENT/RECEPTION & MEETING CAPACITY: The resort holds 450 seated guests.

PRICES: WHAT'S THIS GOING TO COST?

Package Prices: $121–131/person
- Package prices vary depending on the day of the week, time of year, guest count, and package chosen.
- There is also an All-Inclusive Weekday Package for Monday–Thursday weddings, which runs $8,645 for up to 50 guests.
- All packages include the venue rental, food, bridal & groom suites, day-of coordinator, complimentary parking, and many more amenities. The guest minimum varies from 50 to 125 depending on the day of the week and time of year.

AVAILABILITY: Year-round, daily, anytime, excluding major holidays.

SERVICES/AMENITIES:

Catering: in-house
Kitchen Facilities: n/a
Tables & Chairs: provided
Linens, Silver, etc.: provided
Restrooms: wheelchair accessible
Dance Floor: provided
Bride's & Groom's Dressing Areas: yes
AV/Meeting Equipment: some provided
Other: event coordination provided

Parking: large lot
Accommodations: honeymoon suite
Outdoor Night Lighting: provided
Outdoor Cooking Facilities: CBA
Cleanup: provided
View: forest, fountain, garden, hills, lagoon, lake, landscaped grounds, meadow, waterfall, park; panorama of mountains and vineyards

RESTRICTIONS:

Alcohol: in-house
Smoking: designated areas only
Music: amplified OK

Wheelchair Access: yes
Insurance: liability required

Lorimar Vineyards and Winery

Winery

39990 Anza Road, Temecula
951/694-6699
www.lorimarwinery.com/weddings
weddings@lorimarwinery.com

- Rehearsal Dinners
- Ceremonies
- Wedding Receptions
- Private Parties
- Corporate Events
- Meetings
- Film Shoots
- Accommodations

At first sight of Lorimar's impressive Tuscan-inspired tasting room, your guests will know they're in for a treat. With its natural stone walls, terracotta-tiled roof, and soaring campanile, the building would be right at home in the Mediterranean countryside. From this family-owned winery's spot at the center of picturesque Temecula valley, gentle hills of Cabernet Sauvignon, Syrah, Grenache, Muscat, Viognier, and Sangiovese vines stretch out in all directions, and lush orchards scent the air with a delicate bouquet of citrus blossoms.

The Vineyard Lawn is Lorimar's all-outdoor venue, and it's a beauty! Here, you'll follow a paved walkway to exchange vows on a raised platform covered by a wooden arbor wrapped in climbing vines. The space is surrounded by vineyards, and is bathed in a romantic glow as the sun slips down behind the distant mountains. Hold your cocktail hour beneath a shady pergola, then dine on the lawn by the glimmer of bistro lights as a fire crackles in the brick-and-stone hearth. Your band or DJ can set up on the elevated stage (there's even a built-in dance floor!).

The Barrel Room offers the best of both indoors and out. Say "I do" in the Wedding Gazebo just steps away, followed by cocktails in the cozy room itself. Dinner and dancing take place on the adjoining lawn, which has ample space for a lounge area and lawn games, and a gorgeous view of Mount Palomar. As the hour grows later, you can move the party back into the Barrel Room and carry on with the festivities a little longer.

If you're looking for something a bit more intimate (but with plenty of Lorimar's wine country charm), The Coach House may be just the ticket. Tucked away in a secluded corner adjacent to the main grounds, this rustic-chic residence overlooks a small pond, and has its own beautiful reception room with stacked wine half-barrels, a cute bar service walk-up window, and a shaded porch.

You can also rent the Coach House for a weekend stay—it sleeps nine people in its four bedrooms, and has a large common area, gourmet kitchen, and bathrooms with soaking tubs and rain showers. Our favorite feature is the second-floor deck: It's the perfect spot to settle in under the graceful shade sails with a glass of Lorimar's sparkling rosé and watch the sun set.

CEREMONY CAPACITY: The site can seat up to 75 guests indoors and 375 outdoors.

EVENT/RECEPTION CAPACITY: The winery can accommodate 70 seated or 100 standing guests indoors, and 375 seated or 400 standing outdoors.

MEETING CAPACITY: The meeting space holds up to 100 guests.

PRICES: WHAT'S THIS GOING TO COST?

Package Prices: $93–124/person
- Package pricing varies depending on the day of the week, time of year, space reserved, and guest count.
- Packages include the venue rental and food. Each is customized for your unique event.

Service Charge or Gratuity: 20%

AVAILABILITY: Year-round, daily, 9am–10pm.

SERVICES/AMENITIES:

Catering: in-house
Kitchen Facilities: n/a
Tables & Chairs: some provided
Linens, Silver, etc.: some provided
Restrooms: wheelchair accessible
Dance Floor: provided
Bride's Dressing Area: yes
AV/Meeting Equipment: BYO

Parking: several lots throughout the property
Accommodations: The Lorimar Coach House sleeps 9
Outdoor Night Lighting: yes, market lighting
Outdoor Cooking Facilities: no
Cleanup: provided
Other: event coordination

RESTRICTIONS:

Alcohol: in-house
Smoking: designated area only
Music: amplified OK

Wheelchair Access: yes
Insurance: not required

Mount Palomar Winery

Winery

33820 Rancho California Road, Temecula
951/676-5047 X17

www.mountpalomarwinery.com
weddingsandevents@mountpalomar.com

●	Rehearsal Dinners	●	Corporate Events
●	Ceremonies	●	Meetings
●	Wedding Receptions	●	Film Shoots
●	Private Parties		Accommodations

"Wine and love have ever been allies," said Ovid, and the ancient Roman poet certainly got that right. Throughout history, poets, playwrights and novelists have paired the two, and why not? Luscious grapes on the vine, intoxicating aromas, and a seductive first sip (sigh) have turned vineyards into highly coveted wedding venues…perhaps none more so than Mount Palomar Winery.

Gracing the highest hill of Temecula's famous Wine Trail, its ornate iron gates and Italian cypress-lined driveway evoke the Mediterranean countryside, while life-size statues of mythical gods and lovely maidens reinforce the Old World feel of the grounds. Plus, this sprawling 300-acre property with its 50+ acres of planted vineyards includes something most competitors don't: In addition to the multi-tiered guest areas (tasting room, restaurant, picnic spots, etc.), they offer a completely separate hillside for weddings and events—and it's spectacular.

La Bella Vista ceremony site does indeed translate to a beautiful view. From its high perch, you can see for miles over the whole Temecula Valley, an unobstructed panorama extending straight out to the distant mountains. A wide brick center aisle cuts through the lawn to a classic colonnade flanked by a low, white balustrade and urns. The effect is breathtaking. After vows are exchanged, a long bar, set against a backdrop of greenery, beckons your guests to raise a glass of bubbly.

Then, stroll through a picturesque, vine-covered arbor to the expansive al fresco reception space, comprised of the grassy Vista Del Valle and stone-floored Piazza di Arbole. The views are, once again, fantastic and the grounds are abloom with roses, scented herbs and edible grapes. Statuary abounds, along with a large fountain adorned with figurines. Your photographer will love the seemingly endless photo ops here, like dramatic shots on the illuminated staircase leading down to the main welcome center.

Another great thing about Mt. Palomar Winery is that they only host one wedding at a time, so you can spread out and enjoy! In fact, if your wedding revelry isn't ready to wind down when outdoor music ordinances kick in (or the weather isn't cooperating), you're more than welcome to move the bacchanal into their Barrel Room. Yes, it's a real working part of the winery, but so utterly romantic. With crystal chandeliers, a draped ceiling and twinkle lights hidden among the stacked barrels, you'll feel like you've stepped onto a movie set. Photos taken with you posing in front of the larger vats and barrels will give your fantasy night a bit of an industrial edge.

Mt. Palomar, however, is more than just a "pretty face". Their food and wine consistently garner raves, so take advantage of their team of experts to help you pair particular varietals with your menu selections. They provide a multitude of reds, whites and dessert wines to choose from and, in fact, you can even host a private tasting as part of your shower or rehearsal dinner at their pavilion restaurant.

CEREMONY CAPACITY: The site holds 150 seated indoors and 500 seated outdoors.

EVENT/RECEPTION & MEETING CAPACITY: The site accommodates 150 seated or 250 standing guests indoors and 700 seated or 2,000 standing outdoors.

PRICES: WHAT'S THIS GOING TO COST?

Package Prices: $105/person and up
- Package prices vary depending on the day of the week, time of year, guest count, and package chosen.
- All wedding packages include the rental fee and food, and some also include alcohol.
- All-inclusive packages are available.

Service Charge or Gratuity: 20%

AVAILABILITY: Year-round, daily, 10am–midnight.

SERVICES/AMENITIES:

Catering: in-house
Kitchen Facilities: n/a
Tables & Chairs: provided
Linens, Silver, etc.: provided
Restrooms: wheelchair accessible
Dance Floor: yes
Bride's & Groom's Dressing Areas: yes
AV/Meeting Equipment: provided, extra fee

Parking: paved on-site lot for up to 300 cars
Accommodations: no guest rooms
Outdoor Night Lighting: yes (lampposts, market and twinkle lights throughout)
Outdoor Cooking Facilities: no
Cleanup: provided
View: 360-degree panorama of vineyards, valley, and mountains; garden, fountain, landscaped grounds, waterfall

RESTRICTIONS:

Alcohol: in-house
Smoking: designated areas only
Music: amplified OK with restrictions

Wheelchair Access: yes
Insurance: not required

The wedding vendors on our website are the best in the business. How do we know? Read page 425.

South Coast Winery Resort and Spa

Winery, Resort, & Spa

34843 Rancho California Road, Temecula
844/826-4662

www.southcoastwinery.com/weddings
weddings@wineresort.com

- Rehearsal Dinners
- Ceremonies
- Wedding Receptions
- Private Parties
- Corporate Events
- Meetings
- Film Shoots
- Accommodations

This exquisite winery sits on 63 hilltop acres that offer breathtaking views of Temecula's surrounding vineyards and the Palomar Mountains to the east. Nestled among South Coast Winery's own grapevines are the resort's Mediterranean-inspired facilities—tasting rooms, restaurants, guest suites, and hidden gardens—that evoke the Tuscan countryside.

If an all-outdoor wedding is what you've got in mind, you're in luck here! With several al fresco options throughout the property, your only dilemma may be choosing your favorite. Ceremonies are lovely in the Rose Arbor—the namesake arbor is completely covered by climbing roses, and its secluded location boasts a panoramic valley and mountain view. There's also the Vintner's Garden, where you'll find an oversized gazebo and expansive, private lawn large enough to host both your vows and reception. Or perhaps The Courtyard is more your style; this idyllic "sunken" space is sheltered on two sides by the columned main building, and the resort's charming bell tower provides the backdrop for your ceremony.

Once you've said "I do", you can continue the celebration in the Courtyard beneath glowing market lights—your guests will feel as if they're reveling in the piazza of a quaint Italian village. Off to the side, a set of glass doors opens into the atmospheric Barrel Room, where stacked casks lend a "vintage wine cellar" ambiance, making it a very cool place for a hideaway cocktail hour or an intimate reception.

You might also opt to move upstairs to the Back Veranda, a covered terrace that overlooks the Courtyard and affords a bird's-eye view of the landscape. Or, dine and dance until the wee hours in the Grand Ballroom, which features a soaring, open-beamed ceiling and French doors that swing out to reveal a bougainvillea-draped patio.

Because South Coast is a true resort, you can easily spend your entire wedding weekend here. In addition to traditional hotel-style suites, there are The Villas: luxe, stand-alone bungalows with fireplaces, jetted tubs, and private patios. If you feel the need for some serious unwinding, relax with a rejuvenating body treatment at the GrapeSeed Spa, and get your hands and toes looking pretty at the Nail Cellar. You can even hold your rehearsal dinner and morning-after brunch in one of the inviting semi-private dining rooms at the rustic-chic The Vineyard Rose Restaurant.

Two well-structured packages help make planning a breeze, and include many thoughtful extras like a fruit-infused water station and shade umbrellas for your ceremony. Better yet, you and your new spouse receive complimentary Villa accommodations for two nights, ensuring that you get to fully enjoy this utterly romantic setting.

CEREMONY CAPACITY: The facility seats 600 guests indoors and 275 outdoors.

EVENT/RECEPTION CAPACITY: The site accommodates 350 seated or 500 standing indoors and 350 seated or 750 standing outdoors.

MEETING CAPACITY: Meeting spaces hold up to 350 seated guests.

PRICES: WHAT'S THIS GOING TO COST?

Package Prices: $98–152/person
  • Pricing is for peak-season wedding packages, which include the venue rental, food, wine service, and a champagne toast; bar service can be added.

Service Charge or Gratuity: 22%

AVAILABILITY: Year-round, daily, 6am–midnight.

SERVICES/AMENITIES:

Catering: in-house
Kitchen Facilities: n/a
Tables & Chairs: provided
Linens, Silver, etc.: provided
Restrooms: wheelchair accessible
Dance Floor: portable provided
Bride's & Groom's Dressing Areas: CBA
AV/Meeting Equipment: provided, extra fee

Parking: large lot, shuttle service required
Accommodations: 50 guest rooms, 82 villas
Outdoor Night Lighting: yes
Outdoor Cooking Facilities: no
Cleanup: provided
View: garden, landscaped grounds, waterfall; panorama of valley, vineyards, hills, and mountains
Other: event coordination

RESTRICTIONS:

Alcohol: in-house
Smoking: designated areas only
Music: amplified OK with restrictions

Wheelchair Access: yes
Insurance: liability required

Temecula Creek Inn

Inn

44501 Rainbow Canyon Road, Temecula
855/420-8149

www.temeculacreekinn.com
TCIWeddings@TCIResort.com

- Rehearsal Dinners
- Ceremonies
- Wedding Receptions
- Private Parties
- Corporate Events
- Meetings
- Film Shoots
- Accommodations

Located in Southern California's premier wine country, Temecula Creek Inn is framed by rolling hills and lush landscaping and surrounded by historic buildings—all while overlooking a gorgeous 27-hole championship golf course.

If you've envisioned having an intimate outdoor wedding with a rustic ambiance, The Meadows is for you. Here, you'll say "I do" on the ceremony lawn beneath a natural wooden arch that's been exquisitely decorated with flowers and drapes for a sophisticated look. This secluded area also features a unique style, with an arbor-covered lounge outfitted with plush couches, swinging chairs, and fire pits for your guests to cozy up to.

Another stunning option for your celebration is the historic Stone House, a charming cottage that dates back to the 1800s. Originally designed for Temecula's granite quarry workers, it's now a one-of-a-kind venue for events. Your guests are shuttled down the winding path to the house, which sits on a large grassy clearing that's enclosed by split-rail fencing and ringed by woodlands. The building's old wood shutters, little porch, and neat border of colorful flowers give the scene an enchanted feeling. Across the front lawn there's a wooden footbridge that leads to a sylvan ceremony site where everyone awaits your arrival (by horse-drawn carriage, if you wish). Take a moment to bask in the romantic perfection of the setting as you make your grand entrance over that bridge and up the aisle to a bentwood arbor, exchanging vows under a canopy of oak trees strung with lights.

Photo ops are everywhere, thanks to an abundance of 300-year-old oak trees, photogenic buildings, and the Granite Mountains in the background. The beauty of the inn is matched by its experienced wedding planners and award-winning culinary team, who are ready to make your dream wedding day a reality. So go ahead and create your own fairy-tale story at this magical place—you'll be so glad you did!

CEREMONY CAPACITY: The site can accommodate up to 300 seated guests outdoors.

EVENT/RECEPTION CAPACITY: The site holds 220 seated guests indoors, and 300 seated or standing outdoors.

MEETING CAPACITY: Meeting spaces hold 220 seated guests.

PRICES: WHAT'S THIS GOING TO COST?

Rental Fee: *$500–4,000/event*
- The rental fee varies depending on the space reserved.

Food & Beverage Minimum:
- A food & beverage minimum applies and is based on the date of your event and the areas reserved.

Meals (when priced separately): *$65/person and up*
- This pricing is for dinner.

AVAILABILITY: Year-round.

SERVICES/AMENITIES:

Catering: in-house
Kitchen Facilities: fully equipped
Tables & Chairs: provided, upgrades available
Linens, Silver, etc.: provided, upgrades available
Restrooms: wheelchair accessible
Dance Floor: provided
Bride's Dressing Area: yes
AV/Meeting Equipment: provided, upgrades available

Parking: large lot, self-parking
Accommodations: 130 guest rooms
Outdoor Night Lighting: provided, upgrades available
Outdoor Cooking Facilities: no
Cleanup: provided
View: courtyard, fountain, landscaped grounds; golf course fairways; panorama of forest, hills, lake, and mountains
Other: spa services, event coordination

RESTRICTIONS:

Alcohol: in-house
Smoking: designated areas only
Music: amplified OK with restrictions in some areas

Wheelchair Access: yes
Insurance: liability required

Wiens Family Cellars

Winery

35055 Via Del Ponte, Temecula
951/694-9892 x122

www.wienscellars.com
jaime@wienscellars.com

● Rehearsal Dinners		● Corporate Events	
● Ceremonies		● Meetings	
● Wedding Receptions		Film Shoots	
● Private Parties		Accommodations	

Pastoral views, award-winning wines, and exceptional farm-to-table cuisine are a good part of what makes a vineyard wedding so popular. But Wiens Family Cellars goes even further, offering the kind of warm, personalized service that actually makes you feel like you're part of their family.

Set in the rolling hills of SoCal's premier wine country, this Temecula Valley venue is known for its big reds, relaxed atmosphere, and rave reviews from happy couples. Its 10 beautiful acres feature both indoor and outdoor event sites, including two very scenic al fresco options, sure to delight your guests—and your photographer. The Vineyard View's large wooden arbor, that can be adorned with billowy draping and a chandelier, backs up to the grapevines so you're literally getting married right in the vineyard. It's so peaceful, you may want to host appetizers and your reception here as well.

If you prefer sweeping vistas, The Mountain View Amphitheater & Patio is for you. The arbor here, which can be decorated with flowers, is backed by stunning panoramas of the San Jacinto Mountains. The adjacent Patio overlooking the grounds is a great place for a casual or glammed-up reception as the sun sets over the vineyard and stars appear in the night sky. Want a space that's fully enclosed and perfect for a celebration any time of year? The versatile Event Pavilion, decorated in neutral tones accented with dark wood ceiling beams and circular chandeliers, gives you a free hand to add your decorative touches.

But what would a winery be without a charming Cellar Room? Ideal for smaller gatherings of up to 50 guests, this cozy spot boasts a wall of oak barrels on one side and tall, gleaming stainless steel tanks on the other. And since the winery hosts only one wedding per day, you can use this space along with any of the others in whatever combination works best for your big day.

No matter where you celebrate, the food here is outstanding. Their in-house chef sources fresh, local, organic ingredients for an extensive menu of classics and innovative fusion twists for meat-lovers, vegetarians, and vegans alike. Meanwhile, Winemaker Joe Wiens uses his training and experience to make sure that every bottle lives up to the words on their seal: "Quality, Family, Integrity". And if you happen to have beer drinkers in your party, they will not go thirsty—Wiens Family Cellars also owns a craft brewery nearby.

Their array of packages include use of the vineyards for engagement photos, a coordinator to help with planning (even if you're making arrangements from out of town), a pre-wedding wine and food tasting, private bride and groom suites to get ready (with snacks and their signature Amour de L'Orange Sparkling Wine—after all, the valley is known as the "Citrus/Vineyard zone")...and, their Unity Wine Ceremony, which combines both red and white in a glass to be shared by the new couple. Move over Unity Candle—this is more fun!

CEREMONY CAPACITY: The site seats up to 200 guests indoors or outdoors.

EVENT/RECEPTION & MEETING CAPACITY: The site holds 200 seated or standing guests indoors or outdoors.

PRICES: WHAT'S THIS GOING TO COST?

Package Prices: $120–150/person
- Pricing varies depending on the day of the week and package chosen.
- Packages include the venue rental, planning, ceremony, food, alcohol, tables & chairs, linens, and much more.

Service Charge or Gratuity: 20%

AVAILABILITY: Year-round, daily.

SERVICES/AMENITIES:

Catering: in-house
Kitchen Facilities: n/a
Tables & Chairs: provided
Linens, Silver, etc.: provided
Restrooms: wheelchair accessible
Dance Floor: patio or deck
Dressing Areas: yes
AV/Meeting Equipment: CBA
Other: event coordination

Parking: large lot
Accommodations: no guest rooms
Outdoor Night Lighting: market lights provided in Vineyard View
Outdoor Cooking Facilities: BBQ CBA
Cleanup: provided
View: vineyard, mountains, garden, winery, landscaped grounds, forest/wooded area

RESTRICTIONS:

Alcohol: in-house
Smoking: designated areas only
Music: amplified OK

Wheelchair Access: yes
Insurance: not required

Wilson Creek Winery

Winery

35960 Rancho California Road, Temecula
951/699-9463
www.wilsoncreekwinery.com/weddings
weddings@wilsoncreekwinery.com

● Rehearsal Dinners		● Corporate Events	
● Ceremonies		● Meetings	
● Wedding Receptions		● Film Shoots	
● Private Parties		● Accommodations	

With its delectable wines, stellar views, and wonderfully friendly staff, Wilson Creek has long been a Temecula favorite and "must stop" destination for both locals and visitors. This family-owned winery is known for its gracious hospitality—visit their stylish tasting room on a busy Saturday, and you're very likely to run into a member of the Wilson clan, welcoming guests and ensuring things are running smoothly.

Because the grounds are so lovely, outdoor weddings are a specialty here. The Concert Stage, at the very center of the property, overlooks the vineyard and gardens and features a raised stage covered by an arched wooden pergola. The Vineyard View Stage offers a secluded vibe, tucked at the edge of Cabernet vines and accented by ivy-covered arches and petite palm trees. Or, opt for the marvelous White Wedding Gazebo, which is nestled in a lush oasis and encircled by flowering plants and pepper, olive, and other native trees. Cabernet Hill and Merlot Mesa are located in the vines, while Vineyard Row is surrounded by them and sheltered by shade sails.

Wilson Creek's indoor venues provide a wide variety of settings, too: Consider the Barrel Room, with its rows of stacked wine casks illuminated by dramatic uplighting. In the Upper Room, enormous circular chandeliers hang from a peaked, exposed-beam ceiling, and glass double doors open onto a patio overlooking the vineyard and gardens. You might choose the inviting Garden View Terrace Room, where the walls are adorned with romantic vintage-inspired sconces and you have a grand view of the grounds. For a more elegant ambiance, the Champagne Ballroom impresses with beautiful marble columns, a deeply coffered ceiling, and walls covered in a tapestry of wine barrel staves that add both a rustic touch and an artistic backdrop for photos.

Each of the winery's indoor and outdoor event spaces has its own special flair, and you can combine them to suit the size and style of your celebration.

If you're looking to make the most of your wine country wedding weekend, we suggest you book The Manor, Wilson Creek's fantastic vacation retreat—it can accommodate two dozen of your nearest and dearest in 10 luxurious guest rooms. The Grand Salon is the ideal spot for everyone to gather, plus there's a game room (a fun option for a groomsmen's dressing room), commercial kitchen, pool, spa, and large area for grilling and dining. Our favorite feature, though, is the opulent bridal dressing area, which boasts plush lounge furnishings, individual lighted makeup stations, and an enormous 360-degree mirror that makes it easy to see your dress from every angle.

At the end of a perfect day, you and your new spouse will retire to the serene Almond Champagne Suite, named for Wilson Creek's wildly popular sparkling wine. You can even have a personalized label printed onto your preferred vintage—what a special treat to share on your first anniversary!

CEREMONY CAPACITY: The site seats up to 350 outdoors.

EVENT/RECEPTION & MEETING CAPACITY: The winery holds 300 seated guests indoors or 1,000 outdoors and 500 standing guests indoors or 1,200 outdoors.

PRICES: WHAT'S THIS GOING TO COST?

Packages: $85–145/person
  • Wedding packages include: the ceremony space and chairs; 4–5 hours of event time; standard rentals; hors d'oeuvres and entrées; a selection of 3 red wines, 3 white wines, 2 sparkling wines, and 2 beers; and more!

Food & Beverage Minimum: $800–12,000/event

Service Charge or Gratuity: 20%

Additional Info: Pricing varies depending on the day of the week, time of day, time of year, space reserved, event duration, package chosen, and type of event.

AVAILABILITY: Year-round, daily, 6am–midnight.

SERVICES/AMENITIES:

Catering: in-house
Kitchen Facilities: n/a
Tables & Chairs: provided
Linens, Silver, etc.: provided
Restrooms: wheelchair accessible
Dance Floor: yes
Dressing Areas: yes
AV/Meeting Equipment: CBA, extra fee
Other: picnic area, event coordination

Parking: large lot
Accommodations: 10 guest rooms
Outdoor Night Lighting: yes
Outdoor Cooking Facilities: none
Cleanup: provided
View: vineyards, garden, forest/wooded area

RESTRICTIONS:

Alcohol: in-house
Smoking: designated areas only
Music: amplified OK with some restrictions

Wheelchair Access: yes
Insurance: required

Want to find more venues and services? Check out our informative website, www.HereComesTheGuide.com.

San Diego Area

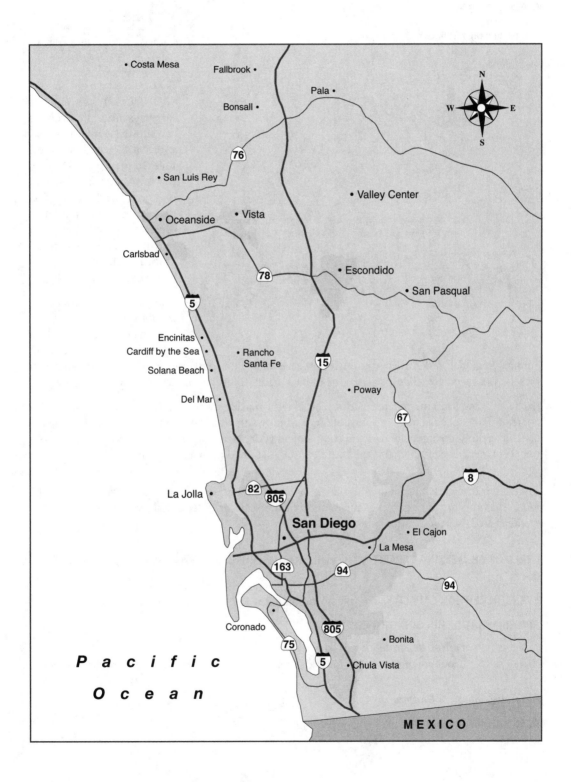

Bonita Golf Course

Golf Course

5540 Sweetwater Road, Bonita
619/267-1103 X17

bonitagolf.net/events
events@bonitagolfclub.com

● Rehearsal Dinners	● Corporate Events
● Ceremonies	● Meetings
● Wedding Receptions	● Film Shoots
● Private Parties	Accommodations

Relaxed yet elegant, Bonita Golf Course brings emerald fairways and picturesque mountain views to every event. It's located just a few miles from busy San Diego in the refreshingly rural suburb of Bonita, and visitors find that it's not uncommon to receive a friendly wave or two from horseback riders ambling along the area's many equestrian trails.

The setting is perfect for indoor/outdoor celebrations. Start with "first look" shots at the nearby Sweetwater Summit Regional Park, where the lush 500-acre waterfront expanse and built-in amphitheater provide photogenic backdrops. Then, head back to BGC for your ceremony and reception.

Exchange vows on a manicured site, which is right outside the newly renovated ballroom. This contemporary space features a series of large windows that fill the room with natural light, and a tasteful, creamy, color palette that will complement your chosen décor. An elevated stage overlooks the permanent dance floor, and the room can be sectioned for smaller events.

In addition to its great facilities, BGC takes pride in offering excellent personalized service. The food selections are varied and creative, and you'll also have a dedicated event manager at your wedding from start to finish.

CEREMONY & MEETING CAPACITY: The facility holds 300 seated guests indoors and 150 seated outdoors.

EVENT/RECEPTION CAPACITY: The site accommodates 300 seated or standing indoors.

PRICES: WHAT'S THIS GOING TO COST?

Meals (when priced separately): $23–40/person
  • The guest count minimum is 125 for Friday night, 150 for Saturday night, and 80 for all other days and times.

Service Charge or Gratuity: 18%

AVAILABILITY: Year-round, daily, 8am–midnight.

SERVICES/AMENITIES:

Catering: in-house
Kitchen Facilities: n/a
Tables & Chairs: provided
Linens, Silver, etc.: provided
Restrooms: wheelchair accessible
Dance Floor: provided
Bride's Dressing Areas: no
AV/Meeting Equipment: some provided

RESTRICTIONS:

Alcohol: in-house
Smoking: outdoors only
Music: amplified OK

Parking: large, private lot
Accommodations: no guest rooms
Outdoor Night Lighting: access only
Outdoor Cooking Facilities: no
Cleanup: provided
View: canyon, creek, forest, fountain, garden, pond, lake, landscaped grounds; panorama of hills, golf course fairways, and mountains

Wheelchair Access: yes
Insurance: not required

The Crossings at Carlsbad

Oceanview Golf Clubhouse

5800 The Crossings Drive, Carlsbad
760/444-1800 x4

www.thecrossingsatcarlsbad.com
catering@thecrossingsatcarlsbad.com

●	Rehearsal Dinners	●	Corporate Events
●	Ceremonies	●	Meetings
●	Wedding Receptions	●	Film Shoots
●	Private Parties		Accommodations

It may seem like the impossible dream to find everything you're looking for in one location—charming coastal community, acres of lush, manicured grounds and a backdrop of the blue Pacific Ocean—but all that and more is waiting for you at The Crossings at Carlsbad.

Perched atop a hillside road just a mile from the beach, this upscale golf club occupies an amazing vantage with views of rolling fairways, sunsets over the horizon, and rugged canyons. The 28,000-square-foot clubhouse incorporates natural materials like stone and wood with lots of glass to showcase the surrounding landscape. Inside the lobby, you'll find comfy, rustic-style leather seating and modern, cylindrical chandeliers.

If you're having your ceremony here, and most couples do, your guests will gather on the Ceremony Lawn, a wide swath of grass framed by feathery trees and shrubbery. Feel the cool sea breezes as you exchange vows against a panorama of the ocean below.

Then it's time to celebrate with a glass of bubbly on the adjacent terrace or upstairs on the wrap-around Canyons Patio where, along with cocktails and hors d'oeuvres, you can drink in the peaceful vistas. Needless to say, the beautiful surroundings offer up lots of great photo ops, from romantic duets at the rock waterfalls, a charming bridge or a verdant knoll…to group shots in front of the very photogenic arched iron gates of the clubhouse.

The Canyons Restaurant, the setting for your main reception, is equally striking. This soaring space features floor-to-ceiling windows and exposed, trestle beams sporting iron rivets for a casually elegant ambiance. There's a long, polished wood bar with black granite top and a large dance floor in front of it. A tall, stacked stone fireplace at one end can be a great focal point for an indoor ceremony, a rehearsal dinner or other intimate event. And of course, wherever you're seated, you'll enjoy a direct sightline to those glorious exteriors.

Their executive chef uses his extensive global experience to lead a topnotch culinary team in creating mouthwatering fare, both casual and gourmet. You can choose from a wide array of menus and complete packages—or even opt to bring in your own caterer, especially for ethnic dishes.

The entire staff offers personalized service, helping you from start to finish so that you can actually relax and enjoy your own event. Whether you'd like a golf tournament, rehearsal dinner, late-night party on the Player's Lounge Patio or overnight accommodations at a local hotel, they're happy to arrange it. They can even help organize a show-stopping entrance via helicopter from nearby Palomar Airport. Oh, and by the way, did we mention that their attention to detail not only takes the cake—it includes a totally customized one!

CEREMONY CAPACITY: The site holds 250 seated outdoors.

EVENT/RECEPTION & MEETING CAPACITY: The site accommodates 220 seated guests indoors and 350 seated or standing outdoors.

PRICES: WHAT'S THIS GOING TO COST?

Package Prices:
- *Ceremony Packages* run $1,000 for Saturday morning, $2,500 for Saturday evening, and $2,000 Sunday–Friday. They include 2 hours of setup time plus ceremony time, white garden chairs, 2 choices of arch, ceremony rehearsal, on-site coordination, and more. Service charge and tax are additional.
- *Reception Packages* start at $100/person for dinner and include 2 hours of setup time and 5 hours of eventing event time; cocktail hour with hosted bar & hors d'oeuvres; 2-course plated meal; tables, chairs, linens, and tableware; Champagne or sparkling cider toast, wedding cake; staffing and day-of coordination; and more. Service charge and tax are additional.

Food & Beverage Minimum: $6,000–15,000/event
- The food & beverage minimum varies depending on the day of the week, time of day, and space reserved.

Service Charge or Gratuity: 21%

AVAILABILITY: Year-round, daily, 7am–midnight.

SERVICES/AMENITIES:

Catering: in-house
Kitchen Facilities: n/a
Tables & Chairs: provided
Linens, Silver, etc.: provided
Restrooms: wheelchair accessible
Dance Floor: portable provided
Bride's Dressing Area: yes
AV/Meeting Equipment: provided

Parking: large complimentary lot
Accommodations: no guest rooms
Outdoor Night Lighting: CBA
Outdoor Cooking Facilities: BBQ CBA
Cleanup: provided
View: panorama of landscaped grounds, golf course, and Pacific Ocean
Other: event coordination; ceremony includes wrought-iron arch and white padded chairs

RESTRICTIONS:

Alcohol: in-house, or BYO with corkage fee
Smoking: designated areas only
Music: amplified OK with restrictions

Wheelchair Access: yes
Insurance: liability required

The Westin Carlsbad Resort and Spa

Coastal Resort Hotel

5480 Grand Pacific Drive, Carlsbad
760/827-2419
joshiro@sheratoncarlsbad.com
www.marriott.com

- Rehearsal Dinners
- Ceremonies
- Wedding Receptions
- Private Parties
- Corporate Events
- Meetings
- Film Shoots
- Accommodations

Mere minutes from a particularly lovely stretch of the California coast, this luxury resort is blessed with cool ocean breezes and even cooler ocean views. The Westin's verdant seaside-bluff setting, extending across some of north San Diego County's most desirable real estate, gives you a sense of getting away from it all—which sounds about perfect for a memorable wedding.

Why not arrive early and get the wedding weekend started with some well-deserved, mother-daughter or bridal party pampering at their Ocean Pearl Spa? Then, follow with a scrumptious rehearsal dinner at 20/Twenty, their casually chic restaurant where you can expect creative cuisine made from the freshest ingredients. Afterwards, you might want to linger on 20/Twenty's patio for a nightcap beside the fire pit.

Your big day officially starts with a ceremony at your choice of two tropically landscaped sites. The secluded Ocean Blue Lawn, situated at the far end of the property, is framed by a lush array of trees and white roses and cooled by tranquil ocean breezes. You can make a dramatic entrance as you head down a long staircase to join your groom and say "I do" against a panorama of the shimmering sea. Or, you can get married on the expansive, Pacific Lawn. Surrounded by towering palms and bordered by a vine-covered pergola, this wide swath of grass is anchored at one end by a circular patio adorned with a truly magnificent magnolia tree. Its spreading branches create a stunning natural backdrop for exchanging vows.

The nearby Palm Courtyard, overlooking the gardens and pool, is a wonderful al fresco reception area. If you prefer something more formal, reserve either the Sunset or Grand Pacific Ballroom. Both come with their own light-filled foyers for cocktails and hors d'oeuvres, as well sweeping, columned terraces that afford sunset and starlit vistas. High ceilings, modern chandeliers, large dance floors and state-of-the-art AV systems set the stage for the kind of celebration you've always imagined. Best of all, you'll be guided by a team of experts that can help you choose everything from décor and lighting packages to your menu.

The service here is amazing. It starts with the warm greeting you receive on arrival and continues every step of the way. Want to turn your event into a mini-vacation? Have the staff arrange accommodations and local activities, like a visit to Legoland (the Westin has its own private entrance to the park!); a round of golf up the hill at The Crossings at Carlsbad; a day at the beach; or shopping for designer clothes at the premium outlet mall nearby. They can also organize a private trolley to take your guests to favorite attractions.

CEREMONY & MEETING CAPACITY: The site holds 900 seated guests indoors and outdoors.

EVENT/RECEPTION CAPACITY: The facility can accommodate 600 seated or 1,000 standing indoors or outdoors.

PRICES: WHAT'S THIS GOING TO COST?

Rental Fee:
• There are no separate rental fees.

Package Prices:
• All-inclusive wedding packages are available.

Meals (when priced separately): *$86/person and up*
• The price varies depending on menu choices. Menus can be customized.

Service Charge or Gratuity: *24%*

AVAILABILITY: Year-round, daily, 6am–midnight.

SERVICES/AMENITIES:

Catering: in-house
Kitchen Facilities: n/a
Tables & Chairs: provided
Linens, Silver, etc.: provided
Restrooms: wheelchair accessible
Dance Floor: portable provided
Bride's Dressing Area: yes
AV/Meeting Equipment: some provided, more CBA

Parking: large lot, valet available
Accommodations: 208 guest rooms
Outdoor Night Lighting: yes
Outdoor Cooking Facilities: no
Cleanup: provided
View: panoramic coastal views from Carlsbad's highest point

RESTRICTIONS:

Alcohol: in-house
Smoking: outdoors only
Music: amplified OK

Wheelchair Access: yes
Insurance: liability required

Orfila Vineyards and Winery

Winery & Vineyard

13455 San Pasqual Road, Escondido
760/738-6500 x314

www.orfila.com
events@orfila.com

- Rehearsal Dinners
- Ceremonies
- Wedding Receptions
- Private Parties
- Corporate Events
- Meetings
- Film Shoots
- Accommodations

Alejandro Orfila, the man behind lovely Orfila Vineyards and Winery, has led an extraordinary life. Formerly Argentina's ambassador to the United States, and later Secretary General of the Organization of American States, he has hobnobbed with every U.S. president from Truman to Clinton. When he retired from his 39-year diplomatic career, he bought a small winery in sleepy San Pasqual Valley and turned its 70 acres into an unexpectedly world-class operation. Credit also goes to winemaker Justin Mund, who joined Orfila in 2010 and continues to maintain and enhance the winery's high-quality standards.

Orfila's grounds are as spectacular as their wines, and they make a decidedly romantic backdrop for a wedding. Ceremonies are held on an expansive lawn with a classic wine country view: countless well-tended rows of Syrah, Sangiovese, Cabernet Sauvignon and Merlot grapes receding towards unspoiled hills rising in the distance. Only the occasional bird chirping interrupts the quiet of this valley, which becomes your cathedral. Its timeless natural beauty complements any celebration, whether formal, relaxed, or somewhere in between.

It's a short stroll from the lawn to the patio, where your guests gather for cocktails. Surrounded by flowers and lit by charming gas lamp-style fixtures, it's the perfect spot for mingling on a balmy summer evening. Bartenders typically dispense libations under the long, vine-covered grape arbor, as your family and friends sample hors d'oeuvres—you may also be inspired to host a wine and cheese tasting!

There is no shortage of photo opportunities at Orfila: down in the vineyard; in the sprawling, grassy park; and up in the aromatic barrel room (you're sure to recall its intoxicating aroma every time you open your wedding album).

Are you planning to invite a lot of people? They'll all fit under the 6,000-square-foot white pavilion adjacent to the patio, with plenty of room left over for your band or DJ and dancing on a hardwood floor. Heaters and ceiling fans provide comfort in any weather; leave the tent sides tied open to enjoy the breeze and the view of the vineyard when the weather is good (which is most of the time). Dramatic spotlights, uplights, and string lights can be adjusted to create whatever mood you like.

In keeping with its commitment to quality, the winery only works with a handpicked coterie of preferred caterers who can handle the full range of events, from a simple down-home dinner to an elaborate gala. In addition, Orfila will assign an event supervisor to make sure everything runs smoothly.

Finally, what would make a more fitting keepsake of your marriage at the winery than a bottle of your favorite Orfila vintage, customized with your own private, commemorative label? Uncork one bottle per table and let your guests raise their glasses together, or give every adult a bottle to take home to remind them this was a very good year.

CEREMONY & EVENT/RECEPTION CAPACITY: The site holds 60 guests indoors and 250 outdoors, seated or standing.

MEETING CAPACITY: Meeting spaces can accommodate 300 seated guests.

PRICES: WHAT'S THIS GOING TO COST?

Rental Fee: $4,450–5,650/event

AVAILABILITY: Year-round, weekdays until 8:30pm, and weekends until 10pm.

SERVICES/AMENITIES:

Catering: select from list
Kitchen Facilities: prep only
Tables & Chairs: provided
Linens, Silver, etc.: through caterer
Restrooms: wheelchair accessible
Dance Floor: yes
Bride's Dressing Area: yes
AV/Meeting Equipment: CBA, extra fee

Parking: self-parking or valet (extra fee)
Accommodations: no guest rooms
Outdoor Night Lighting: provided
Outdoor Cooking Facilities: BBQ CBA
Cleanup: provided
View: hills, landscaped grounds; panorama of vineyards, valley, and mountains
Other: picnic area, event coordination required

RESTRICTIONS:

Alcohol: bar service in-house
Smoking: not allowed
Music: amplified OK outdoors with restrictions

Wheelchair Access: yes
Insurance: not required

This is important! Tell locations you're reading HERE COMES THE GUIDE and ask if our information is still current.

359

Grand Tradition Estate & Gardens

Victorian Mansion & Exotic Gardens

220 Grand Tradition Way, Fallbrook
760/728-6466

www.grandtradition.com
info@grandtradition.com

Rehearsal Dinners	●	Corporate Events
● Ceremonies		Meetings
● Wedding Receptions		Film Shoots
● Private Parties		Accommodations

Grand Tradition Estate & Gardens is one of San Diego's most exclusive and unique wedding venues.

With more than 35 years of professional service devoted to hosting special occasions, Grand Tradition provides a choice of two incredible wedding sites for a completely private ceremony and reception.

Beverly Mansion is an elevated reception space that overlooks Grand Tradition's iconic heart-shaped lake and offers a wonderful indoor/outdoor setting. It's adorned with crystal chandeliers, and glass-panel doors open to a veranda with a picturesque view of the lake. Couples exchange vows at the mansion's lakeside gazebo or in front of the Compass Garden waterfall.

Get married at Arbor Terrace, and you'll feel like you're in a tropical paradise: The ceremony site is shaded by a lush, green canopy of palms and showcases a towering waterfall centerpiece. Receptions follow in an open-air, satin-draped tented pavilion, complete with a terraced stage, outdoor fireplace, and waterfall just above the dance floor.

Weddings are the primary focus of Grand Tradition Estate and Gardens, where the combination of gorgeous landscaping, exceptional service, and gourmet cuisine creates not just spectacular events, but memories you'll keep for a lifetime.

CEREMONY, EVENT/RECEPTION & MEETING CAPACITY: The Beverly Mansion seats up to 300 and the Arbor Terrace holds 220 seated guests.

PRICES: WHAT'S THIS GOING TO COST?

Package Prices: $100–145/person
  • Packages include meals, setup and cleanup, and all site fees.

Service Charge or Gratuity: 20%

Additional Info: Discounted rates are available for events on weekdays, Fridays, and Sundays, and may also be offered for short-notice or off-season bookings.

AVAILABILITY: Year-round, daily. Times vary depending on the season and existing event bookings. Please call to check current date and time availability.

SERVICES/AMENITIES:

Catering: in-house, outside kosher & ethnic catering allowed with approval
Kitchen Facilities: n/a
Tables & Chairs: provided, Chiavari or white padded
Linens, Silver, etc.: provided
Restrooms: wheelchair accessible
Dance Floor: provided
Dressing Suites: yes
AV/Meeting Equipment: podium, easels, DVD projection system, wired & wireless microphones

RESTRICTIONS:

Alcohol: in-house, no BYO
Smoking: outdoors only
Music: provided or BYO; amplified OK indoors with volume limits, outdoors until 10pm

Parking: complimentary parking included, valet CBA
Accommodations: hotels and vacation rentals nearby, shuttle CBA
Outdoor Night Lighting: provided
Outdoor Cooking Facilities: no
Cleanup: provided
View: landscaped grounds, creek, fountain, garden, patio, waterfall, pond, lake
Other: event coordination, indoor specialty lighting

Wheelchair Access: yes
Insurance: not required

El Camino Country Club

3202 Vista Way, Oceanside
760/757-5375
www.countryclubreceptions.com
eventdirector@elcaminoclub.com

Country Club

●	Rehearsal Dinners	●	Corporate Events
●	Ceremonies	●	Meetings
●	Wedding Receptions	●	Film Shoots
●	Private Parties		Accommodations

El Camino Country Club is both relaxed and elegant. The clubhouse's classic décor is timeless, and its meticulous upkeep is evident throughout, from the manicured lawns to the orchids thriving in the foyer.

Ceremonies typically take place outdoors, with the couple exchanging vows in a beautiful white gazebo. Guests seated on the lawn are treated to sweeping views of the lush greens and treelined fairways in the background.

After the ceremony, family and friends enter the charming, sunny Garden Room just off the patio for cocktails and conversation. Meanwhile, the bride and groom are chauffeured in a cart around the golf course for photos in several picturesque spots, including a bi-level lake framed by a graceful weeping willow.

Later, the party moves to the more formal Main Dining Room for the reception. This spacious venue is decorated in neutral colors, and a series of multipaned windows overlook the expansive 18th fairway.

With white linens and chair covers, the room becomes a storybook wedding vision. Silver and crystal gleam in the soft, romantic glow of the chandeliers. When the best man is ready to make his toast or the couple takes to the floor for their first dance, the recessed lights in the ceiling can be turned up to create a theatrical effect.

The club's friendly and accommodating private events office offers a broad array of wedding packages, from a simple and quite affordable afternoon affair to a decadent evening gala with a hosted bar and surf-and-turf dinner.

Regardless of your budget, your wedding at the El Camino Country Club is certain to reflect the class and attention to detail that makes this facility such an enchanting place.

CEREMONY CAPACITY: The lawn holds up to 200 seated guests.

EVENT/RECEPTION & MEETING CAPACITY: The Main Dining Room accommodates up to 200 seated or 250 standing guests; the Patio up to 200 seated or 250 standing; and the Garden Room up to 70 seated or 89 standing. The Cabana can be used by a bride and her bridal party for pre-wedding preparation (up to 15 total).

PRICES: WHAT'S THIS GOING TO COST?

Package Prices: $52/person and up
- Pricing varies based on food, beverage, and rental inclusions. Food & beverage minimums will apply. Menus and packages can be customized to fit your needs and budget. Pricing does not include additional site fees, mandatory service charge, gratuity, and current sales tax.

AVAILABILITY: Year-round, daily.

SERVICES/AMENITIES:

Catering: in-house
Kitchen Facilities: n/a
Tables & Chairs: provided
Linens, Silver, etc.: provided
Restrooms: wheelchair accessible
Dance Floor: provided
Bride's Dressing Area: yes
AV/Meeting Equipment: some provided, more CBA

Parking: large lot
Accommodations: no guest rooms
Outdoor Night Lighting: CBA
Outdoor Cooking Facilities: BBQ CBA
Cleanup: provided
View: garden, pond, hills, grounds, fairways
Other: event coordination

RESTRICTIONS:

Alcohol: in-house
Smoking: outdoors only
Music: amplified OK indoors with restrictions

Wheelchair Access: yes
Insurance: not required

The Condor's Nest Ranch

Private Estate

37537 Magee Road, Pala
949/290-6088
www.thecondorsnestranch.com
thecondorsnest@gmail.com

● Rehearsal Dinners	● Corporate Events
● Ceremonies	● Meetings
● Wedding Receptions	● Film Shoots
● Private Parties	● Accommodations

What if you could spend a few days before your wedding relaxing with your family in the same beautiful country setting where you plan to say "I do?"

And what if, after a few days among mountains, woodlands, dramatic vistas and some delightful farm animals, you could arrive at the altar as relaxed as a cat that's been dozing in a shaft of golden sunlight?

Well, wedding venues that offer this kind of experience are hard to find, but we know of one hidden away in Pala. It's a wonderful "Old California" estate set in a classic San Diego back-country landscape, halfway up a mountain rife with oaks, cactus, palm trees, bougainvillea, and dramatic granite boulders and outcroppings. And, of course, it basks in Southern California's year-round glorious climate. From its expansive picture windows it offers a spectacular overview of the Pala Valley, where coastal fog often lingers until late morning—then melts away to reveal the Pacific Ocean sparkling in the distance.

Called The Condor's Nest Ranch, this delightful property comes with a plethora of charming distractions. The driveway leading to the main house is flanked by a large enclosed barnyard that's home to an extended family of llamas, horses, donkeys, pigs, chickens and goats, as well as lambs, peacocks, a cow, a long-horned steer, and an alpaca! (They have complete run of their yard, but it's up to you whether you want to mingle with them.) The house itself is a low-slung, red-tiled, 5-bedroom/4-bathroom structure, enhanced by patios and trellises. Its west-facing side is lined with huge windows that frame the awesome valley view below. The 6,000-square-foot residence is utterly sophisticated and appealing in its materials and look—furnishings and appliances are state-of-the-art, and carefully selected western-themed art and antique collectibles convey a laid-back air.

Couples and their families often reserve the venue for a week prior to the big event to unwind and spend quality time together. On the wedding day, guests come up the hill to witness and celebrate, then leave after the party. Once they're gone, families easily slip back into the ranch's pre-ceremony serenity. It's not hard to see why: Each bedroom has private access to the outside, while the master bedroom has its own deck and fireplace. When folks want to gather, they chill out in the great room, a combination family room and kitchen beneath a beamed cathedral ceiling. Here, the fireplace and patented valley vista invite warm socializing. The adjoining formal dining room opens out to the foyer (sporting a fountain in its center!) and living room, which features a huge fireplace and plenty of comfortable seating for reading, schmoozing and daydreaming.

Weddings take place on the lawn beside the house and pool, with mountains and woods as a backdrop. Directly over the spot where couples exchange vows, a tall ash tree—perhaps 200 years old—stands majestically. Receptions rock out by the pool or over by the property's second house, a rustic 2-bedroom "cottage" that's decorated with old business signs, license plates and western paraphernalia. Here and there Old West-style relics, including a classic Conestoga wagon, add to the site's appeal. A timeless red barn contributes a final touch to the easygoing retro feel of this country getaway.

The Condor's Nest Ranch is a restful, almost otherworldly place. It will work its magic on you so that no matter how tense you are when you get here, you'll feel totally calm and restored by the time you leave.

CEREMONY CAPACITY: The ranch accommodates 300 seated guests outdoors.

EVENT/RECEPTION CAPACITY: The facility holds 300 seated or standing outdoors.

MEETING CAPACITY: Meeting spaces seat up to 300 outdoors.

PRICES: WHAT'S THIS GOING TO COST?

Package Prices: $16,300/event and up
- All-inclusive packages are available for groups of 50 to 300 guests. Pricing ranges from $16,300 for 50 guests without lodging ($18,750 with it) to $52,250 for 300 guests without lodging ($54,250 with it). Packages include private use of the Ranch for 24 hours with lodging (for up to 20) and 11 hours without; ceremony & reception sites plus tables and gold Chiavari chairs, white linens, and tableware; day-of wedding coordinator and professional staff; catered dinner + bar service; professional DJ/Master of Ceremonies plus 1 sound system setup; setup, takedown, and cleanup; and much much more! For complete package details, please visit the Condor's Nest Ranch website.

AVAILABILITY: Year-round, daily. Call or email for details.

SERVICES/AMENITIES:

Catering: choose from list
Kitchen Facilities: fully equipped
Tables & Chairs: provided
Linens, Silver, etc.: provided
Restrooms: not wheelchair accessible
Dance Floor: portable provided
Bride's Dressing Area: yes
AV/Meeting Equipment: BYO
Other: day-of coordination, pool

Parking: large lot
Accommodations: 7 guestrooms
Outdoor Night Lighting: yes
Outdoor Cooking Facilities: BBQ on site
Cleanup: provided
View: panorama of valley and ocean, forest, mountains; garden courtyard, pool area, landscaped grounds

RESTRICTIONS:

Alcohol: in-house
Smoking: in designated areas only
Music: DJ provided, no BYO

Wheelchair Access: yes
Insurance: included

The Abbey on Fifth Avenue

2825 Fifth Avenue, San Diego
619/686-8700

www.abbeyweddings.com
sd@hornblower.com

Historic Private Event Facility

● Rehearsal Dinners	● Corporate Events
● Ceremonies	● Meetings
● Wedding Receptions	● Film Shoots
● Private Parties	Accommodations

When people step into the Abbey, they're often so awestruck they just stand there with their mouths open. They can't believe what a stunning building it is, and that they can actually have their wedding or special event here.

This striking embodiment of Spanish Colonial Revival architecture boasts two enormous domed stained-glass skylights that bathe the interior in a pale yellow glow, while 12 luminous stained-glass windows cast their own heavenly light. Standing in the middle of this former church, you feel as if you're in a Renaissance cathedral: Dark, polished redwood molding and woodwork is everywhere—framing doors, railings, walls and in curved balconies. Exquisite fixtures made of hand-blown orange-yellow glass are suspended from 50-foot ceilings. No longer a church, the Abbey is a nondenominational venue open to couples of all faiths.

This century-old landmark has undergone several incarnations, and in 1984 an award-winning renovation transformed it into a popular restaurant christened "The Abbey." The statue of Gabriel that crowns the roof was coated in gleaming gold leaf, but with the exception of a little wood refinishing and the replacement of some light fixtures and stained glass, nothing was done to alter the facility's vintage beauty. However, one thing has been added to create an even more beautiful experience: LED lighting is now installed throughout the venue, so you can pick the color you want to enhance the mood of your event.

Today, The Abbey is a private special event facility managed by Hornblower Cruises & Events, two-time recipients of the prestigious "Finest Service Award." They invite you to stage your party, wedding or corporate function in this unique setting, where both traditional and themed events feel equally at home.

Wedding ceremonies take place where the pulpit used to be, and no matter where guests are seated—on the ground floor or up on the mezzanine—they can easily see the goings-on. Add a few candelabras and you have the perfect place for a classic black-tie affair or a Renaissance-themed party (one wedding couple and their entourage actually wore tights!).

When it's time for the reception, guests are treated to an elegant meal featuring gourmet cuisine prepared on site and overseen by Christopher Schlerf, the Food & Beverage Director here for 30 years. Wedding and reception packages are available, but if you prefer, Hornblower's professional planners can custom-design your celebration.

With their expert staff and full services, Hornblower will ensure that your event makes the most of this historic and romantic location.

CEREMONY & EVENT/RECEPTION CAPACITY: Indoors, the site holds 300 seated guests or 475 standing for a cocktail reception.

MEETING CAPACITY: Meeting spaces accommodate 300 seated guests.

PRICES: WHAT'S THIS GOING TO COST?

Meals (when priced separately): $79/person and up

Additional Info: Four hours of room rental fees are waived with a food minimum: $5,500 for daytime events before 4pm; $7,000 for evening events after 6pm. Additional hours can be arranged at $750/hour.

AVAILABILITY: Year-round, daily, anytime.

SERVICES/AMENITIES:

Catering: in-house
Kitchen Facilities: n/a
Tables & Chairs: Chiavari chairs provided
Linens, Silver, etc.: provided
Restrooms: wheelchair accessible
Dance Floor: portable provided
Bride's & Groom's Dressing Areas: yes
AV/Meeting Equipment: CBA

Parking: on street
Accommodations: no guest rooms
Outdoor Night Lighting: provided
Outdoor Cooking Facilities: no
Cleanup: provided
View: no
Other: piano (CBA), complimentary event coordination

RESTRICTIONS:

Alcohol: in-house, or BYO with corkage fee
Smoking: not allowed
Music: amplified OK indoors

Wheelchair Access: limited
Insurance: not required

Overwhelmed? Use the search criteria on www.HereComesTheGuide.com to narrow down your choices.

367

Britt Scripps Manor

406 Maple Street, San Diego
619/795-2937
www.brittscrippsmanor.com
guestrelations@brittscrippsmanor.com

Historic Hotel

- Rehearsal Dinners
- Ceremonies
- Wedding Receptions
- Private Parties
- Corporate Events
- Meetings
- Film Shoots
- Accommodations

Who wouldn't want to take over an amazing historic mansion for an entire wedding weekend in fun-filled San Diego? At Britt Scripps Manor, you'll do just that and experience the privacy, gorgeous grounds, and opulent period trappings of this one-of-a-kind landmark.

Recently renovated and re-imagined as a hideaway for exclusive events, this stunning 1887 Queen Anne-style Victorian soars gracefully over its colorful Banker's Hill neighborhood. It's impossible not to be charmed by the striking architecture—three jewel-toned stories, a gabled roof, and a turret that's right out of a fairy tale. Languid palm trees and manicured hedges hint at the manor's lush rear gardens, and once you pass through the wrought-iron entry gates and beveled-glass front door, you'll think you've stepped into a luxurious 19th-century drawing room.

Welcome arriving guests with cocktails in the lofty foyer—it's embellished by ornate hand-hewn redwood, and houses a gleaming 1880s Steinway grand piano. An extraordinary two-story stained-glass window, featuring intricate depictions of exotic animals and flowers, casts a warm glow over the entire space.

To the left of the foyer, there's an intimate salon—appointed with the same vintage-inspired furnishings found throughout the manor—that's perfect for a dessert table. To the right, a sitting room has been transformed into an inviting lounge, with a custom-made dark wood bar and carved double doors that allow guests to flow in and out of the mansion with ease. That's especially convenient, since the majority of your celebration will take place outside on the home's spacious garden lawns.

On the side lawn, you'll find a pretty arbor backed by a palm tree—a lovely spot for your ceremony, with cool ocean breezes wafting through the surrounding trees. The adjacent brick patio strung with bistro lights is a fantastic location for a congenial cocktail hour, and it makes a great dance floor, too! An enormous camphor tree is the centerpiece of the back garden; setting your sweetheart table beneath its boughs will guarantee some fabulous photos.

At the end of the festivities after most guests have gone home, sneak up to the third floor with your closest friends for a "VIP after-party" in The Loft, a swank common room outfitted with a second custom bar, kitchenette, TV, and oversized plush furniture. This former attic space is home to another intriguing treasure: a cool "hidden room" appointed with everything required to create the perfect bridal dressing suite (think individual makeup mirrors, flattering lighting, luxe décor), and accessible only via top-secret means. We're obliged not to reveal the mystery here, but trust us: It's completely awesome.

Your attentive events manager will guide you on the best use of the mansion's areas and features, but ultimately you get to make all your own decisions—one of them being which of the luxurious guest rooms will be yours for the wedding night! (We particularly love the Balboa Room with its quaint balcony.) Your nearest and dearest will not only enjoy their own five-star accommodations in the other six decadent rooms, they'll also appreciate the mansion's prime location close to the beach, Balboa Park, and the cool Gaslamp Quarter.

From the creativity-inspiring event spaces to the in-house Chef de Cuisine's care in crafting your exquisite personalized menu, everything about Britt Scripps Manor is enchanting and special.

CEREMONY CAPACITY: The site holds 125 seated or standing outdoors.

EVENT/RECEPTION CAPACITY: The site accommodates 25 seated and 50 standing indoors and 125 seated or standing outdoors.

MEETING CAPACITY: The site seats 50 guests indoors and 125 outdoors.

PRICES: WHAT'S THIS GOING TO COST?

Rental Fee: $6,000–11,000/event
- The rental fee varies depending on the day of the week and time of year.
- Saturday or weekend wedding packages require a buyout of Britt Scripps Manor's 7 guest rooms for an additional fee. You may opt to have guests cover the cost of their own rooms.

Meals (when priced separately): $65/person and up
- Customized menus include taxes, gratuities, staffing, event insurance, and day-of wedding coordination. Food & beverage minimums apply.

AVAILABILITY: Year-round, daily. There's an 11pm event curfew, but you may continue the party indoors with your overnight guests.

SERVICES/AMENITIES:

Catering: in-house
Kitchen Facilities: n/a
Tables & Chairs: provided
Linens, Silver, etc.: provided
Restrooms: wheelchair accessible
Dance Area: yes
Bride's & Groom's Dressing Areas: yes
AV/Meeting Equipment: BYO
Other: grand piano; day-of event coordination included with packages

Parking: private garage, included
Accommodations: 7 guest rooms
Outdoor Night Lighting: provided, specialty lighting packages CBA
Outdoor Cooking Facilities: no
Cleanup: provided
View: cityscape, fountain, gardens, garden patio, landscaped grounds, partial ocean

RESTRICTIONS:

Alcohol: in-house
Smoking: designated areas only
Music: amplified OK with restrictions

Wheelchair Access: yes
Insurance: not required

Hilton San Diego Resort & Spa

Historic Hotel

1775 East Mission Bay Drive, San Diego
619/275-8919
www.sandiegohilton.com/weddings
catering@sandiegohilton.com

● Rehearsal Dinners	● Corporate Events
● Ceremonies	● Meetings
● Wedding Receptions	● Film Shoots
● Private Parties	● Accommodations

With San Diego's wealth of pristine beaches, it's no wonder so many couples choose to wed with their "toes in the sand", and this resort's beach ceremony spot is one of the region's loveliest. You'll say "I do" as Mission Bay's tranquil waters lap at the shore and sailboats glide by gracefully in the distance—an iconic snapshot of "America's Finest City", to be sure.

For a celebration with a decidedly South Seas twist, consider the exquisite Garden by the Bay, where towering palm trees form a natural wedding arch. Exchange vows beneath the softly swaying fronds surrounded by lush tropical gardens, all with an unobstructed view of the ocean. Not quite ready to leave the water's edge? Continue the fête right here—this area is wonderful for dining under the stars, and the sunsets aren't to be missed.

You might also hold your reception on the Bayside Terrace, with its cascading waterfall and striking 60-year-old ficus tree. Or, opt for one of the hotel's chic ballrooms, each of which offers a host of fine features, from dazzling Italian glass chandeliers to French doors that open to views of the pool and bay.

With its unique indoor/outdoor feel, the Garden Pavilion is the best of both worlds—it boasts window-lined walls, a soaring ceiling hung with Art Deco-inspired lights, and an adjacent patio with a trickling fountain. For something a bit different, consider Fresco's, an inviting, lounge-style space where you can enjoy the seasonal fireworks from nearby Sea World (and make believe they're just for you!).

Of course, you aren't limited to any one, or even two, of these captivating sites—how you choreograph your party is entirely up to you. The combinations are endless, and your dedicated event specialist will help you work out all the details, including obtaining the permit for your beach vows and accommodating your cultural traditions.

That same flexibility extends to the Hilton's personalized packages, which can be easily tailored to fit your needs and budget. They even offer one exclusively for elopements or very small events: A popular option is an intimate ceremony on the resort's rustic dock on the bay, followed by an open-air reception on Magnolia Patio, with bay breezes rustling through the leaves of the space's namesake tree.

Best yet? The resort is the ideal choice for a wedding weekend. Its central location, just a quick drive to all of the city's most popular attractions, will make this special Hilton a favorite with your out-of-town and local guests alike. And because it's a true resort, with outstanding waterfront rooms, sumptuous dining, enticing pools, the divine Spa Brezza, and much more, you can enjoy a truly San Diego experience without setting foot outside the lavish grounds. On second thought, you may want to extend your stay into a "wedding week"!

CEREMONY CAPACITY: The site seats 600 indoors or 500 outdoors.

EVENT/RECEPTION CAPACITY: The facility accommodates 450 seated and 800 standing indoors and 250 seated or 600 standing outdoors.

MEETING CAPACITY: Meeting spaces seat 50 guests indoors and 125 outdoors.

PRICES: WHAT'S THIS GOING TO COST?

Ceremony Fee: $1,000–2,500/event
- The ceremony fee varies depending on the day of week, time of day, time of year, and space reserved.

Packages: $114/person and up
- Prices vary depending on the day of week, time of day, and package chosen.
- Packages include the venue rental and food.

Service Charge or Gratuity: 25%

AVAILABILITY: Year-round, daily.

SERVICES/AMENITIES:

Catering: in-house, preferred list
Kitchen Facilities: n/a
Tables & Chairs: provided
Linens, Silver, etc.: provided
Restrooms: wheelchair accessible
Dance Area: portable provided
Dressing Areas: CBA
AV/Meeting Equipment: CBA

Parking: large lot, on street, garage, nearby lot
Accommodations: 378 guest rooms
Outdoor Night Lighting: CBA
Outdoor Cooking Facilities: no
Cleanup: provided
View: cityscape, garden, coastline, landscaped grounds

RESTRICTIONS:

Alcohol: in-house
Smoking: designated areas only
Music: amplified OK

Wheelchair Access: yes
Insurance: not required

Hornblower Cruises & Events

1800 North Harbor Drive, San Diego
619/686-8700
www.hornblower.com/san-diego
sd@hornblower.com

- Rehearsal Dinners
- Ceremonies
- Wedding Receptions
- Private Parties
- Corporate Events
- Meetings
- Film Shoots
- Accommodations

One of our acquaintances was married on a yacht, and we can personally attest to the fact that it was a memorable experience for everyone aboard. We enjoyed it all—the glorious day, the light breezes, and the joy that comes with being on the bay. If a wedding on the water sounds like a great idea to you, Hornblower Cruises & Events has a fleet of 49 yachts in eight California ports that can accommodate almost any type of celebration you can think of. Each of Hornblower's vessels has its own individual style.

High Spirits, easily the most romantic yacht in the San Diego fleet, is perfect for groups of 80 to 120. Designed by world-renowned yachtsman John Trumpy, this teak-and-mahogany sloop was built in 1929 and features exquisite antique furniture and detailing, including some classic appointments from the Prohibition Era. *High Spirits* was originally constructed as a sister ship to the USS Sequoia, President Franklin D. Roosevelt's presidential yacht, and now is one of the finest historic yachts available for entertaining on the West Coast.

Emerald Hornblower is a sleek 85-foot Skipper liner, popular for private weddings and reception charters for groups up to 120. The boat's state-of-the-art convertible sunroof lets guests enjoy San Diego's sunshine and fresh sea air at the push of a button. There's also a spacious main dining salon that boasts giant windows, a bar and a full-service galley. Guests can take in San Diego Harbor's stunning views as they eat, then ascend to the Starlight deck for outdoor dancing on the 460-square-foot parquet floor. For those who simply wish to relax after their meal, the plush and contemporary Admiral's Cabin is available for a little luxury at sea. Any Hornblower yacht will also pick up guests at any waterfront hotel guest dock.

For a more intimate celebration of up to 50, *Renown* is an excellent choice. While the ship was constructed mostly out of mahogany, the interior is done in warm dark cherrywood. The roomy and handsome main salon also includes a solid teak bar and touches of hand-rubbed natural walnut throughout. Both the main salon and dining deck provide panoramic views, complemented by a walkway encircling the entire yacht. Topping off *Renown's* extensive list of amenities are three private staterooms, a bar, dance area, stereo system, and an on-board full-service galley.

Hornblower's traditional table service includes white linens, fine china and glassware, and service by an award-winning, nautically attired crew. Whether you're planning an elaborate formal affair or a more casual one, you can be sure this seasoned staff will customize your event to suit your personal tastes.

CEREMONY, EVENT/RECEPTION & MEETING CAPACITY: Seven yachts are regularly available. They differ in size and capacity, accommodating up to 1,000 guests. Other yachts can be arranged. Ceremonies are performed on deck.

PRICES: WHAT'S THIS GOING TO COST?

Package Prices: $99–162/person
- Wedding packages include the boat rental, food, unlimited champagne, and a ceremony performed by the captain. Hourly rates and à la carte services can also be arranged.
- Elopement packages start at $850 for a Brunch Cruise and $950 for a Dinner Cruise. They include: dinner or brunch for the couple, bridal bouquet and groom's boutonnière, bottle of house champagne, 45 minutes private yacht time, ceremony performed by the Hornblower captain, timeless photo package, and more!

AVAILABILITY: Year-round, daily, anytime.

SERVICES/AMENITIES:

Catering: in-house, no BYO
Kitchen Facilities: n/a
Tables & Chairs: provided
Linens, Silver, etc.: provided
Restrooms: inquire for wheelchair access
Dance Floor: provided
Bride's & Groom's Dressing Area: limited
AV/Meeting Equipment: CBA

Parking: fee lots near dock
Accommodations: no guest rooms
Outdoor Night Lighting: yes
Outdoor Cooking Facilities: n/a
Cleanup: provided
View: San Diego Bay, city skyline
Other: complimentary event coordination

RESTRICTIONS:

Alcohol: in-house, no BYO
Smoking: outer decks only
Music: amplified OK

Wheelchair Access: limited
Insurance: not required

Hyatt Regency Mission Bay Spa & Marina

Hotel on the Bay

1441 Quivira Road, San Diego
619/221-4830

missionbay.regency.hyatt.com
sanis-rfp@hyatt.com

● Rehearsal Dinners	● Corporate Events
● Ceremonies	● Meetings
● Wedding Receptions	● Film Shoots
● Private Parties	● Accommodations

Set on the tranquil shore of the bay, the Hyatt Regency Mission Bay Spa and Marina affords fabulous views wherever you look. It also offers a variety of event spaces—from grand ballrooms to a verdant garden patio to a sunny seaside embankment—that will satisfy any couple's desires.

Start with the private Banyan Court and Lawn, a landscaped venue featuring a spreading banyan in the center of a courtyard, ringed by flowering shrubs and water views. Banyans, which symbolize "wish fulfillment" and "eternal life" throughout India and Southeast Asia, make a fitting backdrop for exchanging vows and celebrating a union! There's plenty of room on the expansive adjacent lawn for cocktails and dinner, followed by dancing under the stars. Wedding album alert: The wooden bridge in the court is a charming spot for photos.

If you prefer a ceremony site with the sun sparkling on the water, tie the knot on the Bayside Lawn. From here, it's a short walk to the Bayview Ballroom. Grand in scale, the room boasts floor-to-ceiling windows framing a wide vista that transitions from a colorful sunset at dusk to twinkling lights across Mission Bay at night. An adjoining terrace (also available with the Mission and Palm Ballrooms) creates an indoor/outdoor flow.

The hotel has another option that truly elevates the indoor/outdoor experience to an upscale and glamorous level: The Regatta Pavilion will make you forget anything you ever thought you knew about tented venues. Lushly draped and fully carpeted, the pavilion is a unique, romantic setting where up to 500 guests can revel beside the bay.

Planning a smaller-scale gathering? There are plenty of options for you, too. One of them, The Cabanas, is an intriguing spot for an event-in-the-round. A series of raised, open-air cabanas surround the perimeter of this outdoor venue, which provide seating during the ceremony, or conversation-friendly groupings during the reception.

Hyatt Regency Mission Bay is a great destination for your out-of-town guests: They'll dine splendidly (the catering staff uses the freshest ingredients in deliciously innovative ways); they can be pampered at the spa; there's an award-winning water playground on site; and the hotel is close to a wide range of attractions. And for you, the newlyweds, the perks don't end with the wedding—in addition to receiving a complimentary bridal suite, you actually earn reward points from your event that entitle you to free nights at any Hyatt worldwide for your honeymoon!

CEREMONY CAPACITY: The hotel holds up to 500 seated guests indoors or outdoors.

EVENT/RECEPTION CAPACITY: The site accommodates up to 500 seated or standing guests indoors or outdoors.

MEETING CAPACITY: Meeting rooms hold up to 500 seated guests.

PRICES: WHAT'S THIS GOING TO COST?

Ceremony Fee: $2,000–2,500/event
  • The ceremony fee varies depending on the day of the week, time of day, and space reserved.

Package Prices: $110/person and up

AVAILABILITY: Year-round, daily.

SERVICES/AMENITIES:

Catering: in-house
Kitchen Facilities: n/a
Tables & Chairs: provided
Linens, Silver, etc.: provided
Restrooms: wheelchair accessible
Dance Floor: portable provided
Bride's & Groom's Dressing Areas: CBA
AV/Meeting Equipment: CBA
Other: spa services

Parking: self and valet available
Accommodations: 438 guest rooms
Outdoor Night Lighting: market lights at select outdoor venues
Outdoor Cooking Facilities: no
Cleanup: provided
View: garden, courtyard, pool area, landscaped grounds; panorama of ocean/bay, coastline, and cityscape

RESTRICTIONS:

Alcohol: in-house
Smoking: designated areas only
Music: amplified OK with some restrictions

Wheelchair Access: yes
Insurance: some required

Want to know **WHAT TO ASK** a potential location or vendor? Check out our Questions to Ask starting on page 21.

Kona Kai Resort & Spa

Resort & Spa

1551 Shelter Island Drive, San Diego
619/819-8144
www.resortkonakai.com
jhornick@sdkonakai.com

● Rehearsal Dinners	● Corporate Events
● Ceremonies	● Meetings
● Wedding Receptions	● Film Shoots
● Private Parties	● Accommodations

For decades, Shelter Island has been a favorite escape for both visitors and locals, and Kona Kai Resort and Spa is the getaway many of them choose. Its picturesque, Spanish-influenced buildings are flanked on one side by a sparkling harbor, and on the other by a grassy park overlooking the open bay with the city's sparkling skyline in the background.

A recent $30 million upgrade has made the resort more fabulous than ever for a destination wedding: Two new buildings house 41 suites designed with a relaxed, California vibe, and they've added an adults-only pool. You also have more indoor and outdoor options for hosting your event, and can combine them in whatever way best suits your celebration.

The resort's two newest waterfront venues are absolutely stunning. Skyline View Park hosts ceremonies and receptions on a lawn at the edge of the bay, accompanied by a spectacular panorama of the San Diego skyline. At the Marina View Lawn, you'll exchange vows surrounded by lush greenery against a backdrop of the colorful marina.

For a uniquely "San Diego" experience, you may want to have at least part of your event on the resort's private beach. Here, an expanse of pristine sand brings guests right to the water's edge, where they have a lovely view across the harbor of Point Loma's hills. Naturally, the beach is a coveted ceremony spot, but its permanent fire pits and cabanas set the stage for an awesome cocktail hour or intimate reception, too.

Inside the hotel, you'll find an array of flexible event spaces, each with an adjoining outdoor terrace. Perched over the harbor, the Point Loma Ballroom is perfect for an elegant reception following a ceremony on the adjacent brick-paved Circle Patio. You could easily have your entire wedding in the Cabo Courtyard, notable for its trickling Spanish-style fountain, steps-away landing just right for exchanging vows, and grassy garden areas for mingling and lawn games. With softly glowing market lights that come on at sunset, it just doesn't get any more romantic.

Kona Kai takes the "resort" part of its name seriously—and that means serious fun. You can borrow one of the hotel's fleet of turquoise beach cruisers for a spin around the island, and rent paddle boards or kayaks from the on-site shop. Each guest room is stocked with a stylishly packaged "S'mores Kit" that you can take down to the fire pits, and the full-service spa offers wonderful relaxation and beauty services.

From the gracious accommodations to the customizable wedding packages, Kona Kai works hard to ensure that you won't have to. Throughout the entire resort, you'll notice an artful blend of luxury and attention to detail that makes events easy and enjoyable…so go ahead and enjoy!

CEREMONY CAPACITY: The hotel holds up to 600 seated guests indoors or 300 seated outdoors.

EVENT/RECEPTION CAPACITY: The site accommodates up to 500 seated or 1,000 standing indoors, and 400 seated or 1,000 standing guests outdoors.

MEETING CAPACITY: Meeting rooms hold up to 650 seated guests.

PRICES: WHAT'S THIS GOING TO COST?

Ceremony Fee: $1,000–2,500/event
 • The ceremony fee varies depending on the day of the week, time of day, and space reserved.

Package Prices: $110–160/person

Food & Beverage Minimum: $2,500–30,000/event
 • The food & beverage minimum varies depending on the day of the week, time of day, time of year, and space reserved.

Service Charge or Gratuity: 22%

AVAILABILITY: Year-round, daily, 9am–7pm.

SERVICES/AMENITIES:
Catering: in-house
Kitchen Facilities: n/a
Tables & Chairs: provided
Linens, Silver, etc.: provided
Restrooms: wheelchair accessible
Dance Floor: provided
Bride's & Groom's Dressing Areas: CBA
AV/Meeting Equipment: some provided
Other: grand piano, in-house wedding cake, picnic area

Parking: large lot, on street, valet required
Accommodations: 170 guest rooms
Outdoor Night Lighting: yes in some spaces, CBA in others
Outdoor Cooking Facilities: BBQ CBA
Cleanup: provided
View: cityscape, fountain, garden, courtyard, pool area, landscaped grounds; panorama of bay, hills, and marina

RESTRICTIONS:
Alcohol: in-house
Smoking: not allowed
Music: amplified OK

Wheelchair Access: yes
Insurance: not required

The Lafayette Hotel
Swim Club and Bungalows

2223 El Cajon Boulevard, San Diego
619/780-0355

www.lafayettehotelsd.com
weddings@lafayettehotelsd.com

Hotel

● Rehearsal Dinners	● Corporate Events
● Ceremonies	● Meetings
● Wedding Receptions	● Film Shoots
● Private Parties	○ Accommodations

If you're a fan of old Hollywood glamour but your groom's more a hipster…or you lean toward a garden setting while he prefers an urban vibe, don't despair because there's actually a perfect wedding venue for both of you. The Lafayette Hotel, originally built in the 1940s, ingeniously mixes elements of its storied history with the vibrancy and edginess of its revitalized North Park location in the ultimate mash-up.

A vintage marquee and circular drive lead to the grand, red brick Colonial building, fronted by soaring white columns. Inside, the lobby features ornate coffered ceilings, crown molding and a sparkling crystal chandelier. Among the eclectic décor are a plush round settee and baby grand piano—great for lounging and taking some fun, flirty album shots.

Just beyond two open archways, you'll find their totally unique ceremony site: the Conservatory. This huge space is bathed in natural light streaming in from an entire wall of floor-to-ceiling multi-paned windows and French Doors that serve as the backdrop for your ceremony. Now before you start imagining something prim and proper, take a look up: Suspended from the high, translucent ceiling are dozens of colorful, upside-down parasols giving the entire area a whimsical, garden atmosphere. Seating for your guests offers an equally unexpected twist with a wonderful mélange of wingback, ladder-back, upholstered and Chiavari chairs.

Then when you're ready to pop open the champagne, step outside to the lovely curved Veranda overlooking the hotel's centerpiece swimming pool. Designed in 1946 by Olympic great Johnny Weissmuller, it instantly became a mecca for locals as well as L.A. celebs like Ava Gardner and Bob Hope. Today, after recent renovations, Lafayette's pool scene once again reigns supreme. But if you prefer a more intimate spot for your "I do"s and cocktails, try the tucked-away West Courtyard, where you can have an open-sky affair or one that's covered with a canopy of billowing fabric.

For an unforgettable reception, the *pièce de résistance* is, without doubt, the Mississippi Ballroom. Located on its own floor, it's like stepping into a whole other world of Hollywood soirées and elegant supper clubs. This amazing, two-tiered ballroom features soft recessed lighting inside its circular, coffered ceiling; columns with etched flourishes; and even the original hardwood dance floor. But most stunning of all is the stage with its knockout, backlit clamshell that adds high drama to your live band/DJ, first dance or even sweetheart table. This is just not something you see every day! And there's even a small garden right outside the ballroom where you can smoke a cigar while stargazing.

With comfy rooms for you and your guests, menu selections that'll make you want to try everything, a helpful staff, and an endearing mix of retro touches with modern quirks, this venue may be what marriage is all about—combining diverse elements to create something even better than its individual parts.

CEREMONY & MEETING CAPACITY: The hotel can accommodate 300 seated guests indoors and 125 seated outdoors.

EVENT/RECEPTION CAPACITY: The site holds up to 300 seated or 500 standing indoors and 80 seated or 150 standing outdoors.

PRICES: WHAT'S THIS GOING TO COST?

Rental Fee: $125–2,500/event
• The rental fee varies depending on the day of the week and space reserved.

Meals (when priced separately): $35–85/person

Service Charge or Gratuity: 22%

AVAILABILITY: Year-round; 6am–10pm. The ballroom may be reserved until midnight for an additional fee. Please inquire for more details.

SERVICES/AMENITIES:

Catering: in-house
Kitchen Facilities: n/a
Tables & Chairs: provided
Linens, Silver, etc.: provided or CBA
Restrooms: wheelchair accessible
Dance Floor: yes in one space, CBA for additional fee in other
Bride's Dressing Area: yes
AV/Meeting Equipment: some provided, more CBA

Parking: on street, garage nearby; valet CBA
Accommodations: 133 guest rooms
Outdoor Night Lighting: CBA
Outdoor Cooking Facilities: BBQ on site
Cleanup: provided
View: landscaped grounds
Other: grand piano, event coordination

RESTRICTIONS:

Alcohol: in-house
Smoking: designated areas only
Music: amplified OK

Wheelchair Access: yes
Insurance: not required

Rancho Bernardo Inn

Resort Hotel

17550 Bernardo Oaks Drive, San Diego
858/675-8418

www.ranchobernardoinn.com
rbiweddings@jcresorts.com

- Rehearsal Dinners
- Ceremonies
- Wedding Receptions
- Private Parties
- Corporate Events
- Meetings
- Film Shoots
- Accommodations

Rancho Bernardo Inn has so many spectacular sites for ceremonies, receptions, and photo ops that even the most ardent romantics among us could renew their vows yearly and still find unique spots they hadn't seen before. This 280-acre resort melds its California Rancho history with modern amenities to create a four-star retreat without a hint of stuffiness. So whether you want a wedding that's posh or one that's casual and relaxed, you can host it here and feel pampered in the process.

A beautiful place to start is the Aragon Lawn, an expansive, fairy-tale garden lushly bordered by white roses and trees, where a long center aisle leads to a trellised arbor. Afterwards, serve cocktails and dinner on the adjacent Aragon Terrace, replete with more signature white roses. The terrace wraps around to reveal another grape arbor that's perfect for a sun-dappled reception—there's also an outdoor fireplace to provide a warm glow in the evening. If you prefer a more formal affair, start with cocktails in the Aragon Foyer where arched glass doors open to the terrace, then follow with dinner and dancing in the stately Aragon Ballroom, which boasts honey-toned walls, a high ceiling, and gorgeous pendant chandeliers.

There are several other intimate ceremony sites—including the North and Valencia Lawns—that feature arbors, white roses, or even a dramatic stone backdrop. But if you want sweeping views of the 18-hole championship golf course, check out The Promenade, a brick courtyard with 180-degree fairway panoramas.

Santiago Courtyard is a must-see, partly because of its graceful olive trees and hacienda feel, but mainly because of its magnificent Italian fountain, a centerpiece that truly says "amore": A pair of stone-carved lovers, gazing adoringly at each other, stand above a stunning mosaic waterfall gently cascading into a sculpted pool. This courtyard has an adjacent ballroom, making it easy to flow right into your reception.

Both of the Inn's restaurants are ideal for a rehearsal dinner, pre- or post-wedding brunch, or memorable meal anytime. Menus at the sophisticated AVANT highlight the best that Wine Country cuisine has to offer, showcasing the freshest, locally sourced ingredients—including produce from the on-property garden. Veranda Fireside Lounge & Restaurant, which is inspired by the olive trees, gardens, and villas that dot the Mediterranean coastline, has a sensational patio—complete with outdoor fireplaces and fire pits—that overlooks the rolling fairways.

Frankly, there's so much to love at Rancho Bernardo Inn that we suggest taking a tour. And while you're here, why not stop by The Spa. It's never too early for a little pre-wedding indulgence, and their seasonal Made Fresh Daily treatments are created in-house with ingredients that cleanse the body and nourish the soul.

Rancho Bernardo Inn truly is a venue that caters to all your senses. Between the breathtaking golf course views, award-winning services, and fabulous wedding and dining facilities, you and your guests will have so many reasons to stay.

CEREMONY CAPACITY: The hotel holds 1,000 seated guests indoors and 750 seated outdoors.

EVENT/RECEPTION & MEETING CAPACITY: The site accommodates 840 seated or 1,150 standing guests indoors and 200 seated or 300 standing outdoors.

PRICES: WHAT'S THIS GOING TO COST?

Rental Fee: $2,500–3,500/event
- The rental fee varies depending on the day of the week, time of day, space reserved, and guest count.

Meals (when priced separately): $115–165/person

Service Charge or Gratuity: 25%

AVAILABILITY: Year-round.

SERVICES/AMENITIES:

Catering: in-house, or BYO ethnic caterer with approval
Kitchen Facilities: n/a
Tables & Chairs: provided
Linens, Silver, etc.: provided
Restrooms: wheelchair accessible
Dance Floor: portable provided
Bride's Dressing Area: yes
AV/Meeting Equipment: CBA

Parking: large lot, valet available
Accommodations: 287 guest rooms
Outdoor Night Lighting: CBA
Outdoor Cooking Facilities: BBQ CBA
Cleanup: provided
View: fountain, garden, hills, lake, landscaped grounds, mountains, pool area, waterfall
Other: spa, golf restaurants, café

RESTRICTIONS:

Alcohol: full in-house bar
Smoking: designated areas only
Music: amplified OK indoors only

Wheelchair Access: yes
Insurance: required

Sheraton San Diego Hotel & Marina

Waterfront Hotel

1380 Harbor Island Drive, San Diego
619/692-2730
www.marriott.com/hotels/travel/sansi-sheraton-san-diego
sheratonsandiegosales@sheraton.com

● Rehearsal Dinners	● Corporate Events
● Ceremonies	● Meetings
● Wedding Receptions	● Film Shoots
● Private Parties	● Accommodations

The Sheraton San Diego Hotel & Marina combines the refreshing ambiance of a seaside refuge with the deluxe amenities of the finest resort, including sophisticated dining, a Spa and Fitness Center, and accommodations with private balconies overlooking the bay or the hotel's private marina.

Yet the most spectacular feature of this location has got to be its unmatched panoramic views: The Bay Tower faces the harbor and marina with its ever-changing tableau of colorful boats, while the Marina Tower offers a million-dollar vista—a dazzling display of glittering city lights.

The hotel's waterfront location is ideal for outdoor ceremonies, most often held at the Garden Terrace. Here, fragrant white tea roses, lavender, gardenia, jasmine, and magnolia trees line a latticed arbor walkway, which leads to a fountain that trickles soothingly in the background. Friends and family take their seats on a manicured lawn alongside the water, with the harbor scene providing a gorgeous backdrop. Another site, the Bayview Lawn, is nestled under shade trees near the Marina Tower and affords southerly views of the bay. This lawn is also perfect for hosting a unique rehearsal dinner—one that combines food trucks with hotel catering for a truly special dining experience.

If you prefer a ceremony at sea, board a private yacht and have the captain officiate your wedding. Participate in the tradition of scattering rose petals to the wind, and watch the waves carry them to the horizon.

During the cocktail hour, numerous patios, terraces, and lounges invite guests to mingle in the glow of the setting sun, perhaps taking in the customary evening regatta or departing ocean liners. Clear glass panels surrounding some patios allow unobstructed views, while comfortably protecting everyone from ocean breezes.

Then it's off to one of the Sheraton's half-dozen versatile ballrooms for dinner and dancing. The Catalina Ballroom is a popular choice for larger events, boasting sensational floor-to-ceiling water views, along with its own foyer and terrace. But whether you choose an intimate room for 10 or the 20,000-square-foot tented Pavilion for 1,500 of your closest friends, the hotel can accommodate any size reception.

In addition to the array of impressive event spaces, the food here is topnotch. Named "Best Caterer" multiple times by *San Diego Magazine*, the Sheraton's team of culinary all-stars will serve up a custom menu that showcases fresh, locally sourced ingredients.

The Sheraton San Diego Hotel & Marina is a premier choice for a destination wedding: Your guests will appreciate the luxurious accommodations; recreational activities like sailing, bike riding, and paddle boarding are steps away; and the hotel is just minutes from all of San Diego's attractions. But, most importantly, you can expect a memorable celebration that reflects not only your vision, but the expertise and warmth of this venue's very accommodating staff as well.

CEREMONY CAPACITY: The site holds 900 seated guests, indoors or outdoors.

EVENT/RECEPTION CAPACITY: The hotel can accommodate 900 seated or 1,800 standing guests indoors, and 1,500 seated or 1,800 standing outdoors.

MEETING CAPACITY: A variety of meeting rooms hold 10–2,000 seated guests.

PRICES: WHAT'S THIS GOING TO COST?

Package Prices: $96/person and up

Service Charge or Gratuity: 25%

AVAILABILITY: Year-round, daily, anytime.

SERVICES/AMENITIES:

Catering: in-house; off-site catering available
Kitchen Facilities: fully equipped
Tables & Chairs: provided
Linens, Silver, etc.: provided
Restrooms: wheelchair accessible
Dance Floor: provided
Bride's & Groom's Dressing Areas: CBA
AV/Meeting Equipment: some provided; more CBA, extra fee

Parking: large lot
Accommodations: 1,053 guest rooms
Outdoor Night Lighting: CBA
Outdoor Cooking Facilities: barbecue CBA
Cleanup: provided
View: panorama of bay and marina
Other: grand piano, spa services, picnic area

RESTRICTIONS:

Alcohol: in-house
Smoking: not allowed
Music: amplified OK; must end at 10pm outdoors

Wheelchair Access: yes
Insurance: liability required

The wedding vendors on our website are the best in the business. How do we know? Read page 425.

The University Club Atop Symphony Towers

Private Club

750 B Street, 34th Floor, San Diego
619/702-1986

www.uc-sandiego.com
kristi.saffery@clubcorp.com

- Rehearsal Dinners
- Ceremonies
- Wedding Receptions
- Private Parties
- Corporate Events
- Meetings
- Film Shoots
- Accommodations

The University Club Atop Symphony Towers is one of San Diego's most exclusive urban retreats, and they're happy to extend their VIP treatment to nonmembers hosting a wedding or special event here.

This super-chic, downtown penthouse exudes understated elegance, not to mention jaw-dropping, panoramic views of the entire city. Many of San Diego's elite business and cultural luminaries are among its members, but toss out any preconceived ideas you might have of stuffy rooms and a stodgy atmosphere: With its recent expansion and renovation, this 34th-floor club is modern and stunning.

The elevator whisks you to the stylish entry where a receptionist greets you. Straight ahead is the inviting bar and lounge, highlighted by dark ceramic floors and a striking color palette of crisp white and black punctuated by vibrant splashes of color on high-backed sofas and contemporary club chairs. Huge floor-to-ceiling picture windows frame spectacular vistas that showcase the San Diego Bay, Pacific Ocean, Coronado Islands, and downtown skyline. The club can even provide binoculars on each of the tables so you can get a bird's-eye peek of the Padres in action down at Petco Park.

Speaking of action, to your left is the Media Room, featuring a 103 flat screen TV and an array of signed baseball bats hanging in Lucite boxes, which have been donated by an owner of the hometown team. Glittering chrome chandeliers spiral from the ceiling like tiered sculptures and art is everywhere, from classic oils to a changing display of local artist pieces that you pass en route to the Laureate Ballroom.

This grand space is the hub for your private event. It features ocean-inspired carpet and sleek banquet chairs as part of the recent remodel, and the rich, muted colors of the room make the sensational views of lush Balboa Park through walls of glass even more dramatic. Wooden doors with frosted-glass panels allow you to divide the ballroom and have your ceremony on one side and your reception on the other. On Sundays, you have the option of using the entire club, so you might want to start by exchanging vows in the Founder's Room—which overlooks the Coronado Islands and Pacific Ocean—followed by cocktails and hors d'oeuvres in the awe-inspiring Ebb + Flow Lounge.

Live music is welcome—they've had everything from jazz piano to rock to mariachi bands and even the USC marching band. And, of course, your dining experience will be as impeccable as the venue: The talented chef and culinary team are used to catering to a discerning clientele, and use only local, organic, and sustainable ingredients, putting a contemporary spin on classic favorites and new creations alike.

CEREMONY CAPACITY: The club holds 220 seated guests indoors.

EVENT/RECEPTION & MEETING CAPACITY: The club can accommodate 175 seated or 500 standing guests indoors.

PRICES: WHAT'S THIS GOING TO COST?

Food & Beverage Minimum: $2,000–15,000/event
- The food & beverage minimum varies depending on the day of the week, time of day, and guest count.

Meals (when priced separately): $50–110/person

Service Charge or Gratuity: 24%

AVAILABILITY: Year-round, daily.

SERVICES/AMENITIES:

Catering: in-house
Kitchen Facilities: n/a
Tables & Chairs: provided
Linens, Silver, etc.: provided
Restrooms: wheelchair accessible
Dance Floor: provided
Bride's Dressing Area: yes
AV/Meeting Equipment: provided

Parking: self and valet available
Accommodations: no guest rooms, hotel nearby
Outdoor Night Lighting: no
Outdoor Cooking Facilities: no
Cleanup: provided
View: panorama of city, coastline, Balboa Park, Pacific Ocean
Other: Moët champagne tower, event coordination

RESTRICTIONS:

Alcohol: in-house
Smoking: outdoors only
Music: amplified OK indoors

Wheelchair Access: yes
Insurance: not required

Lomas Santa Fe Country Club

Country Club

1505 Lomas Santa Fe Drive, Solana Beach
858/755-6768

www.countryclubreceptions.com
eventdirector@lomassantafecc.com

●	Rehearsal Dinners	●	Corporate Events
●	Ceremonies	●	Meetings
●	Wedding Receptions	●	Film Shoots
●	Private Parties		Accommodations

Set on a hill just a few miles from the blue Pacific, Lomas Santa Fe Country Club is an in-demand wedding location for good reason: Their landscaped grounds are an open-air delight, and the newly renovated indoor spaces lend a fresh, contemporary sophistication to events.

As guests arrive, they step through solid oak doors into the lobby, which has the inviting ambiance of a casual-chic living room. Crisp white walls and furniture clad in an elegant cobalt blue fabric provide a cool contrast to the warm, pine-beamed ceiling high overhead.

Ceremonies are typically held outdoors to take advantage of the stunning ocean vista and almost year-round fabulous weather. And if you want to make a grand entrance, you'll have the perfect opportunity here: A gently terraced walkway leads from the clubhouse down to the golf course where your seated guests wait in anticipation. As you slowly descend, all eyes will be on you! Vows are exchanged on an expansive lawn, with acres of tree-studded fairways and a distant ocean view as your backdrop. Time your ceremony just right, and you'll also have a gorgeous sunset.

While the wedding party poses for photos wherever they like on the grounds, everyone else heads up to the shaded clubhouse terrace for mingling over drinks and hors d'oeuvres. Designed with a wall of windows and outfitted with heaters, this space allows guests to enjoy themselves as well as the lovely panorama while staying comfortable in any season.

After the cocktail hour, guests step from the terrace into the adjoining ballroom for the reception. Here, the look is an appealing modern-meets-rustic: The rich, midnight blue carpet laced with a silvery pattern is a bold complement to the white walls and natural, pine-beamed ceiling and wrought-iron chandeliers. A working fireplace adds warmth, and couples often decorate its mantel with flowers, candles or other items to personalize the space. A parquet dance floor in the center of the room and wraparound windows ensure that both the action inside and the view outside are visible from every seat. The terrace is also available throughout your event, creating a fun, indoor/outdoor experience.

Three wedding packages and a tempting selection of hors d'oeuvres and entrées let you customize your celebration to your taste and budget. Lomas Santa Fe also makes it easy to turn your big day into a wedding weekend for family and friends. Shuttle service to the club is offered by a few recommended local hotels, and there's a lot to do nearby: shopping, dining and beach activities in the cute town of Solana Beach, plus the Del Mar Fairgrounds just two miles away.

San Diego

Their friendly, experienced staff will help with all your decisions, from choosing the right linens to selecting your menu and signature drinks. The combination of topnotch services and a beautiful setting definitely makes Lomas Santa Fe Country Club a winning choice for a San Diego wedding.

CEREMONY CAPACITY: The ceremony site holds up to 250 seated guests.

EVENT/RECEPTION CAPACITY: The ballroom accommodates up to 230 seated or 350 standing.

MEETING CAPACITY: The club seats 300 guests theater-style.

PRICES: WHAT'S THIS GOING TO COST?

Package Prices: $78/person and up
- Pricing varies based on food, beverage, and rental inclusions. Food & beverage minimums will apply. Menus and packages can be customized to fit your needs and budget. Pricing does not include additional site fees, mandatory service charge, and current sales tax.

AVAILABILITY: Year-round.

SERVICES/AMENITIES:

Catering: in-house; outside catering allowed with approval, extra fee may apply
Kitchen Facilities: fully equipped, extra fee with outside catering
Tables & Chairs: provided
Linens, Silver, etc.: provided
Restrooms: wheelchair accessible
Dance Floor: provided
Bride's Dressing Area: yes
AV/Meeting Equipment: some provided

Parking: large complimentary lot
Accommodations: no guest rooms
Outdoor Night Lighting: CBA
Outdoor Cooking Facilities: BBQ CBA
Cleanup: provided
View: fairways, pond, ocean, grounds
Other: ceremony coordination, florals

RESTRICTIONS:

Alcohol: in-house, BYO allowed with corkage fee
Smoking: outside only
Music: amplified OK

Wheelchair Access: yes
Insurance: not required

Shadowridge Golf Club

Golf Club

1980 Gateway Drive, Vista
760/727-7700 X2148
www.shadowridgecc.com
anna.williams@clubcorp.com

●	Rehearsal Dinners	●	Corporate Events
●	Ceremonies	●	Meetings
●	Wedding Receptions	●	Film Shoots
●	Private Parties		Accommodations

Enveloped by flowering shrubs and bougainvillea, Shadowridge Country Club's hilltop ceremony site provides the sheltered privacy of a secret garden. Tall hedges embrace the intimate spot, where a classic gazebo at the far end overlooks the Vista hills. As perfect as this setting is, you're welcome to add your own unique touches, from lanterns and draping to a rose petal aisle or even crystals. Sculptural boulders, trees and sweeping hillsides around the perimeter serve as ideal backdrops for wedding photos and a post-ceremony champagne toast.

Once vows are exchanged, you and your guests will be shuttled aboard luxury buses to the modern, Mediterranean-style clubhouse with its wide circular drive, white-washed exterior and red-tiled roof. A graceful staircase leads up past feathery palms to your exclusive entrance and a small "welcome" patio overlooking the immaculate golf course.

Double French doors open to the newly renovated reception wing, whose rooms can be used in whatever combination best suits your event. The light-filled Ballroom has wraparound picture windows, offering magnificent views of the verdant fairways and distant hills dotted with upscale homes. A raised white ceiling and contemporary cylindrical chandeliers lend an open, airy feel, while seagrass-covered walls add texture to the neutral palette.

Want to increase your square footage? The Champagne Lounge just across the hall can be utilized for a separate cocktail reception.

Flexibility is Shadowridge's specialty. No matter which spaces or package you choose, the highly trained staff will work with you every step of the way to make sure your celebration matches your style and budget so that you get the best possible value. The club's accomplished Executive Chef can also help design the right menu for your affair—with popular selections like Almond Crusted Mahi Mahi, Char-Grilled Filet Mignon and Chicken Fontina—or plan a buffet with fun options like a Potato Martini Bar.

Thanks to service like this, it's no wonder Shadowridge hosts so many special events, including Sweet 16s, bar/bat mitzvahs and quinceañeras. But with one of the prettiest ceremony sites to grace a golf club, it's easy to see why weddings top the list.

CEREMONY CAPACITY: The facility accommodates 200 seated guests outdoors.

EVENT/RECEPTION CAPACITY: The site holds 185 seated or standing guests indoors and 800 seated (beneath a tent) or standing outdoors.

MEETING CAPACITY: Meeting spaces hold 200 seated guests indoors.

PRICES: WHAT'S THIS GOING TO COST?

Package Prices: *$75–105/person*
   • Prices include tax and service fee.

Food & Beverage Minimum: *$8,000/event and up*
   • The food & beverage minimum varies depending on the day of the week, time of day, space reserved, and guest count.

AVAILABILITY: Year-round, daily, 6am–midnight.

SERVICES/AMENITIES:

Catering: in-house
Kitchen Facilities: n/a
Tables & Chairs: provided
Linens, Silver, etc.: provided
Restrooms: wheelchair accessible
Dance Floor: portable provided
Bride's Dressing Area: yes
AV/Meeting Equipment: provided

Parking: large complimentary lot
Accommodations: no guest rooms
Outdoor Night Lighting: CBA
Outdoor Cooking Facilities: BBQ on site
Cleanup: provided
View: garden, lagoon; panorama of landscaped grounds, fairways, and mountains
Other: day-of event coordinator provided

RESTRICTIONS:

Alcohol: in-house
Smoking: designated areas only
Music: amplified OK

Wheelchair Access: yes
Insurance: not required

Vista Valley Country Club

Country Club

29354 Vista Valley Drive, Vista
760/842-6689

www.vistavalley.com
lmitchell@vistavalley.com

● Rehearsal Dinners	● Corporate Events
● Ceremonies	● Meetings
● Wedding Receptions	● Film Shoots
● Private Parties	Accommodations

Old World romance, rich history, and plenty of California charm are the hallmarks of this unique country club, nestled in a quiet valley of northern San Diego County. There are no "cookie cutter" weddings here—the staff delights in each couple's individual style and story, and is devoted to helping you use their uncommonly special spaces to create an event that feels exclusively "you".

You'll start your day in the exquisite Bridal Suite and Salon, where natural light streams through oversized, opulently draped windows, and two step-out balconies allow you to sneak a peek at the activities below. While you're prepping and making memories with your bridal party, the guys will be all set up in the Library, with its inviting club-style leather furniture, wood bar, and walls hung with antique maps.

Vista Valley's most extraordinary outdoor venue is referred to as "Provence Gardens" for the elaborate 18th-century French gates and pillars that mark its entrance. Along the garden's perimeter, you'll find viewing portals—stone half-walls and open window frames that hail from L'Orangerie in the south of France and date from the 1700s. The portals are favorite spots for photos, and add a pastoral, rustic feel to the space. Ceremonies are held beneath a wooden pergola with stone columns, and guests look on from a lawn area bordered by towering timbers. Not only do these stately sentinels create a striking effect, they've got a fascinating history, having been ordered in the 1730s by George Washington for the construction of naval ships. Graceful sails can be attached to the timbers to provide shade on sunny days.

Once you've said "I do", you can host an al fresco cocktail hour in the garden's Parkside setting, sheltered by mature native trees and lit by strings of market lights. You have the option to continue the evening here, or move to the expansive Driving Range, which accommodates large fêtes and can be tented if desired.

Indoor celebrations are held in the Mission Revival-style Clubhouse, which is reminiscent of a traditional Mediterranean abbey, with huge wood doors, soaring archways, and a pale stone exterior.

The interior is just as stunning—the two-story ballroom is filled with incredible European-inspired details: an open-raftered ceiling, tiered wrought-iron candelabra chandeliers, delicate wall sconces, impressive tapestries, and an intricately carved wood fireplace that serves as a frame for your sweetheart table.

You'll have ultimate privacy at Vista Valley—only one wedding is held per day, and the areas you reserve will be closed to all club activities for the duration of your event. They also offer a huge array of enhancements to help personalize your party and round out your wedding weekend, including farm tables, antique furniture, golf outings, spa treatments from the pros at neighboring Cal-a-Vie Health Spa, and enticing late-night snacks. Warm, house-made mini donuts? Yes, please!

CEREMONY CAPACITY: The facility accommodates 400 seated guests outdoors.

EVENT/RECEPTION CAPACITY: The site holds 250 seated or 350 standing guests indoors and 500 seated or 600 standing outdoors.

MEETING CAPACITY: Meeting spaces can seat up to 250 guests indoors.

PRICES: WHAT'S THIS GOING TO COST?

Rental Fee: $2,500/event and up
- The rental fee varies depending on the day of the week, space reserved, and type of event.

Meals (when priced separately): $95–175/person
- All menu packages include hors d'oeuvres, salad, and entrées.

Service Charge or Gratuity: 20%

AVAILABILITY: Year-round, daily.

SERVICES/AMENITIES:

Catering: in-house
Kitchen Facilities: n/a
Tables & Chairs: provided
Linens, Silver, etc.: provided
Restrooms: wheelchair accessible
Dance Floor: portable provided
Dressing Areas: yes
AV/Meeting Equipment: some provided
Other: grand piano, event coordination

Parking: large lot
Accommodations: no guest rooms
Outdoor Night Lighting: market lighting included
Outdoor Cooking Facilities: BBQ CBA
Cleanup: provided
View: forest/wooded area, garden, landscaped grounds, golf course fairways

RESTRICTIONS:

Alcohol: in-house
Smoking: designated areas only
Music: amplified OK

Wheelchair Access: yes
Insurance: not required

Want to find more venues and services? Check out our informative website, www.HereComesTheGuide.com.

391

Greater Palm Springs

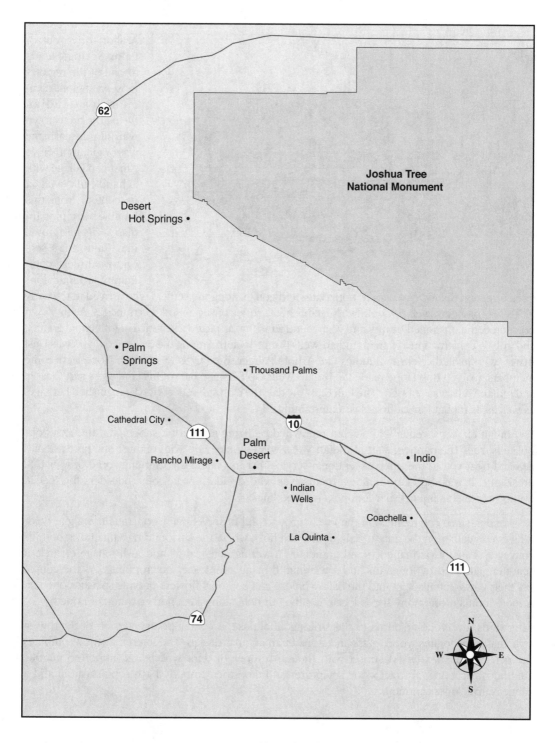

Indian Wells Country Club

46-000 Club Drive, Indian Wells
760/834-6018
www.indianwellsclub.com
morgan.oleary@clubcorp.com

Country Club

● Rehearsal Dinners	● Corporate Events
● Ceremonies	● Meetings
● Wedding Receptions	● Film Shoots
● Private Parties	Accommodations

A short drive out of Palm Springs leads to one of the region's most prestigious communities—Indian Wells. The pretty town with the unusual name was originally a Native American village with a hand-built well at its center. From this humble beginning Indian Wells has grown into California's second-wealthiest community, a miraculous transformation that owes a debt to both dates and golf. Among the settlers who arrived in the early 1900s was pioneer Caleb E. Cook, who established a series of successful date ranches. As the town prospered, the unspoiled beauty and year-round sunshine attracted the notice of influential golfers, and in 1955 construction began on Indian Wells Country Club. Among the original owners was Desi Arnaz, who invited celebrity buddies like Arnold Palmer, Bing Crosby and Bob Hope to become members. In 1960 Bob Hope made the Indian Wells Golf Course part of his famous Desert Classic, and Indian Wells was dubbed "The Fun Club." Today, the club still reflects its distinguished heritage, as well as its reputation for first-class entertaining.

You might expect a venue with such a renowned pedigree to be a bit snooty, but the exact opposite is true. The banquet staff at Indian Wells will embrace you with enthusiastic professionalism and treat you to the same exceptional service that has made the Club a favorite of four U.S. presidents. It was the club members themselves who decided to welcome outsiders for special events, expressing a particular fondness for weddings.

No wonder, since ceremonies on the lovely grounds fill observers with romantic nostalgia. Wedding guests gather on the grassy plain of the 18th hole, where the surrounding Santa Rosa foothills convey a sense of permanence and grandeur. Towering date palms and lush foliage encircle a sparkling lake, fed by fountains and a waterfall flowing over rocky outcroppings. As the couple say their vows, cattails lean into the balmy breeze and seasonal flowers provide splashes of color. A more intimate ceremony site is located at the 9th hole alongside another waterfall pond.

Afterwards, everyone adjourns to the striking clubhouse, a contemporary version of Southwest style that incorporates wood, glass and stone in an angular design. The interior artfully combines the rich palette of a desert sunset with the earth tones of dark woods and imported marble. Luxurious carpeting, abstract stone sculptures and tapestries embody both sophistication and a subtle Native American motif.

Cocktail receptions for smaller events are held in the Main Lounge, a split-level area with a crescent-shaped bar and a distinctive wooden ceiling. Relax in the comfy armchairs and watch the ducks cavorting in a pair of ponds, just beyond the floor-to-ceiling windows. Receptions feel right at home in the Main Dining Room, a sunken banquet space with lofty windows overlooking manicured fairways. An imposing mantel of smooth stone frames a fireplace, and ornate chandeliers with matching sconces adorn the cut-stone walls—details that impart both classic formality and convivial warmth.

Your most lavish gala will come alive in the expansive Bob and Dolores Hope Ballroom. Crystal prisms dangle from the extravagant lighting elements, and an entire wall of windows lets in the view of that gorgeous 18th hole. An adjoining veranda invites guests outside to enjoy the stunning starscape of a desert night. The staff at Indian Wells knows how to bring out the Ballroom's elegance, and they'll help you merge the best of their delicious menu and the finest vendors to create an event worthy of their sterling reputation.

CEREMONY CAPACITY: Outdoors, the 9th Hole holds 120 seated with a view of the Classic Course, and the 18th Fairway acoomodates 500 seated. Indoors, the Ballroom seats 500 and the Main Dining Room 100.

EVENT/RECEPTION CAPACITY: The facility holds 500 seated or 700 standing in the Bob and Dolores Hope Ballroom, and various rooms accomodate 30–200 seated or 50–400 for a standing reception. Complete outdoor receptions are also possible on the 1st or 18th fairways of the Classic Golf Course.

MEETING CAPACITY: Several rooms hold 22–600 seated guests.

PRICES: WHAT'S THIS GOING TO COST?

Ceremony Fee: $1,500–3,000/event
- The ceremony fee varies depending on the space reserved.

Package Prices: $60/person and up
- Packages vary and may include: hors d'oeuvres, champagne toast, meal, open bar and beverages, valet service, linens, and room fees.

Service Charge or Gratuity: 22%

AVAILABILITY: Year-round, daily, 6am–2am.

SERVICES/AMENITIES:

Catering: in-house
Kitchen Facilities: n/a
Tables & Chairs: provided
Linens, Silver, etc.: provided
Restrooms: wheelchair accessible
Dance Floor: provided
Bride's & Groom's Dressing Area: yes
AV/Meeting Equipment: full range, extra fee

Parking: large lot, valet available
Accommodations: no guest rooms, hotel partnership
Outdoor Night Lighting: yes
Outdoor Cooking Facilities: BBQs
Cleanup: provided, extra fee
View: fairways, mountains, lake, and waterfall
Other: grand piano

RESTRICTIONS:

Alcohol: in-house, or wine corkage $15+/bottle
Smoking: outdoors only
Music: amplified OK indoors, outdoors OK with volume limits

Wheelchair Access: yes
Insurance: not required

Heritage Palms

Golf Club

44291 South Heritage Palms Drive, Indio
760/797-8643 or 760/797-8641
www.heritagepalmsweddings.com
ralcorn@heritagepalms.org

● Rehearsal Dinners	● Corporate Events
● Ceremonies	● Meetings
● Wedding Receptions	● Film Shoots
● Private Parties	Accommodations

Many Coachella Valley venues say that they offer flexibility, but at Heritage Palms Golf Club they take the concept so seriously they even prepare a customized wedding package especially for you. Why such a personalized approach? Very simple: The accommodating staff wants you to feel that Heritage Palms is your club for your unique event.

Located near the site of the famed Coachella arts and music festival, the entry to the Heritage Palms clubhouse is an impressive, three-story-high rotunda Lobby lined with classic columns around the periphery. Light streams in through clerestory windows just below the coved ceiling, as well as through a wall of windows showcasing the golf course. Glass pendant chandeliers and a gleaming grand piano add touches of elegance to what is already a beautiful spot for an indoor ceremony. However, if you'd like to get married outdoors, exchange vows overlooking the verdant greens next to the clubhouse, then come back inside the Lobby for a swanky cocktail hour.

Either way, the adjacent Library, with its curved wall of windows and dramatic chandelier, serves as your very spacious bridal party lounge. Down the hallway, the Pool Room with billiard and card tables is a perfect hangout for the groom and his attendants.

The smartly decorated, modern San Jacinto Room and Terrace is a great choice for an indoor/outdoor reception. Normally a members-only dining room, it's yours to enjoy exclusively during your celebration. The comfortable space features plush seating, soft lighting, a soothing water wall and a low bar that runs the length of the room. Picture windows frame a lovely view of the terrace, fairways and jagged San Jacinto Mountains in the distance.

A short walk from the main clubhouse is the Heritage Room, which is not just a room but a separate building and grounds that offer a completely different setting for your festivities. Say "I do" beneath a pyramid-topped pavilion facing your guests seated on tiers of grass, then proceed inside for cocktails in the cool, marble-floored foyer. The dining room, visible beyond an etched-glass wall, treats everyone to a glorious vista of the fairways and mountains, enhanced here by two shimmering ponds edged with palm trees right outside the door. There's even an attached dance studio that can double as a club/lounge.

For brides who want to pull out all the stops, check out the newly renovated ballroom. In this large, neutral-toned banquet space you can unlock your creativity: It's easy to transform the look of the room with uplighting, draping, and any décor that strikes your fancy. The full-sized, raised stage (including dressing rooms) is ideal for a band, humorous toasts or producing your own YouTube video sensation. A sound control booth helps your DJ rock the house, and a drop-down HD screen by the dance floor lets you share home movies.

Heritage Palms hosts a wide range of social and business events with equal finesse, including more intimate gatherings like meetings, welcome brunches or rehearsal dinners. Remember, at this golf club you can mix and match the spaces and configure them however you like. After all, it's your wedding, your way.

CEREMONY & EVENT/RECEPTION CAPACITY: The facility holds 250 seated or standing guests indoors and 500 seated or 1,000 standing outdoors.

MEETING CAPACITY: Meeting spaces can seat up to 300 guests.

PRICES: WHAT'S THIS GOING TO COST?

Rental Fee: $800–2,000/event
  • The rental fee varies depending on the time of year.

Meals (when priced separately): $28–60/person

Service Charge or Gratuity: 20%

AVAILABILITY: Year-round, daily, 10am–3pm for lunches; 7am–midnight for meetings; and 3pm–midnight for weddings.

SERVICES/AMENITIES:

Catering: in-house
Kitchen Facilities: fully equipped
Tables & Chairs: provided
Linens, Silver, etc.: provided
Restrooms: wheelchair accessible
Dance Area: provided
Bride's Dressing Area: yes
AV/Meeting Equipment: provided

Parking: large lot, valet CBA
Accommodations: no guest rooms
Outdoor Night Lighting: CBA
Outdoor Cooking Facilities: BBQ CBA
Cleanup: provided
View: landscaped grounds; panorama of mountains, fairways, hills, and lake
Other: grand piano, picnic area

RESTRICTIONS:

Alcohol: full in-house bar; or BYO wine with corkage fee
Smoking: not allowed
Music: amplified OK

Wheelchair Access: yes
Insurance: not required

Desert Falls Country Club

Golf Club

1111 Desert Falls Parkway, Palm Desert
760/340-5646 x225
www.desert-falls.com
contactus@desert-falls.com

● Rehearsal Dinners	● Corporate Events
● Ceremonies	● Meetings
● Wedding Receptions	● Film Shoots
● Private Parties	Accommodations

Beyond the gate to Desert Falls Country Club, a long drive lined with stately palms hugs the golf course as it leads you up the gentle hill. At the top, you arrive at your destination: the sprawling clubhouse set against a panorama of distant mountains.

To the right of the building, mere steps away, is the Lakeside Ceremony site. Here, in the midst of green fairways, your guests will be seated on a wide swath of lawn landscaped with beautiful trees to await your entrance. As you make your way past a petite rose garden and down the aisle, you'll join your groom beneath the wedding arch and exchange vows with a sparkling lake behind you.

After this picturesque beginning, it's time to celebrate with a glass of champagne. The clubhouse Grand Foyer, a large central space with a grand piano, is just one of several settings for a cocktail hour—and it's also a terrific alternative for an indoor ceremony. The building's distinctive three-tiered roofline creates a "stepped" ceiling with multiple skylights that soars more than 30 feet high, giving the room a sense of drama.

If you prefer cocktails al fresco, serve them on the Lakeview Terrace along the back of the clubhouse. The view from here is glorious and encompasses the lake as well as a pond and rock-strewn brook. At sunset, tiki torches and outdoor heaters are lit so you can enjoy the Terrace in comfort throughout the evening.

Your reception takes place in the Lakeview Room, a two-level dining room featuring white walls with dark wood accents and floor-to-ceiling windows. Seating on the main floor as well as up a few stairs on the "balcony," affords everyone an unobstructed view of the action (think first dance…). Also, consider expanding the festivities into the adjacent Grill Room. Decorated with soft leather banquettes, a long black granite bar and a more sophisticated, clubby ambiance, it's just right for cocktails or after-dinner drinks.

Rehearsal dinners and other more intimate gatherings are held in the Private Dining Room just off the Grand Foyer. Like many of the spaces here, it has a high ceiling with an intricate design of carved wood and lots of natural light streaming in through a wall of windows. It comes with its own private patio, too.

Desert Falls offers enormous flexibility and the staff will work with you to create the best package and value for your specific needs. For example, in addition to the popular and varied catering menu, the chef is not only happy to add ethnic dishes but will even recreate one of your cherished, family recipes. Now that's customizing!

CEREMONY CAPACITY: The site holds 200 seated indoors and 250 seated outdoors.

EVENT/RECEPTION CAPACITY: The facility can accommodate 200 seated or 250 standing indoors.

MEETING CAPACITY: The site holds 200 seated guests.

PRICES: WHAT'S THIS GOING TO COST?

Rental Fee: $500–2,000/event
- The rental fee varies depending on the space reserved.

Package Prices: $32/person and up
- Packages vary and may include: hors d'oeuvres, champagne toast, meal, open bar and beverages, valet service, linens, and room fees.

Service Charge or Gratuity: 20%

AVAILABILITY: Year-round, daily, 6am–1pm.

SERVICES/AMENITIES:

Catering: in-house, or BYO ethnic caterer with approval
Kitchen Facilities: fully equipped
Tables & Chairs: provided
Linens, Silver, etc.: provided
Restrooms: wheelchair accessible
Dance Floor: portable provided
Bride's Dressing Area: yes
AV/Meeting Equipment: provided

Parking: large lot, valet optional
Accommodations: no guest rooms
Outdoor Night Lighting: CBA
Outdoor Cooking Facilities: BBQ CBA
Cleanup: provided
View: fairways, lake, landscaped grounds, mountains
Other: grand piano, event coordination

RESTRICTIONS:

Alcohol: in-house
Smoking: outdoors only
Music: amplified OK

Wheelchair Access: yes
Insurance: not required

Desert Willow Golf Resort

Golf Club

38-995 Desert Willow Drive, Palm Desert
760/346-7060 x103

www.desertwillow.com
RLomes@desertwillow.com

●	Rehearsal Dinners	●	Corporate Events
●	Ceremonies	●	Meetings
●	Wedding Receptions	●	Film Shoots
●	Private Parties		Accommodations

Your Desert Willow experience begins with a mile-long drive through a serene landscape, where the resort's deep green fairways are interspersed with the subtle hues of regional flora: silvery sage, golden-tipped brittlebush, and tiny lavender blooms of the namesake desert willow. A flicker of white is a cottontail rabbit scampering through the fields, and tawny roadrunners take respite beneath the shade of a yucca. Leaving the well-planned town behind, visitors get the sense they're embarking on a desert safari. However, upon spying the award-winning clubhouse in the distance, any expectation of "roughing it" is instantly dispelled and replaced by the blissful anticipation of luxury.

Desert Willow's sleek contemporary clubhouse sports a bold portico, yet is warmed by the generous use of flagstone and wood that harmonize with the earthy surroundings. Honored for its environmentally sensitive design that includes the skillful integration of native plants, Desert Willow has even graced the cover of Smithsonian magazine. Environmental awareness extends to aesthetic elements as well; the club is active in Palm Desert's acclaimed Art in Public Places program, and commissioned special sculptural fences around their golf courses to ensure unobstructed views. Inside, the lobby offers a stunning example of their cultural sensibility: Suspended from the high ceiling is artist Dale Chihuly's flamboyant blown-glass sculpture, whose gumdrop colors and whimsical curlicues are a treat for the eyes.

However, the most eye-catching element at Desert Willow is its scenic panorama, captured through an entire side of double-tall glass walls. Celebrations in the Firecliff Ballroom look out across beautiful terraces and landscaped walkways to the mountain-rimmed links dotted with trees and lakes. Large enough for a picturesque reception for 200 guests, the ballroom can easily be divided into separate salons.

Wedding ceremonies are simply divine outside on the Palm Desert Terrace, which overlook s the scenic Firecliff Golf Course. The lake and oasis below, along with the sun-drenched Chocolate Mountains as a backdrop, make wedding photos look like picture postcards. Another wonderful setting is the Event Lawn, a sweep of grass that faces the 18th fairway and the shimmery lake.

Where cuisine is concerned, Desert Willow surpasses expectations. Their award-winning chef creates meals that rival those served in the finest restaurants.

As classy and exacting as many exclusive venues, Desert Willow is actually a public facility that welcomes residents and resort visitors alike. Once you take a tour, you'll no doubt have the same thought we had: "I can't believe it's not private!"

CEREMONY CAPACITY: The site accommodates over 300 seated guests outdoors.

EVENT/RECEPTION CAPACITY: Indoors, the Firecliff Ballroom accommodates 200 seated. Outdoors, the Event Lawn holds over 150 seated and the Terraces accommodate up to 300 seated.

MEETING CAPACITY: The club holds up to 300 seated guests.

PRICES: WHAT'S THIS GOING TO COST?

Rental Fee: $500–2,500/event
- The rental fee varies depending on the day of the week and time of day.

Package Prices: $65/person and up

Service Charge or Gratuity: 22%

AVAILABILITY: Year-round, daily, 6:30am–1:30am.

SERVICES/AMENITIES:

Catering: in-house
Kitchen Facilities: n/a
Tables & Chairs: provided
Linens, Silver, etc.: provided
Restrooms: wheelchair accessible
Dance Floor: provided
Bride's Dressing Area: yes
AV/Meeting Equipment: full range

Parking: large lot
Accommodations: no guest rooms
Outdoor Night Lighting: yes
Outdoor Cooking Facilities: BBQ CBA
Cleanup: provided
View: mountains, fairways, lake, pond, garden
Other: event coordination, WiFi

RESTRICTIONS:

Alcohol: in-house or BYO with corkage fee
Smoking: outdoors only
Music: amplified OK

Wheelchair Access: yes
Insurance: not required

This is important! Tell locations you're reading HERE COMES THE GUIDE and ask if our information is still current.

401

Palm Valley Country Club

Country Club

39205 Palm Valley Drive, Palm Desert

760/345-2737

www.countryclubreceptions.com
privateevents@palmvalley-cc.com

●	Rehearsal Dinners	●	Corporate Events
●	Ceremonies	●	Meetings
●	Wedding Receptions	●	Film Shoots
●	Private Parties		Accommodations

There's a friendly competition amongst the many fine country clubs in Greater Palm Springs, each one laying claim to the prettiest mountain view, best banquet room, or superior chef. That sense of pride and desire for excellence is good news for anyone planning a wedding or special event in the desert. At Palm Valley Country Club, the good news is even better—not only does the club boast great views, banquet space and food, but it's also one of the best regional values for weddings and hosted events.

To reach the country club, visitors first pass through a private gated community of luxury condos that flank Palm Valley's two picturesque golf courses. A long curving avenue lined with robust palms culminates at a rectangular fountain pool and waterfall, a refreshing introduction to the large clubhouse.

A bright, inviting interior continues the congenial welcome, courtesy of double-high ceilings, skylights, and generous use of glass accents. The lobby flows right into the Main Dining Room, a favorite space for receptions—and gazing out the wall of windows it's easy to see why! Guests are treated to a panorama of the club's palm-lined fairways, with flowing brooks and waterfalls embraced by a mountainous skyline. Opposite the windows, a long built-in bar affords effortless drink and buffet service for your event, while a double-sided hearth with a marble mantel adds warmth and a touch of elegance. Next door, the cocktail lounge has an extra wall of view-filled windows opening to a small outdoor patio. At the other end of the Dining Room are two adjoining salons dubbed Palm and Valley, where indoor ceremonies enjoy an up-close view of the waterfalls. These spaces can even be opened up to the Dining Room to hold a super-sized gala.

Whatever the length of your guest list, everyone can be accommodated on the club's outdoor ceremony site—an expanse of manicured lawn spreading out like a sea of green velvet. White lawn chairs are set facing a lush grove, and a white arch between two majestic trees awaits your florist's talents. Above the treetops the jagged silhouette of the San Andreas Mountains is a dynamic counterpoint to the clear blue sky.

Palm Valley offers attractively priced wedding packages, including spa and salon options at their on-site facilities. Customized menus are provided with a smile, and the attentive staff will happily arrange add-ons like decorative string lights. With scenery, service and savings all at one location, Palm Valley is sure to keep their rivals on their toes!

CEREMONY CAPACITY: Outdoors, the lawn holds 300 seated guests; indoors, the Main Dining Room holds up to 300 seated.

EVENT/RECEPTION & MEETING CAPACITY: The club accommodates 300 seated guests.

PRICES: WHAT'S THIS GOING TO COST?

Package Prices: $58/person and up
  • Pricing varies based on food, beverage, and rental inclusions. Food & beverage minimums will apply. Menus and packages can be customized to fit your needs and budget. Pricing does not include additional site fees, mandatory service charge, gratuity, and current sales tax.

AVAILABILITY: Year-round, daily, 6:30am–midnight.

SERVICES/AMENITIES:

Catering: in-house, no BYO

Kitchen Facilities: n/a

Tables & Chairs: provided

Linens, Silver, etc.: provided

Restrooms: wheelchair accessible

Dance Floor: provided

Bride's Dressing Area: yes

Meeting Equipment: some provided, more CBA

Other: coordination, spa services, grand piano, golf

Parking: large lot, valet optional

Accommodations: no guest rooms, condo rentals available

Outdoor Night Lighting: CBA

Outdoor Cooking Facilities: BBQ

Cleanup: provided

View: fairways, pool, mountains, lake, grounds, fountains

RESTRICTIONS:

Alcohol: in-house, no BYO

Smoking: outdoors only

Music: amplified OK

Wheelchair Access: yes

Insurance: not required

Historic Cree Estate

Private Estate

Address withheld to ensure privacy. Palm Springs
760/772-8313 Locations Unlimited
www.creeestate.com
thies@LocationsUnlimited.com

● Rehearsal Dinners	● Corporate Events
● Ceremonies	● Meetings
● Wedding Receptions	● Film Shoots
● Private Parties	● Accommodations

Many Palm Springs residents know of pioneer Raymond Cree only because a local school is named after him. In fact, Cree was one of the area's most important developers who recognized early on the exciting potential of the Coachella Valley's wide open spaces and captivating beauty. One of Cree's spectacular contributions is the lavish hacienda he built back in the 1930s as his own private hideaway. Sprawled over two and a half acres of lush landscaping, the Cree Estate captures the simplicity and warmth of old-fashioned Mexican architecture, while artfully incorporating modern amenities in a way that makes them seem as apropos as the Spanish red-tile roof. For your most important celebration, this embodiment of Old World charm can become your personal desert paradise.

A grand Spanish fountain greets guests as they approach the large driveway that circles around a grassy island. Orange and lemon trees filter the sunlight alongside a cluster of lofty palms—an impressive 78 of those graceful emblems of the desert are scattered over the grounds. The hacienda is a genuine all-adobe home, and the front wall has cunning miniature alcoves that showcase antique statuary. A wrought-iron gate leads to a wide lawn just right for a wedding ceremony, and a vine-covered arbor along one side makes a picturesque aisle. Whitewashed adobe walls decked with autumn-hued lantana enclose the grass, and include two old wooden doors, delightfully weathered and worn, that evoke a sense of timelessness and tradition.

Delicate tree branches form a natural archway from the ceremony site to an attractive poolside plaza, adorned with several patches of emerald lawn. A black-bottomed swimming pool, one of two on the estate, features a tiled border reminiscent of an intricately embroidered ribbon. In the first rays of twilight guests savor their glasses of bubbly amidst stone benches and classical statuary, accompanied perhaps by the stirring strains of a Spanish guitar.

Stepping-stones lead to the gently rolling greens of the reception area, highlighted by the dramatic main swimming pool. One of the largest and most beautiful pools in all of Palm Springs, it is elaborately tiled in Catalina blue, and has both a spa and waterfall. It has the look of a tropical lagoon, enhanced by its curving shape, a swim-up bar, and birdcages and lanterns strung from surrounding trees. Twinkle lights on the trees, candles and floral displays afloat in the water, and a lifelike statue resembling Michelangelo's David further heighten the exotic ambiance. Near the pool a built-in dance pavilion inspires guests to tango in the moonlight. If anyone is feeling sporting, a lighted tennis court is also at hand, and some brides add astroturf and a tent in order to hold their reception courtside.

The best way to appreciate all of the Cree Estate's attractions is to book the entire place for a wedding weekend. With six bedrooms, three kitchens and a formal dining room, the Cree can effortlessly take you from rehearsal dinner to post-wedding brunch. The estate's interior décor has an authentic Mission quality, and the living room's rustic wood-beam ceiling, whitewashed brick walls, and hearth all create a mood of intimacy. Romance is in the air in the Bridal Suite, where a skylight invites the newlyweds to "wish upon a star," and the scent of burning logs in the fireplace kindles earthy desires.

At the Cree you and your guests can party in style and then unwind, enveloped by the estate's romantic atmosphere. Why not take your cue from the many Hollywood couples who've stayed here and make the Cree Estate your *own* love nest?

CEREMONY CAPACITY: The Wishing Well Lawn holds up to 200 seated guests.

EVENT/RECEPTION & MEETING CAPACITY: The venue accommodates up to 200 guests.

PRICES: WHAT'S THIS GOING TO COST?

Rental Fee: $8,500/event
  • The rental fee includes a 2-night stay in six bedrooms (up to 16 guests).

AVAILABILITY: Year-round, music curfew 10pm, event curfew 11pm.

SERVICES/AMENITIES:

Catering: BYO
Kitchen Facilities: for house guests only
Tables & Chairs: BYO
Linens, Silver, etc.: BYO
Restrooms: not wheelchair accessible
Dance Floor: provided
Bride's & Groom's Dressing Area: provided
AV/Meeting Equipment: BYO

Parking: some on site, shuttle or valet suggested
Accommodations: for up to 16 guests
Outdoor Night Lighting: CBA
Outdoor Cooking Facilities: BBQs
Cleanup: provided, extra fee
View: San Jacinto Mountains

RESTRICTIONS:

Alcohol: BYO
Smoking: outdoors only
Music: amplified OK with volume restrictions

Wheelchair Access: yes
Insurance: not required
Other: no rice or confetti

The O'Donnell House and The Willows Historic Inn

Historic Inn

412 West Tahquitz Canyon Way, Palm Springs
800/525-7634

odonnellhouse.com
laurie@eventsdepartment.com

● Rehearsal Dinners	● Corporate Events
● Ceremonies	● Meetings
● Wedding Receptions	● Film Shoots
● Private Parties	● Accommodations

Imagine: You arrive at your private mountainside hideaway, where you have exclusive use of a distinctive venue that radiates Old World charm. This is the O'Donnell House, poised on a plateau above The Willows Historic Inn under the shade of towering palms. A scenic shuttle ride ascends past trailing magenta bougainvillea, picturesque rocks, and cactus to the enchanting villa itself. The estate's wrought-iron gates open, admitting only you and your privileged guests. The gates bear the sign "Ojo del Desierto"—Eye of the Desert. Surveying the sweeping valley vistas from on high, everyone certainly has a sense that all the desert's delights are theirs to command.

A spacious cliffside stone terrace seems to float above the world, making receptions here both dramatic and exhilarating. It's an ideal vantage from which to survey the transformation from technicolor sunset to star-filled sky. The house itself is a two-story Spanish Revival hacienda that boasts a red-tile roof and a long balcony, a perfect spot for the bouquet toss. Behind the home, rock archways lead to a lawn dotted with colorful native blooms, a supremely romantic milieu for wedding ceremonies. Meanwhile, guests are free to explore the interior of this elite haven, and mingle amongst the Mediterranean-style furnishings and rooms. Whether sealing your vows with a kiss in this dramatic mountainside setting or dancing cheek to cheek on the terrace, you'll savor being close to nature and yet so very pampered.

Speaking of pampering: Newlyweds and their families can splurge on a buyout of the 17 stunning guest rooms at the Willows Historic Inn down the hill. Not only will you be treated to elegant accommodations, but you'll also have the Inn's other living spaces all to yourselves. The Great Room, with its high, open-beam ceiling, grand piano and antiques, evokes an air of refined luxury. Cozy up by the fireplace, and you'll begin to sense what it was like back when The Willows hosted movie stars, powerful politicos, world-class intellectuals…and now, you. The adjacent Dining Room features a magnificent frescoed ceiling, and glass doors open onto a patio where a waterfall cascades into a tranquil garden pool. Enjoy this dreamy vision over breakfast, and take a few photos while you're at it.

The Willows' seductive guest rooms each have their own character: The Italianate Marion Davies Room is tempting, with sumptuous pearl-white bedding, and a satin chaise lounge alongside a clawfoot tub big enough for two. A balcony overlooks the pool, and loveseats beckon by the fireplace. Clark Gable and Carole Lombard spent part of their honeymoon in the Library, which boasts rich mahogany furniture, an elaborate coffered ceiling, and French doors opening to a private garden courtyard. Or cuddle up to the Loft's serene mountain views, and be lulled to sleep by the sound of the waterfall...

Originally built in 1925, The O'Donnell House and The Willows have been lovingly restored to their former magnificence and have received numerous awards and raves. Steeped in vintage glamour, these unique venues pay homage to a storied past and inspire couples to create lasting memories of their own.

CEREMONY CAPACITY: The O'Donnell House seats 125 outdoors.

EVENT/RECEPTION & MEETING CAPACITY: The O'Donnell House holds 125 seated or 250 standing outdoors. Indoor space is available for guest mingling.

PRICES: WHAT'S THIS GOING TO COST?

Rental Fee: $8,000–12,000/event
  • The rental fee varies depending on the guest count.

Additional Info: Destination events may want to take advantage of the Deluxe Event Packages which include almost all the services and amenities you'll need, providing greater overall value. Please inquire for details.

AVAILABILITY: September–June, daily, noon–10pm.

SERVICES/AMENITIES:

Catering: preferred caterers
Kitchen Facilities: no
Tables & Chairs: limited number provided
Linens, Silver, etc.: BYO
Restrooms: not wheelchair accessible
Dance Floor: yes
Bride's & Groom's Dressing Areas: provided
AV/Meeting Equipment: BYO

Parking: valet and/or shuttle service required
Accommodations: 17 guest rooms in The Willows, 4 guest rooms in The O'Donnell
Outdoor Night Lighting: CBA
Outdoor Cooking Facilities: no
Cleanup: through caterer
View: San Jacinto Mountains, waterfall, garden, cityscape from The O'Donnell House

RESTRICTIONS:

Alcohol: preferred caterer or BYO, licensed server
Smoking: no
Music: amplified OK until 10pm

Wheelchair Access: limited
Insurance: liability required
Other: no rice, birdseed, confetti, or sparklers

The Saguaro Palm Springs

Boutique Hotel

1800 East Palm Canyon, Palm Springs
760/969-6481

thesaguaro.com/palm-springs
swilder@thesaguaro.com

- Rehearsal Dinners
- Ceremonies
- Wedding Receptions
- Private Parties
- Corporate Events
- Meetings
- Film Shoots
- Accommodations

No question about it: The Saguaro Palm Springs is an oasis of cool. Inspired by the desert's spectacular annual display of wildflowers, this Sydell Group boutique hotel incorporated splashes of purple, red, blue, green, and yellow into its boldly inventive, Technicolor design…and then took it up a notch, merging that burst of rainbow hues with mid-century architecture and Southwestern décor. Add in the relaxed vibe, lively pool scene, and uncomplicated approach to event planning, and it's easy to see why it's a top choice for couples seeking a fun, fabulous, destination wedding.

Your first hint that things are different here is in the Skittles-color-scheme lobby, where local art and witty dioramas of Ken and Barbie are spotlighted. (Second hint: being offered a margarita before your initial tour!) As you explore the hotel you'll find that all of its spaces are wonderfully diverse, and having the option to mix and match them just makes this place even more special.

The Lawn, a favorite for ceremonies as well as receptions, has great views of the pool and the peaks of the surrounding San Jacinto and Santa Rosa mountains. Nearby, Hammock Village offers canopies, hammocks, sofas, and even bocce ball for a very unique cocktail or dinner reception. Prefer an indoor/outdoor approach? Check out the upper-level Sago Terrace, featuring a retractable roof, a striking ceremony backdrop embedded with stained glass that captures the sunlight, and bird's-eye vistas of the property and mountains.

When it's time to party, you have several possibilities starting with the adjacent Sago Ballroom. It's a stunning, all white, loft-like space with a dramatic, trussed ceiling and walls of glass that look out to the colorful courtyard. Alternatively, the Agave Ballroom has a high, coffered ceiling, tall windows overlaid with etched aluminum palm trees, and plenty of room for an indoor ceremony, cocktails, dinner, and dancing to your DJ or live band.

For more intimate affairs, as well as welcome dinners and after-parties, there's the edgy multi-level Palmetto and its patio, where hip industrial meets mood lighting and cozy fire pits.

Regardless of the setting, you can customize the décor, flow, and menus to suit your style. Choose one of the chef's curated packages or add a taco bar or seafood station—they'll even create a signature drink for you. Their event manager can help guide you, providing a list of recommended vendors for additional services you might desire and arranging overnight accommodations for you and your guests. Each of the vibrantly appointed rooms includes a private balcony or patio, along with access to the huge pool, hot tubs, relaxing spa, fitness facility, and yoga al fresco, plus complimentary bikes and shuttles to downtown and the airport.

Whether you linger to explore the area, hike the hills, arrange tequila tastings with their sommelier, or kick back and chill, you'll probably be planning a return visit to The Saguaro Palm Springs by the time you get home.

CEREMONY CAPACITY: The hotel seats 250 indoors or outdoors.

EVENT/RECEPTION CAPACITY: The hotel accommodates 225 seated or 800 standing guests indoors and 175 seated or 300 standing outdoors.

MEETING CAPACITY: The hotel seats up to 300.

PRICES: WHAT'S THIS GOING TO COST?

Rental Fee: $750–6,500/event
  • The rental fee varies depending on the day of the week, time of year, and space reserved.

Package Prices: $125/person and up
  • Customized alcohol packages are additional.

Service Charge or Gratuity: 22%.

AVAILABILITY: Year-round, daily, 6am–2am. Overtime charges may apply for late-night events.

SERVICES/AMENITIES:

Catering: in-house
Kitchen Facilities: n/a
Tables & Chairs: provided
Linens, Silver, etc.: provided
Restrooms: wheelchair accessible
Dance Area: parquet floor
Dressing Areas: CBA
AV/Meeting Equipment: CBA, extra fee
Other: in-house wedding cake, picnic area; event coordination available, extra fee

Parking: large complimentary lot
Accommodations: 244 guest rooms
Outdoor Night Lighting: bistro lighting available, extra fee
Outdoor Cooking Facilities: no
Cleanup: provided
View: garden patio, landscaped grounds, pool area, mountains

RESTRICTIONS:

Alcohol: in-house
Smoking: designated areas only
Music: amplified OK with restrictions

Wheelchair Access: yes
Insurance: liability required

Overwhelmed? Use the search criteria on www.HereComesTheGuide.com to narrow down your choices.

Smoke Tree Ranch

Ranch Resort

1850 Smoke Tree Lane, Palm Springs
800/525-7634

www.smoketreeranch.com
laurie@eventsdepartment.com

● Rehearsal Dinners	● Corporate Events
● Ceremonies	● Meetings
● Wedding Receptions	Film Shoots
● Private Parties	● Accommodations

Walt Disney loved Smoke Tree Ranch so much it became his home away from home. Since 1925, this exclusive 375-acre gated western-style resort in historic Palm Springs has been a favorite of celebrities, heads of state and anyone lucky enough to discover it—and savvy enough to spend time on its scenic grounds. If you're looking for gold in the desert, you might as well stop right here.

Strangers to the area probably won't find Smoke Tree Ranch, which accounts for the privacy that those who own and rent its handsome ranch-style houses and guest cottages enjoy. This versatile getaway is not only a unique choice for an elegant indoor/outdoor wedding, it's also a great place for a dynamic corporate function, a relaxing retreat, or an exuberant family reunion. And while you're at the ranch you'll have your very own playground, including an Olympic-size pool, world-class tennis courts, a three-hole golf course, bowling green, and miles of trails for birding, hiking, jogging, and horseback riding.

Quail, squirrels, roadrunners and jackrabbits, peering from behind the barrel cactus, towering saguaro, and feathery smoke trees might note your progress along the private drive that leads into this captivating hideaway. You'll park in the spacious lot near the old-style Ranch House, where guest registration, greetings and smaller meetings and gatherings take place. Its gracefully rustic interior is replete with a wood-beamed ceiling, stone floors and fireplaces, hand-carved chairs and suede-soft couches in rich chocolate browns.

Just a short walk away, the Kiva Room and Disney Hall offer poolside entertaining possibilities. The ocean blue-tiled Kiva Room, with its three walls of sliding glass windows and ample bar, is ideal for pre-dinner appetizers and passed hors d'oeuvres. An adjacent living room, warmed by a fireplace, is an inviting space for even more socializing. Disney Hall, named after the celebrated animator, features spot lighting in its vaulted ceiling, sand-colored carpets, and an entire wall of windowed sliders that lead to patio and pool. Dine or dance inside, or allow your celebration to flow into the great outdoors.

The sun shines year-round in this desert oasis, so why not let the bright blue sky or the dusky night sky tent your event? There's plenty of room for a band under the loggia or on the patio next to the pool. There's even a children's play area complete with treehouse close at hand. If your wedding dreams are cast in green, you might want to take over the entire three-hole golf course for your ceremony and, after a cocktail break, for a fabulous dinner al fresco. Imagine your guests on the perfect lawn framed by regal trees and a 360-degree surround of soaring mountain ranges.

Visiting family, friends and colleagues who want to make your event the trip of a lifetime should definitely book one of the charming cottages and sally forth to enjoy the fine restaurants, shows, casinos, shopping and parklands that make Palm Springs a five-star destination. It's a California dreamscape like no other: naturally inspiring and wildly beautiful. If you hear coyotes howling or owls hooting at midnight it might just be your happy guests.

CEREMONY & EVENT/RECEPTION CAPACITY: The ranch holds 125 seated or 300 standing guests indoors and 500 seated or 750 standing outdoors.

MEETING CAPACITY: Meeting spaces accommodate 100 seated guests.

PRICES: WHAT'S THIS GOING TO COST?

Rental Fee: $5,000/event and up
  • The rental fee varies depending on the space reserved and guest count.

Meals (when priced separately): $65/person and up
  • Price includes service charge.

AVAILABILITY: November–April, daily, 8am–midnight.

SERVICES/AMENITIES:

Catering: in-house
Kitchen Facilities: n/a
Tables & Chairs: some provided
Linens, Silver, etc.: some provided
Restrooms: wheelchair accessible
Dance Floor: CBA
Bride's Dressing Area: CBA
AV/Meeting Equipment: CBA, extra charge

Parking: large lot
Accommodations: 49 guest cottages
Outdoor Night Lighting: CBA
Outdoor Cooking Facilities: no
Cleanup: provided
View: panorama of mountains, garden, hills and fairways; pool area, landscaped grounds
Other: tennis courts, bowling lawn, horseback riding, croquet lawn, hiking trails, Olympic-size pool

RESTRICTIONS:

Alcohol: in-house
Smoking: in designated areas only
Music: amplified OK with restrictions

Wheelchair Access: yes
Insurance: liability required

Mission Hills Country Club

Country Club

34-600 Mission Hills Drive, Rancho Mirage
760/324-9400
www.missionhills.com
Rochelle.Bang@clubcorp.com

● Rehearsal Dinners	● Corporate Events
● Ceremonies	● Meetings
● Wedding Receptions	● Film Shoots
● Private Parties	● Accommodations

For more than 20 years at Mission Hills Country Club, it's been a tradition for the winner of one of the LPGA's most prestigious championships to jump into the lake surrounding the celebrated 18th green. So far, to the relief of friends and family, no bride or groom has decided to "take the plunge" in quite that way, preferring instead to soak up the sights, sounds and splendor of this desert oasis while staying picture-perfect dry.

With the jagged Santa Rosa Mountains reaching skyward in the background, you drive through the wrought-iron gates and truly feel that you've left the world behind as you arrive at those famous jade-green fairways studded with enormous rustling palms. For your ceremony, you have a choice of two stunning locations—The Lakefront or The Grove.

At the Lakefront, your family and friends will be seated overlooking the renowned 18th green, an island reachable by a footbridge anchored by a bronze statue of Dinah Shore (who first created the women's tournament here in 1974). As your guests take their seats facing the lake, everyone has a perfect line of sight to watch you make your entrance down the stairs from the clubhouse.

The Grove is an equally spectacular setting. Guests are welcomed into a secluded orchard of young citrus trees, whose fragrant blossoms offer a seasonal surprise. Lush green hedges and bright splashes of colorful flowers surround a carpet of manicured lawn where seated guests face an elevated altar. Then you and your fiancé say "I do" against a majestic backdrop of Mount San Jacinto and mature palms gently swaying in the breeze.

Afterwards, celebrate the moment with cocktails and hors d'oeuvres, served either on the spacious clubhouse veranda overlooking the golf course or inside the air-conditioned lounge with floor-to-ceiling, wraparound windows that seem to bring the outside in.

The clubhouse offers an understated elegance with a modern take on mid-century themes. There's a subtle interplay between soft and hard, like the placement of plush carpets and a red velvet settee around a marble fireplace...and an inventive use of natural materials, like panels of polished picture quartz, backlit and set into the textured stone wall behind the bar. Directly over the bar, dramatic circular teak chandeliers descend from the coffered ceiling. The entire lounge area is large, bright and inviting, with a mixture of traditional tables and chairs in the center and more intimate, curved banquettes around the perimeter.

The adjoining banquet rooms continue the same design themes, and have the flexibility to be opened fully to accommodate 215 people or reconfigured for smaller gatherings. As with the lounge area, the full-length windows allow the tall, exterior columns and vibrant pinks, yellows and greens of the outside landscaping to become part of the room.

And if one day is just not enough to contain your bliss, Mission Hills Country Club offers a full spa on the property for pre-wedding pampering, plus a separate compound of four villas ranging in size from 1,700 to 3,200 square feet. With a combined total of 13 bedrooms to house you and your out-of-town guests, this very private, gated area includes a party-sized barbecue grill, putting green, and hot tub and pool, where everyone will most definitely enjoy each other and the relaxing ambiance.

CEREMONY CAPACITY: The site can accommodate 215 seated guests indoors or 350 seated outdoors.

EVENT/RECEPTION CAPACITY: The site holds 215 seated or 350 standing indoors.

MEETING CAPACITY: The site seats 215 guests.

PRICES: WHAT'S THIS GOING TO COST?

Rental Fee: $700–2,000/event
- The rental fee varies depending on the space reserved.

Packages:
- Pricing for all-inclusive wedding packages for up to 100 guests is $12,000 for Sunday, $19,000 for Friday, and $13,000 for Saturday. Smaller weddings are welcomed as well.
- Packages include: 1-hour wedding rehearsal, choice of ceremony site plus white garden folding chairs, fruitwood Chiavari reception chairs, cash bar with professional bartender, cocktail hors d'oeuvres and staffed reception meal, silver or gold chargers, complimentary valet parking, and more!

Service Charge or Gratuity: 22%

AVAILABILITY: Year-round, daily.

SERVICES/AMENITIES:

Catering: in-house
Kitchen Facilities: n/a
Tables & Chairs: provided
Linens, Silver, etc.: provided
Restrooms: wheelchair accessible
Dance Floor: provided
Bride's & Groom's Dressing Areas: yes
AV/Meeting Equipment: some provided

Parking: large lot, valet provided
Accommodations: 4 villas
Outdoor Night Lighting: yes
Outdoor Cooking Facilities: BBQ on site
Cleanup: provided
View: panorama of mountains and fairways, lake
Other: spa services, golf, tennis, pre- and after-parties

RESTRICTIONS:

Alcohol: in-house, or wine corkage $17/bottle
Smoking: outdoors only
Music: amplified OK with restrictions

Wheelchair Access: yes
Insurance: not required

Index

Event Venues

d

e

f

g

h

r

s

t

All of the Event Services profiled on HereComesTheGuide.com have been

1. We only represent the best professionals in the biz.

The professionals featured on our website aren't plucked from a random Google search. They're a carefully selected group of vendors who we'd recommend to our friends and business associates without hesitation.

2. Because we're picky, you don't have to worry about who to hire for your event.

We've thoroughly checked the professional track record of our event pros so you can be as confident about their abilities as we are. The companies we highlight have passed our reference check with flying colors, and we're honored to represent each of them. They've all been *Certified By The Guide.* To see all of our prescreened vendors, go to HereComesTheGuide.com.

3. Getting into Here Comes The Guide is tough.

The service providers we represent are topnotch. We put each one through a rigorous reference check, which involves interviewing up to 15 couples who used their services. We contact every single reference and ask about the professionalism, technical competency, and service orientation of the advertiser in question.

When you invest so much time talking to that many wedding couples, and professionals, you get a crystal clear picture of who's doing a superb job and who isn't. Those candidates who received consistent, rave reviews made it into HereComesTheGuide.com's VENDOR section. Those who didn't were (nicely) turned down.

About the Authors

Jan Brenner has co-authored and edited all of Hopscotch Press' books. Although she received a BA in English from UC Berkeley, she backed into writing only after spending ten years in social work and four in publishing. Along the way she got a couple of other degrees that have never been put to official use. A lifelong dilettante, she's quasi-conversant in 3.1 languages, dabbles in domestic pursuits, and spends an inordinate amount of time hanging out with her dog Luigi.

Jolene Rae Harrington has been with Hopscotch Press since she first fell in love with their groundbreaking publications while planning her own beach wedding in 1995. In addition to co-authoring and editing the *Here Comes The Guide* books, she serves as Media & Communications Director and Venue Specialist for HereComesTheGuide.com and is a frequently quoted expert on the bridal industry. Beyond her work at Here Comes The Guide, Jolene's writing credits range from an award-winning television script to a best-selling children's computer game. She lives in her native Southern California with her husband and various animal children.

Who's got the #1 Bridal Show Calendar?
HereComesTheGuide.com, that's who!

Use our calendar to find a bridal fair or wedding expo in your area to check off a bunch of wedding TO-DOs all in one place on the same day. You'll get to:

- soak up tons of wedding inspo

- check out the latest trends in fashion, food, décor, music, photography, and other wedding services

- meet with vendors face-to-face

- sample hors d'oeuvres, cake bites, and cocktails

- attend DIY Seminars

- enter giveaways

- receive a swag bag (if you're lucky!)

This is a budget-friendly way to plan, plus you'll have a blast!

And many of the shows listed in our online calendar also offer special promo codes for discounted tickets!

Notes

Notes

Notes

Notes

Notes

Notes